STRIKE A BLOW TO VIVIFY

STRIKE A BLOW TO VIVIFY
STRIKE A BLOW TO VIVIFY
STRIKE A BLOW TO VIVIFY
STRIKE A BLOW TO VIVIFY
STRIKE A BLOW TO VIVIFY
STRIKE A BLOW TO VIVIFY
STRIKE A BLOW TO VIVIFY
STRIKE A BLOW TO VIVIFY

2

矢上裕
Presented by YU YAGAMI

Translation – Christine Schilling
Adaptation – Kai Connick
Editorial Assistant – Mallory Reaves
Retouch and Lettering – Team Pokopen
Production Manager – James Dashiell
Editor – Brynne Chandler

A Go! Comi manga

Published by Go! Media Entertainment, LLC

Hikkatsu Volume 2
© YU YAGAMI 2006
First published in 2006 by Media Works Inc., Tokyo, Japan.
English translation rights arranged with Media Works Inc.
English Text © 2007 Go! Media Entertainment, LLC. All rights reserved.

Visit us online at www.gocomi.com
e-mail: info@gocomi.com

ISBN 978-1-933617-58-9

First printed in December 2007

1 2 3 4 5 6 7 8 9

Manufactured in the United States of America

Hikkatsu!
STRIKE A BLOW TO VIVIFY

STORY AND ART BY
YU YAGAMI

VOLUME 2

go!comi

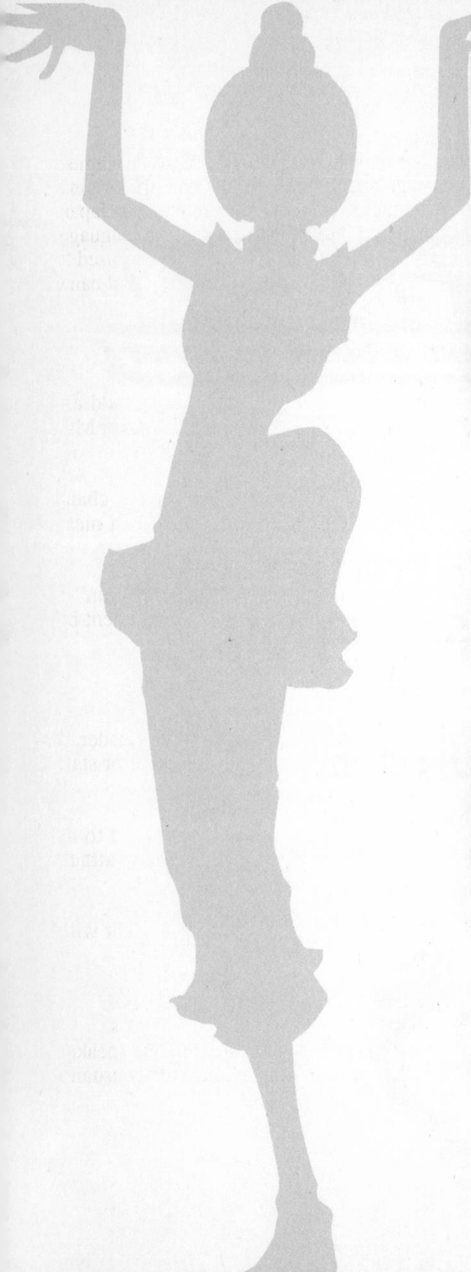

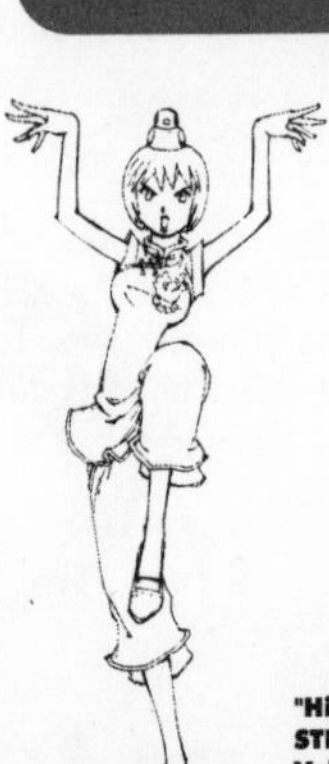

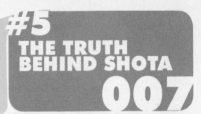

"Hikkatsu!"
STRIKE A BLOW TO VIVIFY
Vol. 2
Presented By YU YAGAMI

Concerning Honorifics

At Go! Comi, we do our best to ensure that our translations read seamlessly in English while respecting the original Japanese language and culture. To this end, the original honorifics (the suffixes found at the end of characters' names) remain intact. in Japan, where politeness and formality are more integrated into every aspect of the language, honorifics give a better understanding of character relationships. They can be used to indicate both respect and affection. Whether a person addresses someone by first name or last name also indicates how close their relationship is.

Here are some of the honorifics you might encounter in reading this book:

-san: This is the most common and neutral of honorifics. The polite way to address someone you're not on close terms with is to use "-san." it's kind of like Mr. or Ms., except you can use "-san" with first names as easily as family names.

-chan: Used for friendly familiarity, mostly applied towards young girls. "-chan" also carries a connotation of cuteness with it, so it is frequently used with nick-names towards both boys and girls (such as "Na-chan" for "Natsu").

-kun: Like "-chan," it's an informal suffix for friends and classmates, only "-kun" is usually associated with boys. it can also be used in a professional environment by someone addressing a subordinate.

-sama: indicates a great deal of respect or admiration.

Sempai: in school, "sempai" is used to refer to an upperclassman or club leader. it can also be used in the workplace by a new employee to address a mentor or staff member with seniority.

Sensei: Teachers, doctors, writers or any master of a trade are referred to as "sensei." When addressing a manga creator, the polite thing to do is attach "-sensei" to the manga-ka's name (as in Yagami-sensei).

Onii: This is the more casual term for an older brother. Usually you'll see it with an honorific attached, such as "onii-chan."

Onee: The casual term for older sister, it's used like "onii" with honorifics.

[blank]: Not using an honorific when addressing someone indicates that the speaker has permission to speak intimately with the other person. This relationship is usually reserved for close friends and family.

A young girl raised by pigeons. She fell in love with Shota at first sight and now travels with him.

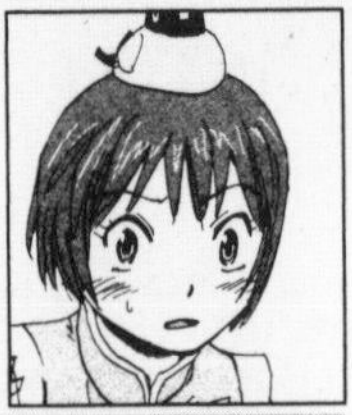

MOMOKO モモコ

A young boy learning to channel his karate skills into a repair blow technique, which he uses to whack broken things into working order.

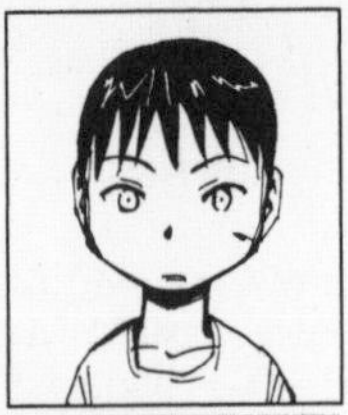

CHILD SHOTA ショータ(子供時代)

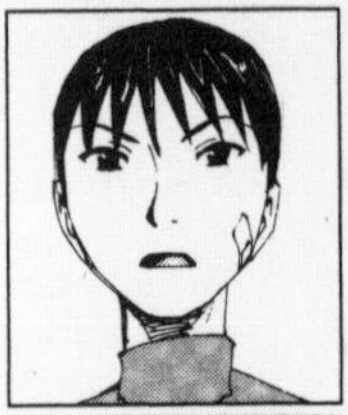

SHOTA ショータ

Shota's karate instructor and Asuka's father. He taught Shota the basics of martial arts.

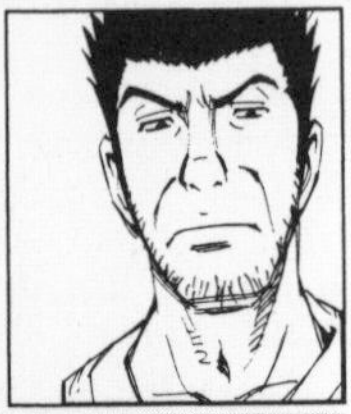

INSTRUCTOR 師範

A former karate classmate of Shota's. She's sworn revenge on Shota for killing her father, their instructor.

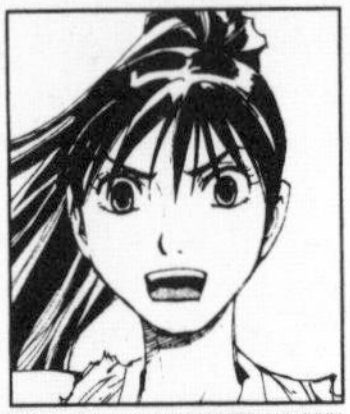

ASUKA アスカ

Self-proclaimed trickster. He doesn't have much to say, except about money.

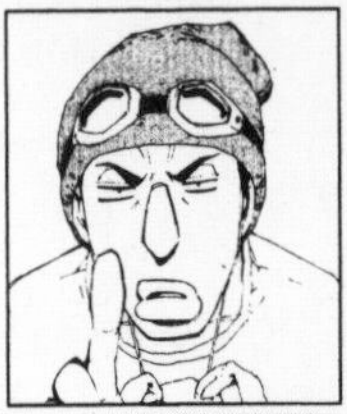

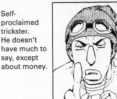

KANJI カンジ

Character & Story

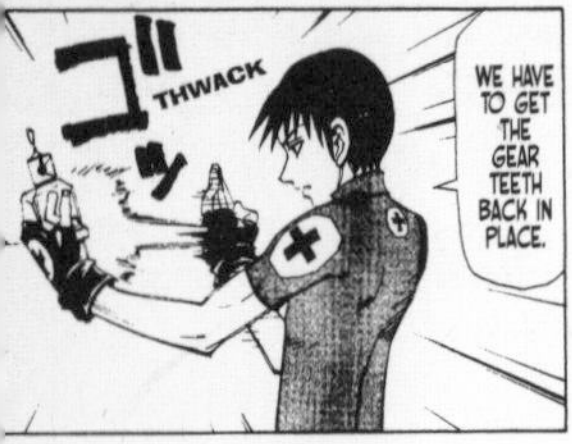
THWACK
WE HAVE TO GET THE GEAR TEETH BACK IN PLACE.

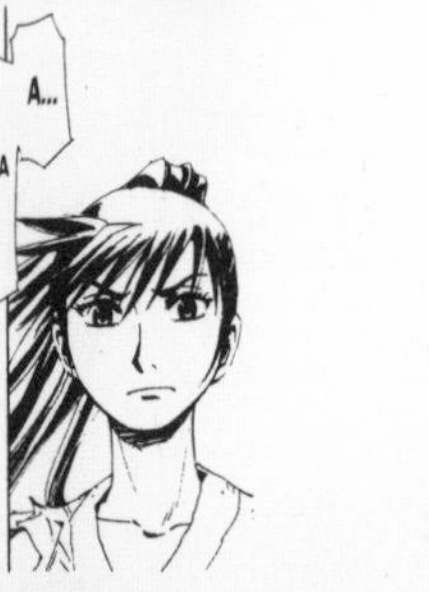
A...
ASUKA ...!?

In this, the "Malfunctioning Era," geomagnetic abnormalities cause machines to malfunction, seriously affecting the quality of life. When Shota was a child learning karate, he witnessed a broken television repaired with a firm whack. This inspired him to develop his "Repair Blow" which he can use to fix broken-down machinery with a few well-placed attacks.
The eruption of Mt. Fuji ends Shota's mountain-top training, and he decides that he has mastered his technique enough to continue his studies in the city.

Though his efforts show little success, his skills are enough to impress Momoko, who falls in love with him at first sight. Later, the smooth-talking, enterprising Kanji can see the business potential of Shota's abilities. They join him on his journey.
Soon after, a city-to-city bus that Momoko was riding breaks down, sending it dangerously out of control. Shota's Repair Blow miraculously stops the bus, saving Momoko and its passengers. Celebrations are cut short when Asuka appears, challenging Shota to a fight for the honor of her slain father!

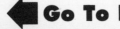

← Go To Next Page

#5 The Truth Behind Shota

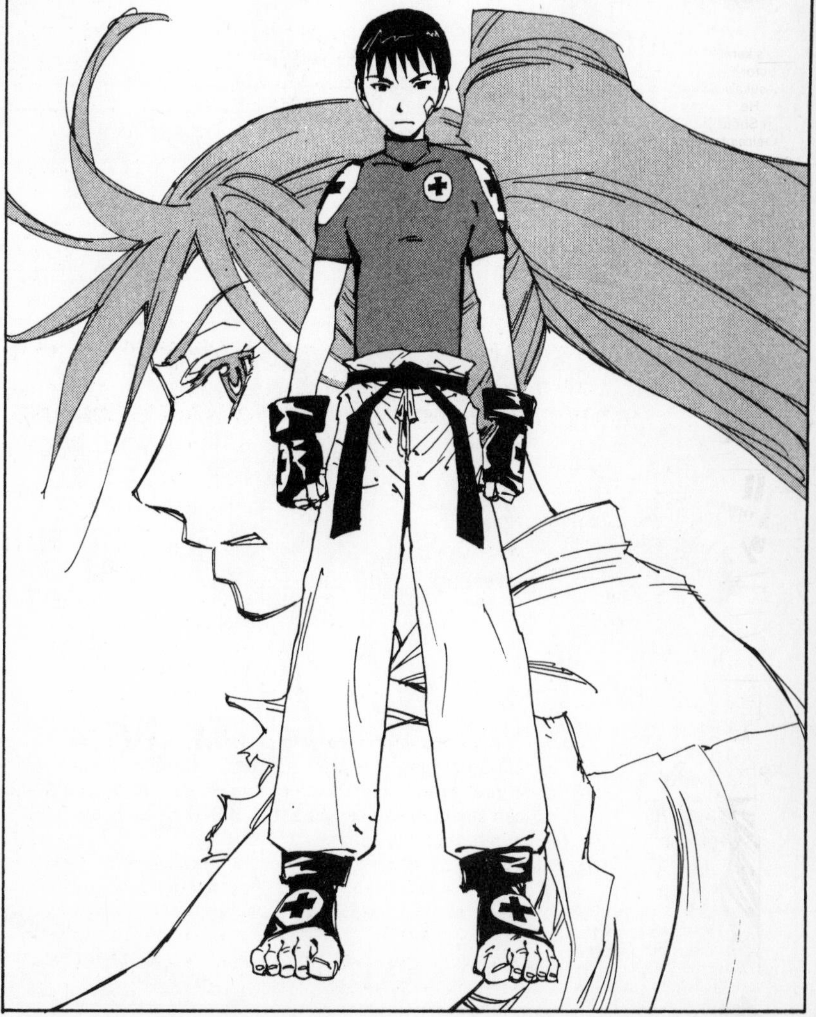

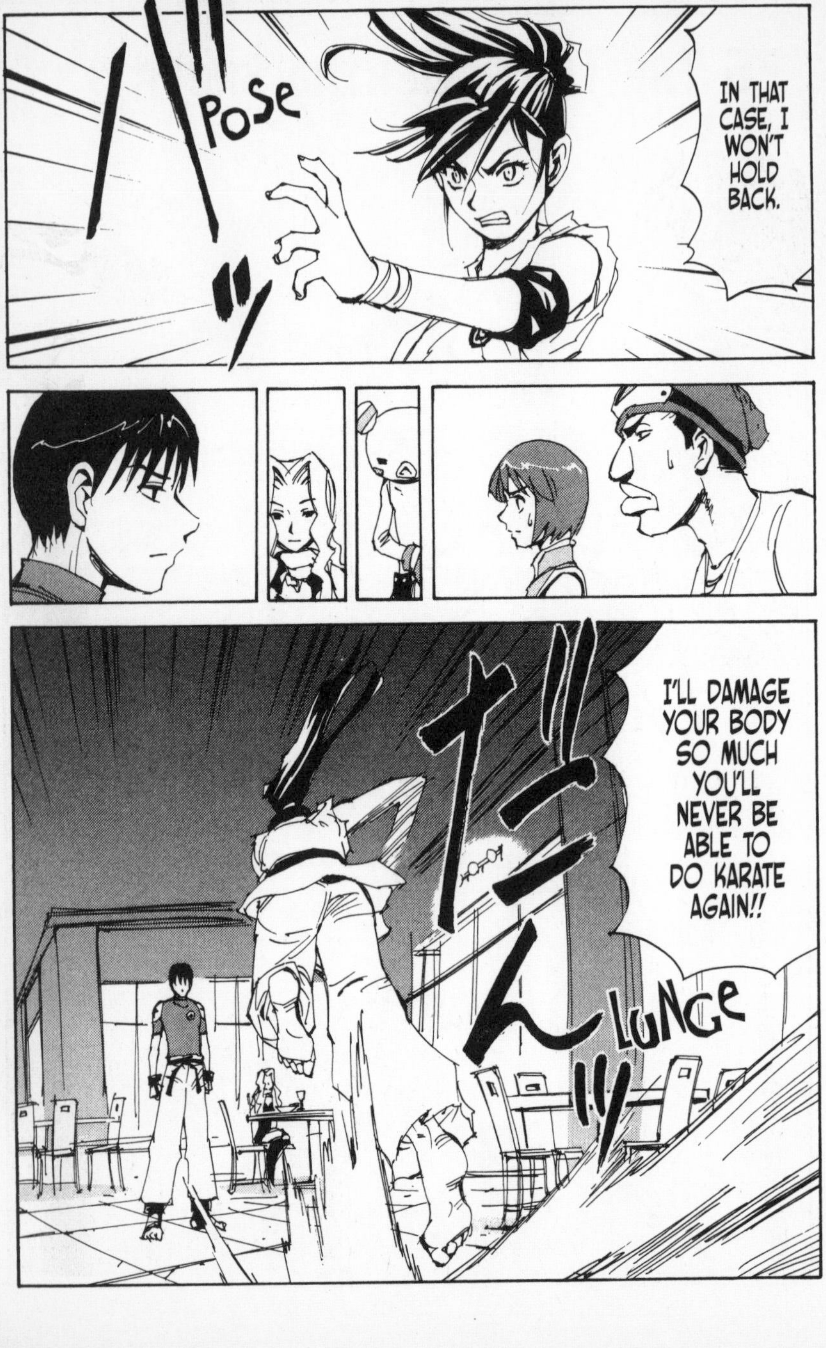
IN THAT CASE, I WON'T HOLD BACK.
POSE
I'LL DAMAGE YOUR BODY SO MUCH YOU'LL NEVER BE ABLE TO DO KARATE AGAIN!!
LUNGE

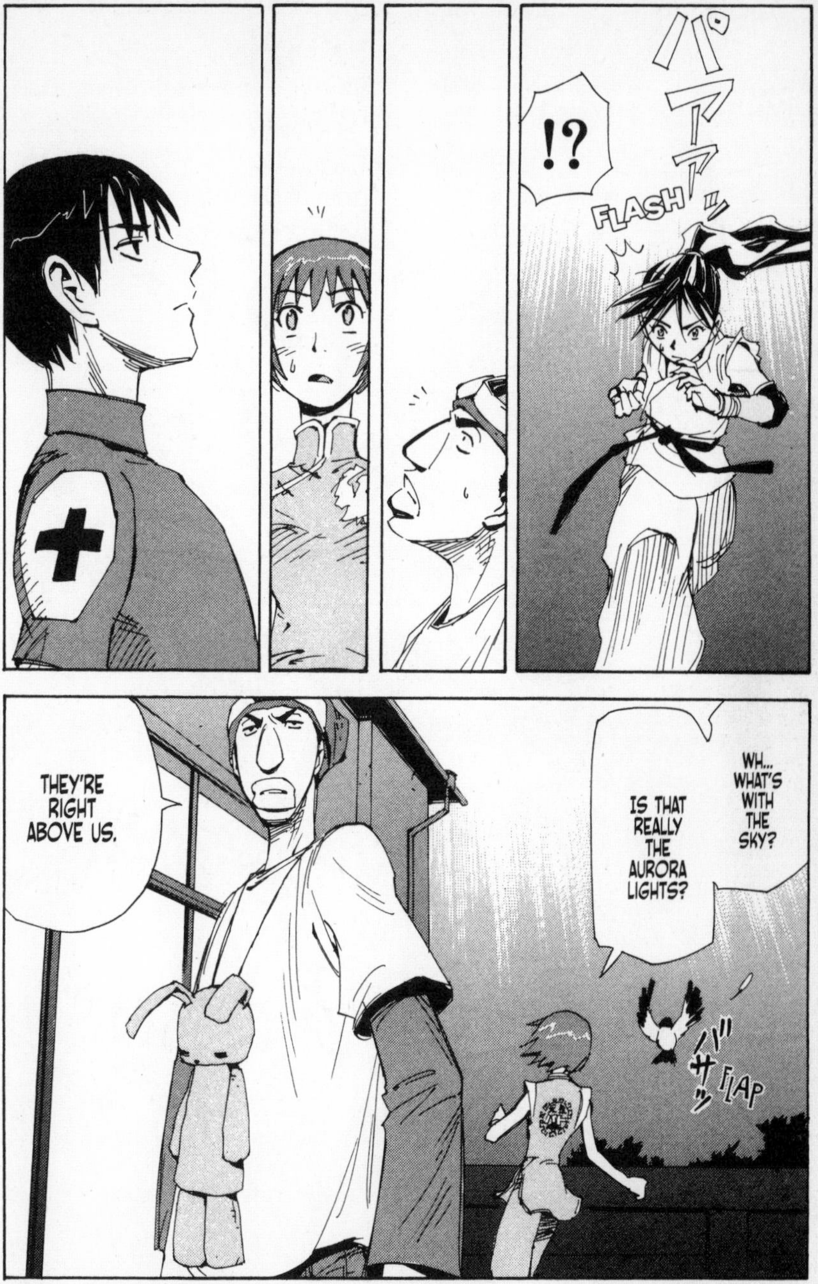

パアァッ
FLASH
!?
WH... WHAT'S WITH THE SKY?
IS THAT REALLY THE AURORA LIGHTS?
バサッ
FLAP
THEY'RE RIGHT ABOVE US.

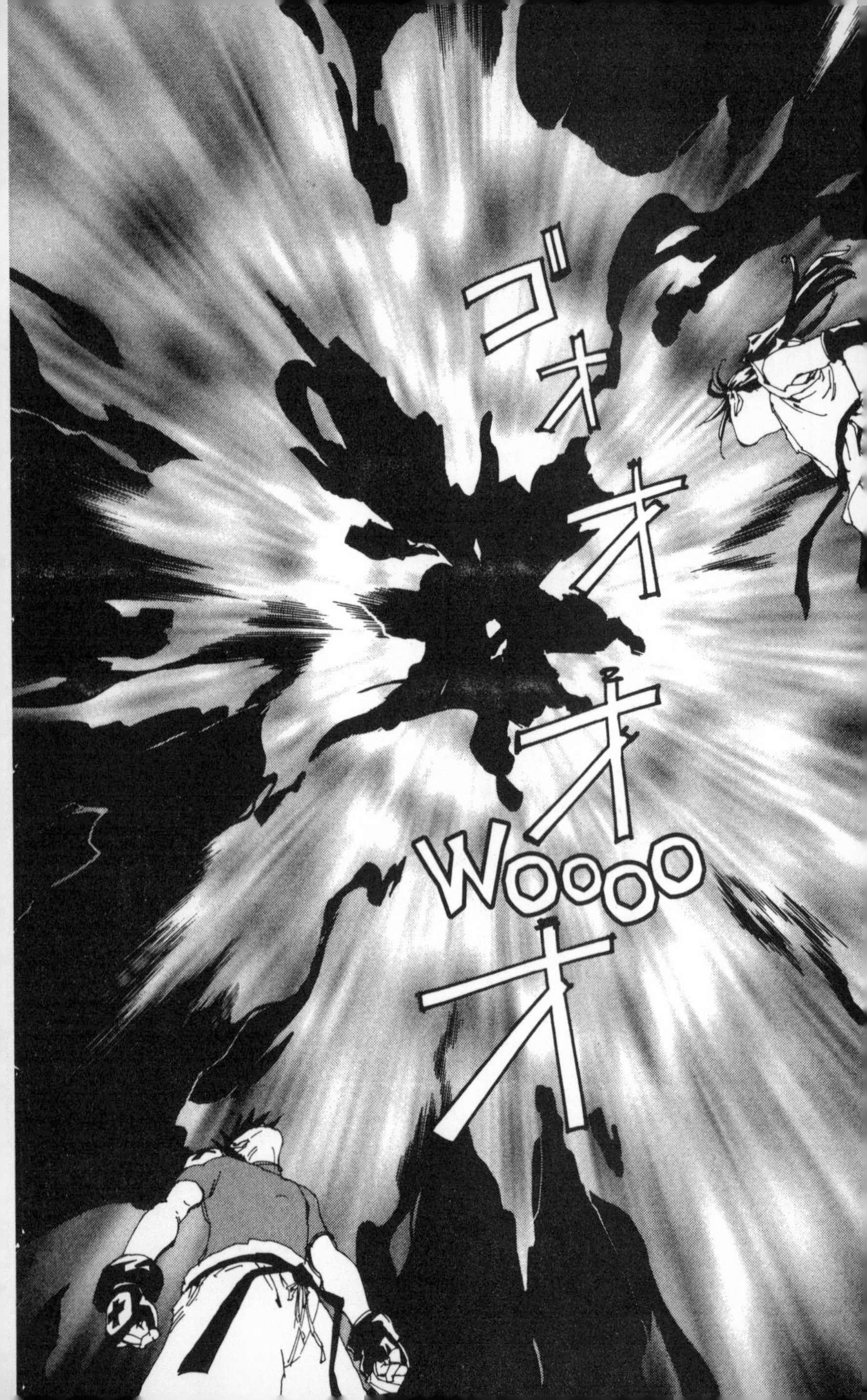
ゴオオオオ
WOOOO

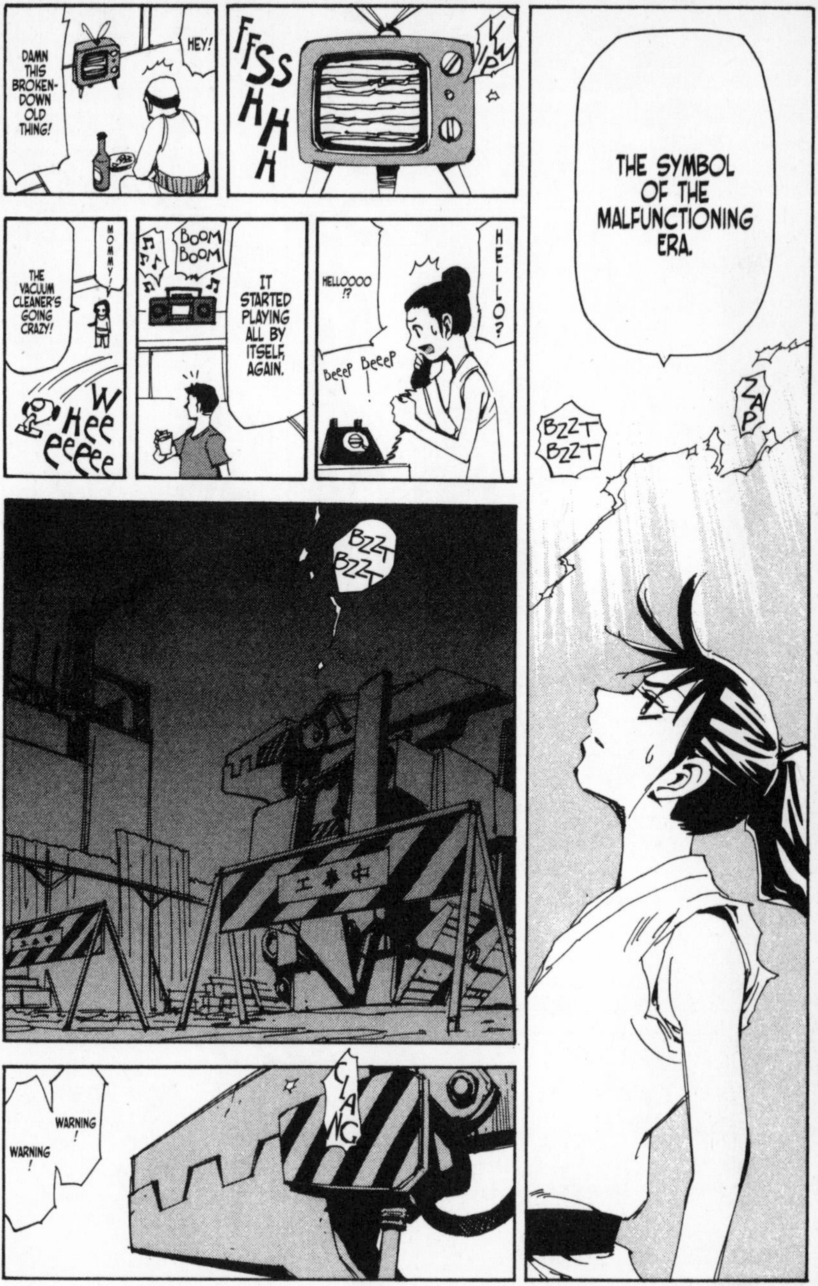
THE SYMBOL OF THE MALFUNCTIONING ERA.
ZAP
BZZT BZZT
VWIP
FFSSHHHH
HEY!
DAMN THIS BROKEN-DOWN OLD THING!
HELLO?
HELLOOOO!?
Beeep Beeep
IT STARTED PLAYING ALL BY ITSELF, AGAIN.
BOOM BOOM
MOMMY!
THE VACUUM CLEANER'S GOING CRAZY!
WHEEeeeee
BZZT BZZT
CLANG
WARNING!
WARNING!

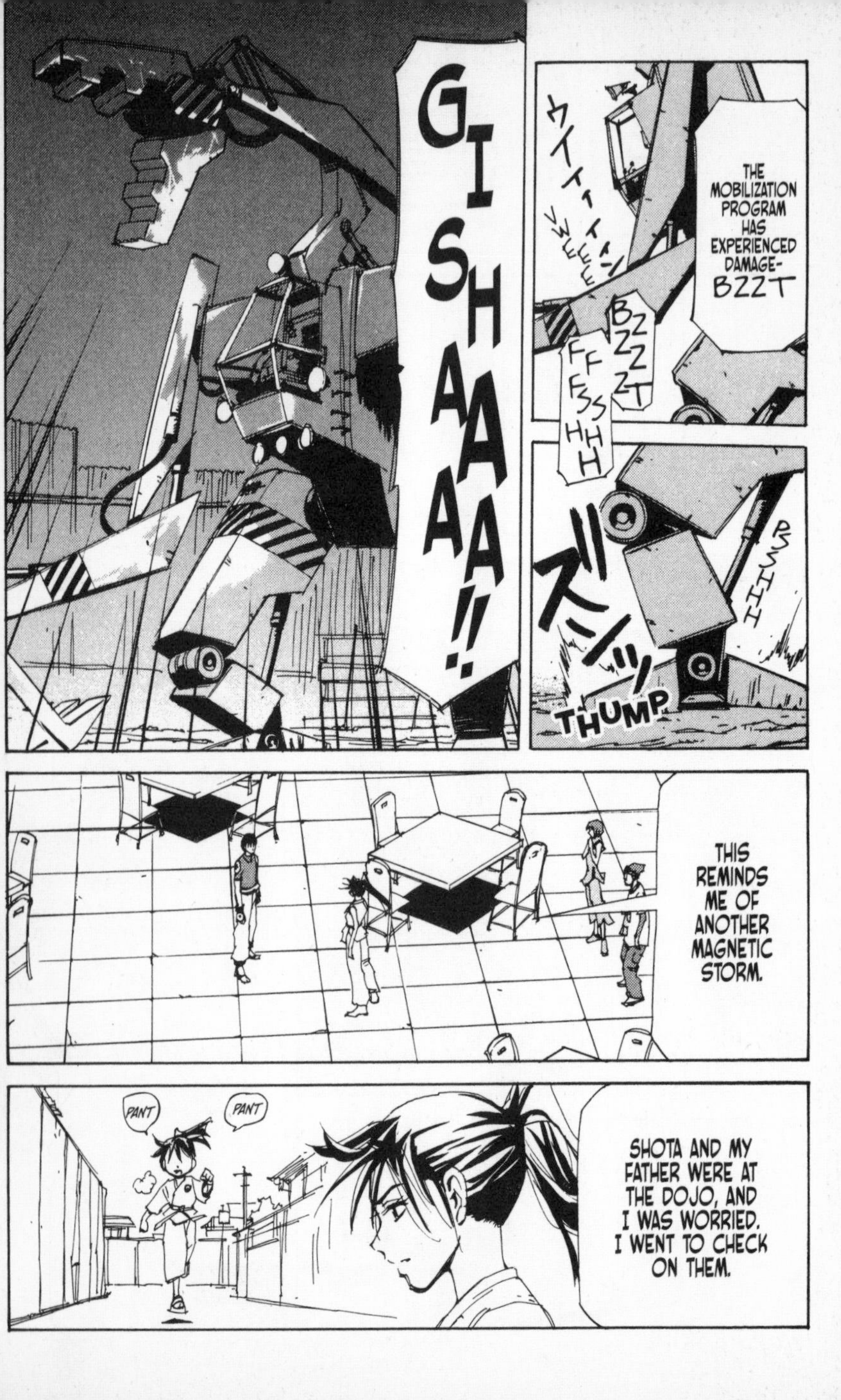
VWEEEE
THE MOBILIZATION PROGRAM HAS EXPERIENCED DAMAGE- BZZT
BZZZT
FFFSSHHH
PSSHHH
THUMP
GISHAAAAA!!
THIS REMINDS ME OF ANOTHER MAGNETIC STORM.
SHOTA AND MY FATHER WERE AT THE DOJO, AND I WAS WORRIED. I WENT TO CHECK ON THEM.
PANT
PANT

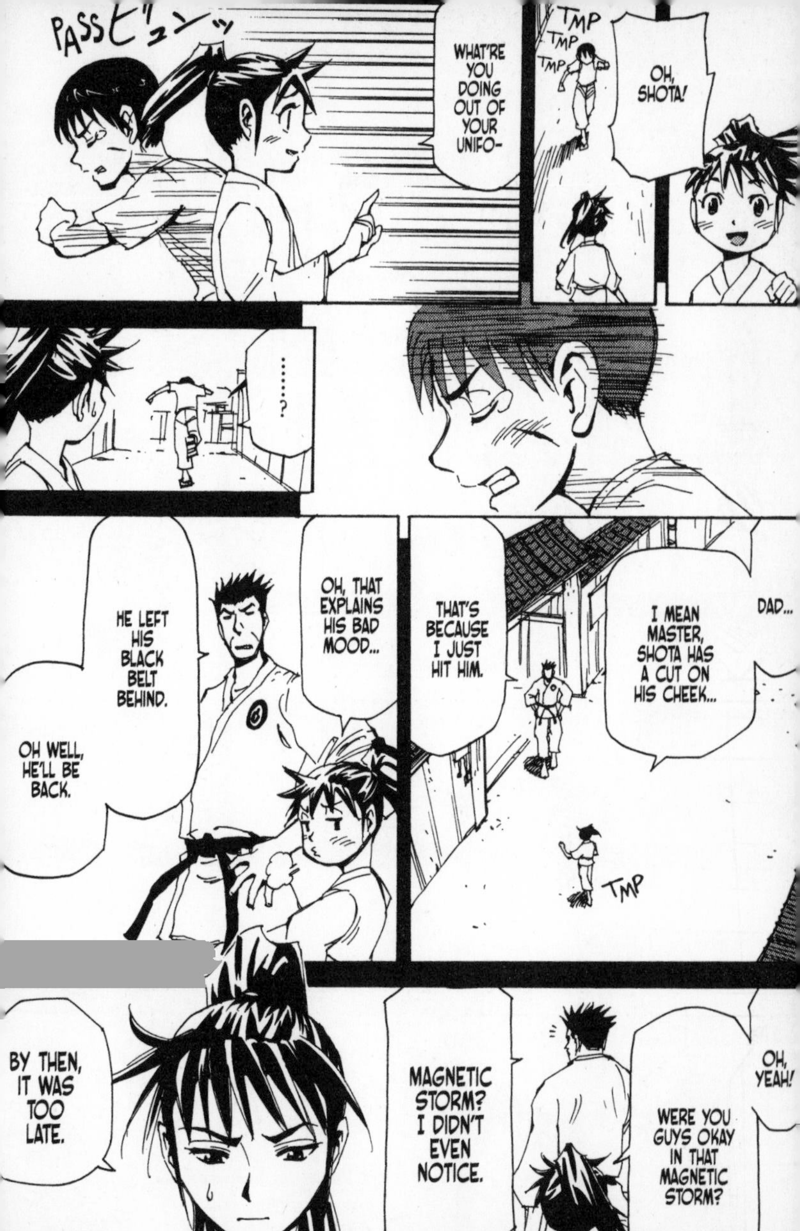
TMP
TMP
TMP
OH, SHOTA!
WHAT'RE YOU DOING OUT OF YOUR UNIFO-
PASS ビュンッ
......?
DAD...
I MEAN MASTER, SHOTA HAS A CUT ON HIS CHEEK...
THAT'S BECAUSE I JUST HIT HIM.
TMP
OH, THAT EXPLAINS HIS BAD MOOD...
HE LEFT HIS BLACK BELT BEHIND.
OH WELL, HE'LL BE BACK.
OH, YEAH!
WERE YOU GUYS OKAY IN THAT MAGNETIC STORM?
MAGNETIC STORM? I DIDN'T EVEN NOTICE.
BY THEN, IT WAS TOO LATE.

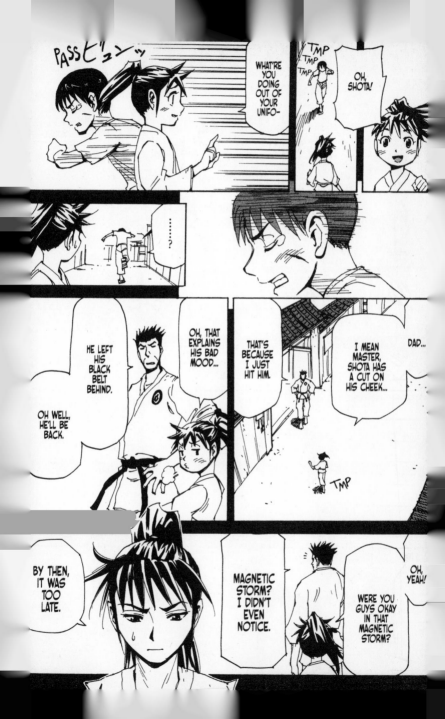

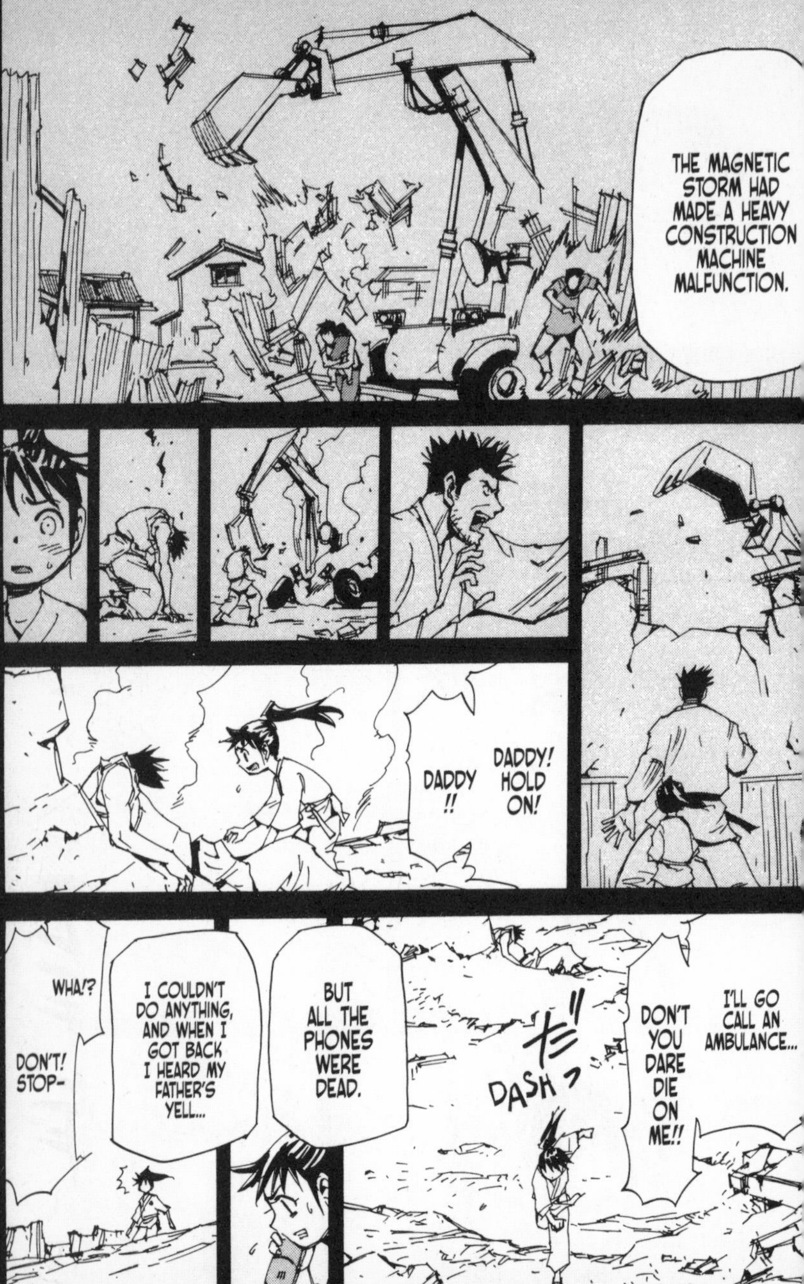
THE MAGNETIC STORM HAD MADE A HEAVY CONSTRUCTION MACHINE MALFUNCTION.
DADDY! HOLD ON!
DADDY !!
I'LL GO CALL AN AMBULANCE...
DON'T YOU DARE DIE ON ME!!
DASH
BUT ALL THE PHONES WERE DEAD.
I COULDN'T DO ANYTHING, AND WHEN I GOT BACK I HEARD MY FATHER'S YELL...
WHA!?
DON'T! STOP-

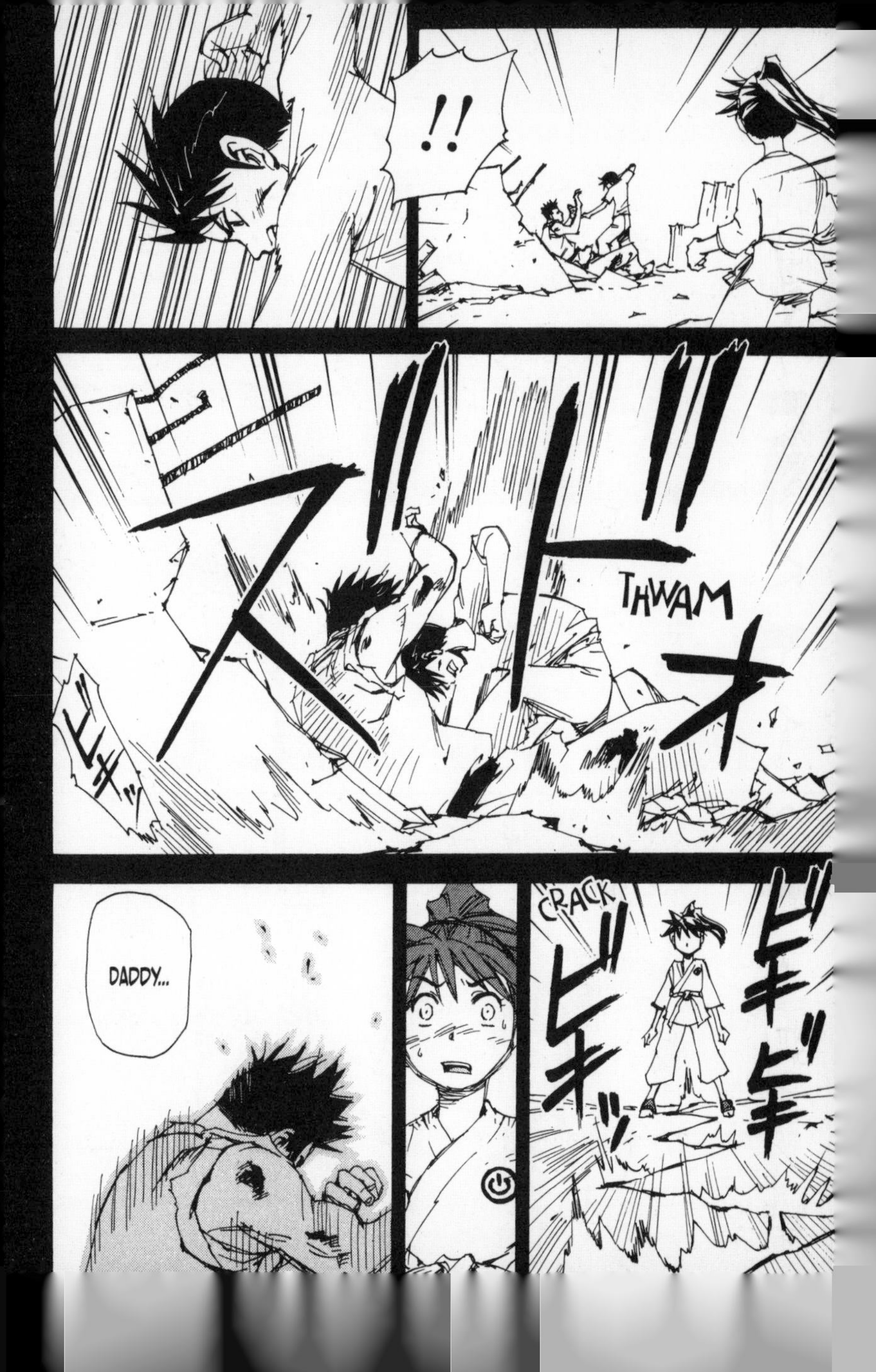

!!
THWAM
CRACK
DADDY...

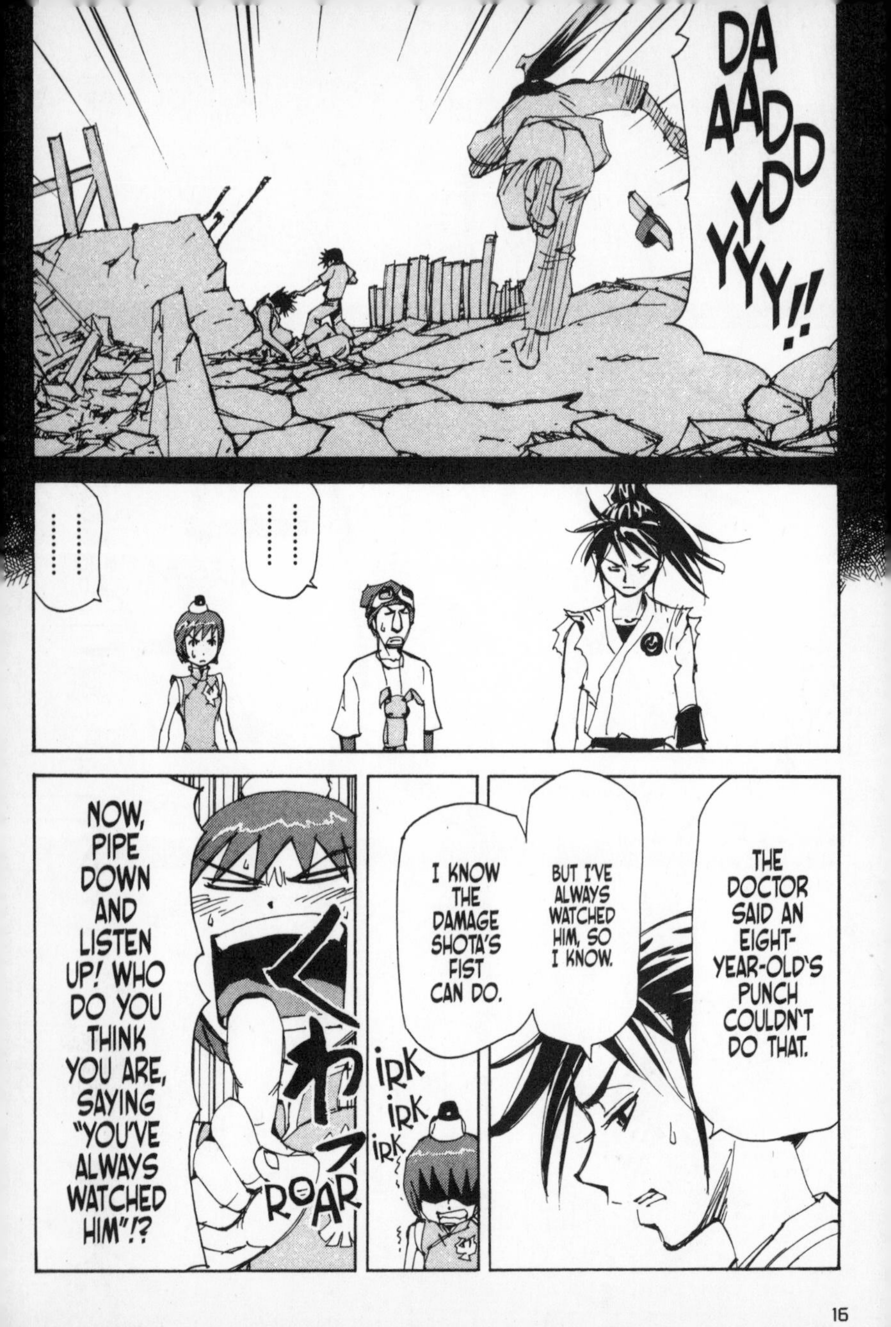
DAAADDYDDYYY!!
……
……
THE DOCTOR SAID AN EIGHT-YEAR-OLD'S PUNCH COULDN'T DO THAT.
BUT I'VE ALWAYS WATCHED HIM, SO I KNOW.
I KNOW THE DAMAGE SHOTA'S FIST CAN DO.
IRK IRK IRK
NOW, PIPE DOWN AND LISTEN UP! WHO DO YOU THINK YOU ARE, SAYING "YOU'VE ALWAYS WATCHED HIM"!?
わッ
ROAR

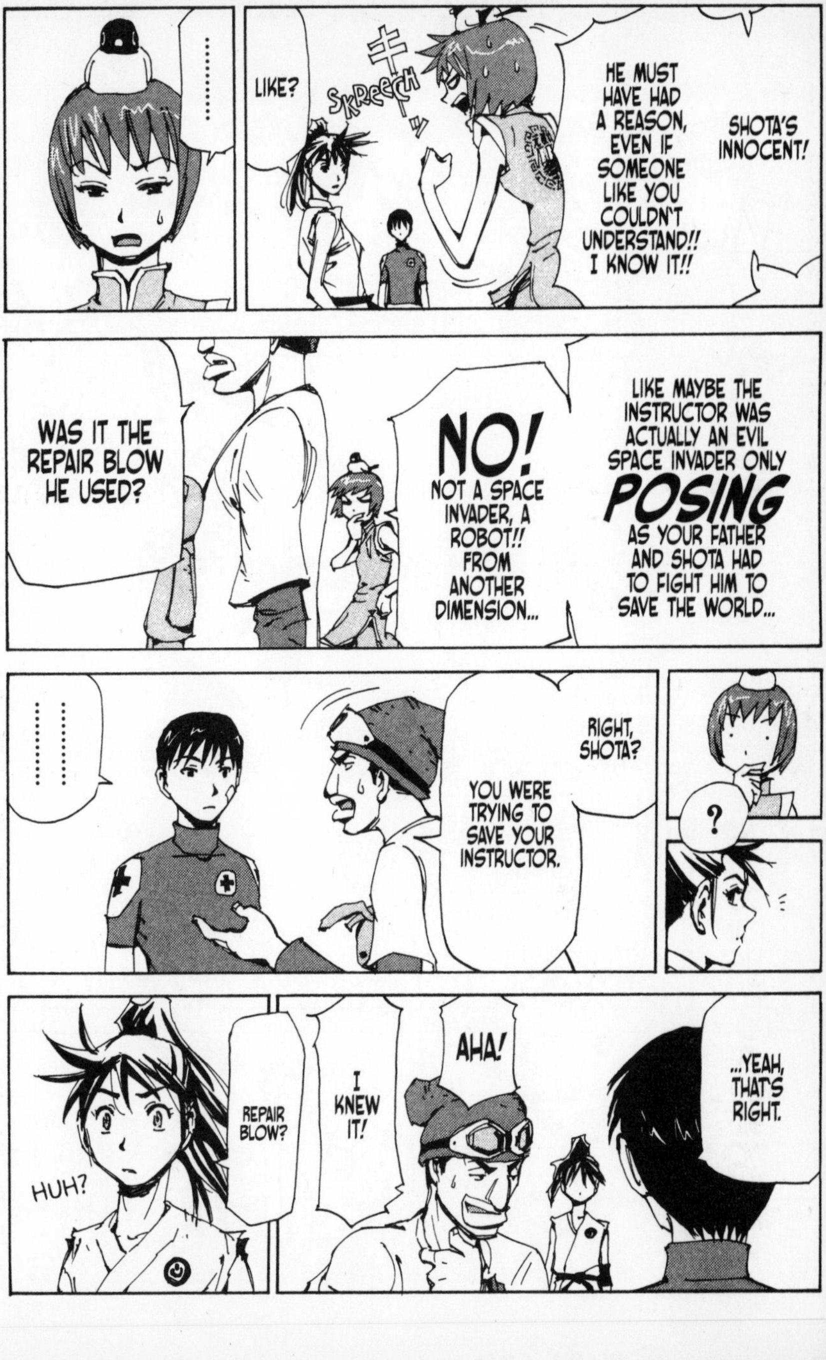
SHOTA'S INNOCENT!
HE MUST HAVE HAD A REASON, EVEN IF SOMEONE LIKE YOU COULDN'T UNDERSTAND!! I KNOW IT!!
SKREECH
LIKE?
......
LIKE MAYBE THE INSTRUCTOR WAS ACTUALLY AN EVIL SPACE INVADER ONLY POSING AS YOUR FATHER AND SHOTA HAD TO FIGHT HIM TO SAVE THE WORLD...
NO! NOT A SPACE INVADER, A ROBOT!! FROM ANOTHER DIMENSION...
WAS IT THE REPAIR BLOW HE USED?
?
RIGHT, SHOTA?
YOU WERE TRYING TO SAVE YOUR INSTRUCTOR.
......
...YEAH, THAT'S RIGHT.
AHA!
I KNEW IT!
REPAIR BLOW?
HUH?

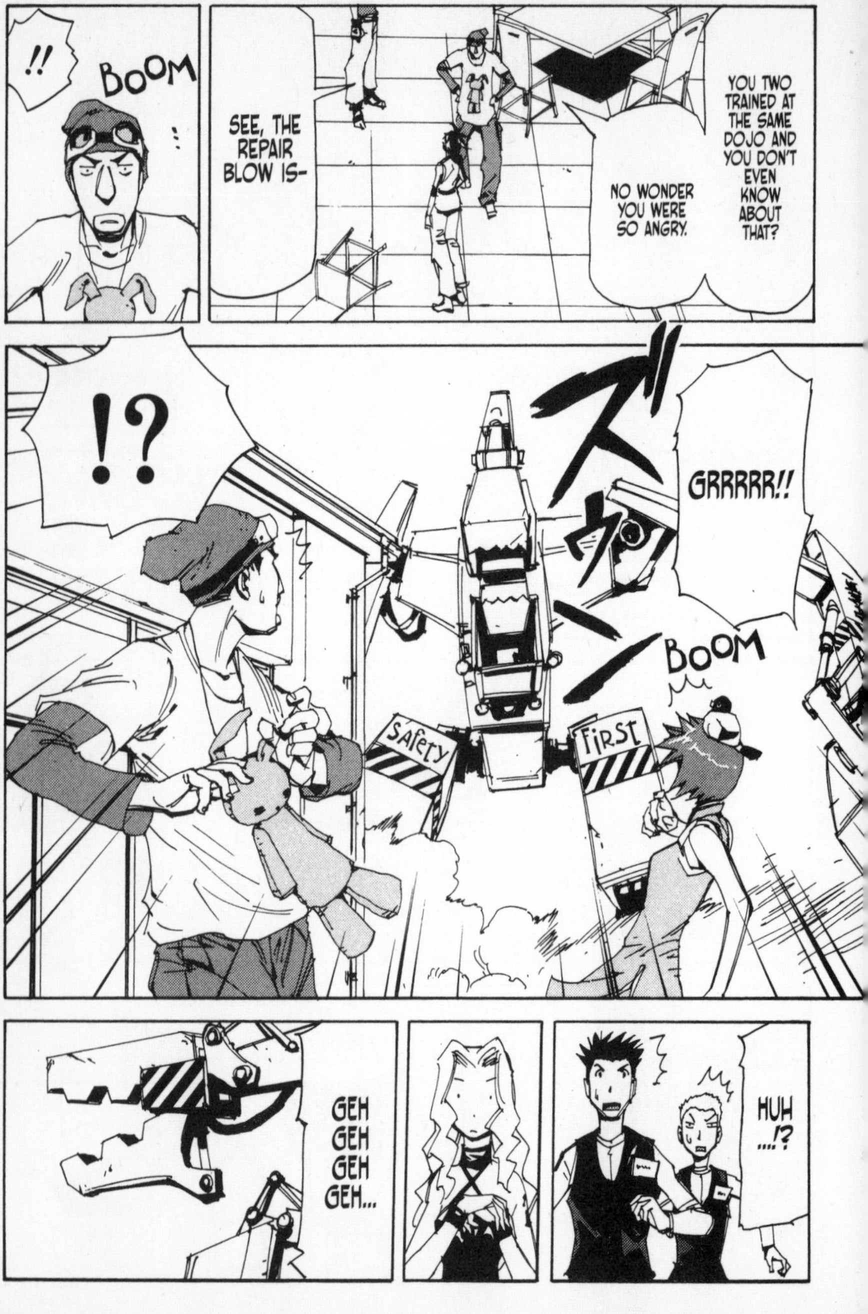
YOU TWO TRAINED AT THE SAME DOJO AND YOU DON'T EVEN KNOW ABOUT THAT?
NO WONDER YOU WERE SO ANGRY.
SEE, THE REPAIR BLOW IS-
!!
BOOM
GRRRRR!!
BOOM
First
Safety
!?
HUH ...!?
GEH GEH GEH GEH...

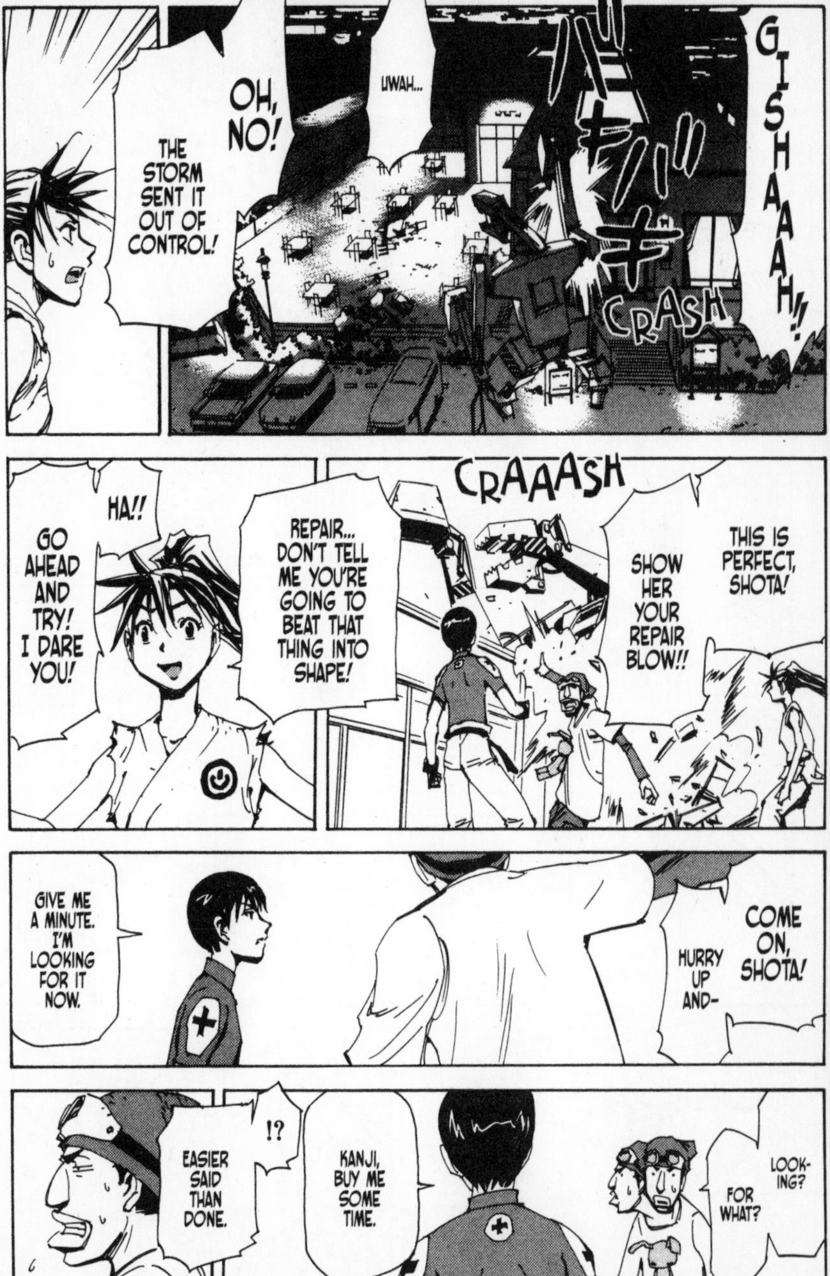
GISHAAAAH!!
CRASH
UWAH...
OH, NO!
THE STORM SENT IT OUT OF CONTROL!
CRAAASH
THIS IS PERFECT, SHOTA!
SHOW HER YOUR REPAIR BLOW!!
REPAIR... DON'T TELL ME YOU'RE GOING TO BEAT THAT THING INTO SHAPE!
HA!!
GO AHEAD AND TRY! I DARE YOU!
COME ON, SHOTA!
HURRY UP AND-
GIVE ME A MINUTE. I'M LOOKING FOR IT NOW.
LOOKING?
FOR WHAT?
KANJI, BUY ME SOME TIME.
!?
EASIER SAID THAN DONE.

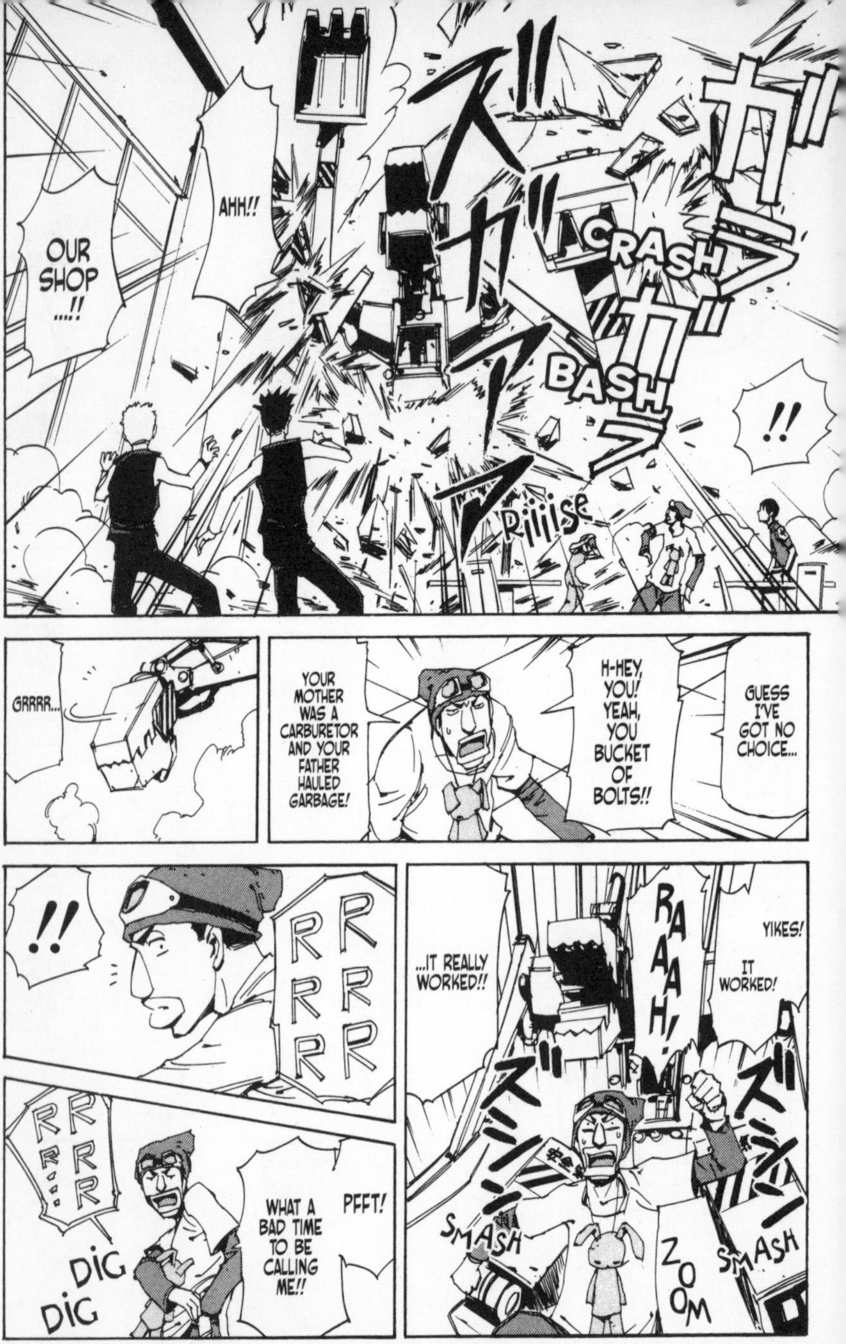
CRASH
BASH
!!
Riiiise
AHH!!
OUR SHOP ...!!
GUESS I'VE GOT NO CHOICE...
H-HEY, YOU! YEAH, YOU BUCKET OF BOLTS!!
YOUR MOTHER WAS A CARBURETOR AND YOUR FATHER HAULED GARBAGE!
GRRRR...
YIKES!
IT WORKED!
RAAAH!!
...IT REALLY WORKED!!
SMASH
ZOOM
SMASH
RRRRRR
!!
PFFT!
WHAT A BAD TIME TO BE CALLING ME!!
RRRRR
DIG
DIG

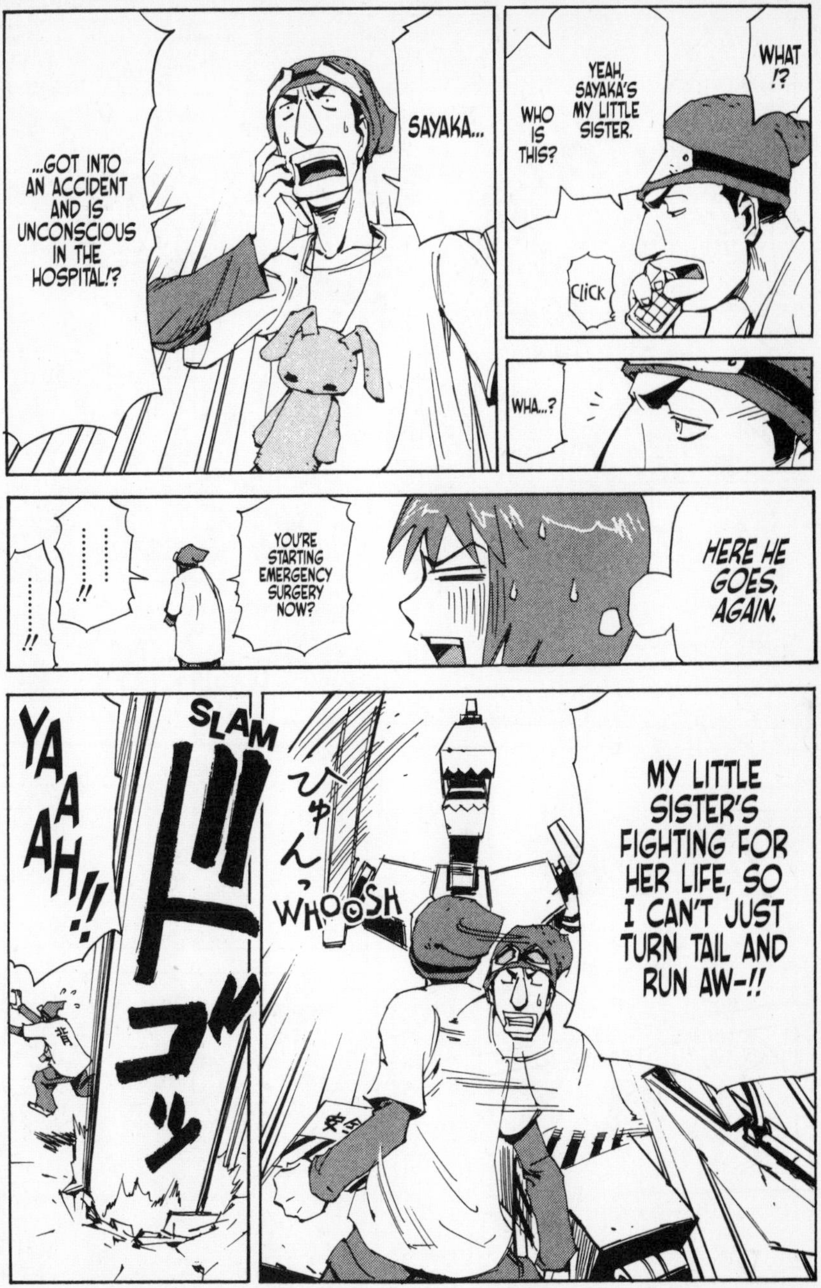
WHAT!?
YEAH, SAYAKA'S MY LITTLE SISTER.
WHO IS THIS?
CLICK
WHA...?
SAYAKA...
...GOT INTO AN ACCIDENT AND IS UNCONSCIOUS IN THE HOSPITAL!?
HERE HE GOES, AGAIN.
YOU'RE STARTING EMERGENCY SURGERY NOW?
......!!
......!!
MY LITTLE SISTER'S FIGHTING FOR HER LIFE, SO I CAN'T JUST TURN TAIL AND RUN AW-!!
ひゅんっ
WHOOSH
SLAM
ドゴッ
YAAAAH!!!

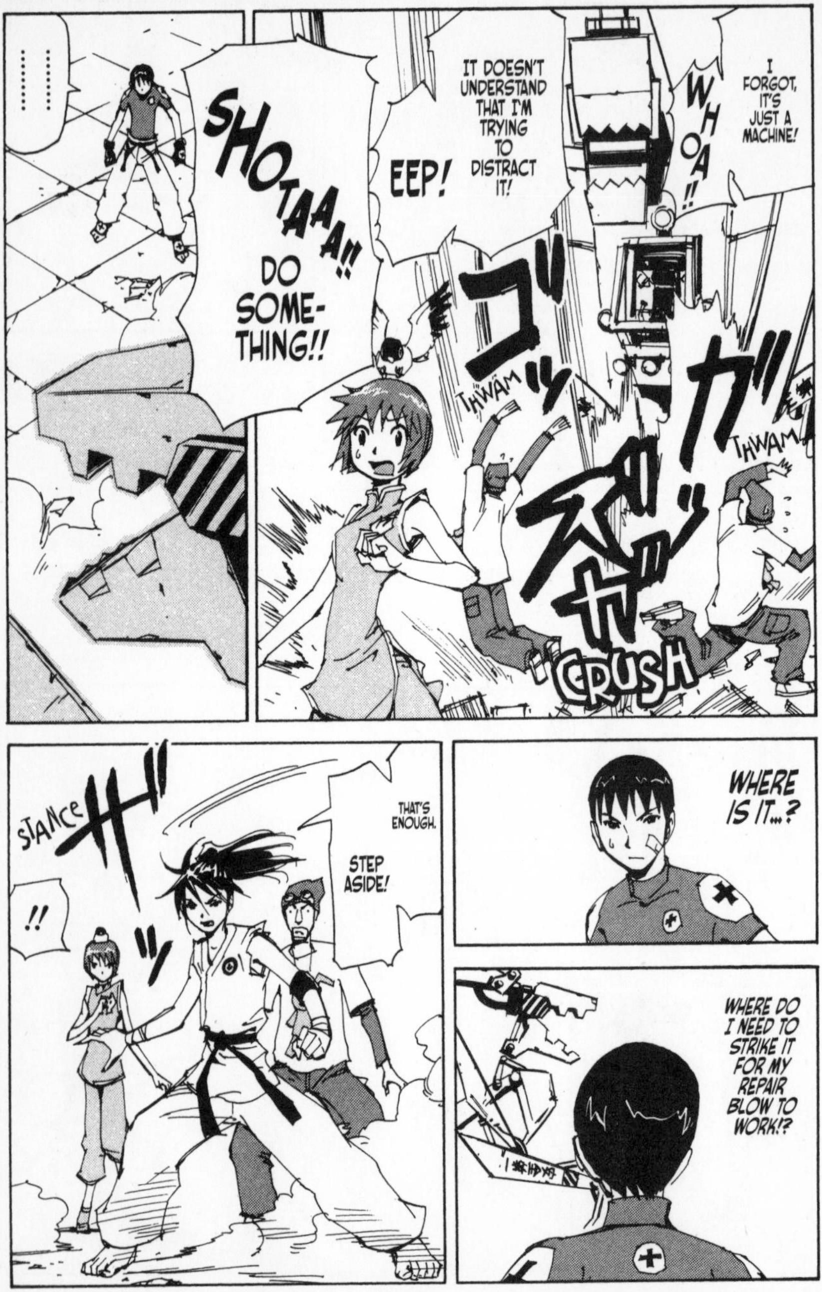
I FORGOT, IT'S JUST A MACHINE!
WHOA!!
IT DOESN'T UNDERSTAND THAT I'M TRYING TO DISTRACT IT!
EEP!
SHOTAAAA!! DO SOMETHING!!
THWAM
THWAM
CRUSH
......
WHERE IS IT...?
WHERE DO I NEED TO STRIKE IT FOR MY REPAIR BLOW TO WORK!?
THAT'S ENOUGH.
STEP ASIDE!
STANCE
!!

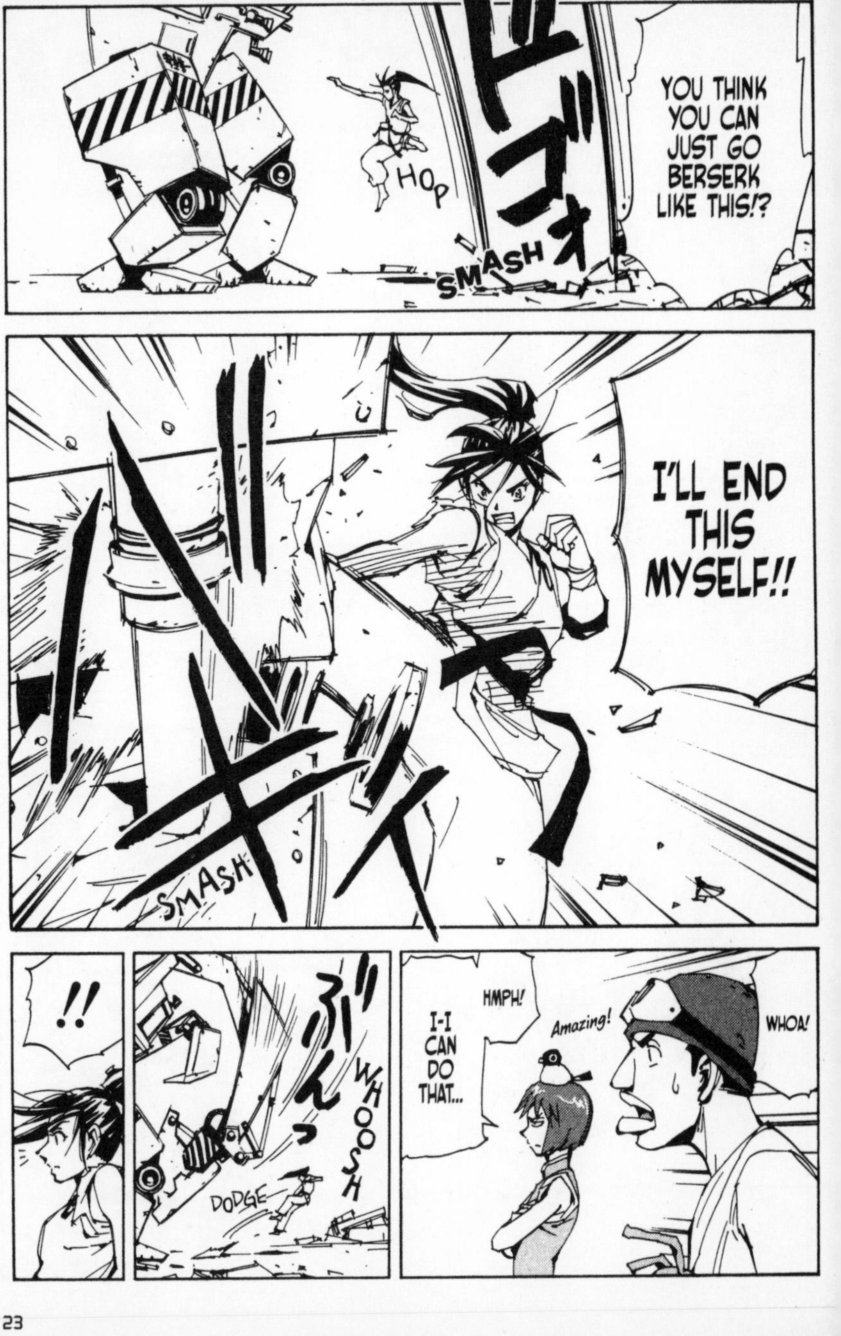
YOU THINK YOU CAN JUST GO BERSERK LIKE THIS!?
ドゴォ
SMASH
HOP
I'LL END THIS MYSELF!!
バキィ
SMASH
WHOA!
Amazing!
HMPH!
I-I CAN DO THAT...
ぶんっ
WHOOSH
DODGE
!!

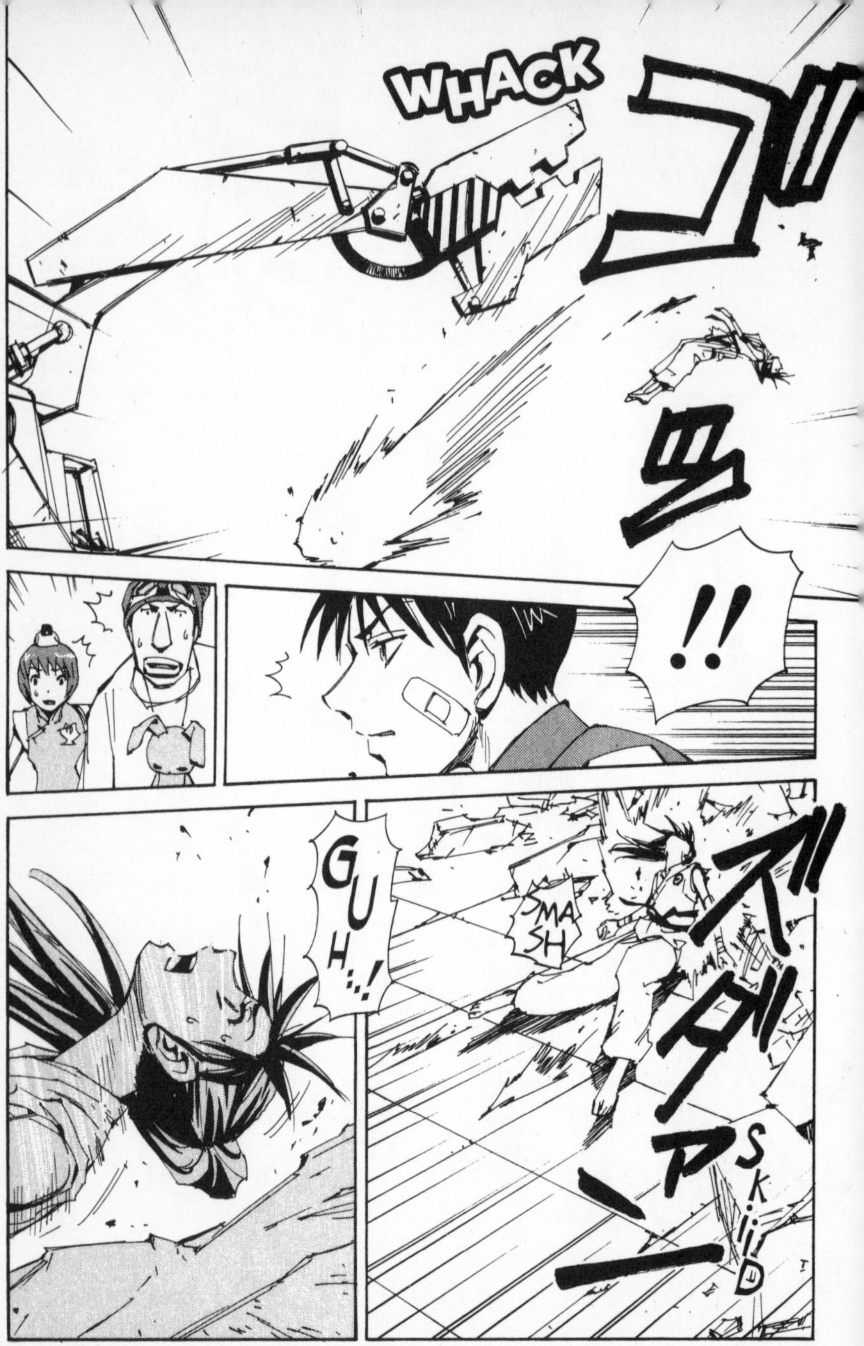
WHACK
!!
SMASH
SKIIID
GUH...!

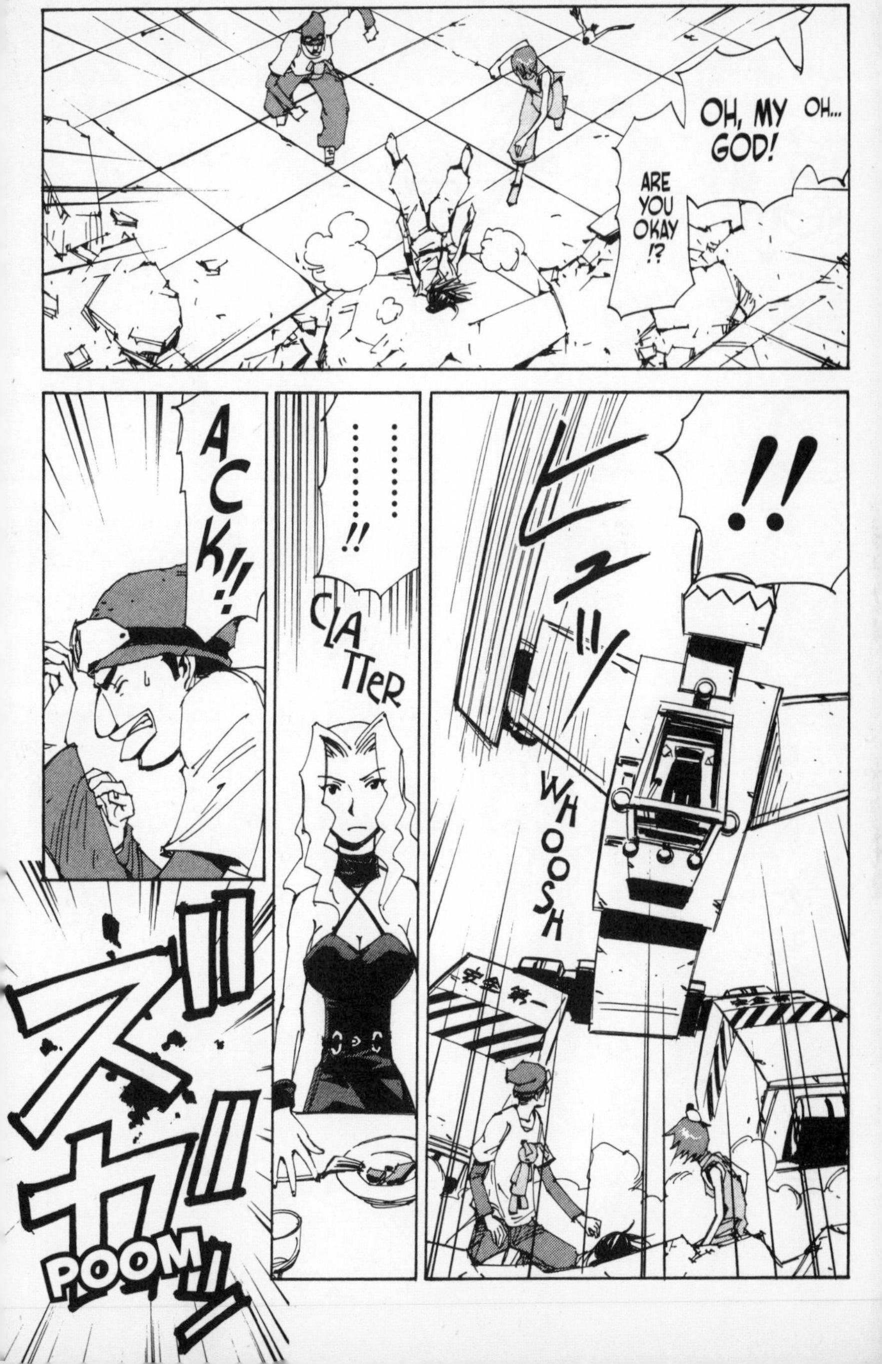
OH...
OH, MY GOD!
ARE YOU OKAY!?
!!
WHOOSH
......!!
CLATTER
ACK!!
POOM!!

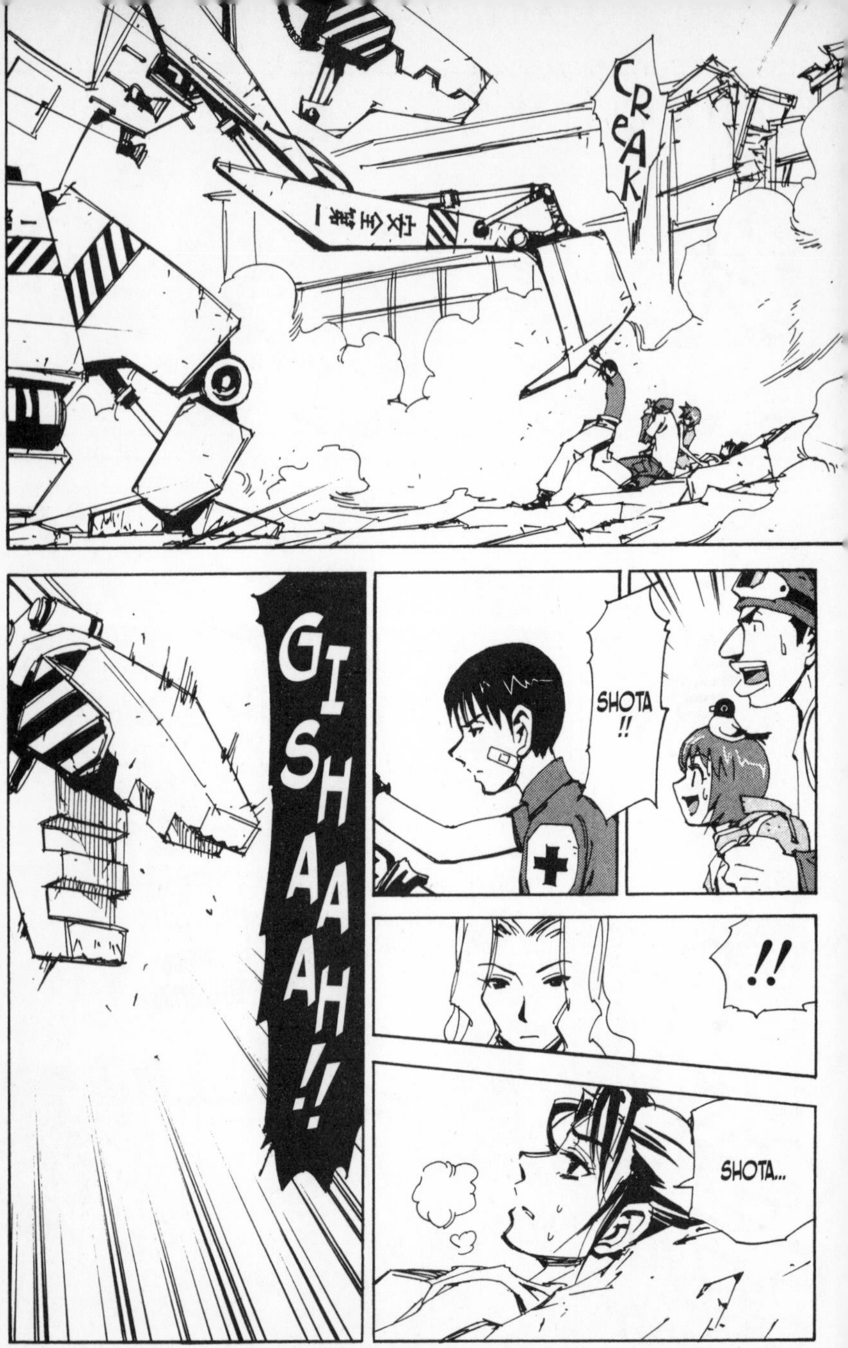
CREAK
SHOTA !!
!!
SHOTA...
GISHAAAH!!

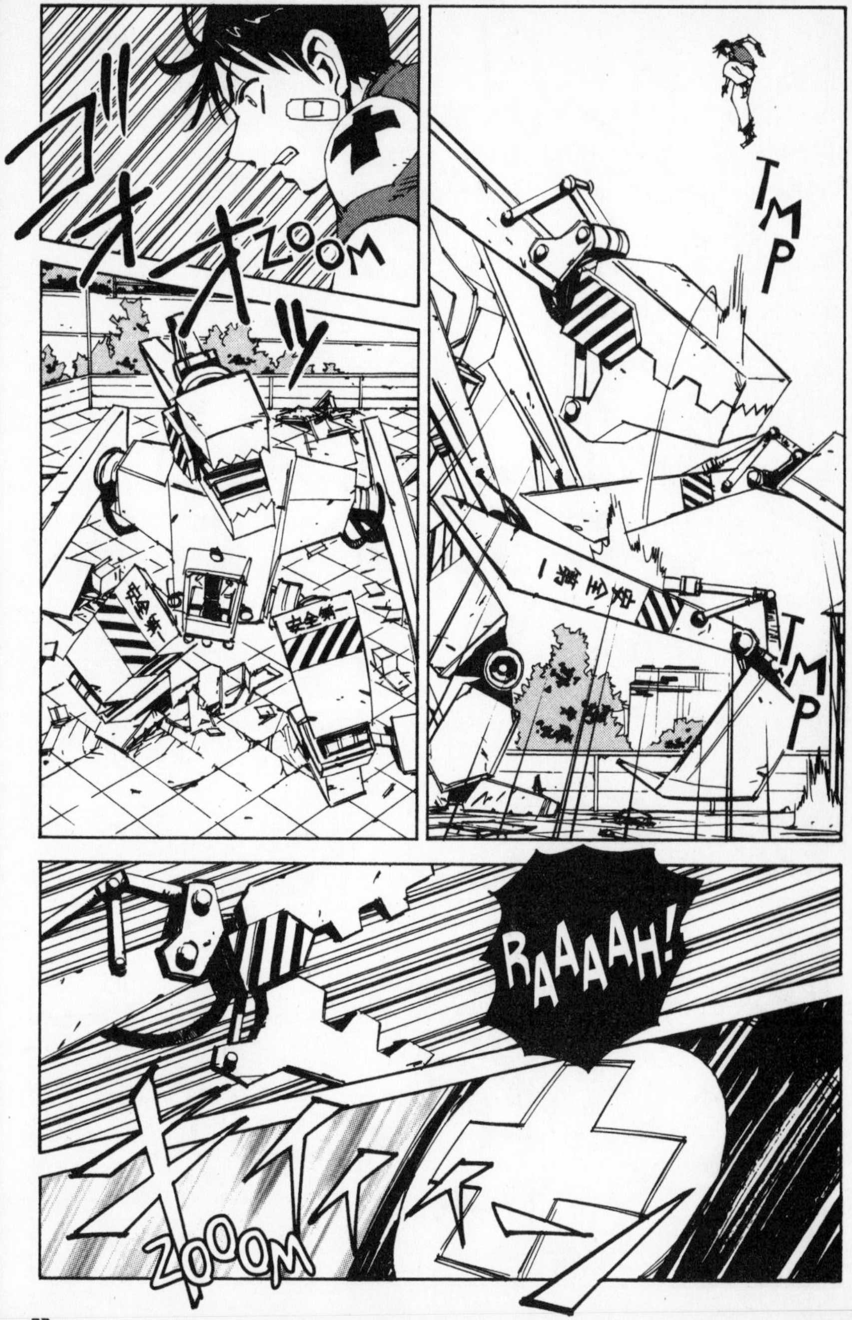
TMP
TMP
ゴオオッ
ZOOM
安全第一
RAAAAH!
ZOOOM

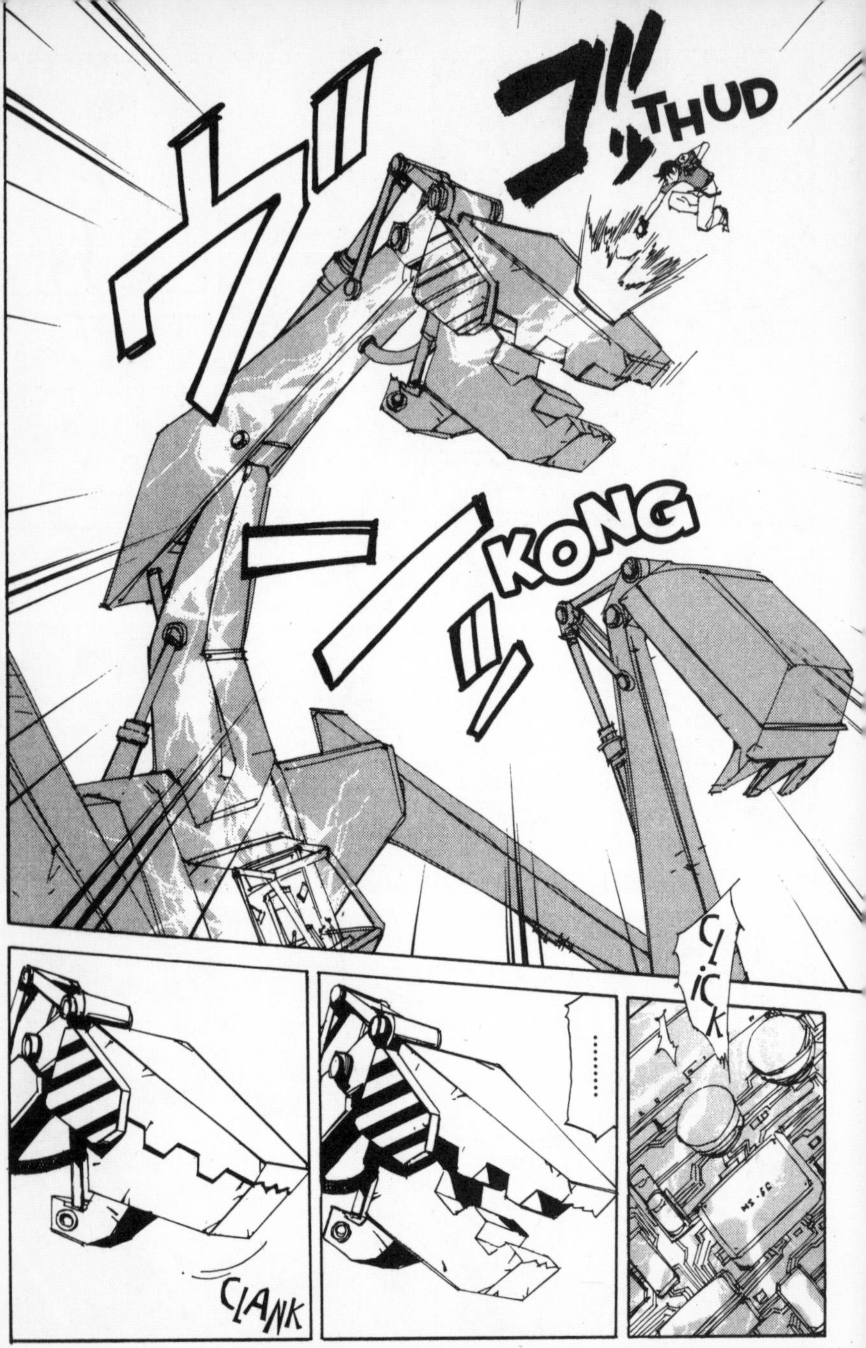
ゴッ
THUD
KONG
CLICK
......
CLANK

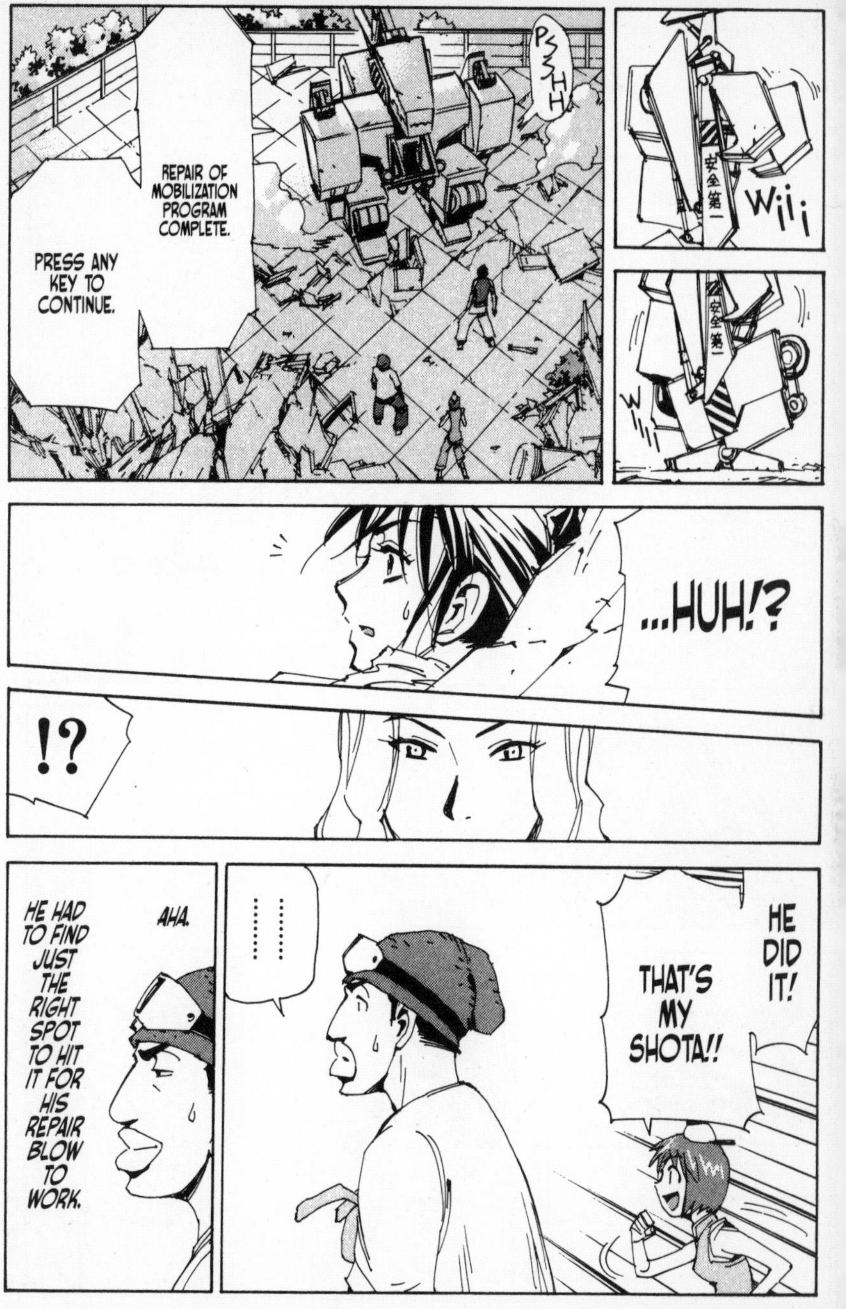
安全第一
Wiii
安全第一
Wiii
PSSHH
REPAIR OF MOBILIZATION PROGRAM COMPLETE.
PRESS ANY KEY TO CONTINUE.
...HUH!?
!?
HE DID IT!
THAT'S MY SHOTA!!
......
AHA.
HE HAD TO FIND JUST THE RIGHT SPOT TO HIT IT FOR HIS REPAIR BLOW TO WORK.

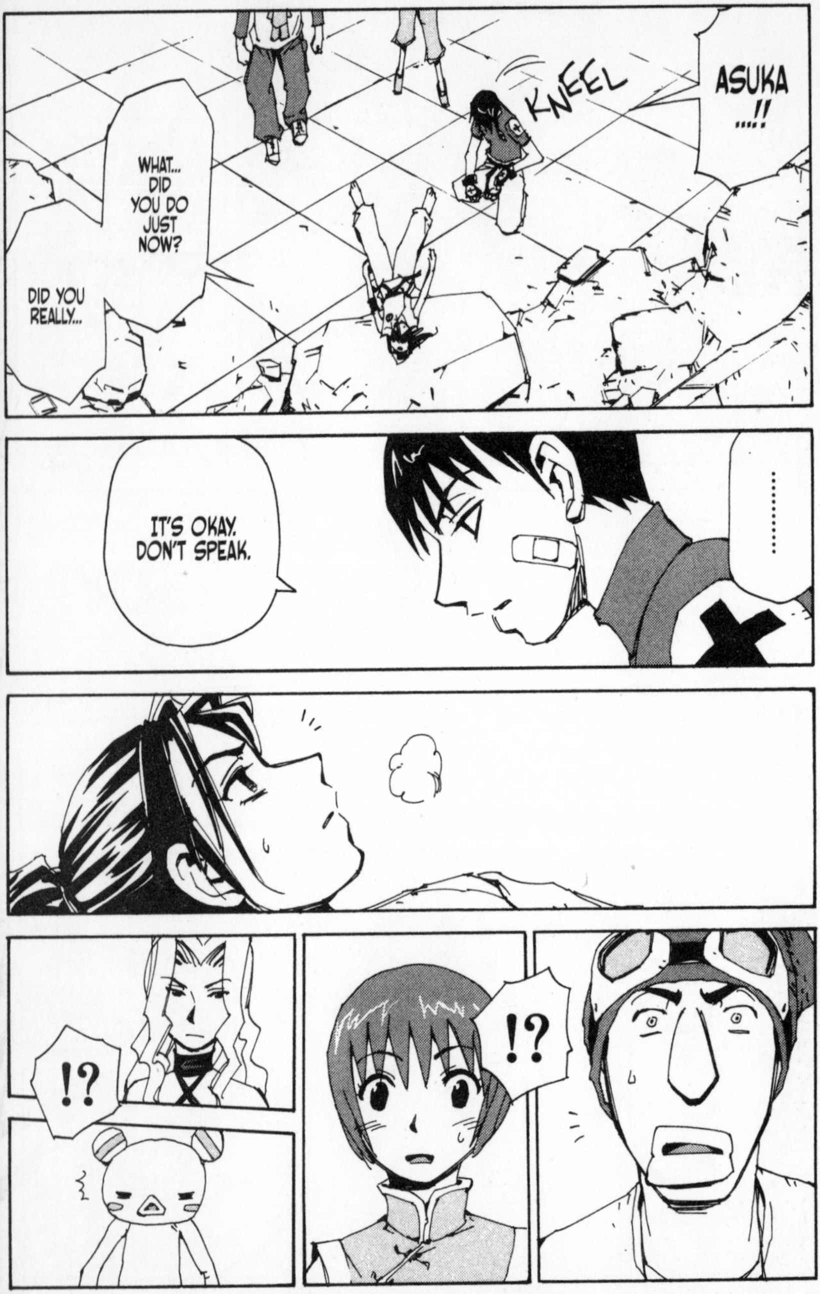
ASUKA ....!!
KNEEL
WHAT... DID YOU DO JUST NOW?
DID YOU REALLY...
......
IT'S OKAY. DON'T SPEAK.
!?
!?

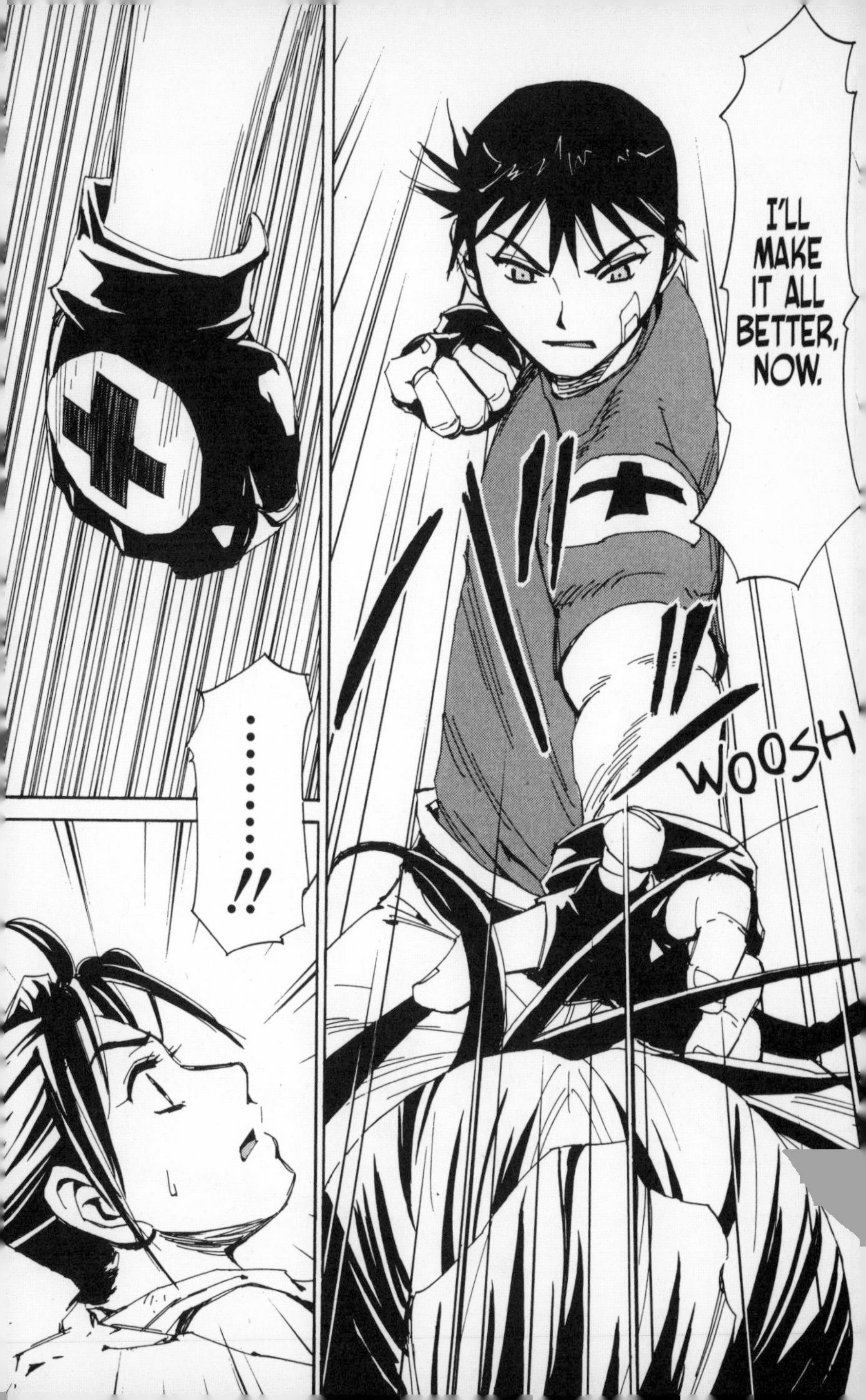
I'LL MAKE IT ALL BETTER, NOW.
WOOSH
.........!!

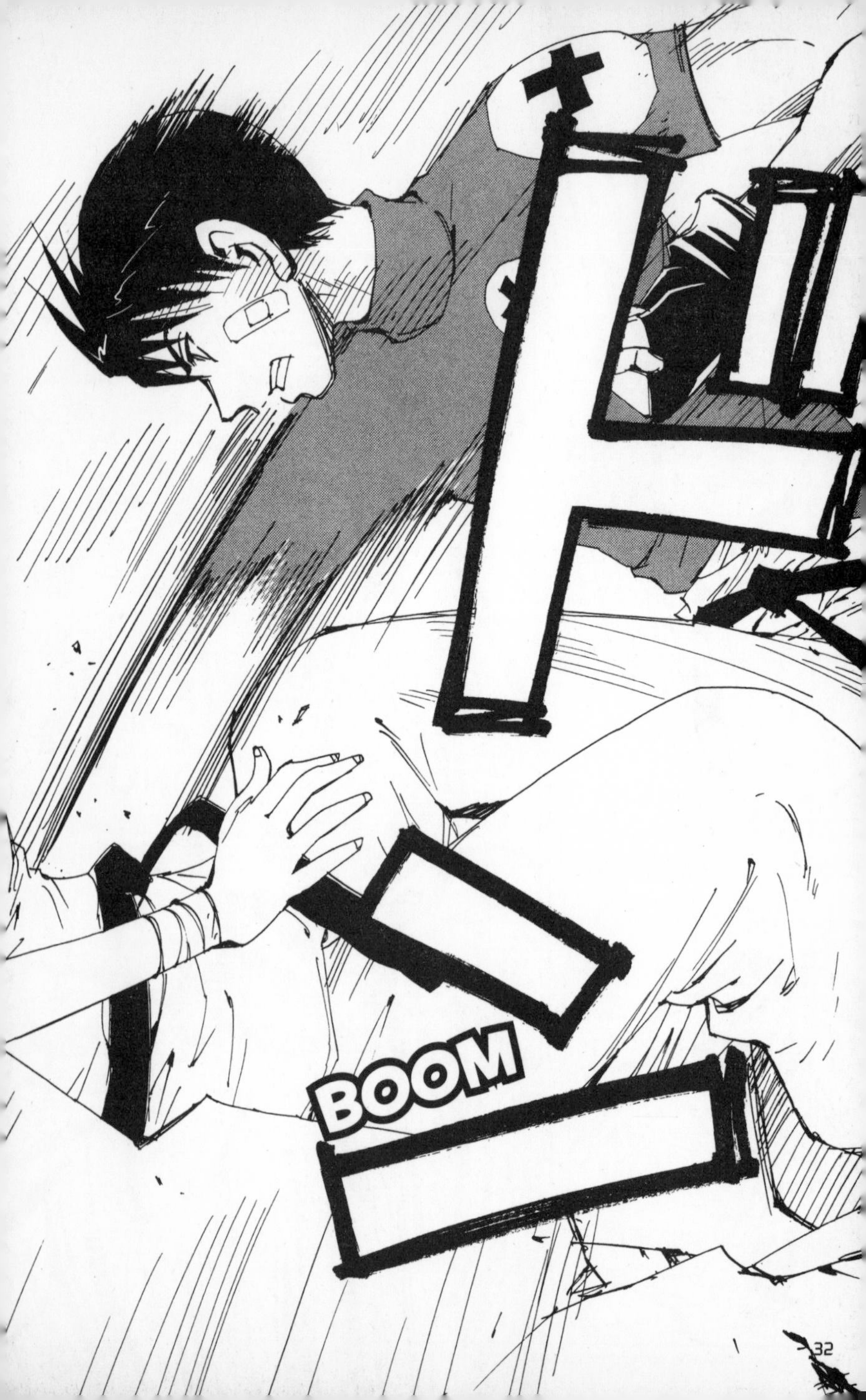
BOOM

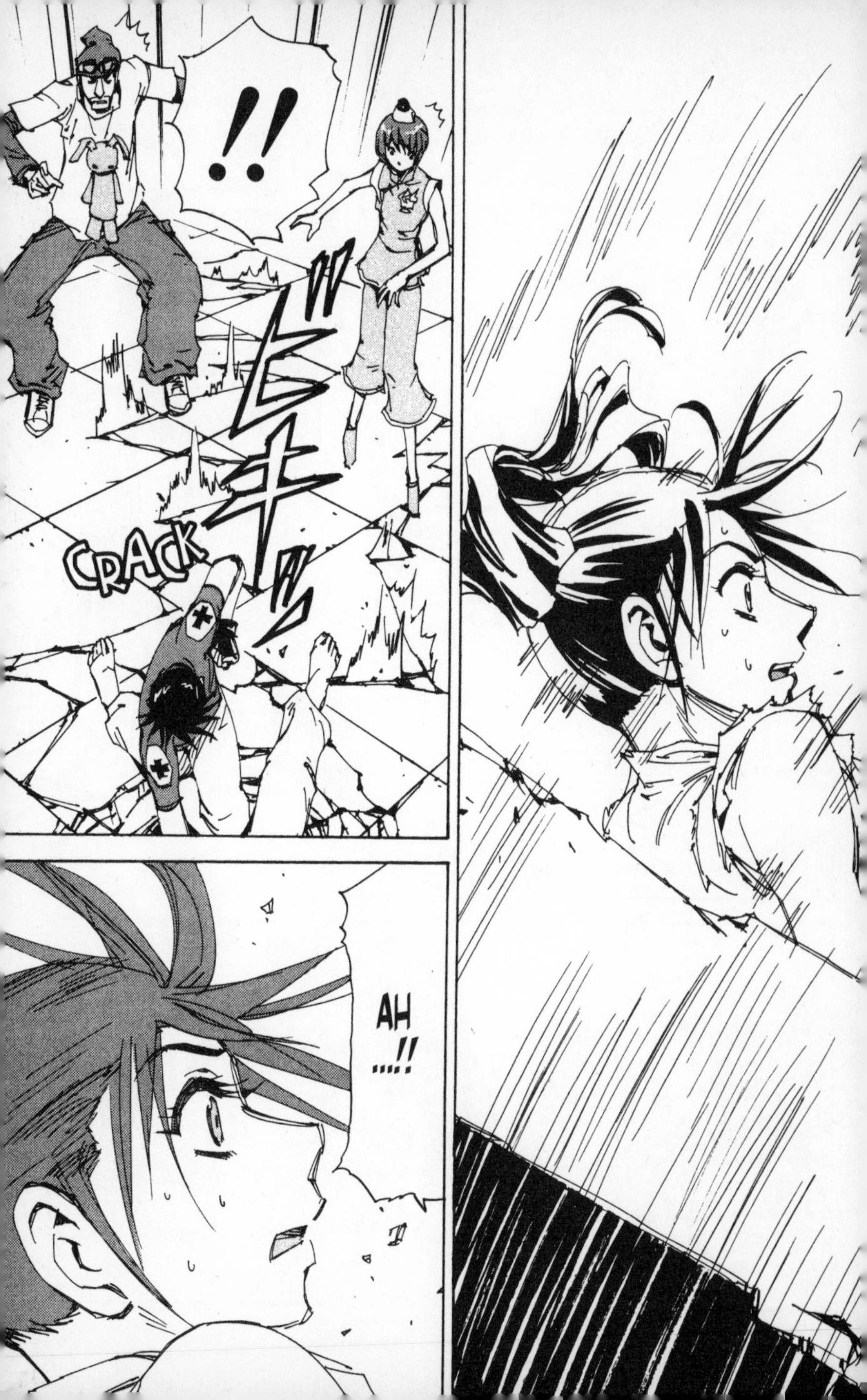
!!
ビキッ
CRACK
AH ...!!

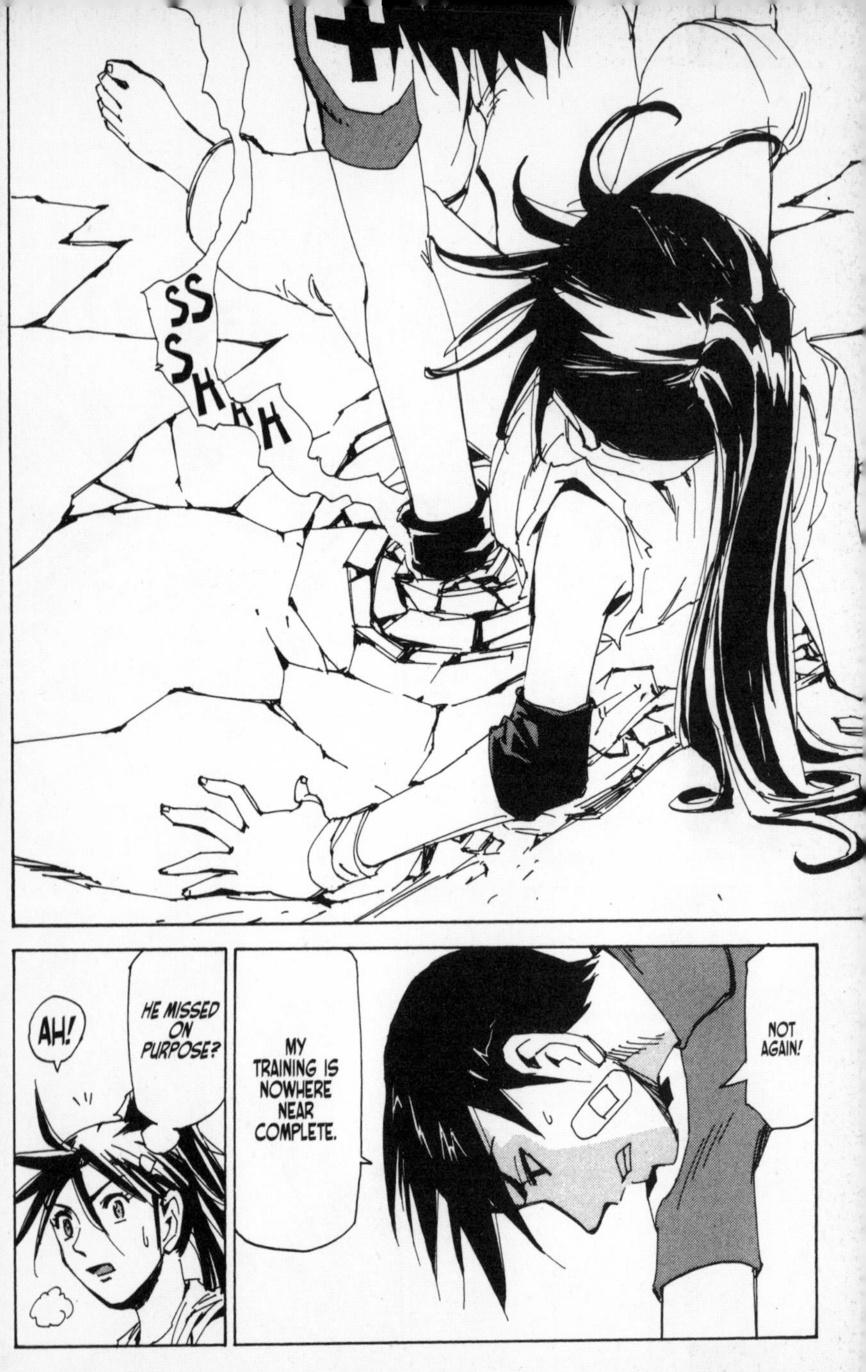
SSSHHHH
NOT AGAIN!
MY TRAINING IS NOWHERE NEAR COMPLETE.
HE MISSED ON PURPOSE?
AH!

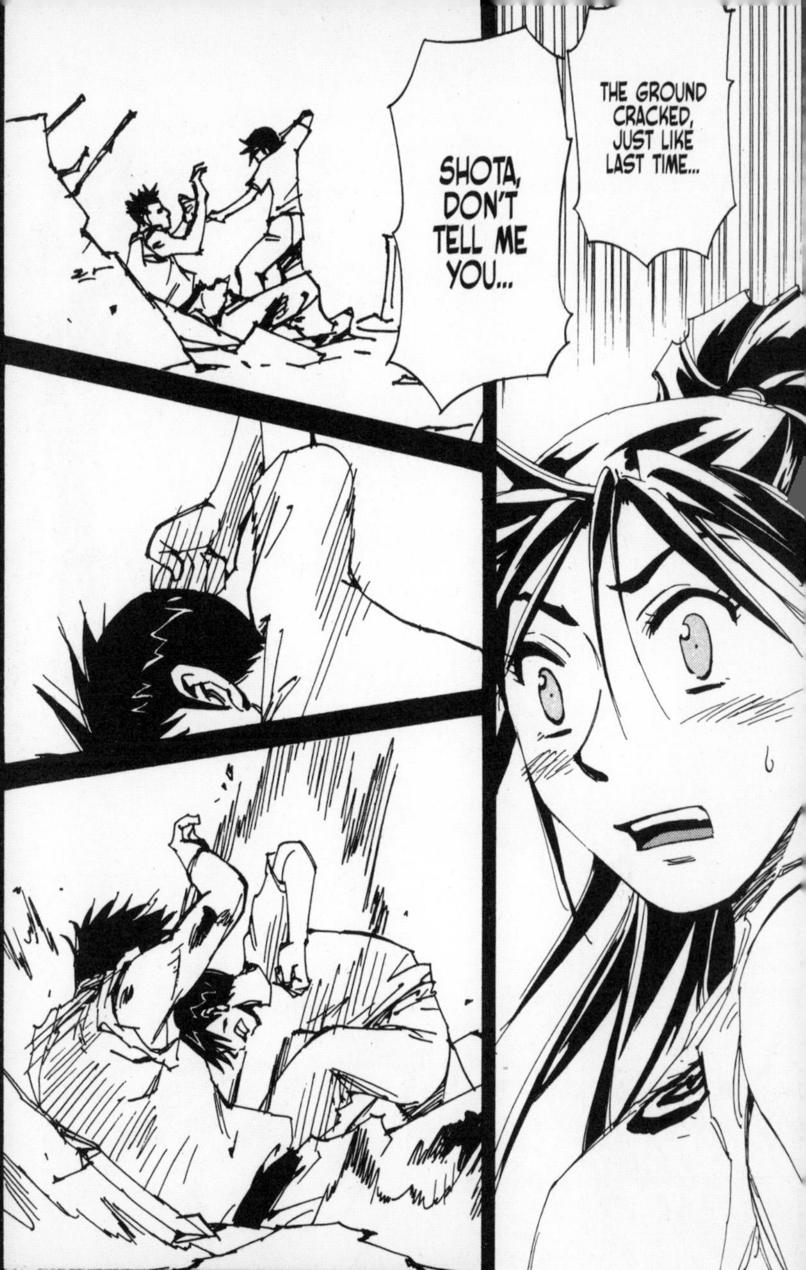
THE GROUND CRACKED, JUST LIKE LAST TIME...
SHOTA, DON'T TELL ME YOU...

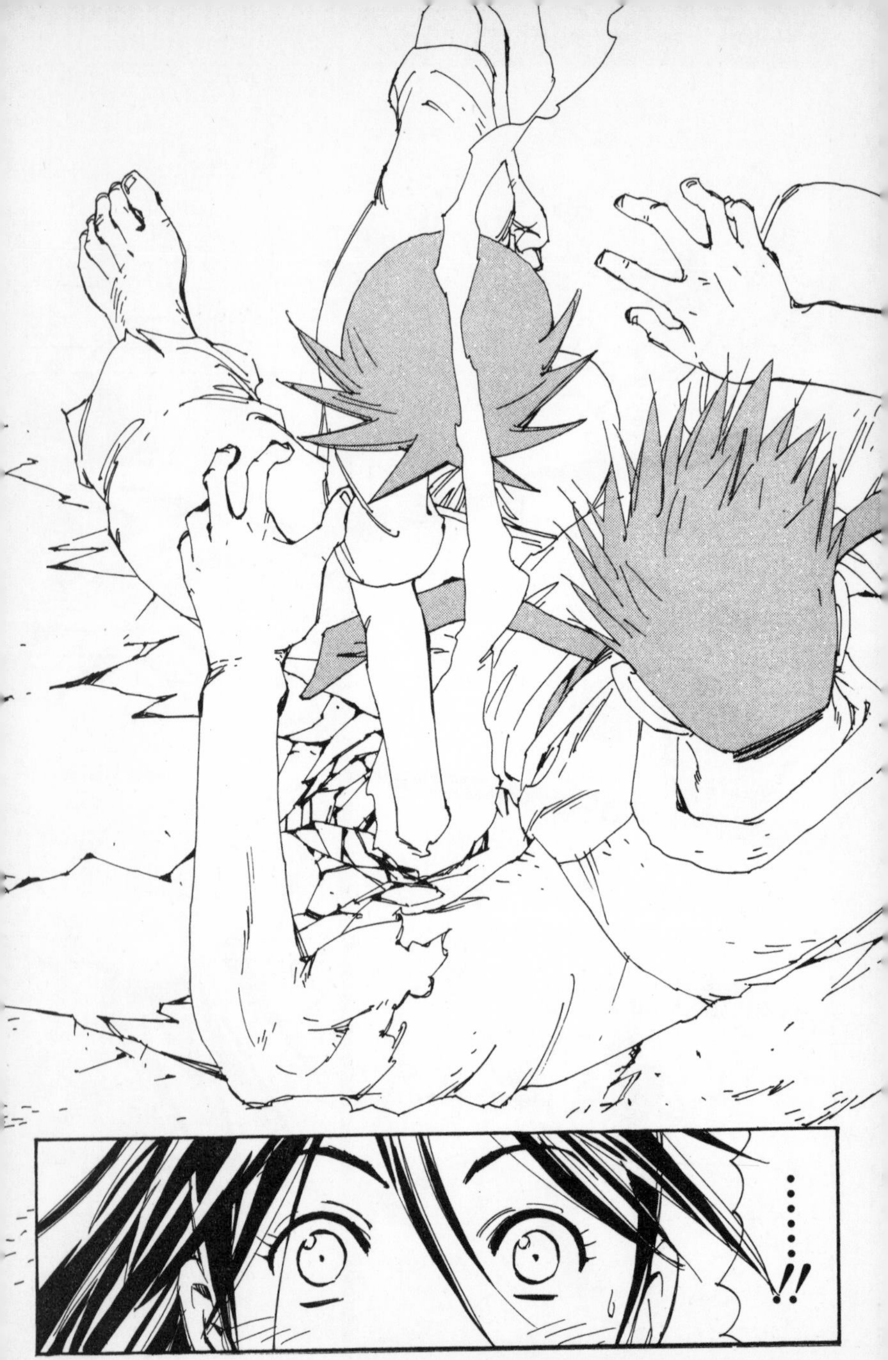
......!!

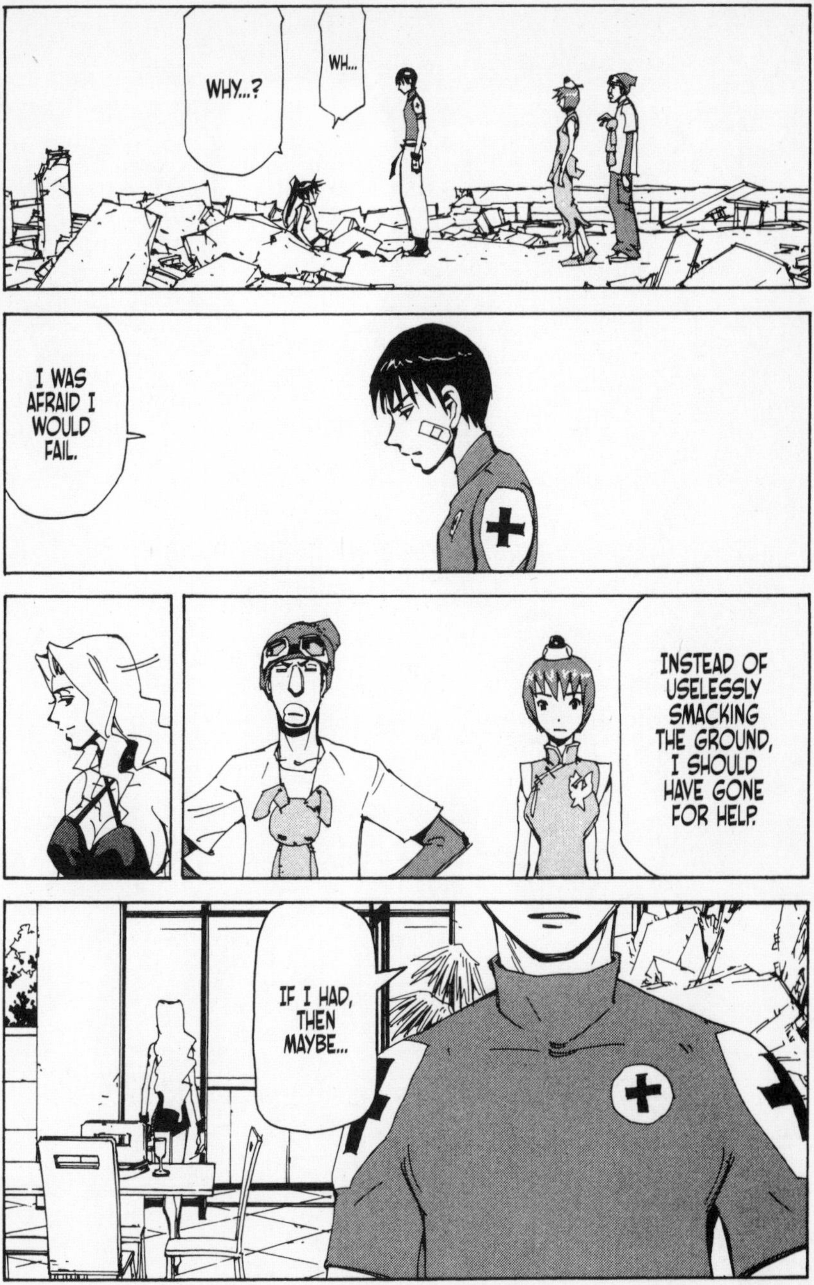
WH...
WHY...?
I WAS AFRAID I WOULD FAIL.
INSTEAD OF USELESSLY SMACKING THE GROUND, I SHOULD HAVE GONE FOR HELP.
IF I HAD, THEN MAYBE...

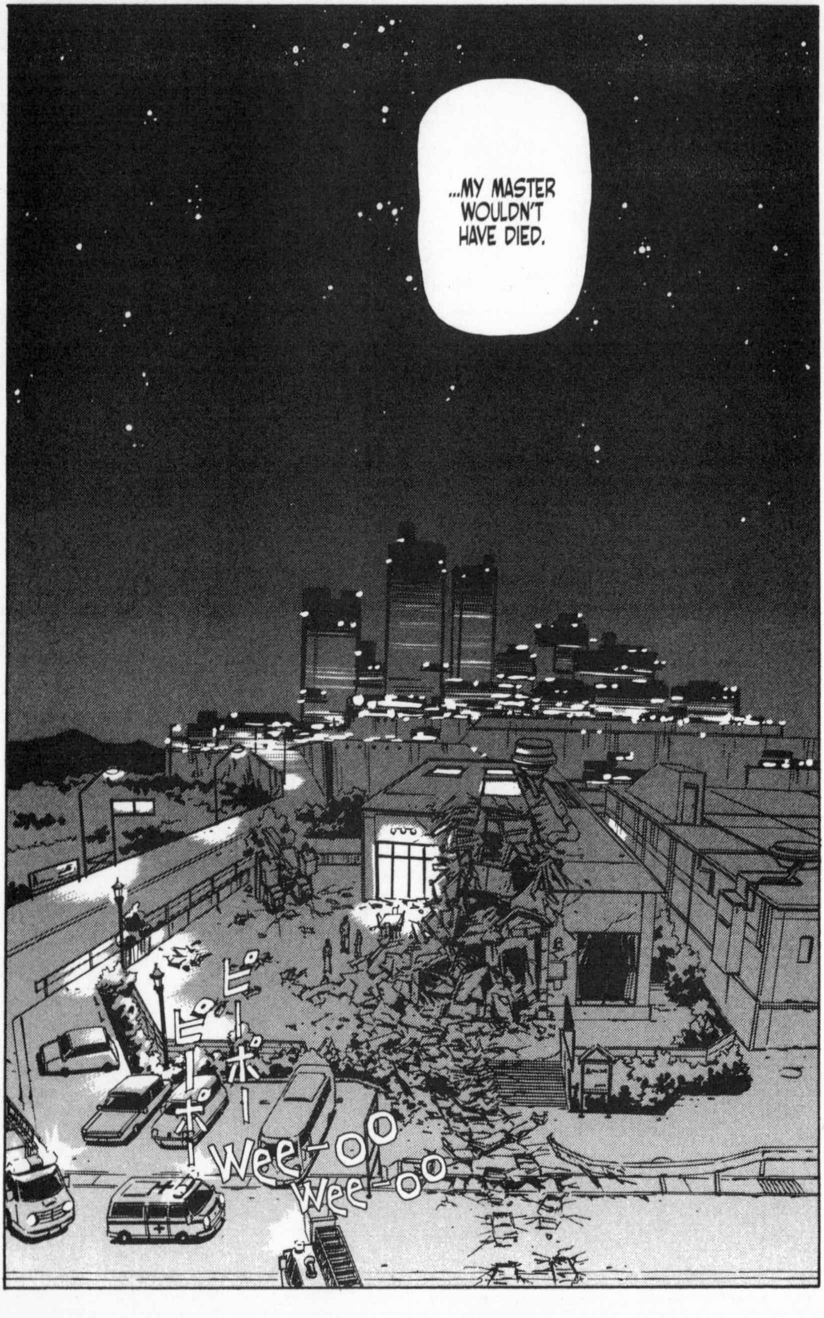
...MY MASTER WOULDN'T HAVE DIED.
ピーポー
ピーポー
WEE-OO
WEE-OO

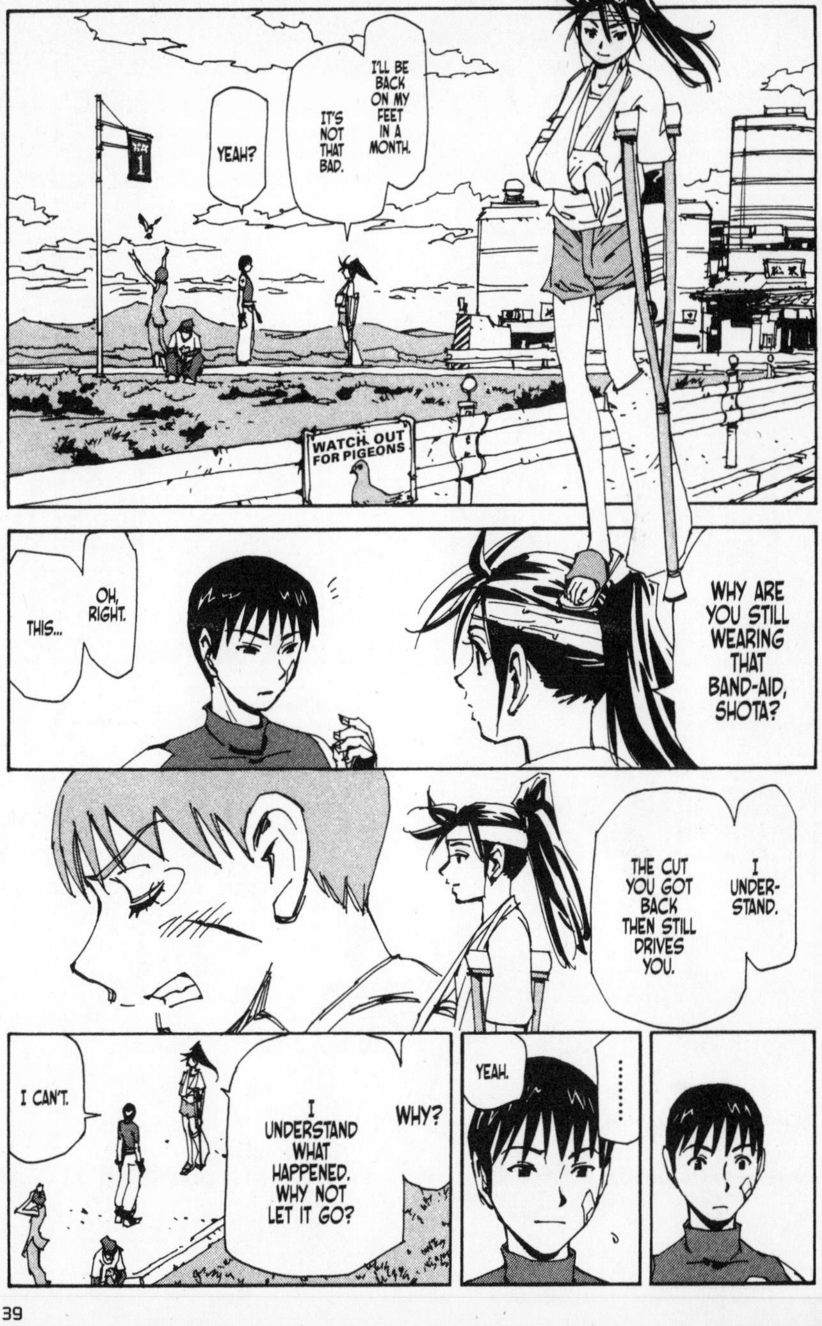
I'LL BE BACK ON MY FEET IN A MONTH.
IT'S NOT THAT BAD.
YEAH?
1
WATCH OUT FOR PIGEONS
WHY ARE YOU STILL WEARING THAT BAND-AID, SHOTA?
OH, RIGHT.
THIS...
I UNDERSTAND.
THE CUT YOU GOT BACK THEN STILL DRIVES YOU.
......
YEAH.
WHY?
I UNDERSTAND WHAT HAPPENED. WHY NOT LET IT GO?
I CAN'T.

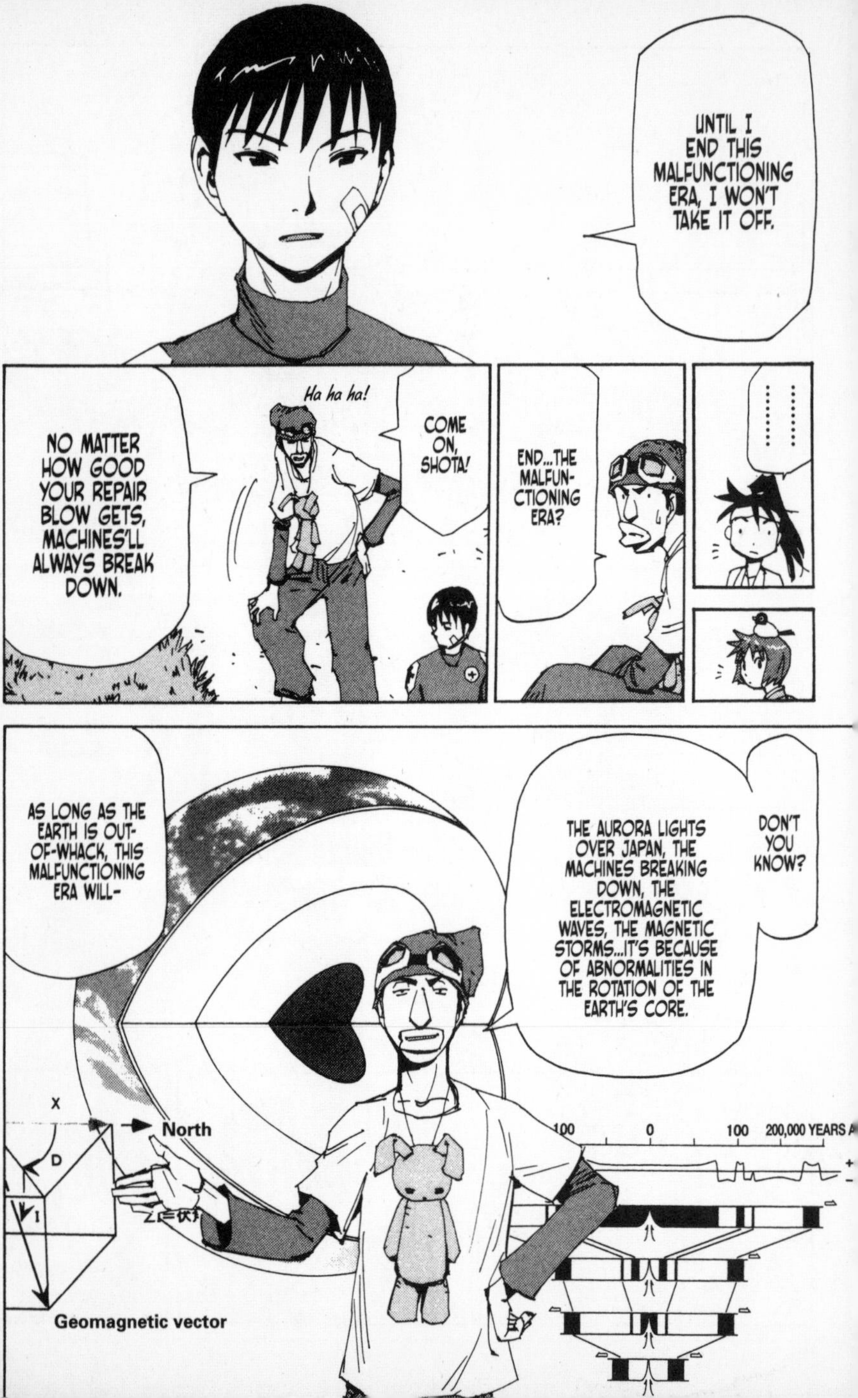
UNTIL I END THIS MALFUNCTIONING ERA, I WON'T TAKE IT OFF.
......
END...THE MALFUNCTIONING ERA?
COME ON, SHOTA!
Ha ha ha!
NO MATTER HOW GOOD YOUR REPAIR BLOW GETS, MACHINES'LL ALWAYS BREAK DOWN.
DON'T YOU KNOW?
THE AURORA LIGHTS OVER JAPAN, THE MACHINES BREAKING DOWN, THE ELECTROMAGNETIC WAVES, THE MAGNETIC STORMS...IT'S BECAUSE OF ABNORMALITIES IN THE ROTATION OF THE EARTH'S CORE.
AS LONG AS THE EARTH IS OUT-OF-WHACK, THIS MALFUNCTIONING ERA WILL-
X
North
D
I
Geomagnetic vector
100
0
100
200,000 YEARS A
+
–

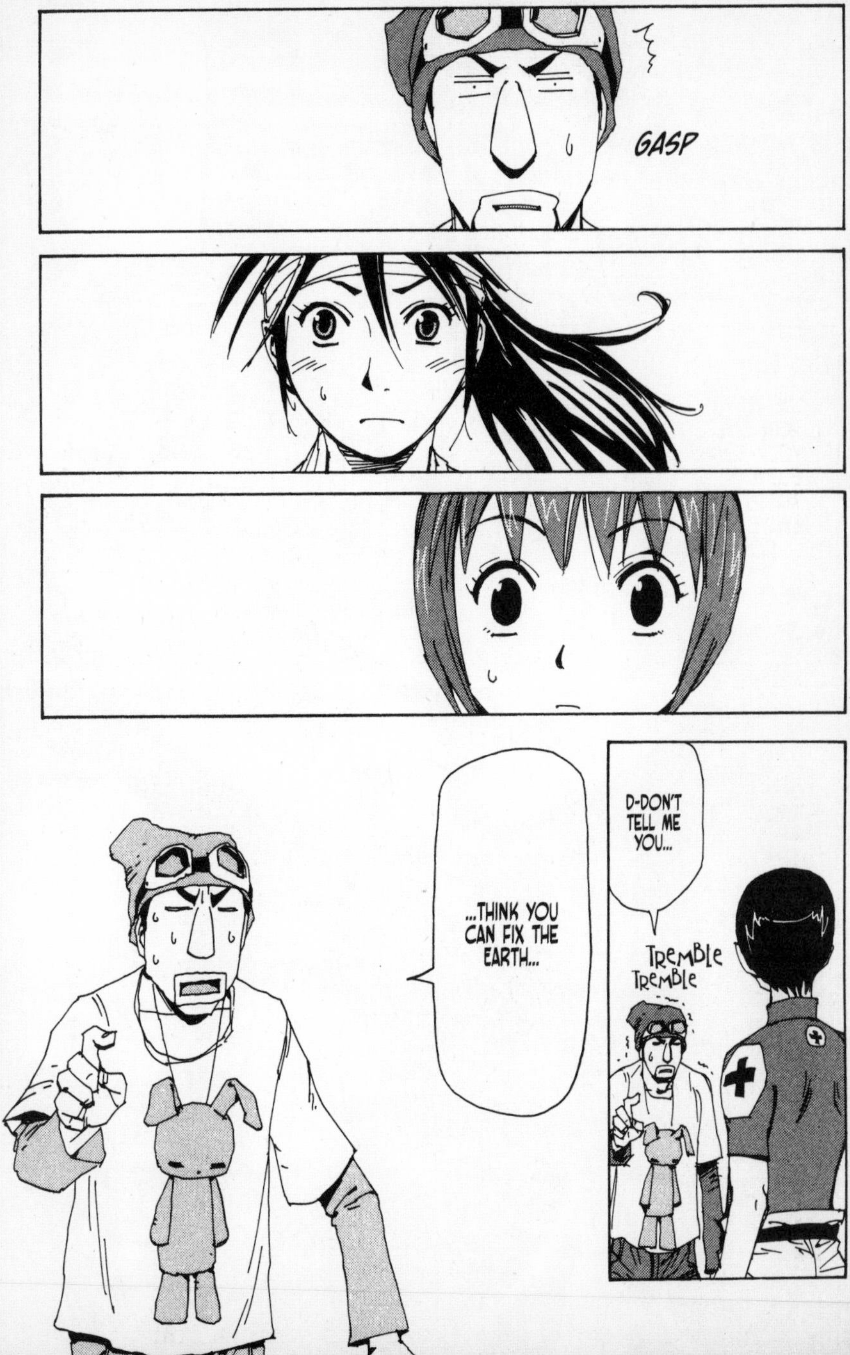
GASP
D-DON'T TELL ME YOU...
TREMBLE TREMBLE
...THINK YOU CAN FIX THE EARTH...

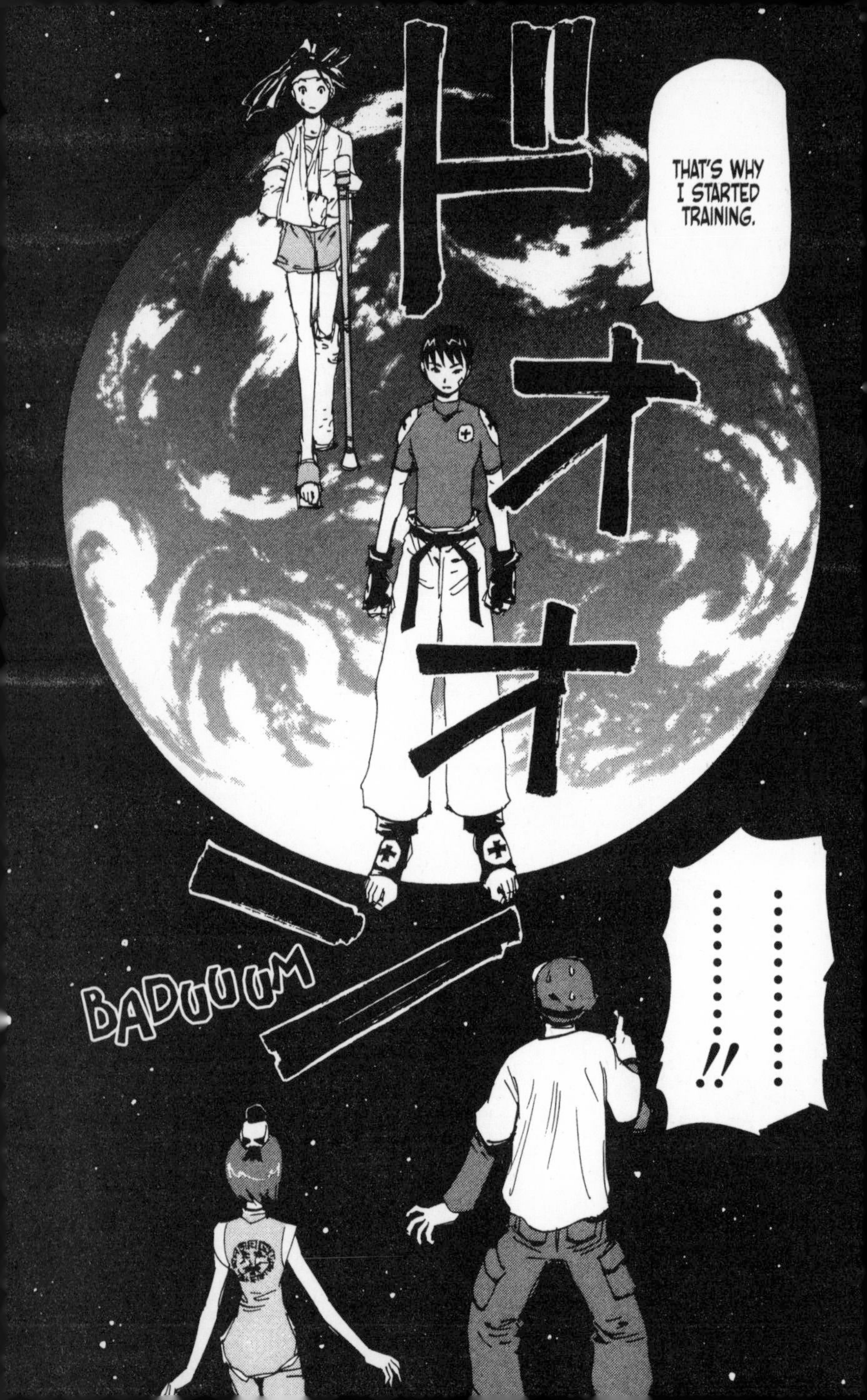
THAT'S WHY I STARTED TRAINING.
ドオオン
BADUUUM
......!!
......

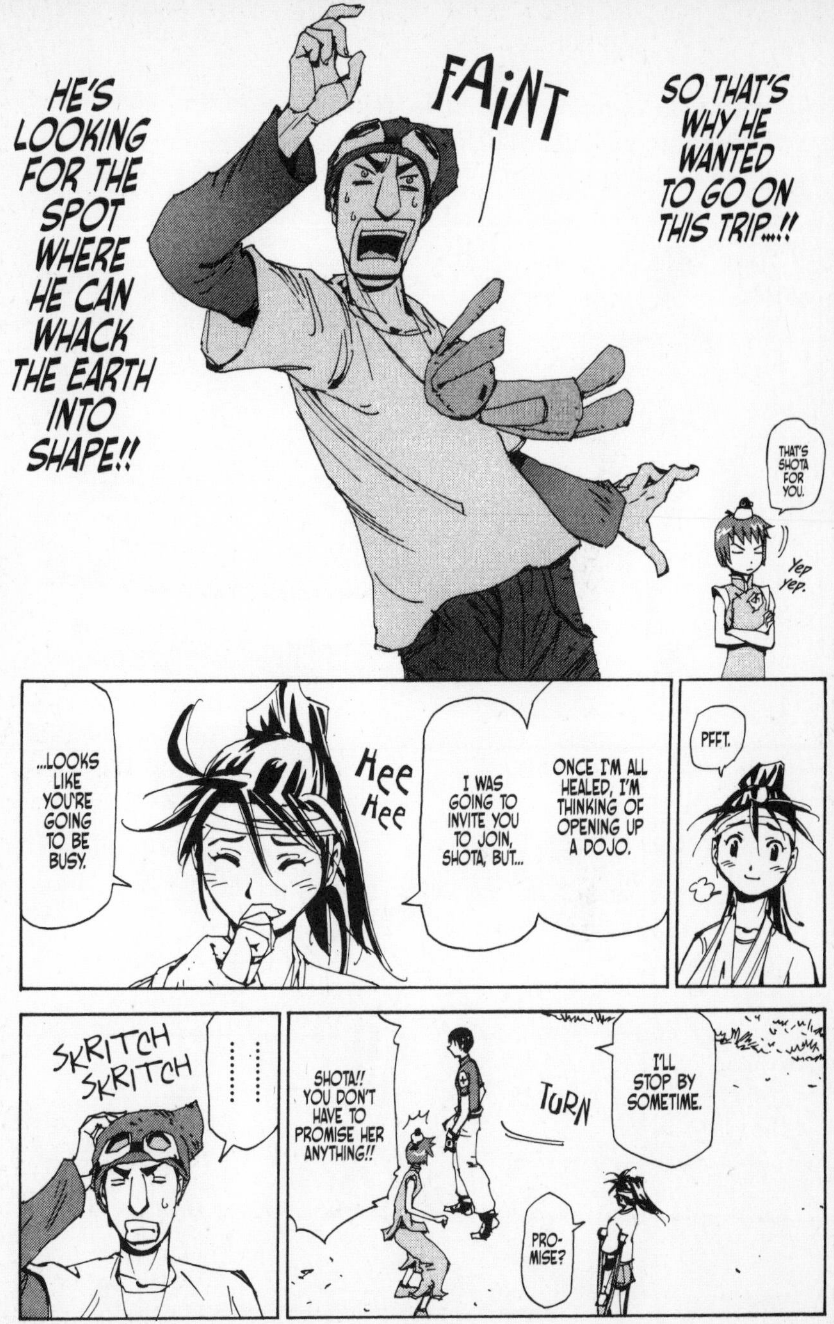
SO THAT'S WHY HE WANTED TO GO ON THIS TRIP...!!
FAINT
HE'S LOOKING FOR THE SPOT WHERE HE CAN WHACK THE EARTH INTO SHAPE!!
THAT'S SHOTA FOR YOU.
Yep yep.
PFFT.
ONCE I'M ALL HEALED, I'M THINKING OF OPENING UP A DOJO.
I WAS GOING TO INVITE YOU TO JOIN, SHOTA, BUT...
Hee Hee
...LOOKS LIKE YOU'RE GOING TO BE BUSY.
I'LL STOP BY SOMETIME.
TURN
SHOTA!! YOU DON'T HAVE TO PROMISE HER ANYTHING!!
PRO-MISE?
......
SKRITCH SKRITCH

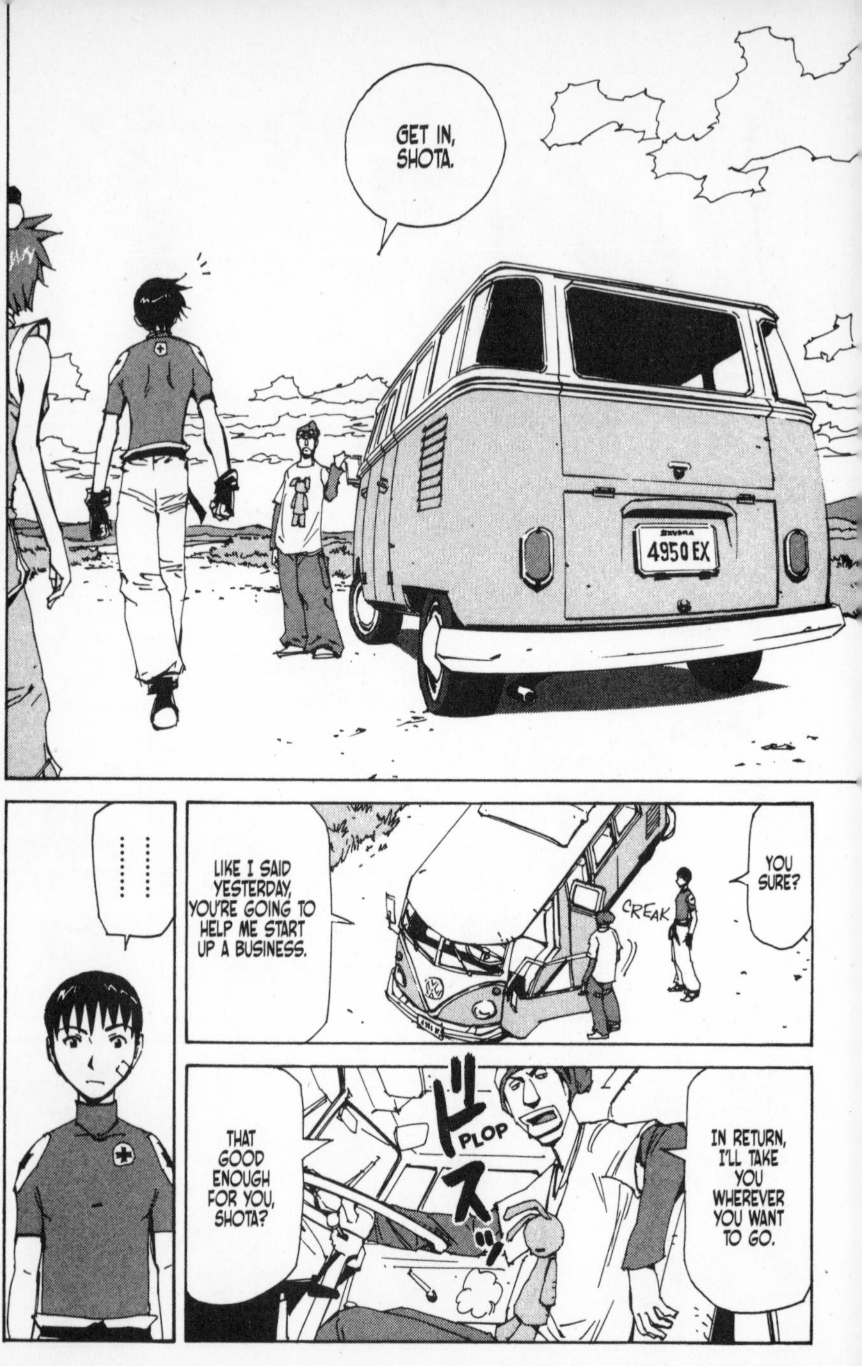
GET IN, SHOTA.
4950 EX
YOU SURE?
CREAK
LIKE I SAID YESTERDAY, YOU'RE GOING TO HELP ME START UP A BUSINESS.
IN RETURN, I'LL TAKE YOU WHEREVER YOU WANT TO GO.
ドス
PLOP
THAT GOOD ENOUGH FOR YOU, SHOTA?
......

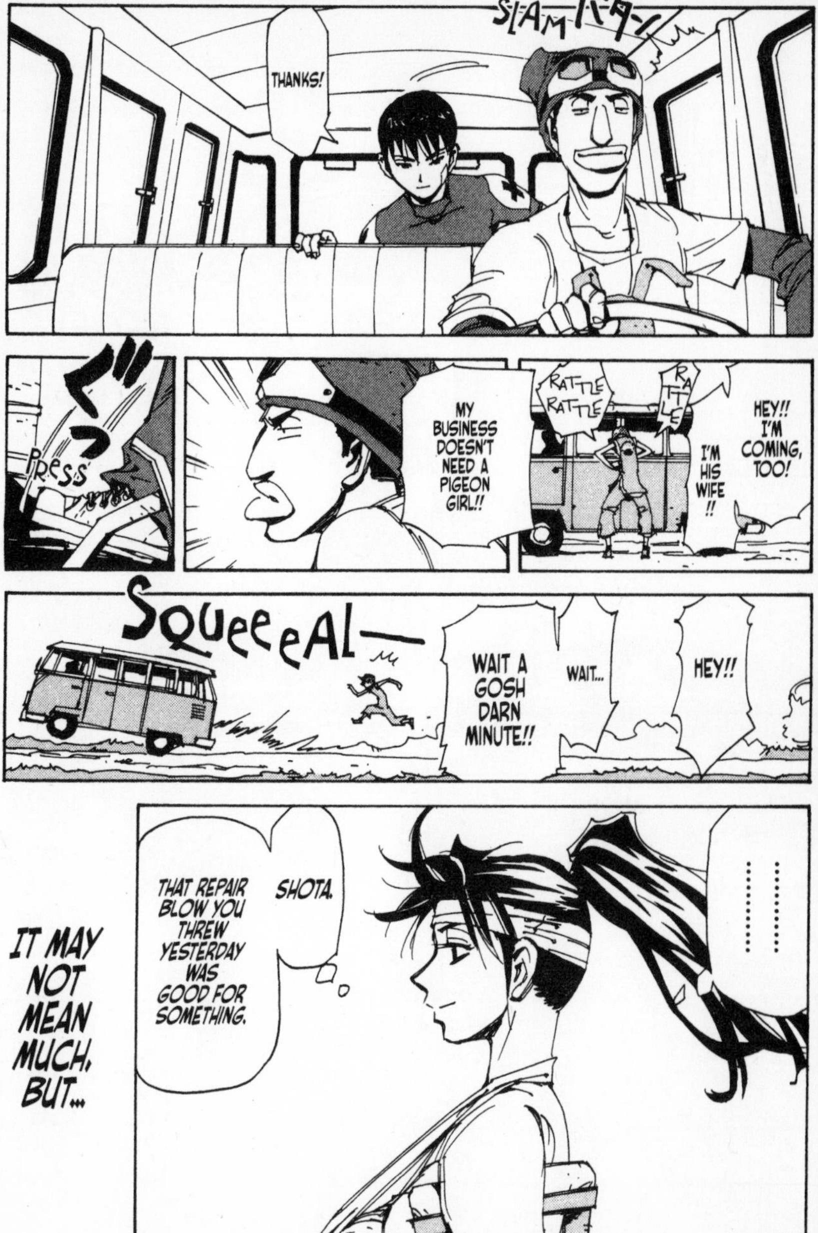
SLAM
THANKS!
HEY!! I'M COMING, TOO!
RATTLE
RATTLE RATTLE
I'M HIS WIFE!!
MY BUSINESS DOESN'T NEED A PIGEON GIRL!!
PRESS
HEY!!
WAIT...
WAIT A GOSH DARN MINUTE!!
SQUEEEAL—
......
SHOTA.
THAT REPAIR BLOW YOU THREW YESTERDAY WAS GOOD FOR SOMETHING.
IT MAY NOT MEAN MUCH, BUT...

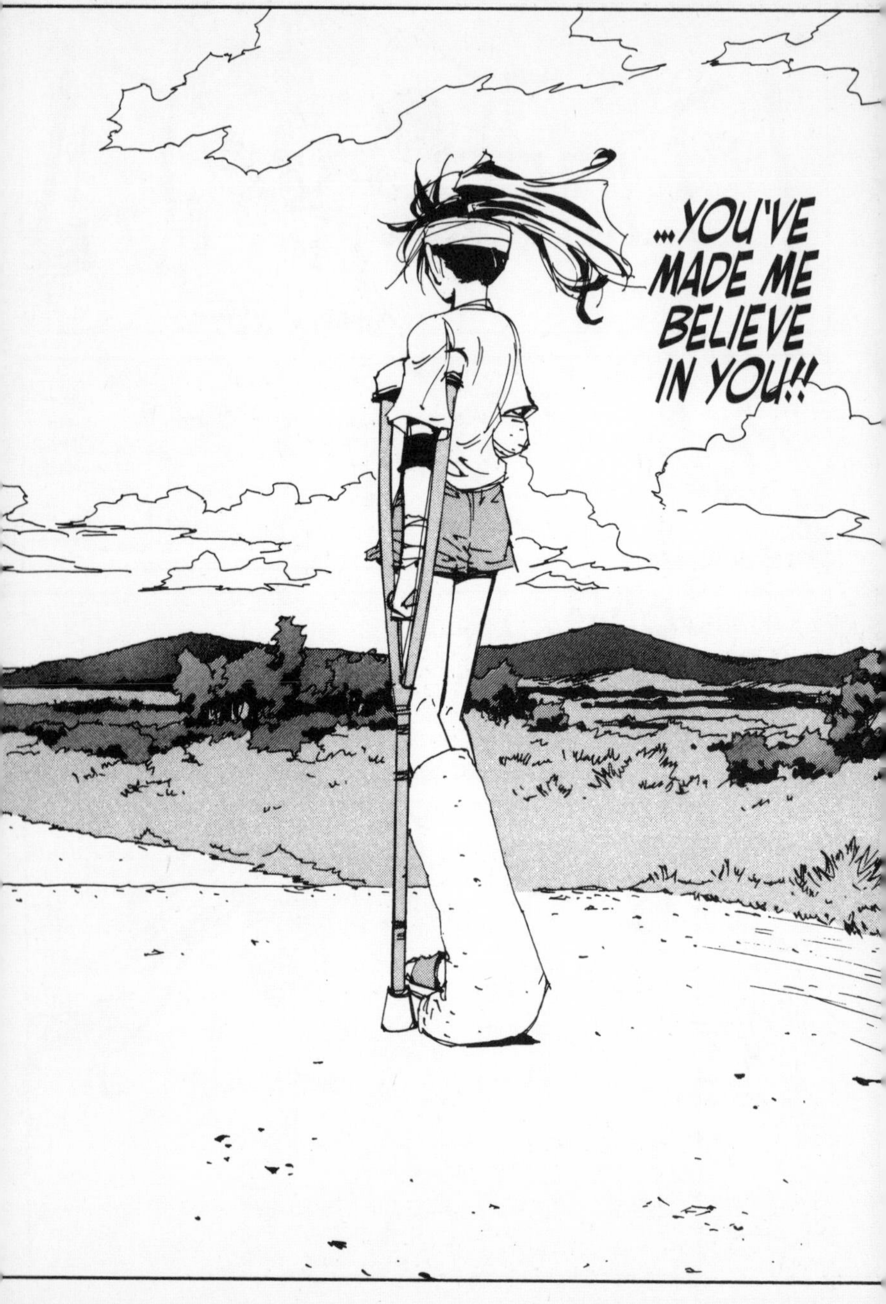
...YOU'VE MADE ME BELIEVE IN YOU!!

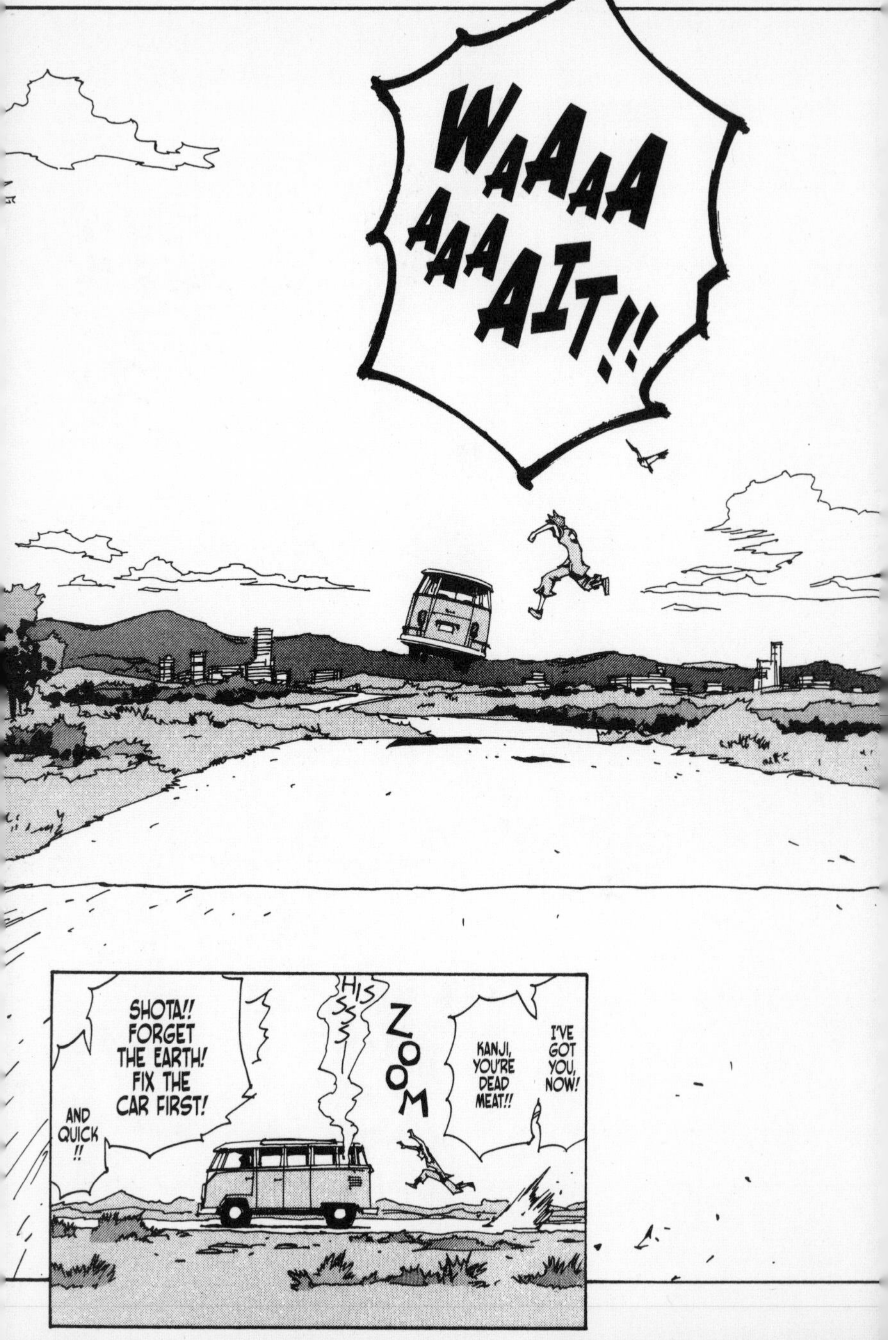
WAAAA AAAAIT!!
I'VE GOT YOU, NOW!
KANJI, YOU'RE DEAD MEAT!!
ZOOM
HISSSS
SHOTA!! FORGET THE EARTH! FIX THE CAR FIRST!
AND QUICK!!

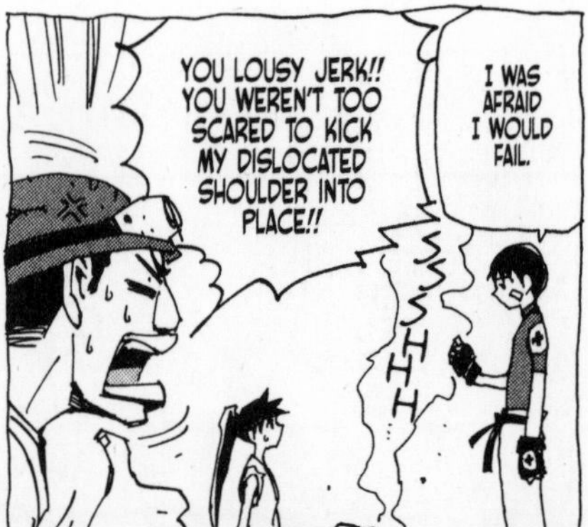
I WAS AFRAID I WOULD FAIL.
SSSHHH...
YOU LOUSY JERK!! YOU WEREN'T TOO SCARED TO KICK MY DISLOCATED SHOULDER INTO PLACE!!

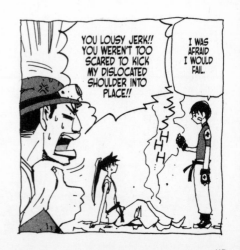

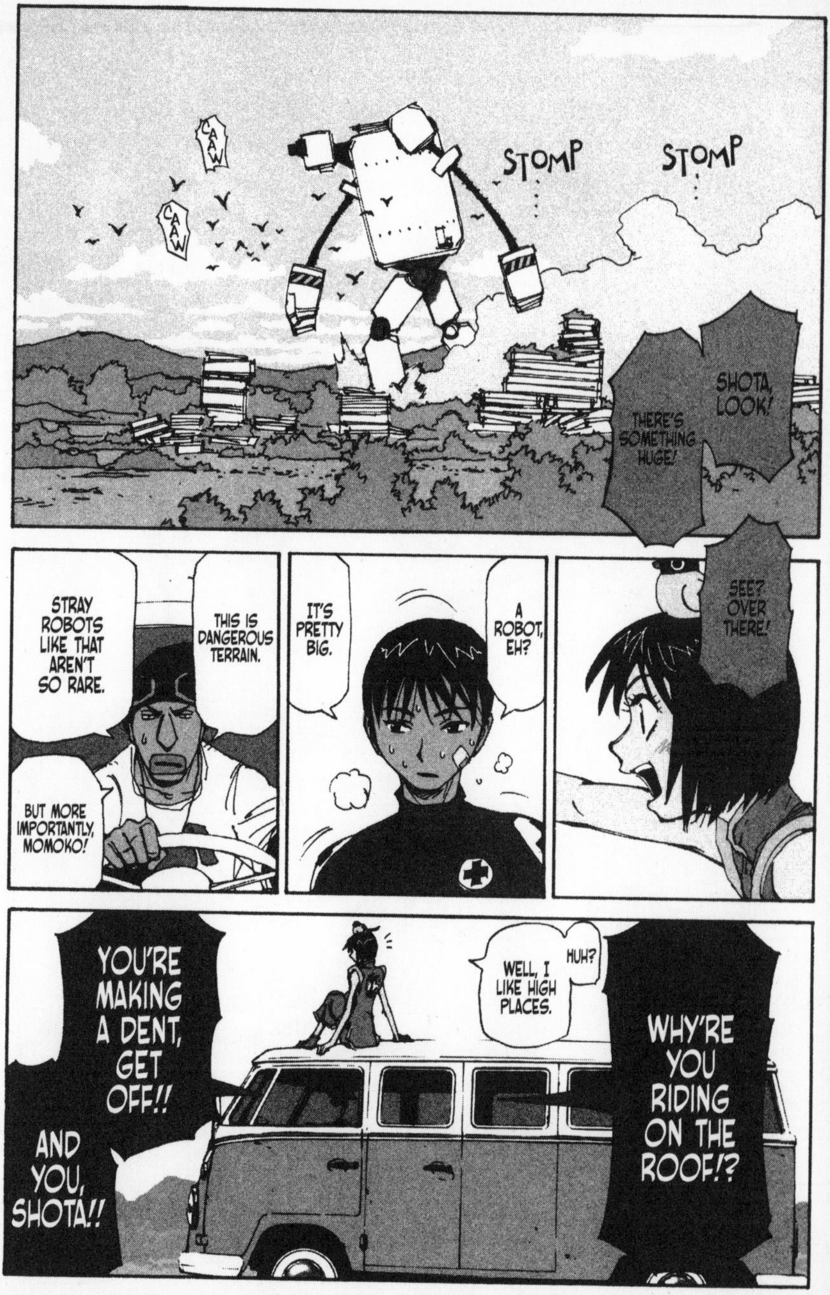
SHOTA, LOOK!
THERE'S SOMETHING HUGE!
STOMP
STOMP
CAAW
CAAW
SEE? OVER THERE!
A ROBOT, EH?
IT'S PRETTY BIG.
THIS IS DANGEROUS TERRAIN.
STRAY ROBOTS LIKE THAT AREN'T SO RARE.
BUT MORE IMPORTANTLY, MOMOKO!
HUH?
WHY'RE YOU RIDING ON THE ROOF!?
WELL, I LIKE HIGH PLACES.
YOU'RE MAKING A DENT, GET OFF!!
AND YOU, SHOTA!!

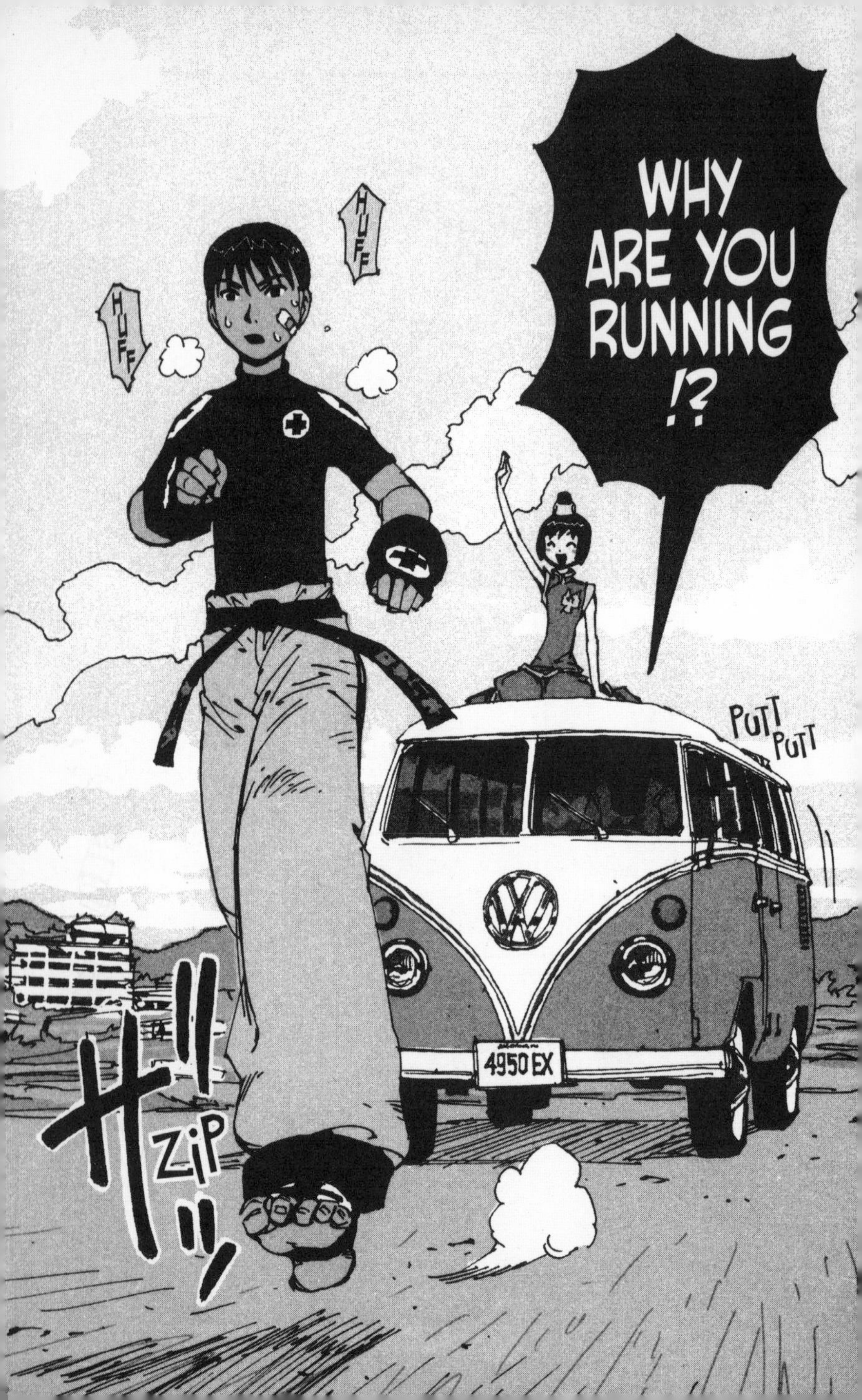
WHY ARE YOU RUNNING !?
HUFF
HUFF
PUTT PUTT
4950 EX
ZIP

#6 PITFALL

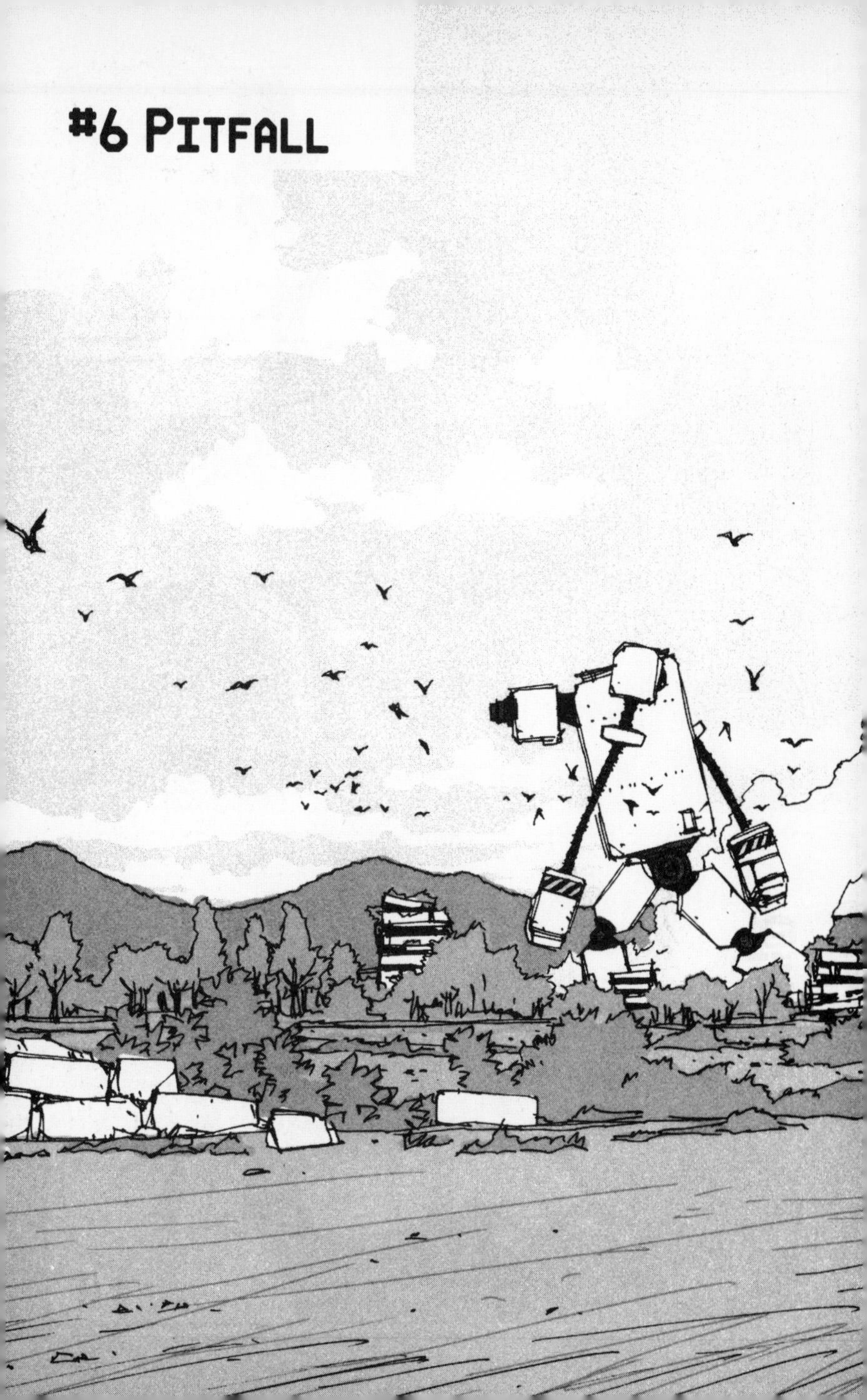

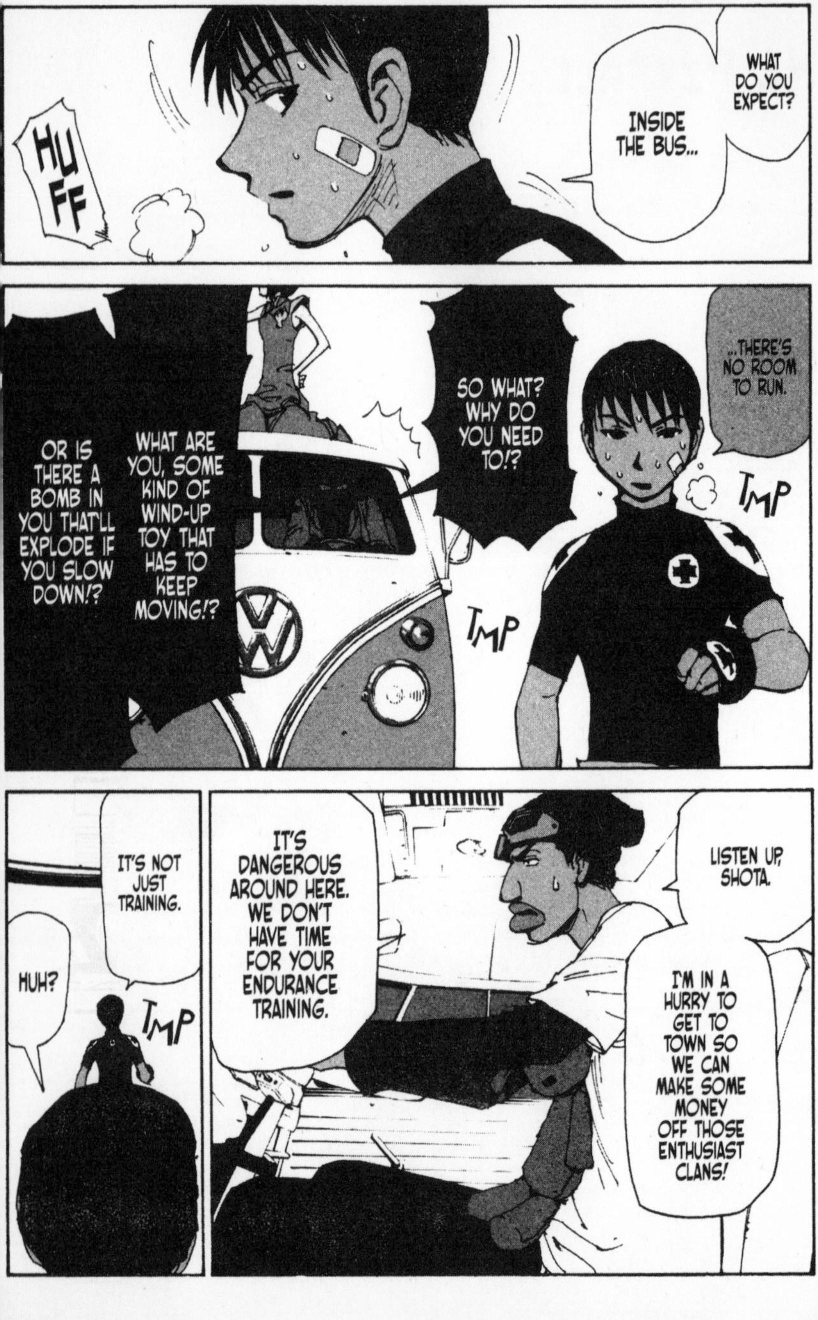
WHAT DO YOU EXPECT?
INSIDE THE BUS...
HUFF
...THERE'S NO ROOM TO RUN.
TMP
SO WHAT? WHY DO YOU NEED TO!?
TMP
WHAT ARE YOU, SOME KIND OF WIND-UP TOY THAT HAS TO KEEP MOVING!?
OR IS THERE A BOMB IN YOU THAT'LL EXPLODE IF YOU SLOW DOWN!?
LISTEN UP, SHOTA.
I'M IN A HURRY TO GET TO TOWN SO WE CAN MAKE SOME MONEY OFF THOSE ENTHUSIAST CLANS!
IT'S DANGEROUS AROUND HERE. WE DON'T HAVE TIME FOR YOUR ENDURANCE TRAINING.
IT'S NOT JUST TRAINING.
TMP
HUH?

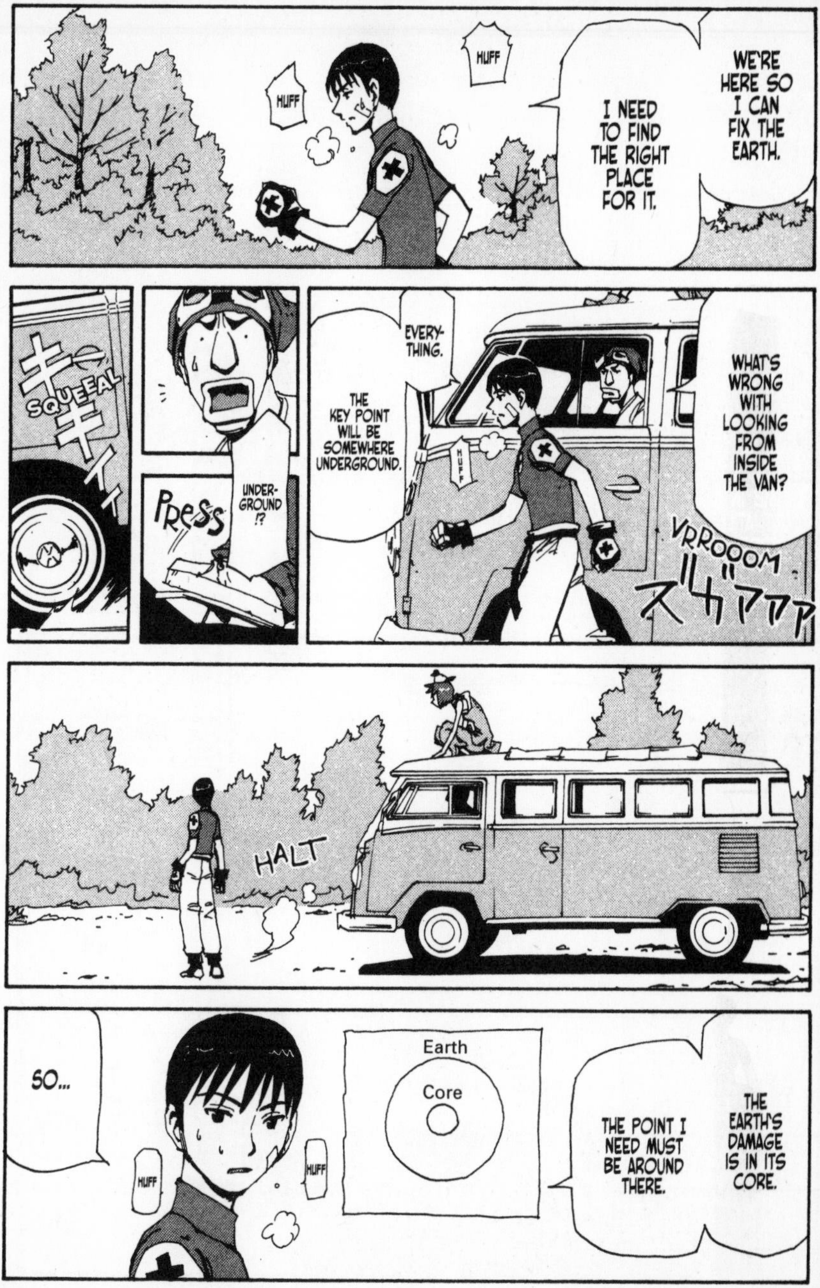
WE'RE HERE SO I CAN FIX THE EARTH.
I NEED TO FIND THE RIGHT PLACE FOR IT.
HUFF
HUFF
WHAT'S WRONG WITH LOOKING FROM INSIDE THE VAN?
EVERYTHING.
THE KEY POINT WILL BE SOMEWHERE UNDERGROUND.
HUFF
VRROOOM
UNDERGROUND!?
PRESS
SQUEEAL
HALT
THE EARTH'S DAMAGE IS IN ITS CORE.
THE POINT I NEED MUST BE AROUND THERE.
Earth
Core
HUFF
HUFF
SO...

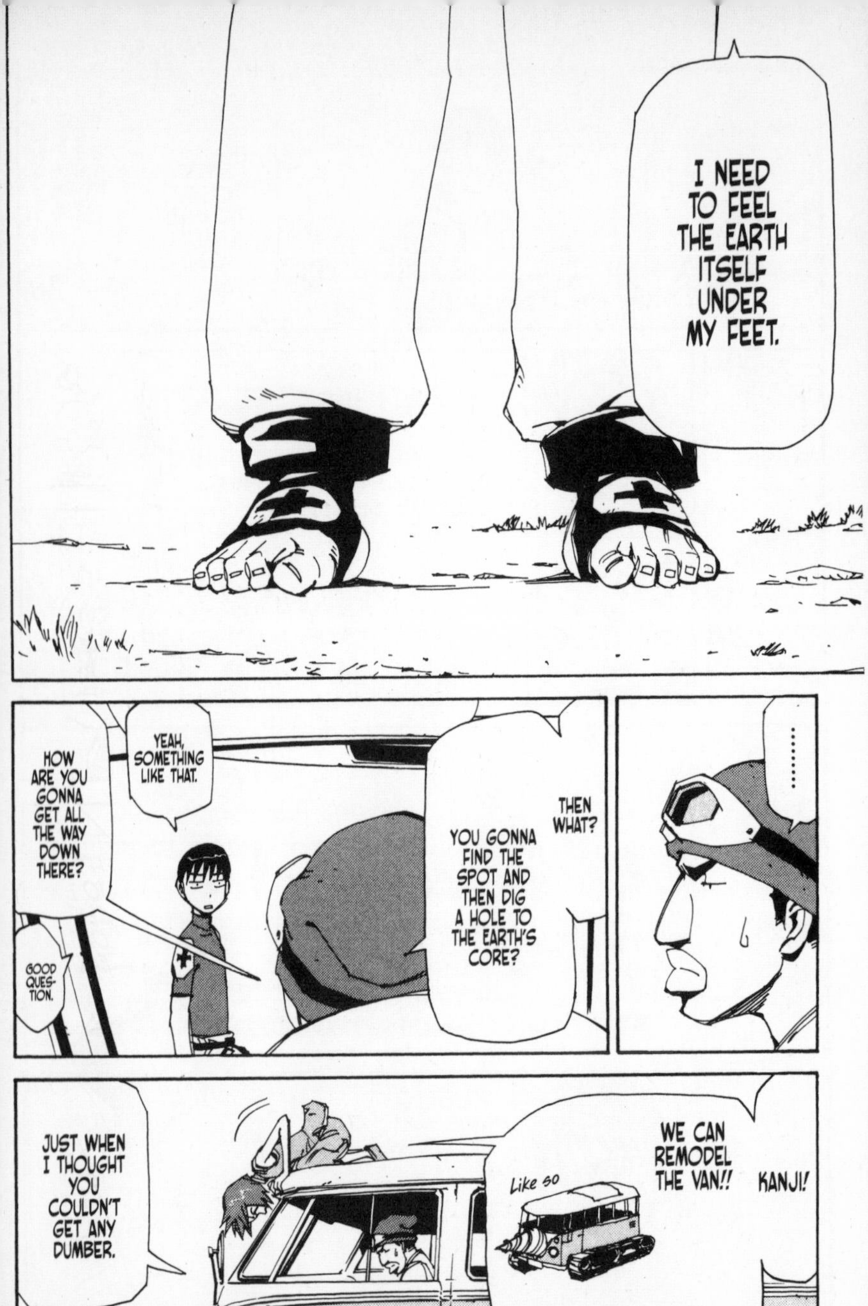
I NEED TO FEEL THE EARTH ITSELF UNDER MY FEET.
......
THEN WHAT?
YOU GONNA FIND THE SPOT AND THEN DIG A HOLE TO THE EARTH'S CORE?
YEAH, SOMETHING LIKE THAT.
HOW ARE YOU GONNA GET ALL THE WAY DOWN THERE?
GOOD QUES-TION.
KANJI!
WE CAN REMODEL THE VAN!!
Like so
JUST WHEN I THOUGHT YOU COULDN'T GET ANY DUMBER.

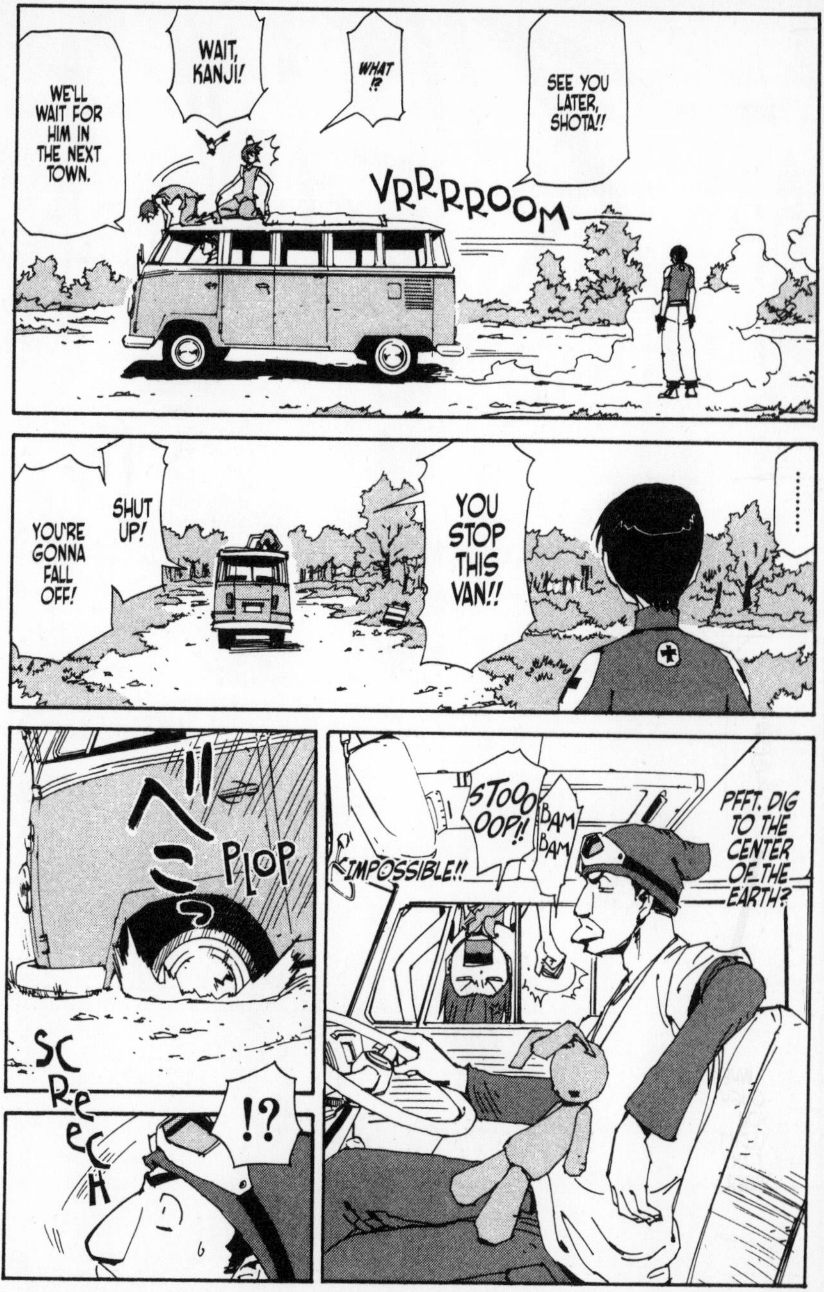
SEE YOU LATER, SHOTA!!
WHAT !?
WAIT, KANJI!
WE'LL WAIT FOR HIM IN THE NEXT TOWN.
VRRRROOM
......
YOU STOP THIS VAN!!
SHUT UP!
YOU'RE GONNA FALL OFF!
PFFT. DIG TO THE CENTER OF THE EARTH?
BAM BAM
STOOOOOP!!
IMPOSSIBLE!!
べこっ
PLOP
SCREECH
!?

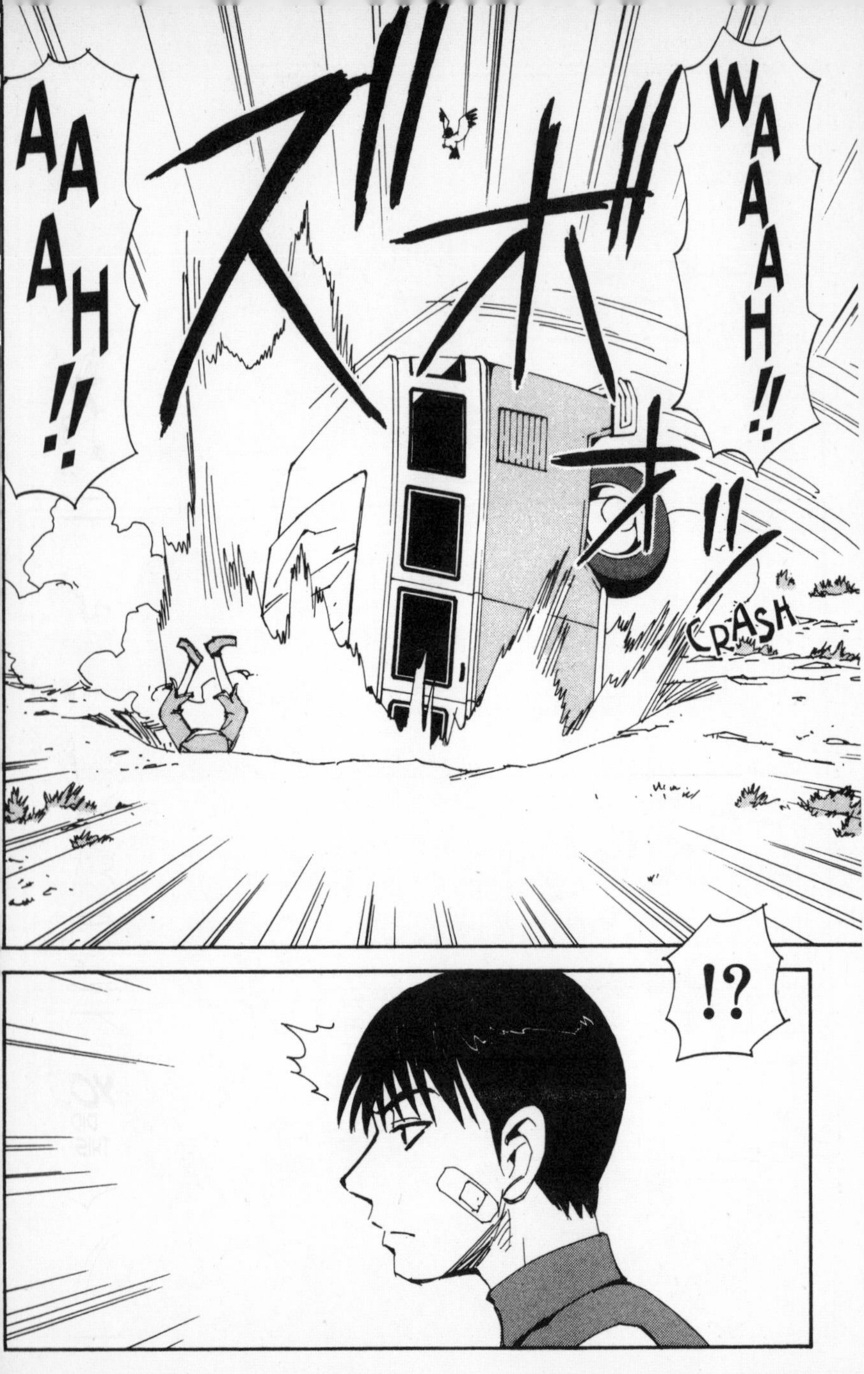
WAAAH!!
CRASH
AAAH!!
!?

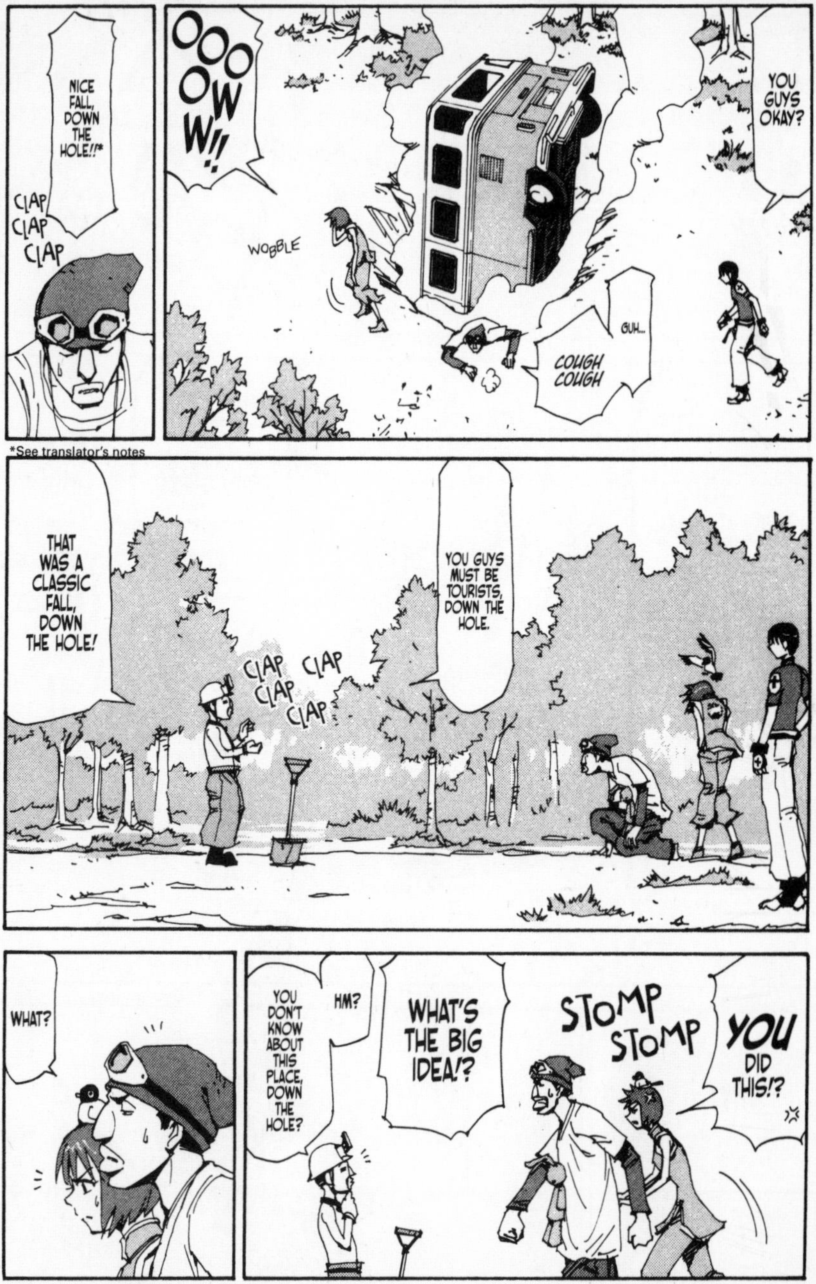
YOU GUYS OKAY?
GUH...
COUGH COUGH
WOBBLE
OOOOWW!!
NICE FALL, DOWN THE HOLE!!*
CLAP CLAP CLAP
YOU GUYS MUST BE TOURISTS, DOWN THE HOLE.
CLAP CLAP CLAP CLAP
THAT WAS A CLASSIC FALL, DOWN THE HOLE!
YOU DID THIS!?
STOMP STOMP
WHAT'S THE BIG IDEA!?
HM?
YOU DON'T KNOW ABOUT THIS PLACE, DOWN THE HOLE?
WHAT?

*See translator's notes

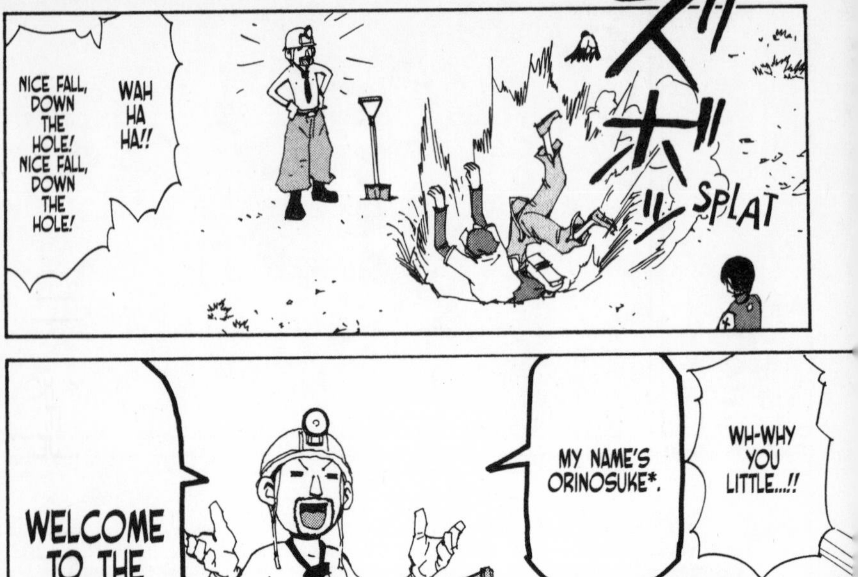
ズボッ
SPLAT
WAH HA HA!!
NICE FALL, DOWN THE HOLE! NICE FALL, DOWN THE HOLE!
WH-WHY YOU LITTLE...!!
RiSe
がばっ
MY NAME'S ORINOSUKE*.
WELCOME TO THE PITFALL ENTHUSIAST CLAN, DOWN THE HOLE!

*See translator's notes

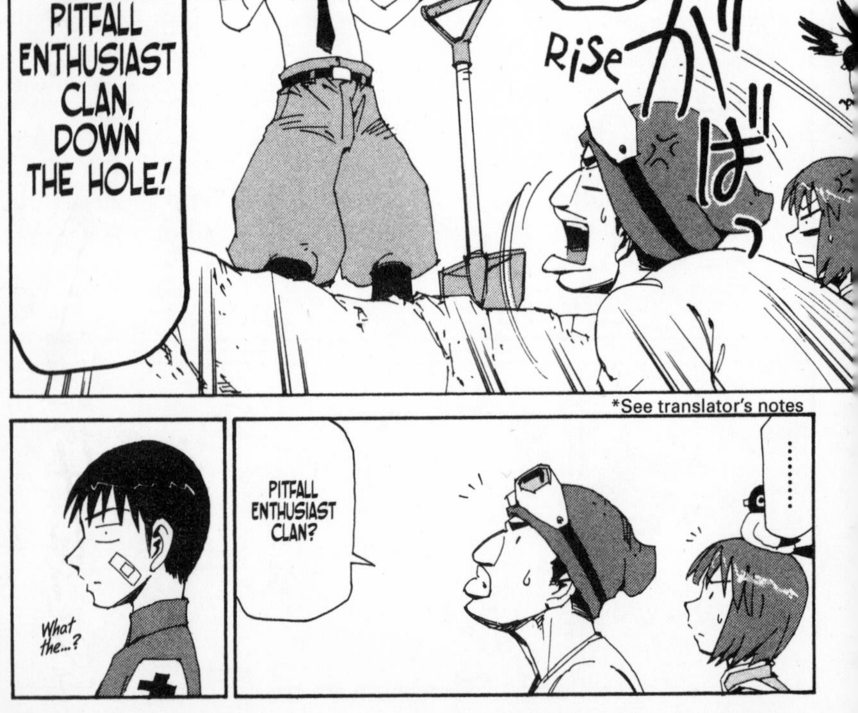
......
PITFALL ENTHUSIAST CLAN?
What the...?

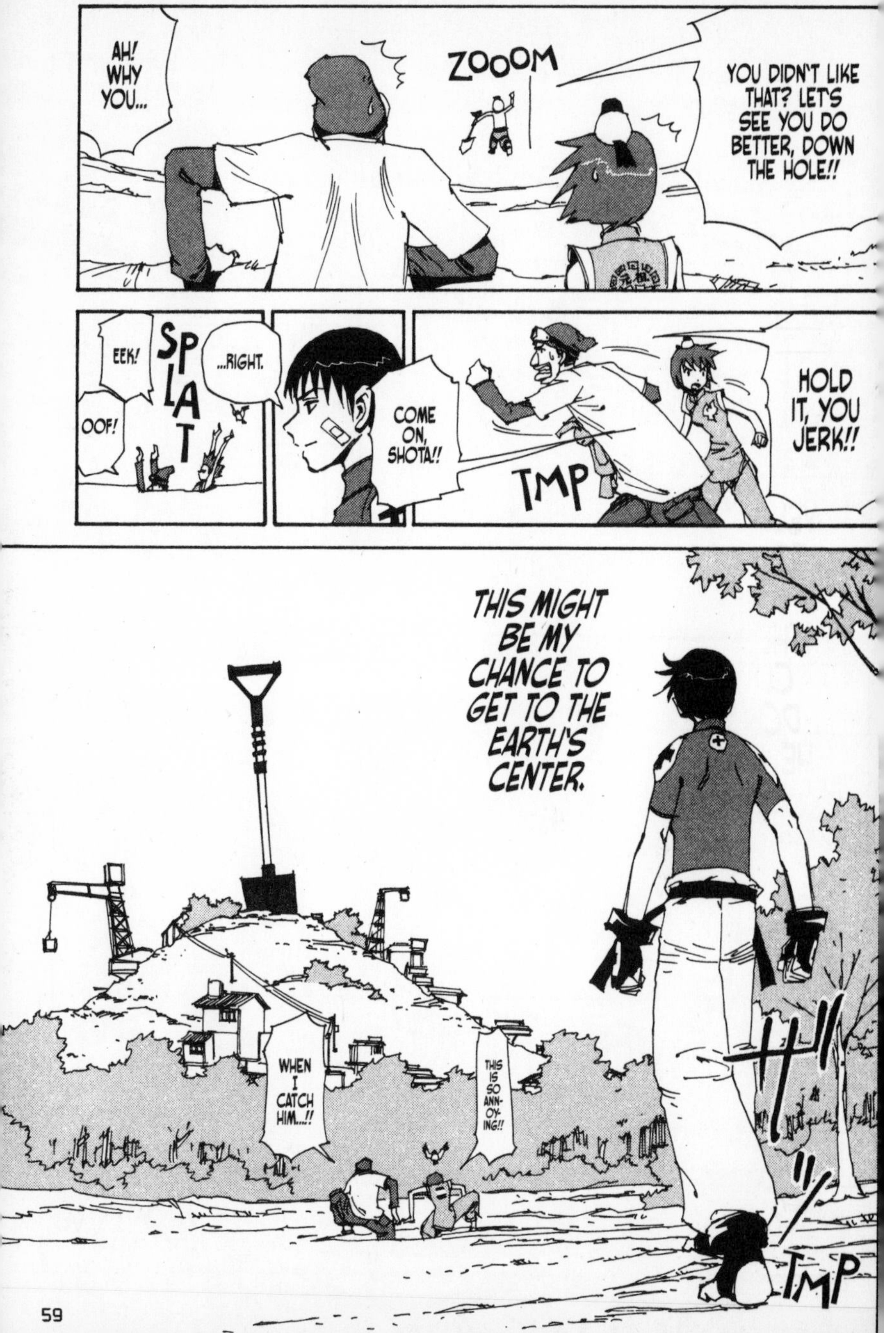
YOU DIDN'T LIKE THAT? LET'S SEE YOU DO BETTER, DOWN THE HOLE!!
ZOOOM
AH! WHY YOU...
HOLD IT, YOU JERK!!
TMP
COME ON, SHOTA!!
...RIGHT.
SPLAT
EEK!
OOF!
THIS MIGHT BE MY CHANCE TO GET TO THE EARTH'S CENTER.
THIS IS SO ANN-OY-ING!!
WHEN I CATCH HIM...!!
TMP

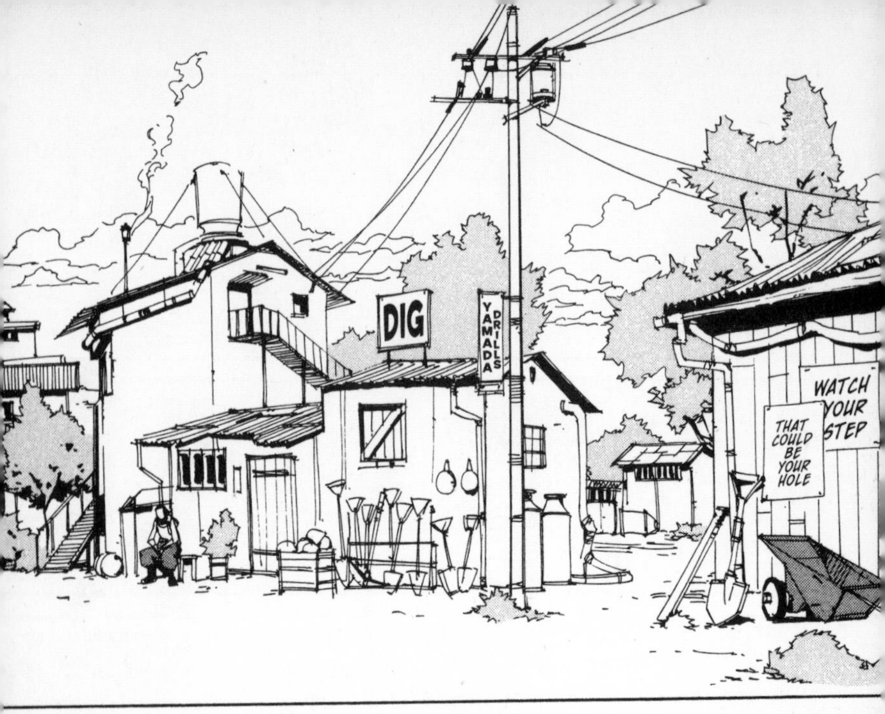
WATCH YOUR STEP
THAT COULD BE YOUR HOLE
YAMADA DRILLS
DIG

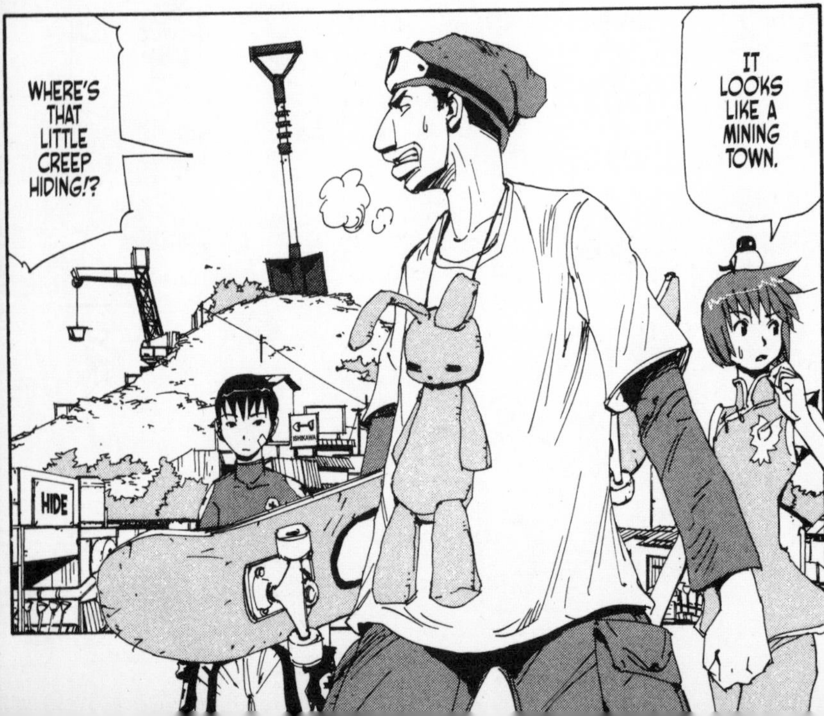
IT LOOKS LIKE A MINING TOWN.
WHERE'S THAT LITTLE CREEP HIDING!?
ISHIKAWA
HIDE

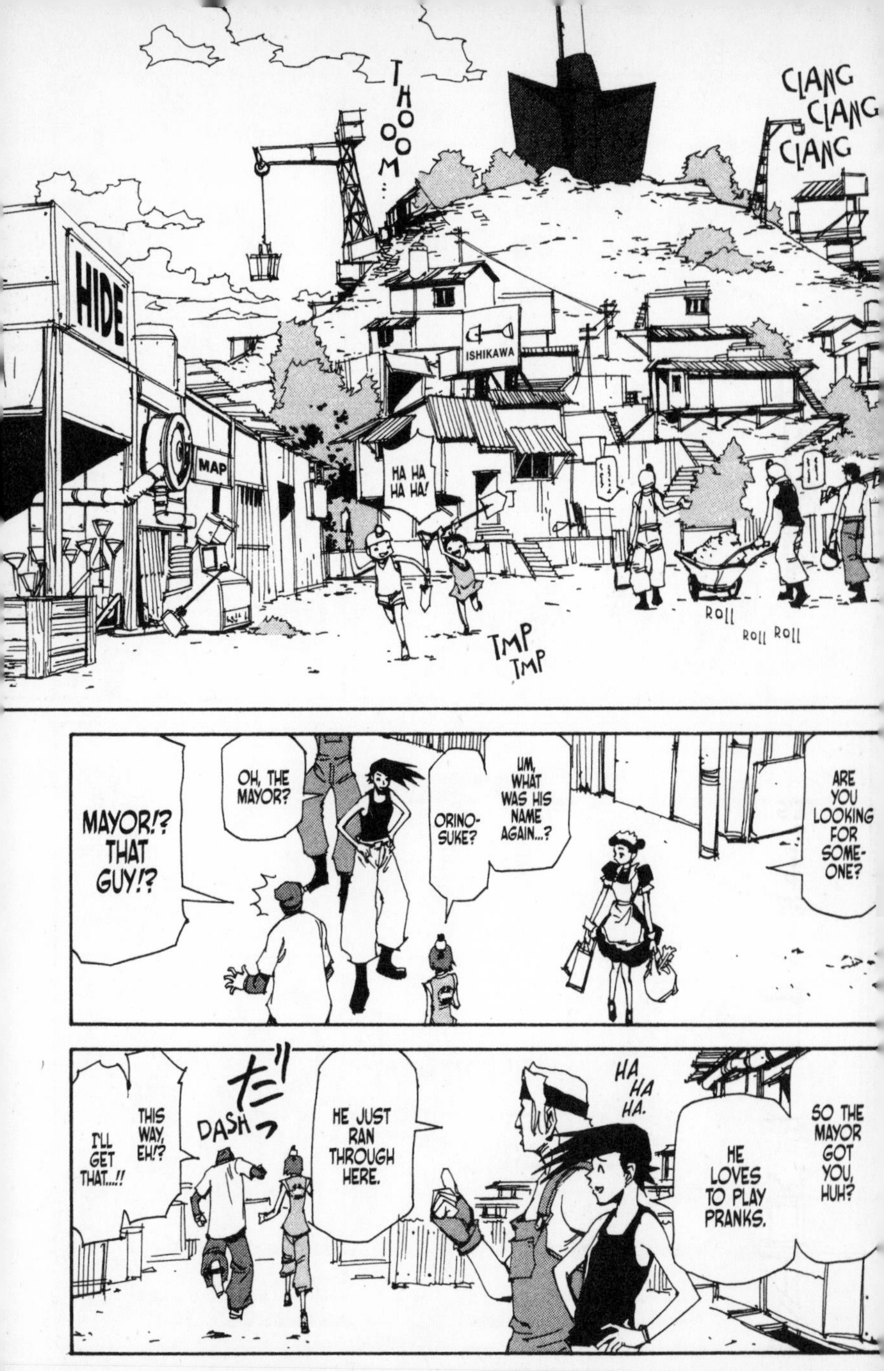
CLANG CLANG CLANG
THOOOOM...
HIDE
ISHIKAWA
MAP
HA HA HA HA!
ROLL ROLL ROLL
TMP TMP
ARE YOU LOOKING FOR SOME-ONE?
UM, WHAT WAS HIS NAME AGAIN...?
ORINO-SUKE?
OH, THE MAYOR?
MAYOR!? THAT GUY!?
SO THE MAYOR GOT YOU, HUH?
HE LOVES TO PLAY PRANKS.
HA HA HA.
HE JUST RAN THROUGH HERE.
だっ
DASH
THIS WAY, EH!?
I'LL GET THAT...!!

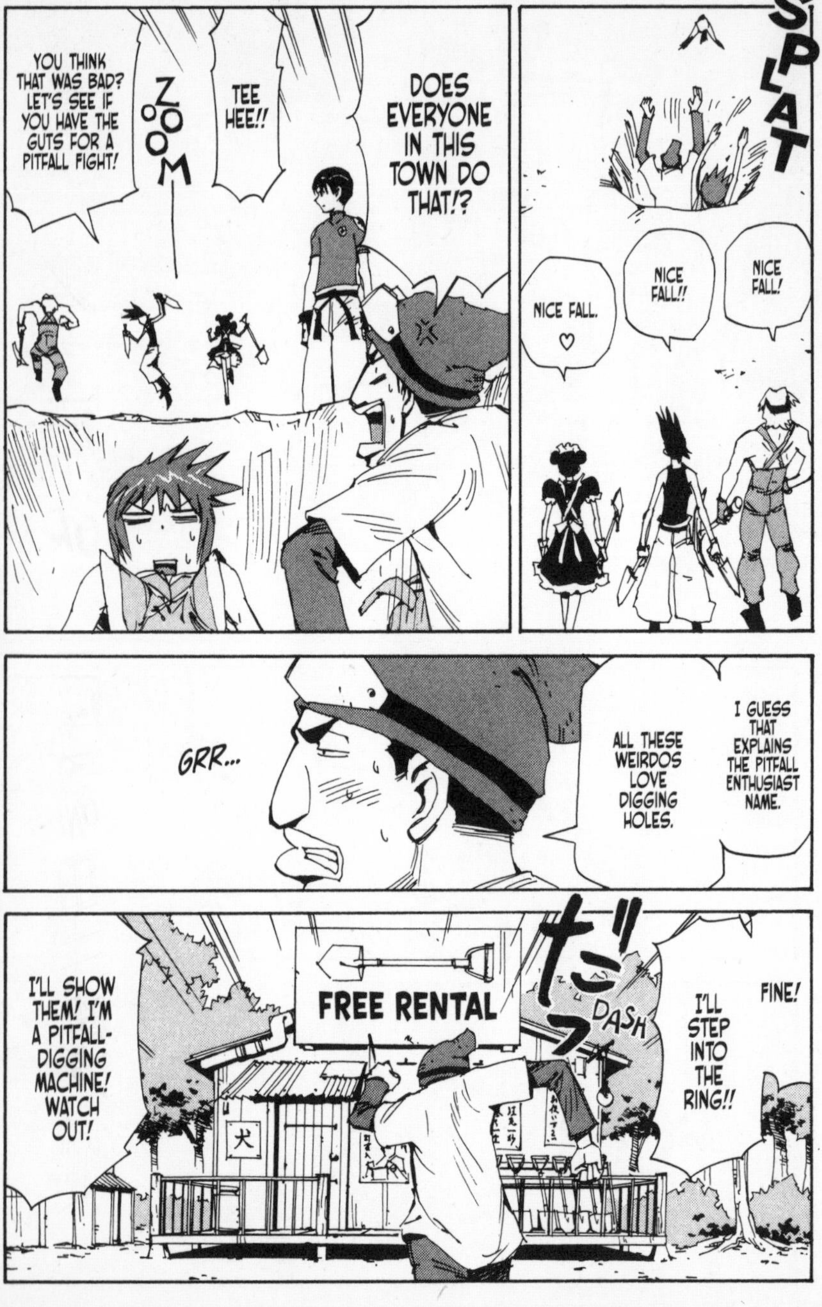
SPLAT
NICE FALL!
NICE FALL!!
NICE FALL. ♡
DOES EVERYONE IN THIS TOWN DO THAT!?
TEE HEE!!
ZOOOOM
YOU THINK THAT WAS BAD? LET'S SEE IF YOU HAVE THE GUTS FOR A PITFALL FIGHT!
I GUESS THAT EXPLAINS THE PITFALL ENTHUSIAST NAME.
ALL THESE WEIRDOS LOVE DIGGING HOLES.
GRR...
FINE!
I'LL STEP INTO THE RING!!
DASH
FREE RENTAL
I'LL SHOW THEM! I'M A PITFALL-DIGGING MACHINE! WATCH OUT!

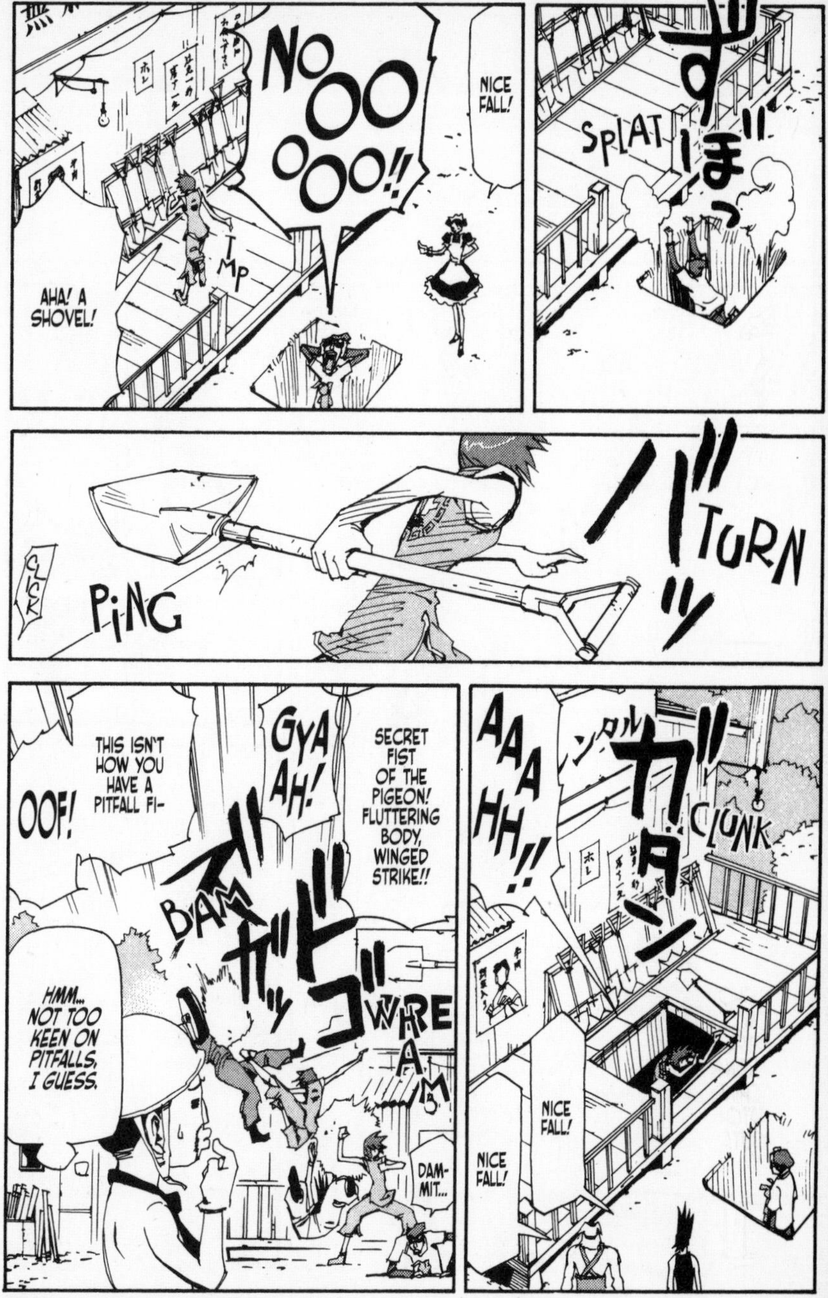
ずぼっ
SPLAT
NICE FALL!
NOOOOOOO!!
TMP
AHA! A SHOVEL!
バッ
TURN
PING
CLICK
ガタン
CLUNK
レンタル
AAAAHH!!
NICE FALL!
NICE FALL!
SECRET FIST OF THE PIGEON! FLUTTERING BODY, WINGED STRIKE!!
GYAAH!
THIS ISN'T HOW YOU HAVE A PITFALL FI-
OOF!
ズドッ
BAM
ガッ
ゴッ
WHAM
DAM-MIT...
HMM... NOT TOO KEEN ON PITFALLS, I GUESS.

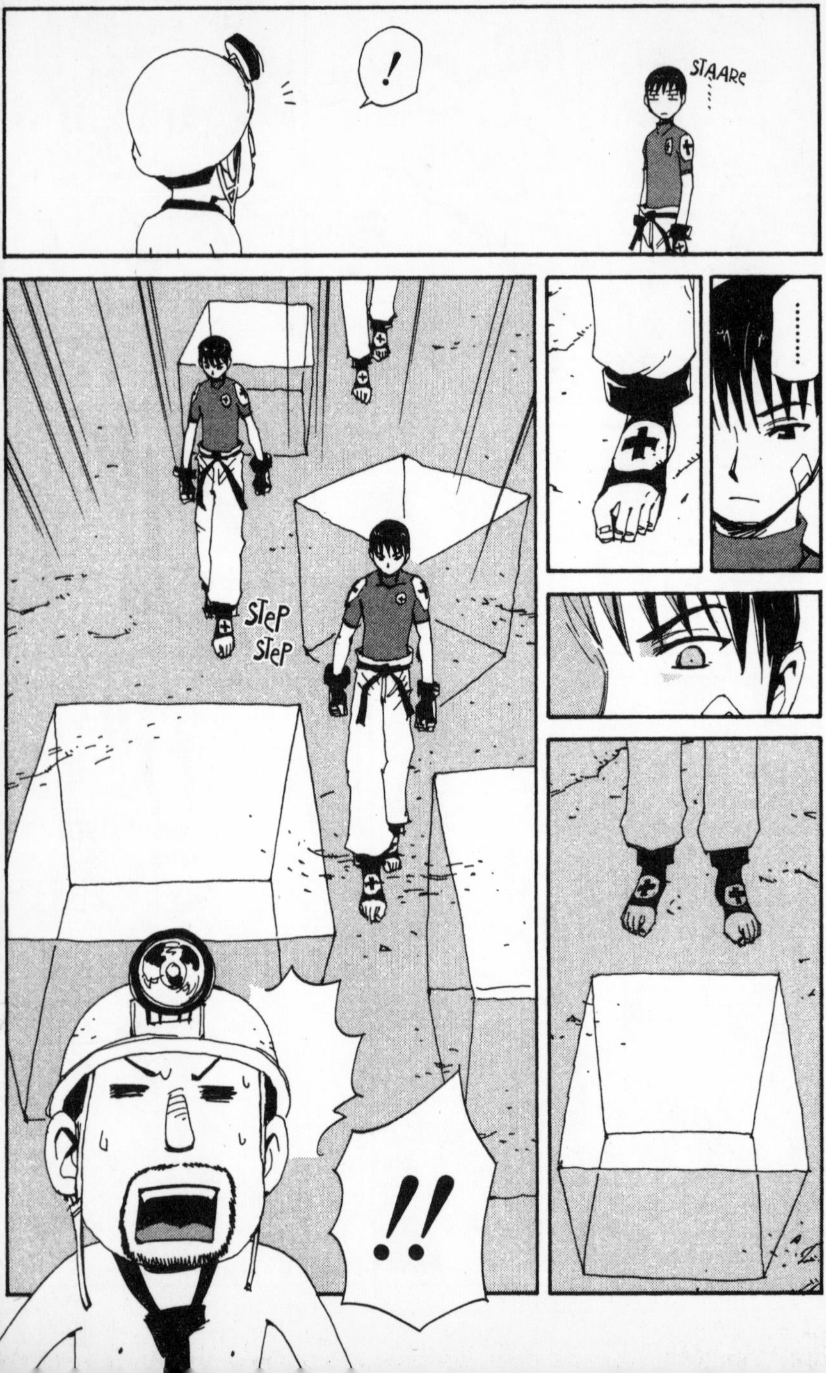
STAARE
!
......
STEP
STEP
!!

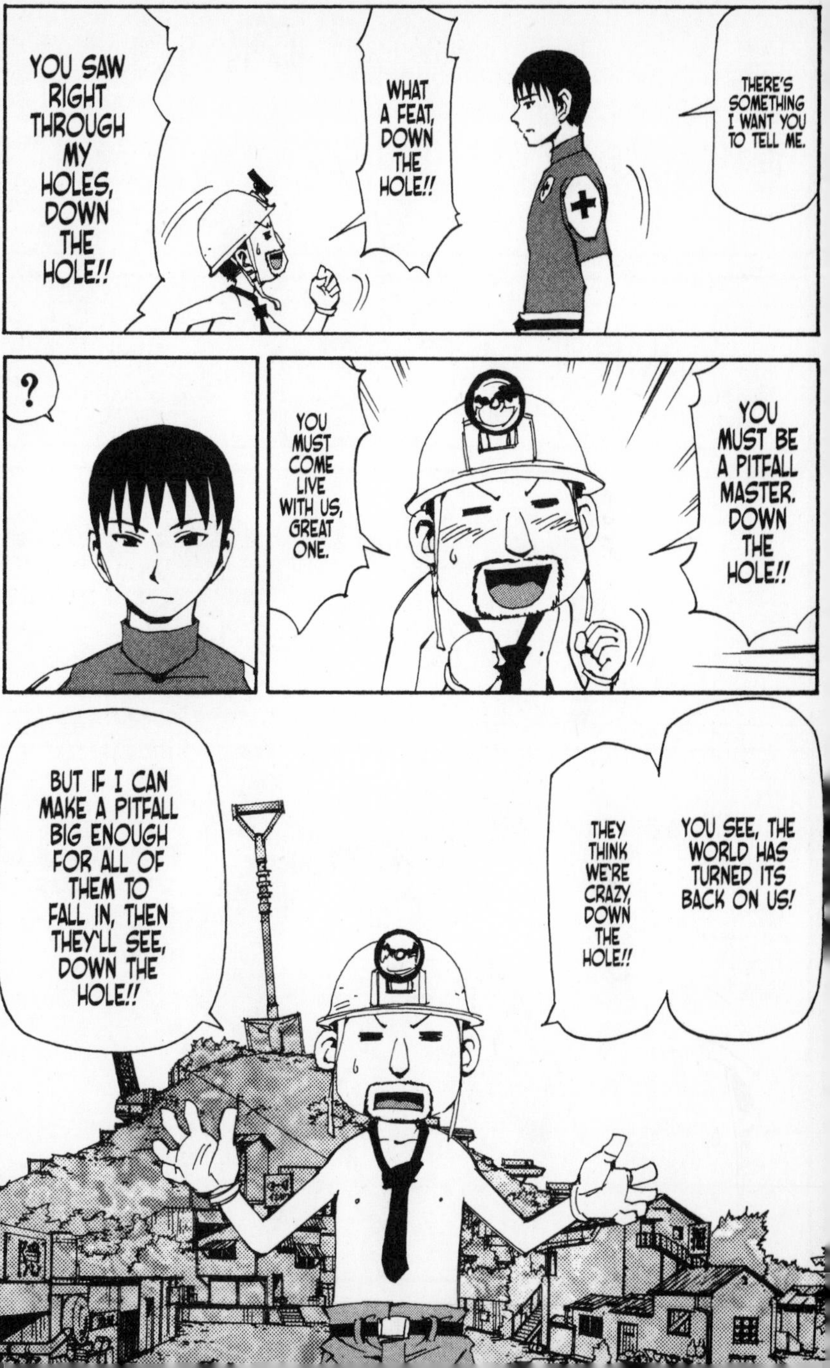
THERE'S SOMETHING I WANT YOU TO TELL ME.
WHAT A FEAT, DOWN THE HOLE!!
YOU SAW RIGHT THROUGH MY HOLES, DOWN THE HOLE!!
YOU MUST BE A PITFALL MASTER. DOWN THE HOLE!!
YOU MUST COME LIVE WITH US, GREAT ONE.
?
YOU SEE, THE WORLD HAS TURNED ITS BACK ON US!
THEY THINK WE'RE CRAZY, DOWN THE HOLE!!
BUT IF I CAN MAKE A PITFALL BIG ENOUGH FOR ALL OF THEM TO FALL IN, THEN THEY'LL SEE, DOWN THE HOLE!!

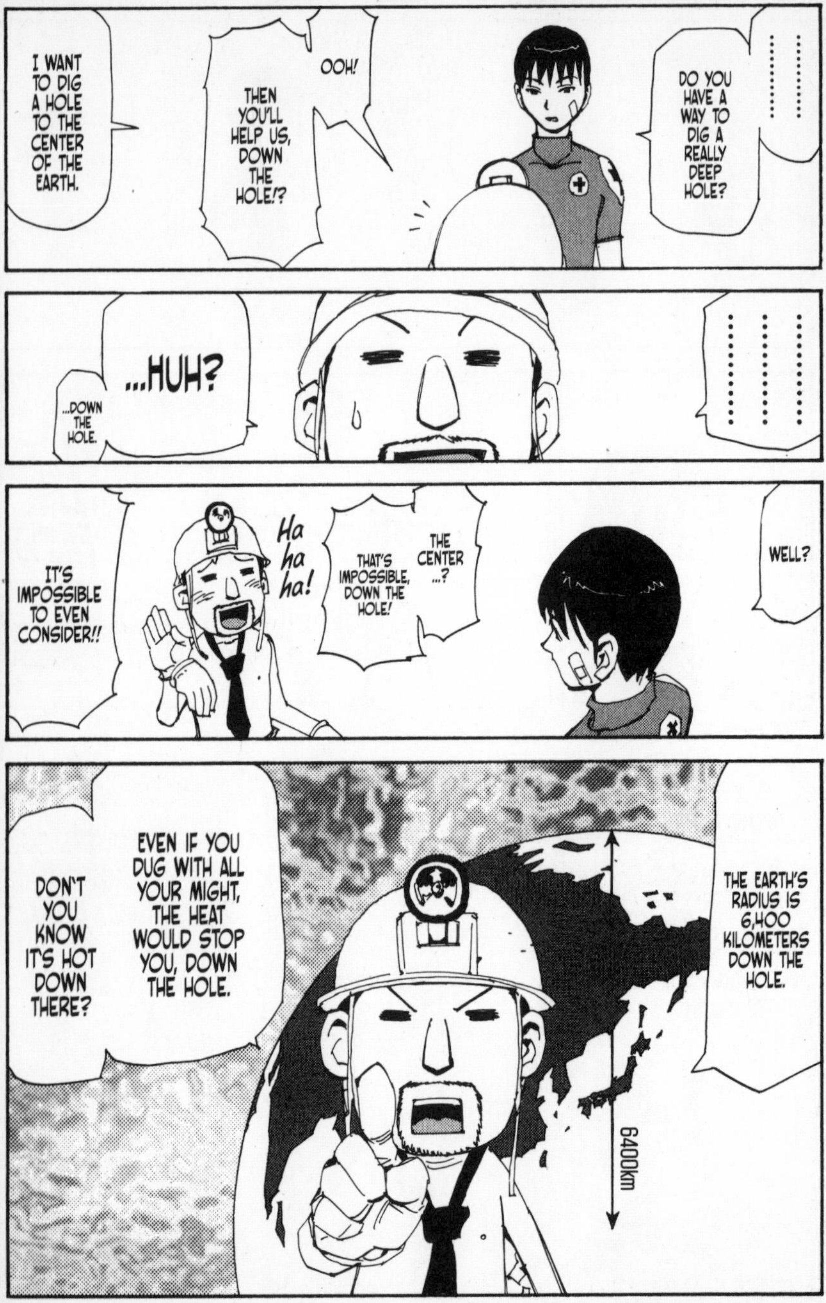
......
DO YOU HAVE A WAY TO DIG A REALLY DEEP HOLE?
OOH!
THEN YOU'LL HELP US, DOWN THE HOLE!?
I WANT TO DIG A HOLE TO THE CENTER OF THE EARTH.
......
...HUH?
...DOWN THE HOLE.
WELL?
THE CENTER ...?
THAT'S IMPOSSIBLE, DOWN THE HOLE!
Ha ha ha!
IT'S IMPOSSIBLE TO EVEN CONSIDER!!
THE EARTH'S RADIUS IS 6,400 KILOMETERS DOWN THE HOLE.
6400km
EVEN IF YOU DUG WITH ALL YOUR MIGHT, THE HEAT WOULD STOP YOU, DOWN THE HOLE.
DON'T YOU KNOW IT'S HOT DOWN THERE?

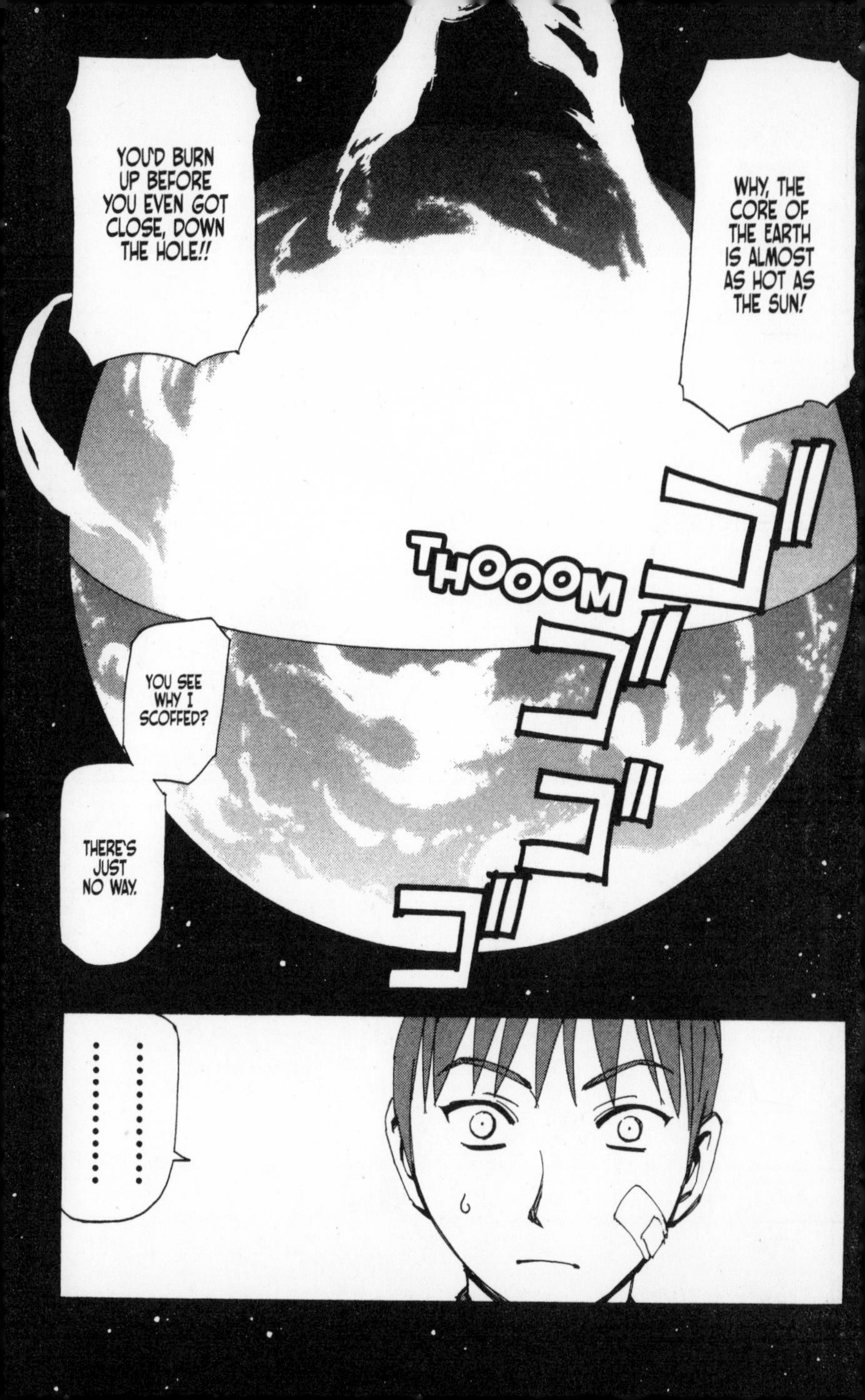

WHY, THE CORE OF THE EARTH IS ALMOST AS HOT AS THE SUN!
YOU'D BURN UP BEFORE YOU EVEN GOT CLOSE, DOWN THE HOLE!!
ゴゴゴゴ
THOOOM
YOU SEE WHY I SCOFFED?
THERE'S JUST NO WAY.
......

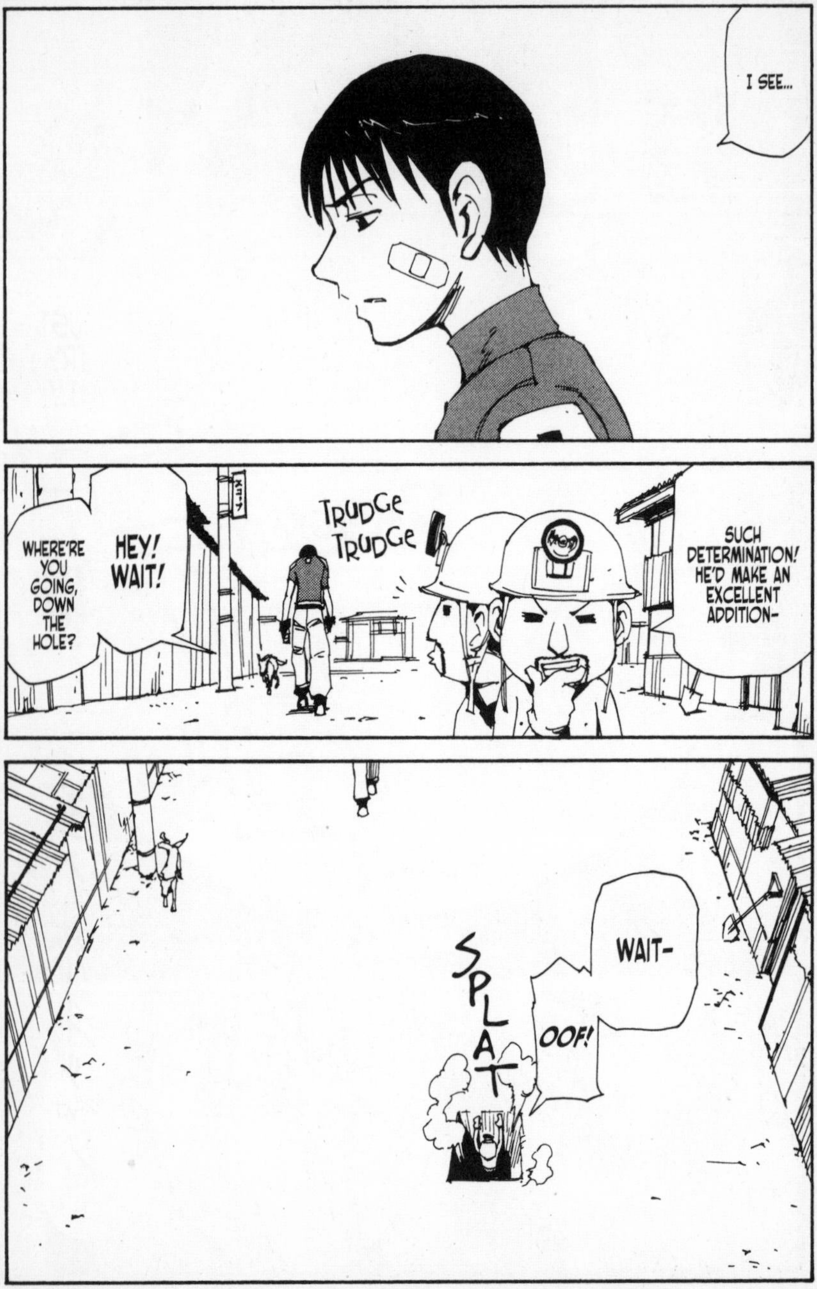
I SEE...
SUCH DETERMINATION! HE'D MAKE AN EXCELLENT ADDITION-
TRUDGE TRUDGE
HEY! WAIT!
WHERE'RE YOU GOING, DOWN THE HOLE?
WAIT-
OOF!
SPLAT

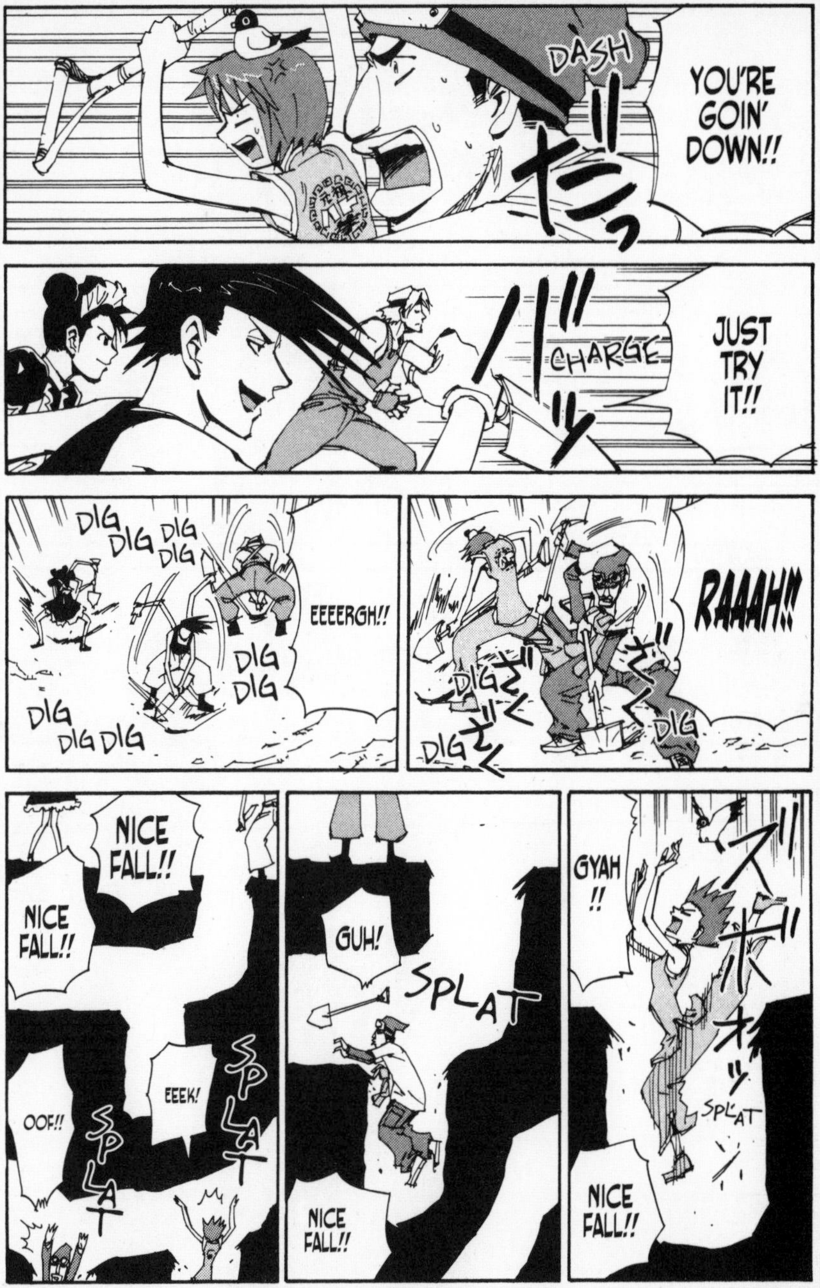
YOU'RE GOIN' DOWN!!
DASH
JUST TRY IT!!
CHARGE
RAAAH!!
DIG
DIG
DIG
DIG
EEEERGH!!
DIG DIG DIG DIG
DIG DIG
DIG DIG DIG
GYAH!!
SPLAT
NICE FALL!!
GUH!
SPLAT
NICE FALL!!
NICE FALL!!
NICE FALL!!
SPLAT
EEEK!
SPLAT
OOF!!

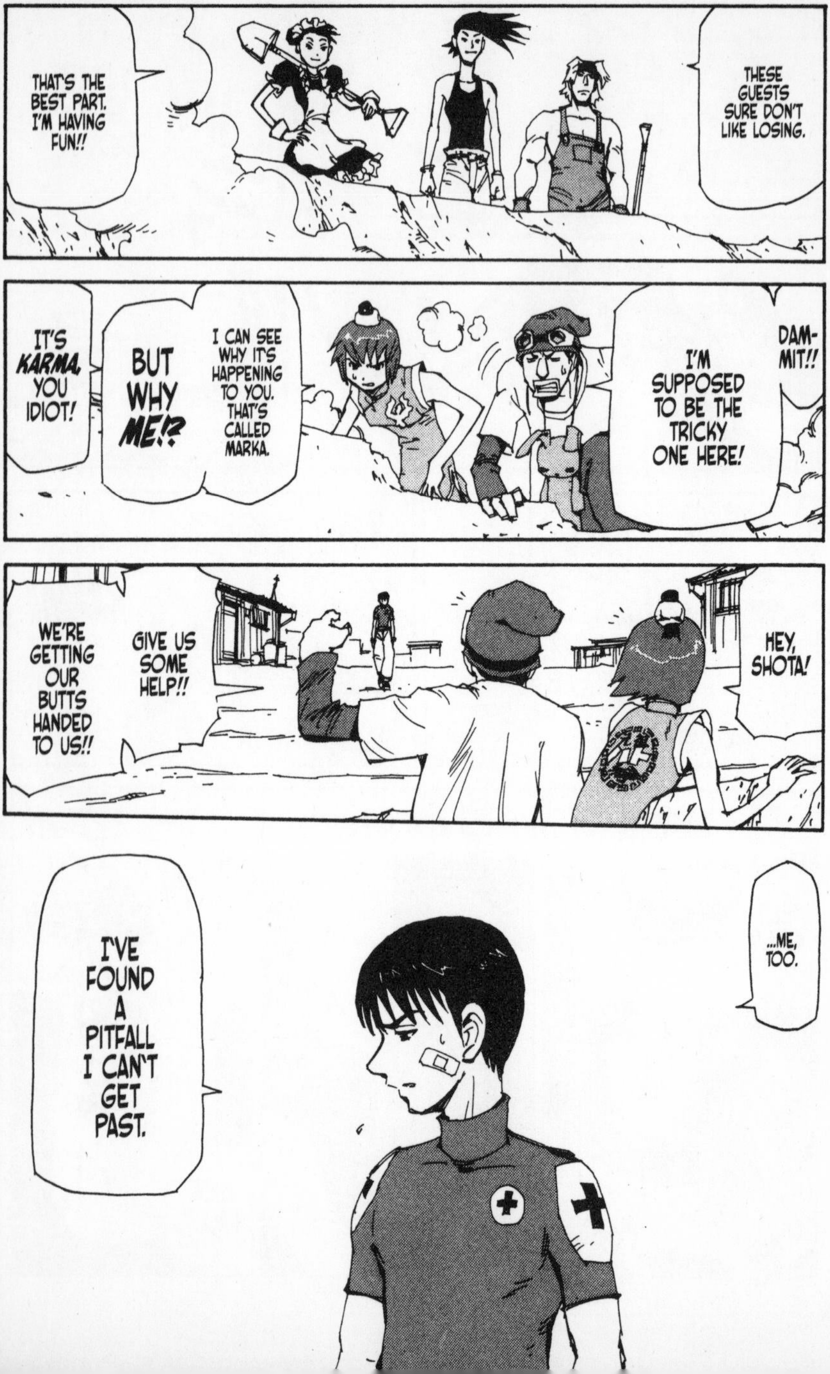
THESE GUESTS SURE DON'T LIKE LOSING.
THAT'S THE BEST PART. I'M HAVING FUN!!
DAM-MIT!!
I'M SUPPOSED TO BE THE TRICKY ONE HERE!
I CAN SEE WHY IT'S HAPPENING TO YOU. THAT'S CALLED MARKA.
BUT WHY ME!?
IT'S KARMA, YOU IDIOT!
HEY, SHOTA!
GIVE US SOME HELP!!
WE'RE GETTING OUR BUTTS HANDED TO US!!
...ME, TOO.
I'VE FOUND A PITFALL I CAN'T GET PAST.

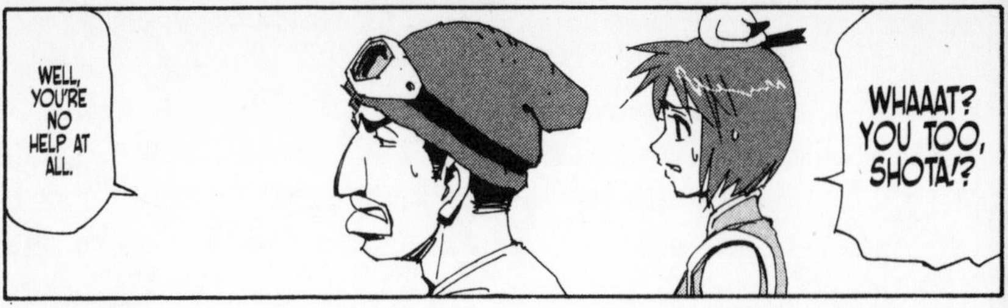
WHAAAT? YOU TOO, SHOTA!?
WELL, YOU'RE NO HELP AT ALL.

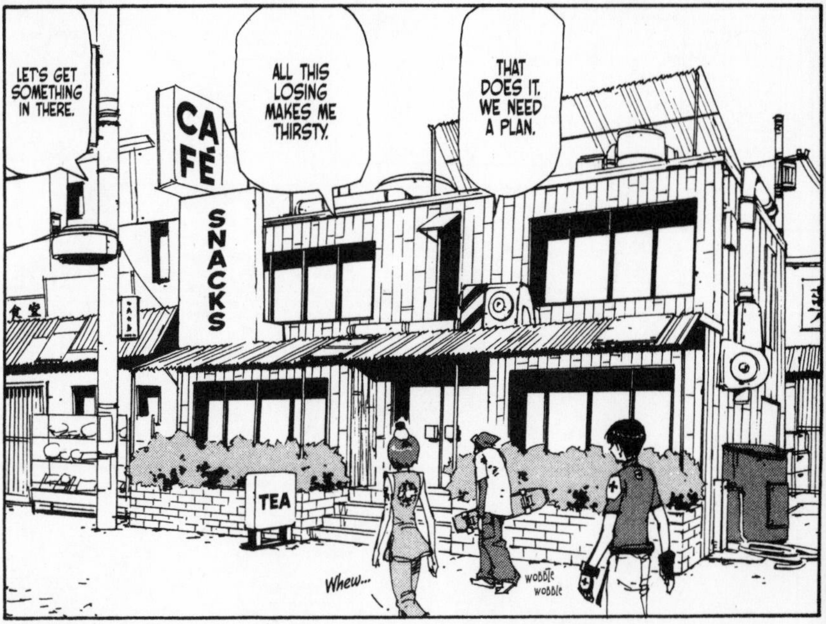
THAT DOES IT. WE NEED A PLAN.
ALL THIS LOSING MAKES ME THIRSTY.
LET'S GET SOMETHING IN THERE.
CAFÉ
SNACKS
TEA
WOBBLE WOBBLE
Whew...

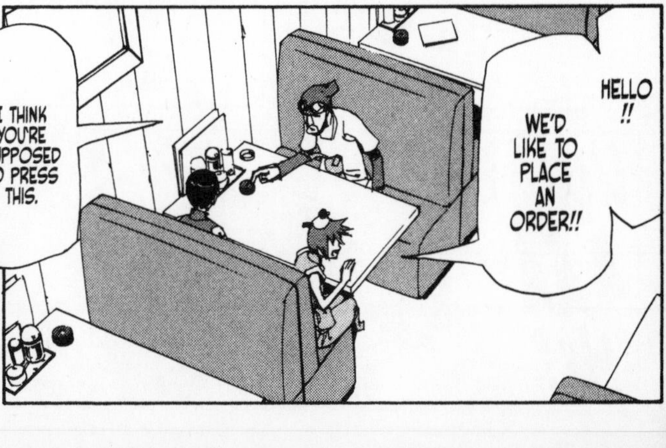
HELLO!!
WE'D LIKE TO PLACE AN ORDER!!

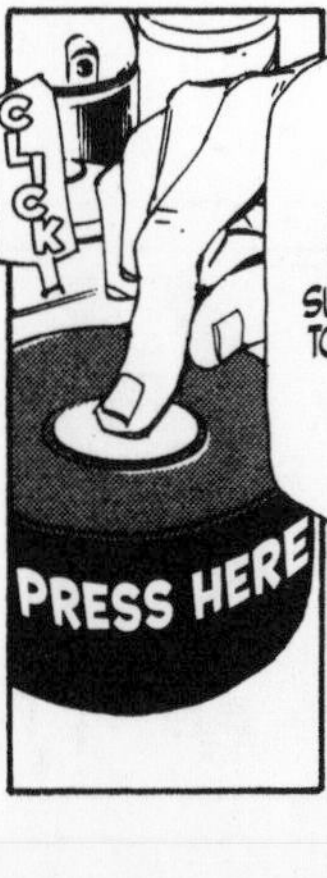
I THINK YOU'RE SUPPOSED TO PRESS THIS.
CLICK
PRESS HERE

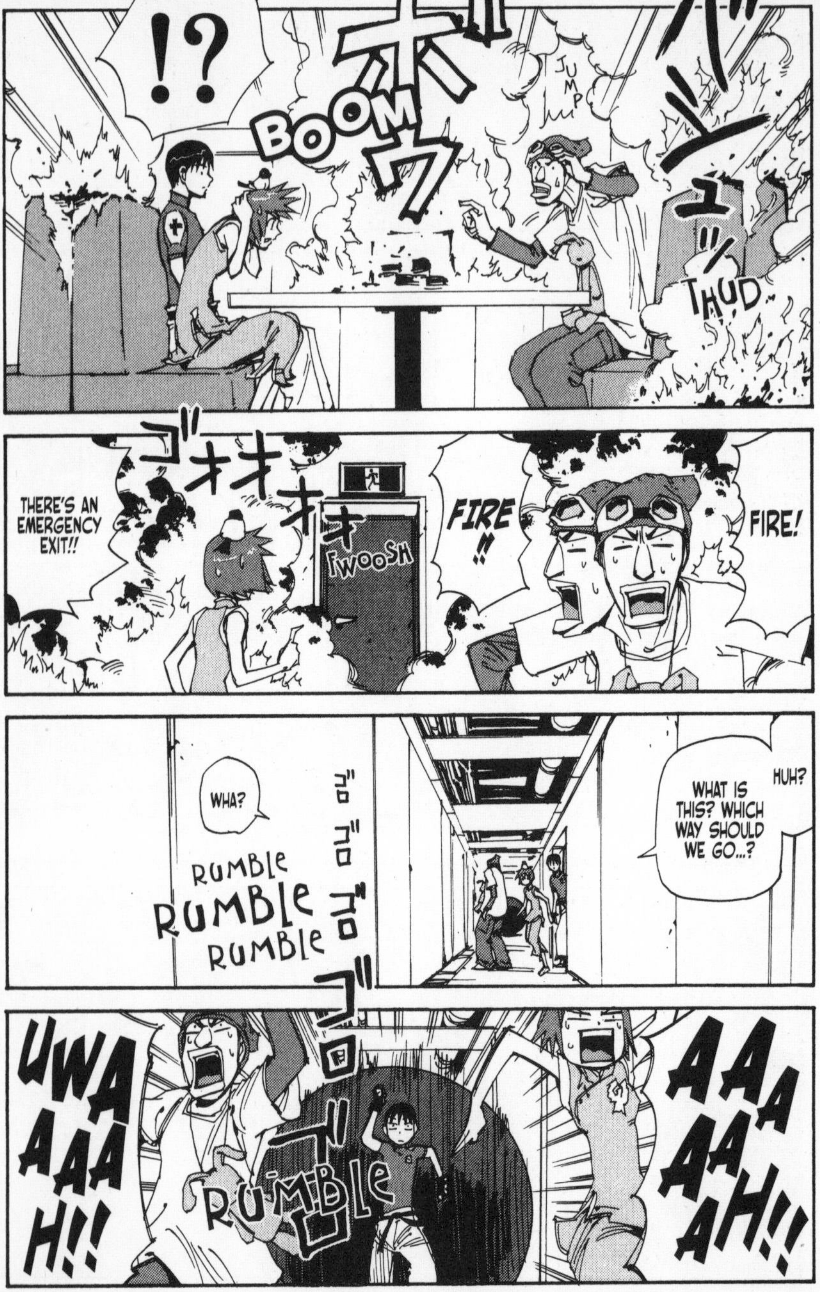
THUD
JUMP
ボウ
BOOM
!?
FIRE!
FIRE!!
ゴオオオ
FWOOSH
THERE'S AN EMERGENCY EXIT!!
HUH?
WHAT IS THIS? WHICH WAY SHOULD WE GO...?
ゴロゴロゴロ
WHA?
RUMBLE RUMBLE RUMBLE
AAAAAAAH!!
ゴロゴロ
RUMBLE
UWAAAAAH!!

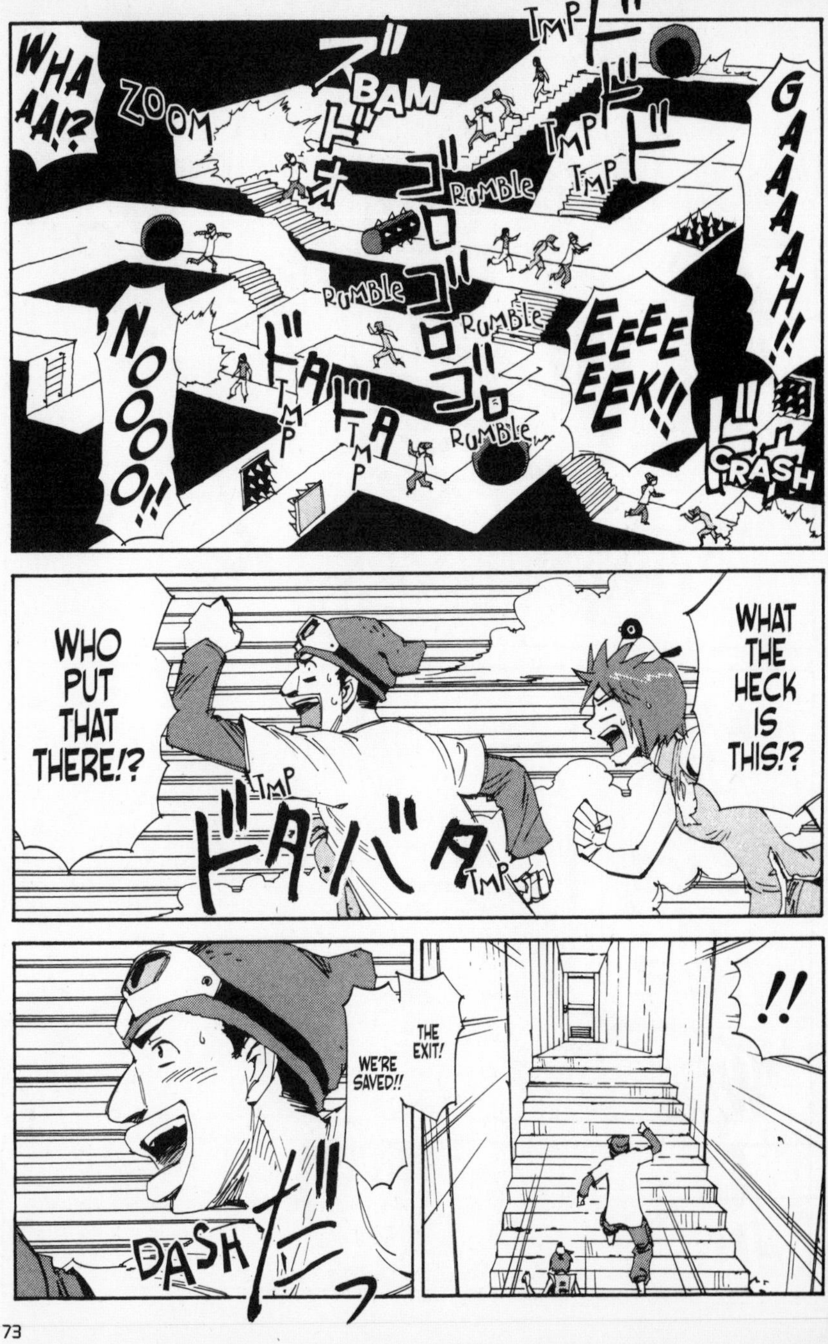
GAAAAAH!!
TMP ドドド TMP TMP
ズドォ BAM
ZOOM
WHAAAA!?
ゴロゴロゴロ RUMBLE RUMBLE RUMBLE RUMBLE
EEEEEEK!!
CRASH
NOOOOO!!
ドタドタ TMP TMP
WHAT THE HECK IS THIS!?
WHO PUT THAT THERE!?
ドタバタ TMP TMP
!!
THE EXIT!
WE'RE SAVED!!
DASH

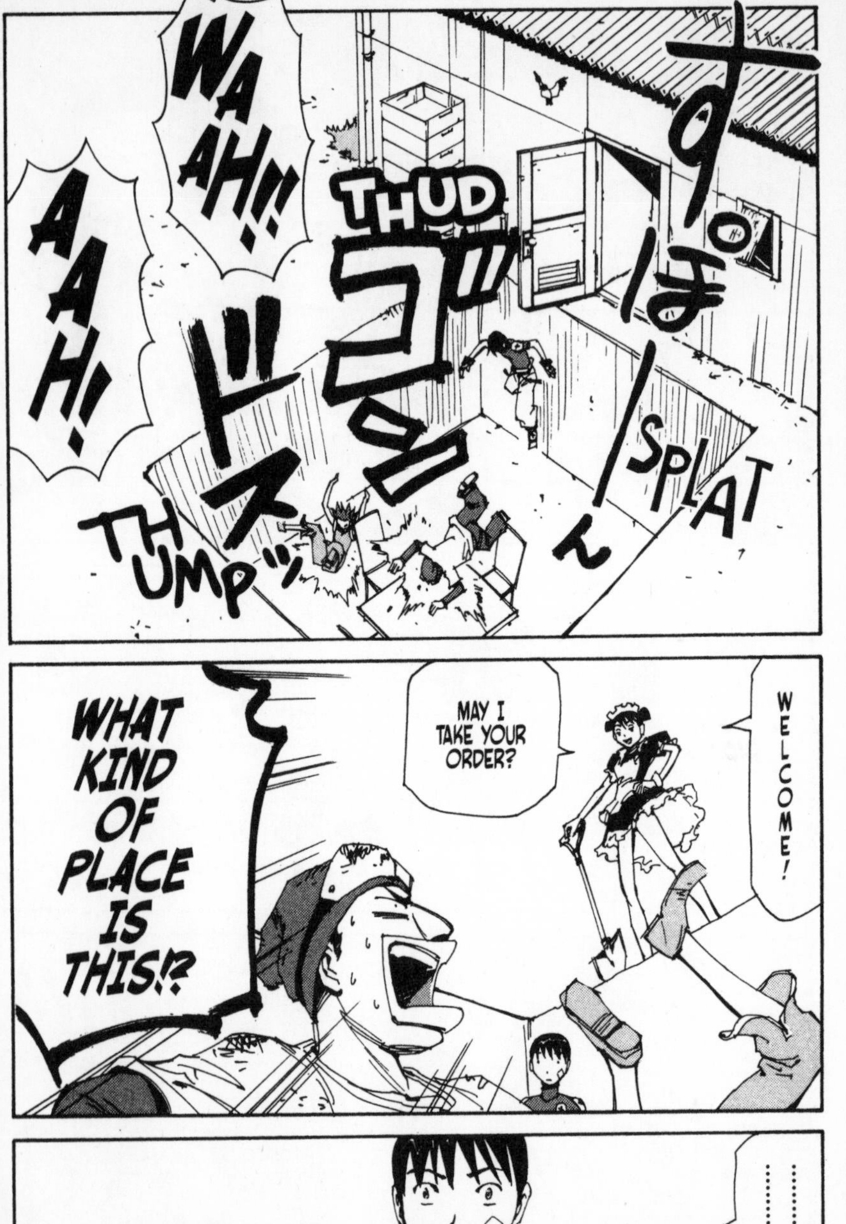
すぽーん
SPLAT
THUD
ゴン
WA AH!!
AAAH!
ドスッ
THUMP
WELCOME!
MAY I TAKE YOUR ORDER?
WHAT KIND OF PLACE IS THIS!?
......

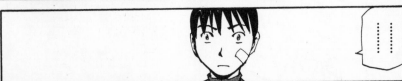

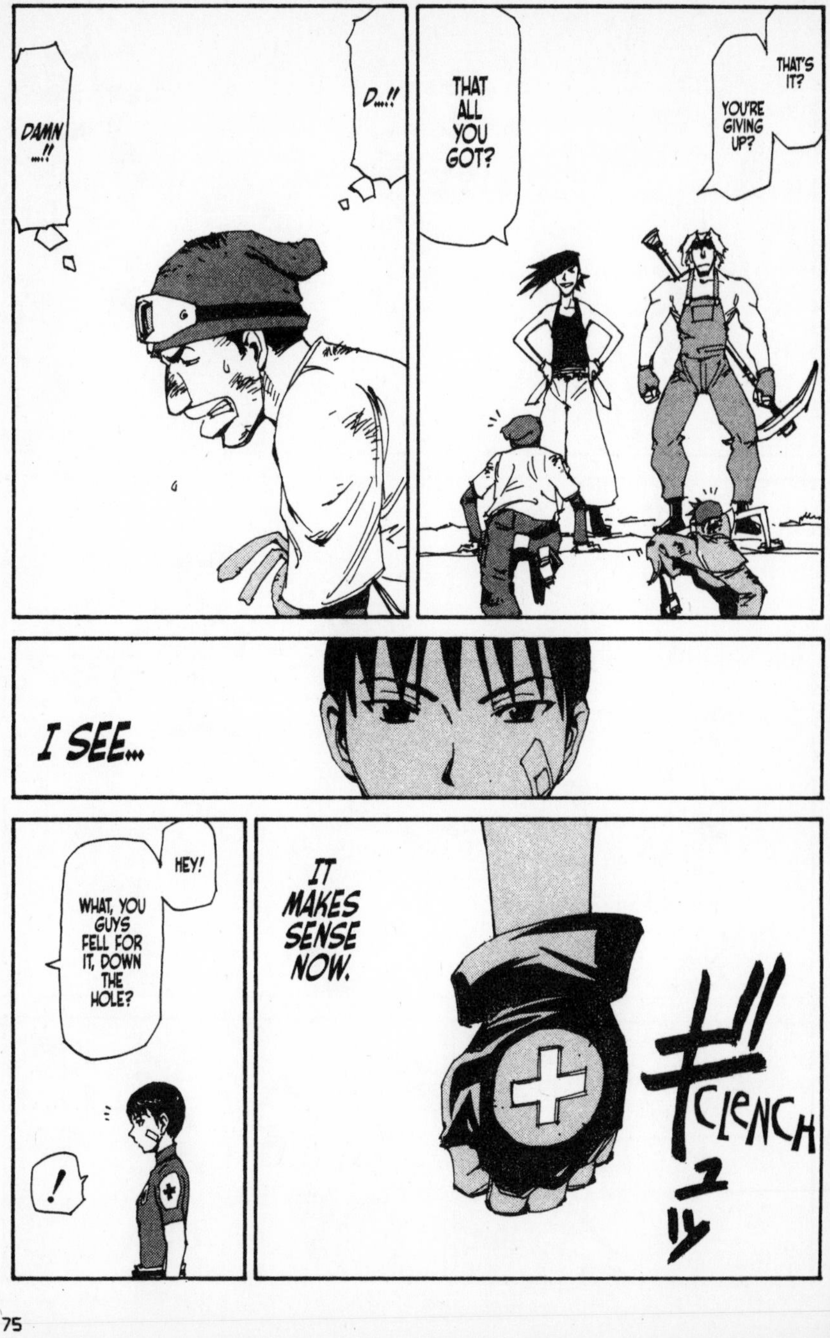
THAT'S IT? YOU'RE GIVING UP?
THAT ALL YOU GOT?
D...!!
DAMN ...!!
I SEE...
IT MAKES SENSE NOW.
CLENCH
ギュッ
HEY! WHAT, YOU GUYS FELL FOR IT, DOWN THE HOLE?
!

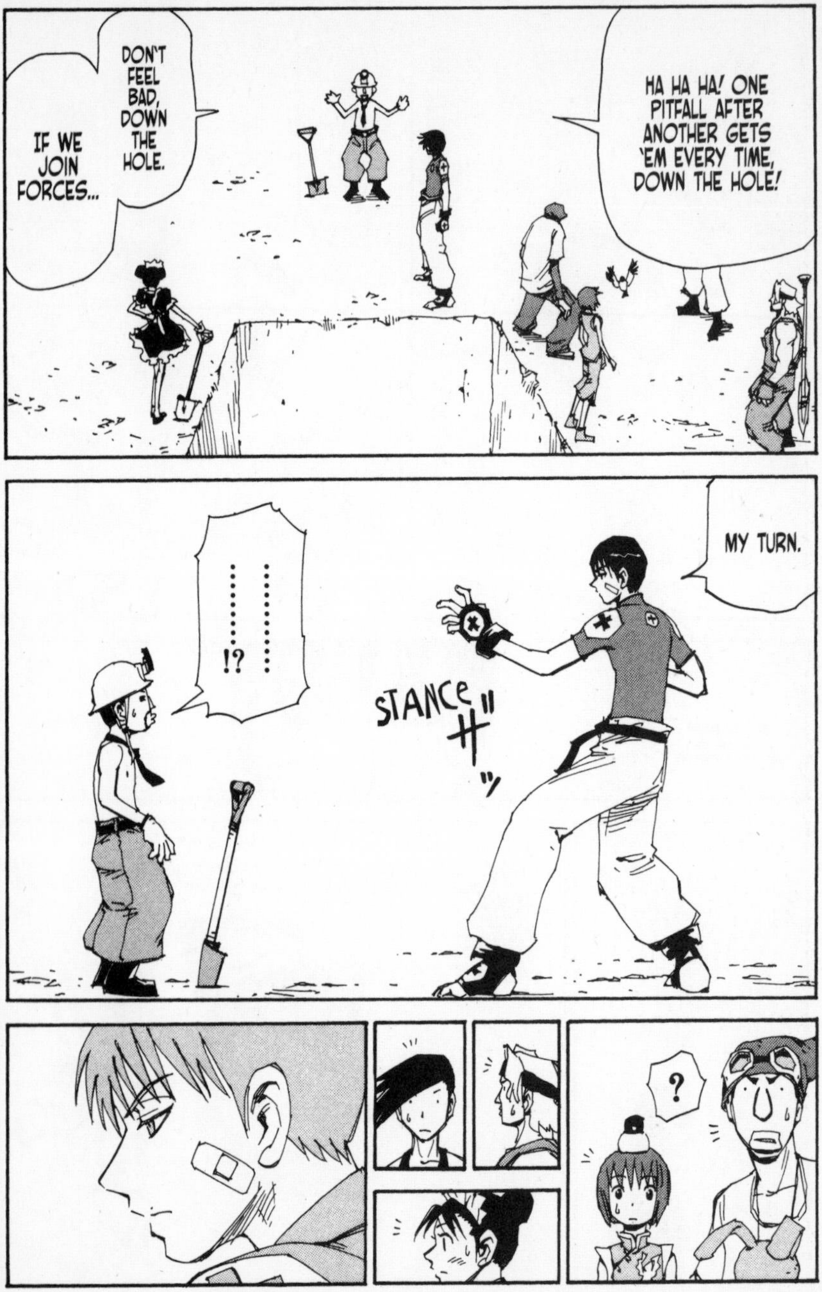
HA HA HA! ONE PITFALL AFTER ANOTHER GETS 'EM EVERY TIME, DOWN THE HOLE!
DON'T FEEL BAD, DOWN THE HOLE.
IF WE JOIN FORCES...
MY TURN.
STANCE
ザッ
......!?
?

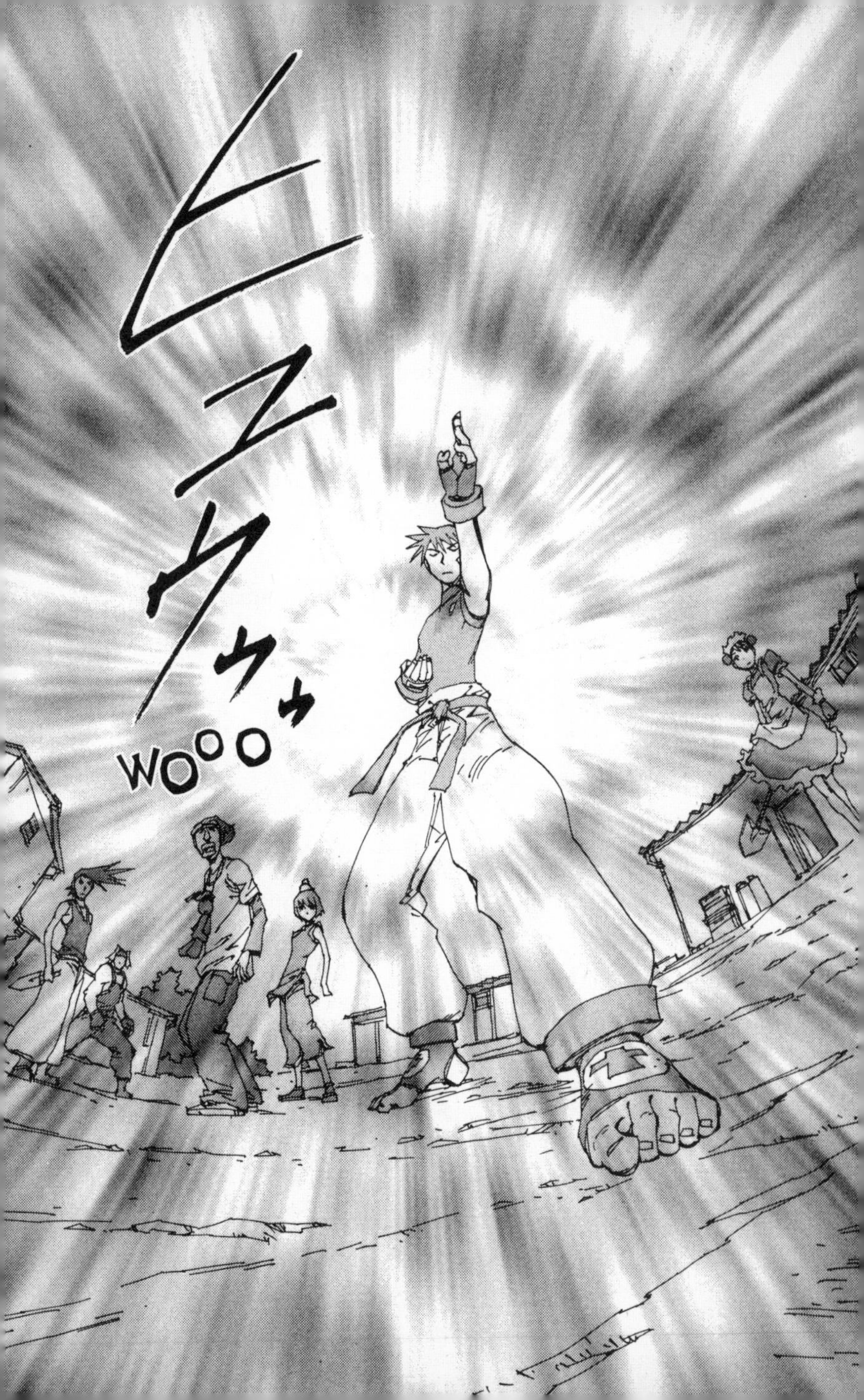
WOOO

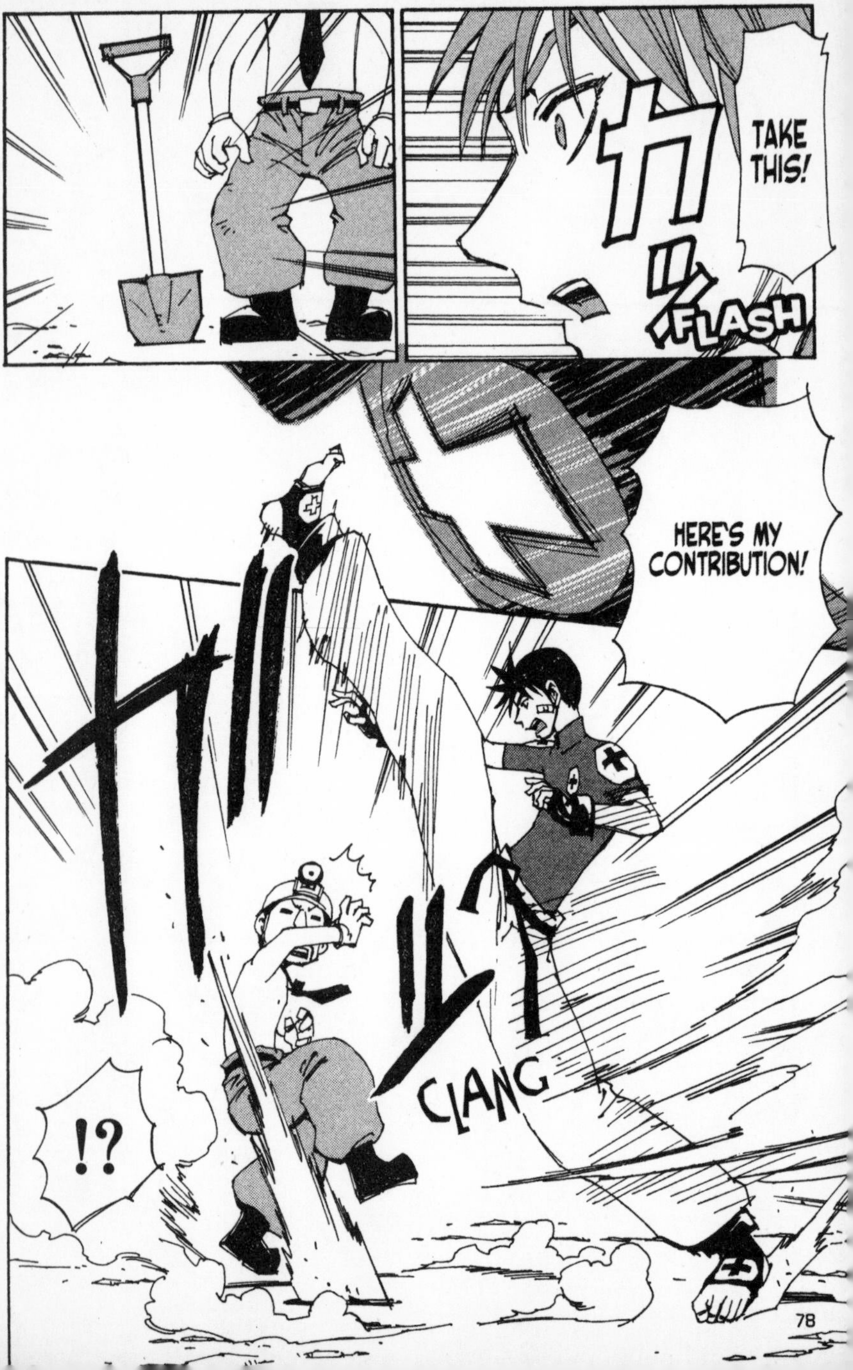
TAKE THIS!
カッ
FLASH
HERE'S MY CONTRIBUTION!
CLANG
!?

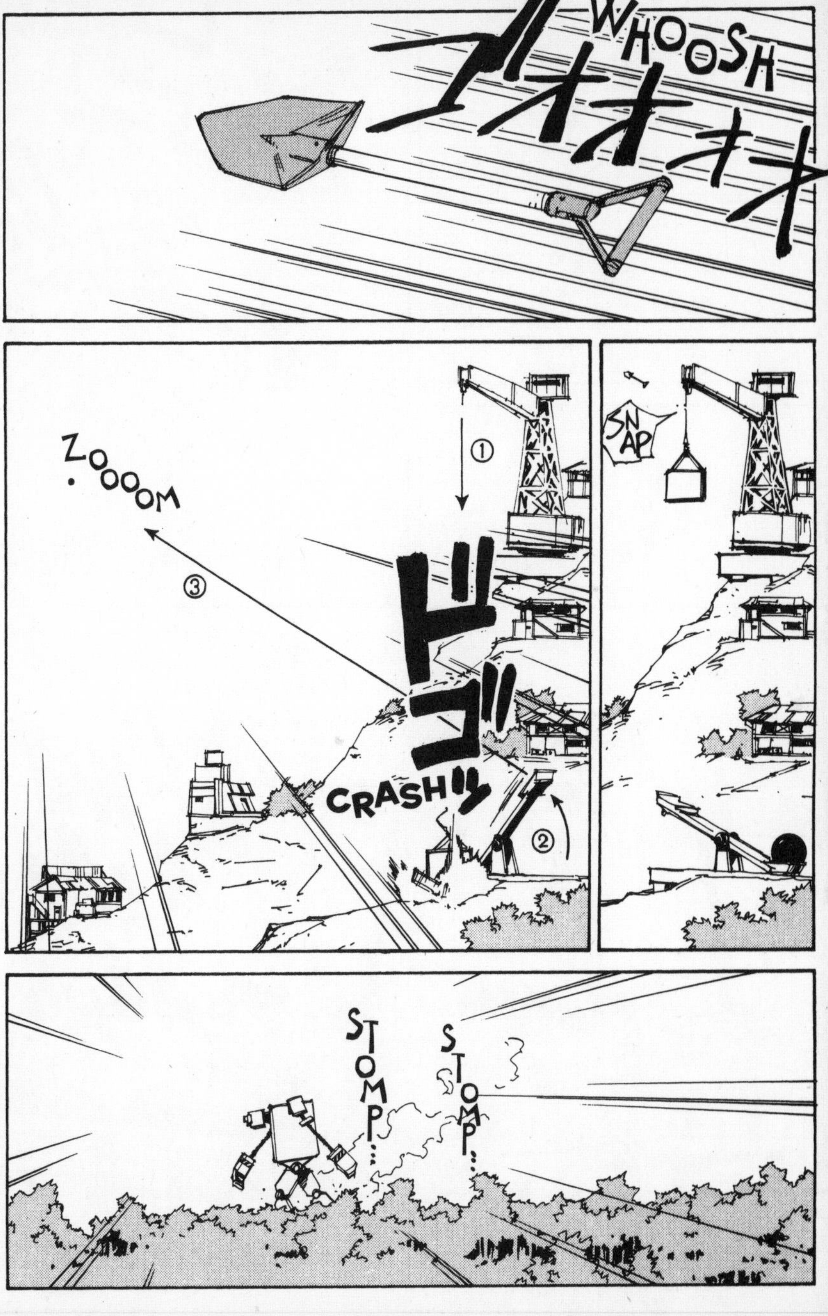
ゴオオオオ
WHOOSH
SNAP
①
ドゴ
CRASH!!
②
③
ZOOOOM
STOMP...
STOMP...

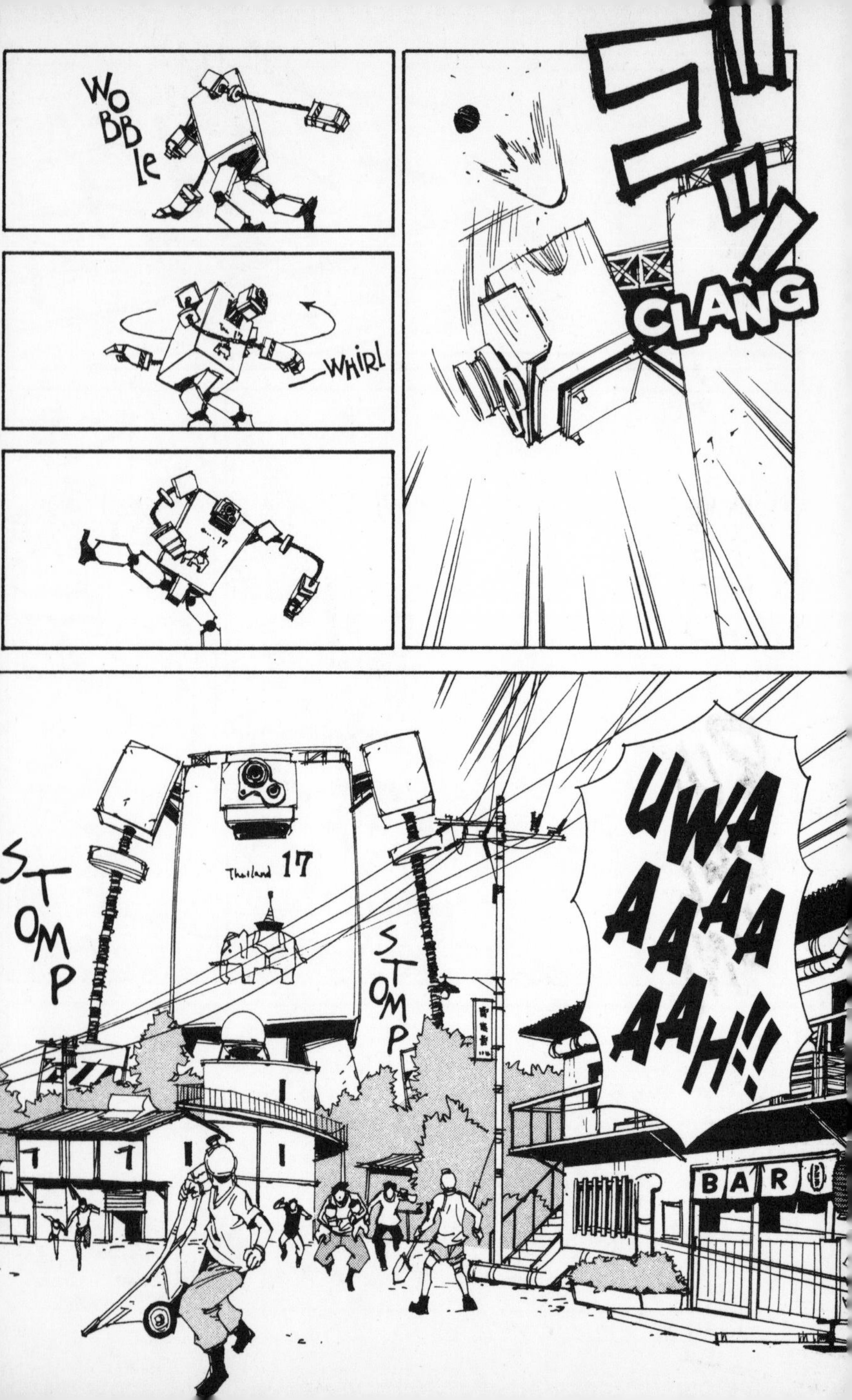
ゴッ!
CLANG
WOBBLE
WHIRL
Thailand 17
STOMP
STOMP
UWAAAAAAAH!!
BAR

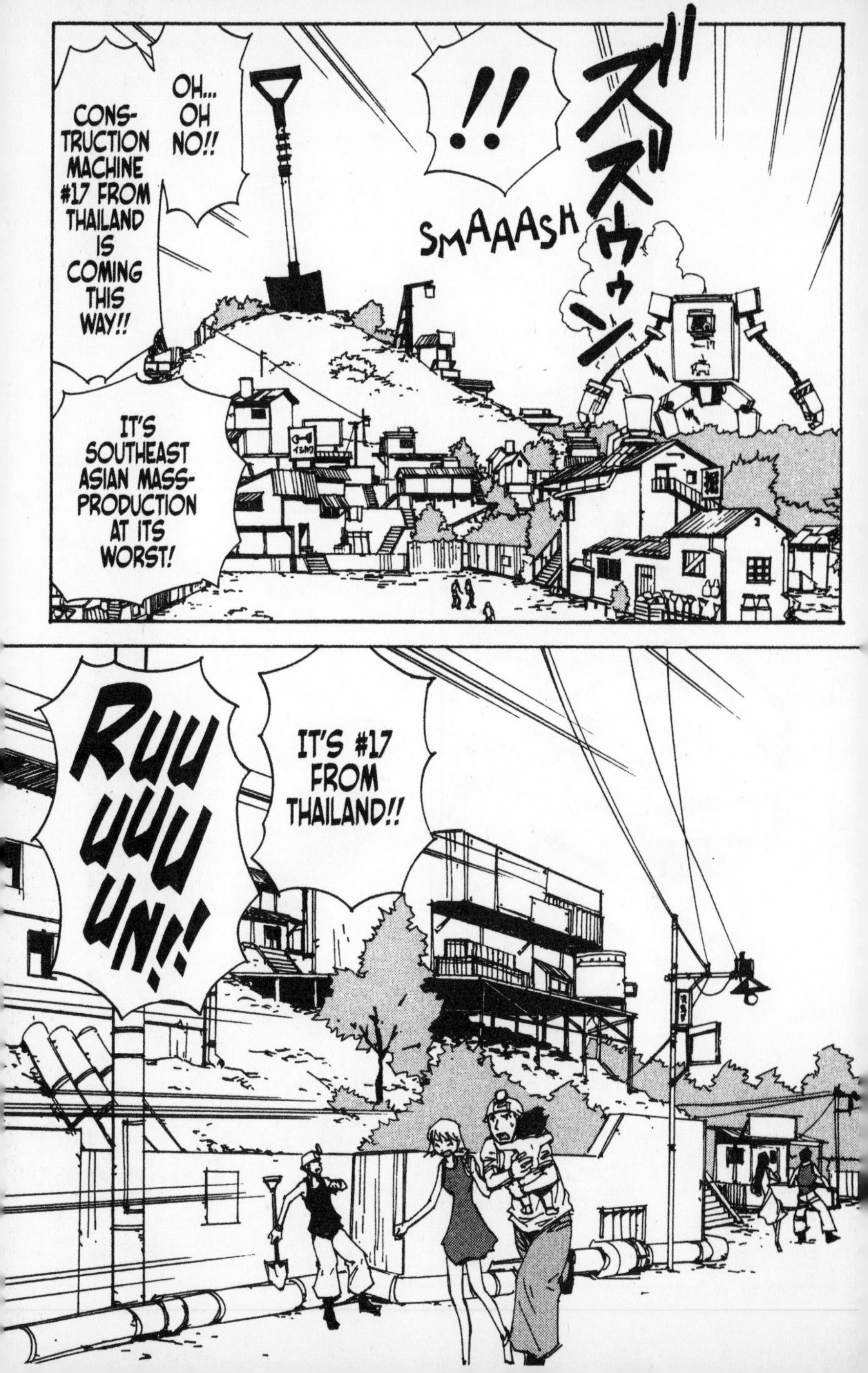
!!
ズズウゥン
SMAAASH
OH... OH NO!!
CONS-TRUCTION MACHINE #17 FROM THAILAND IS COMING THIS WAY!!
IT'S SOUTHEAST ASIAN MASS-PRODUCTION AT ITS WORST!
IT'S #17 FROM THAILAND!!
RUUUUUUN!!

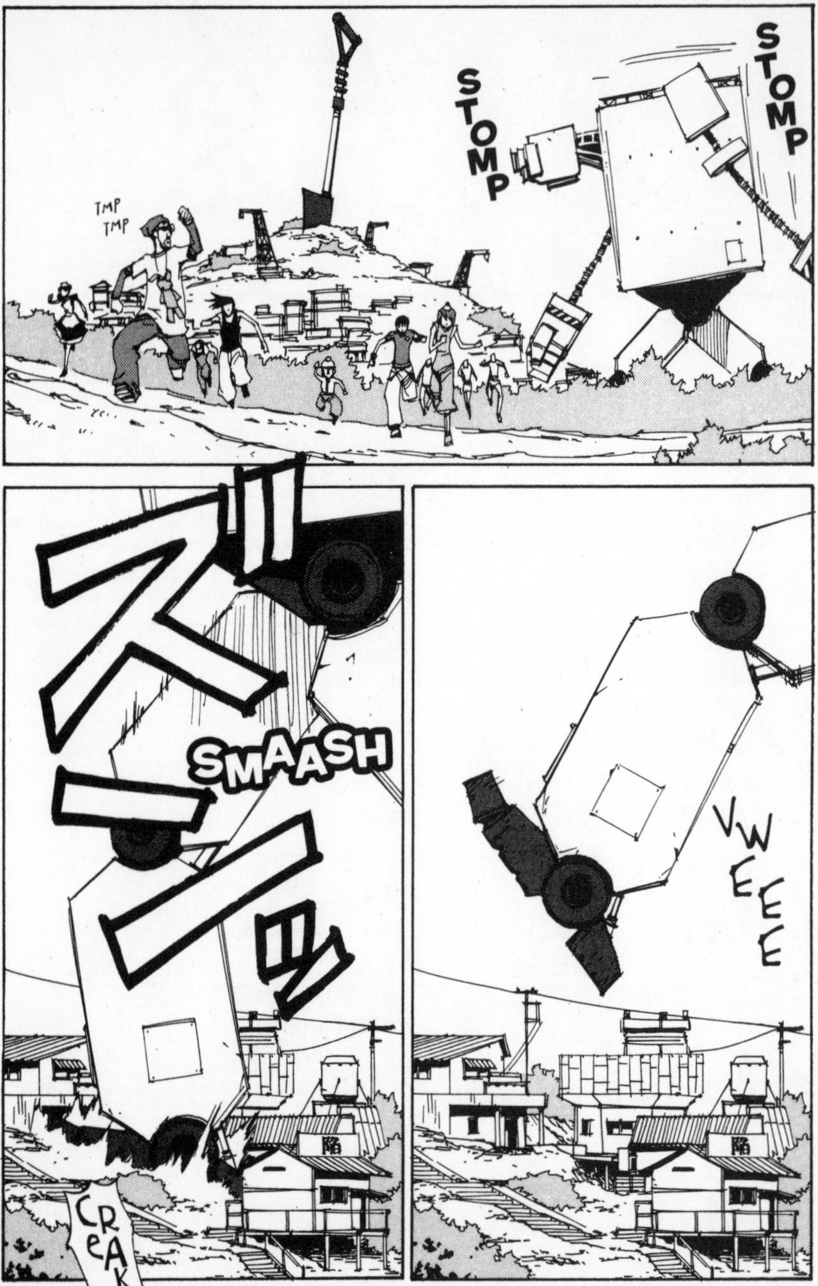
STOMP
STOMP
TMP TMP
VWEEE
SMAASH
CReAK

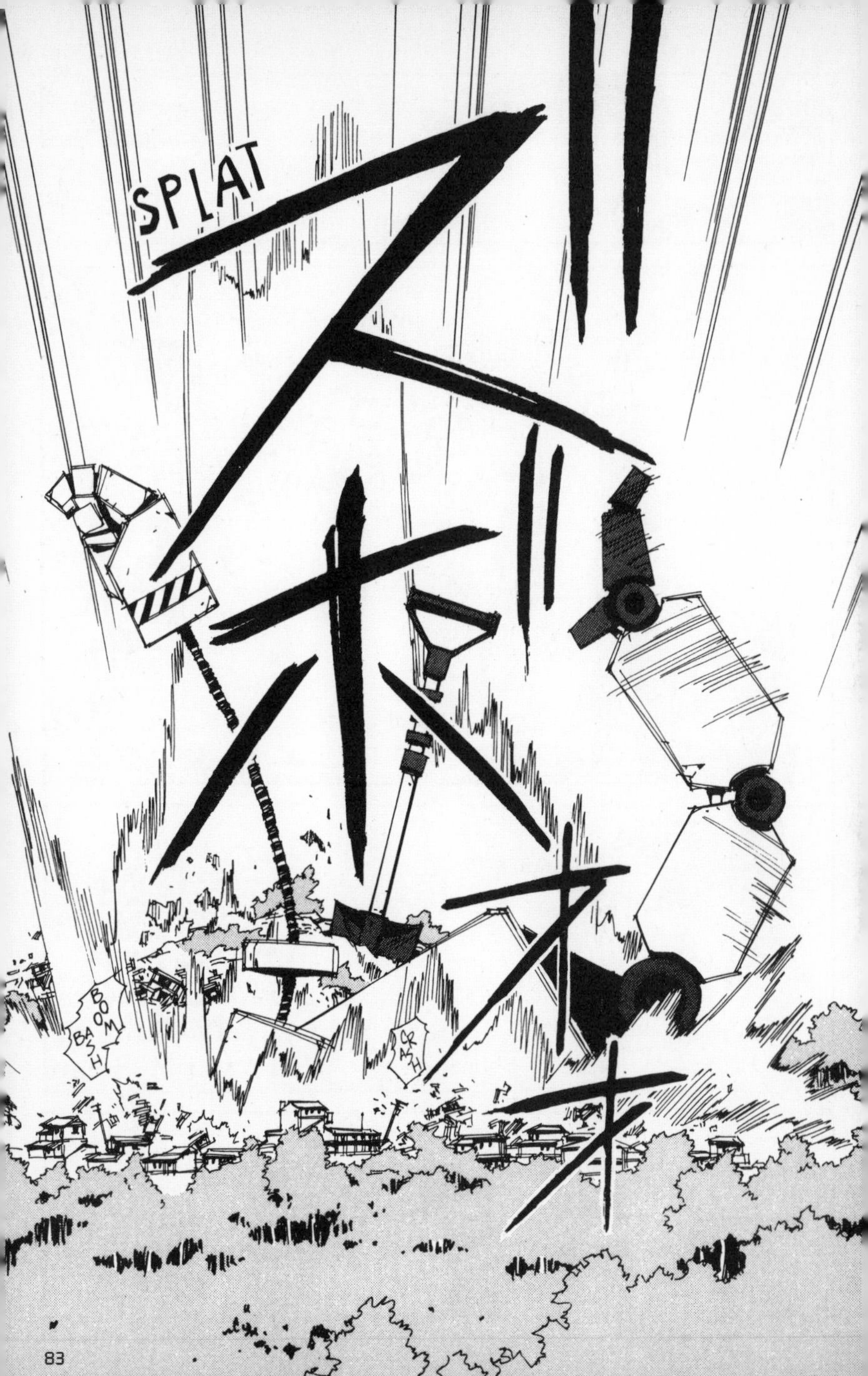
SPLAT
CRASH
BOOM
BASH

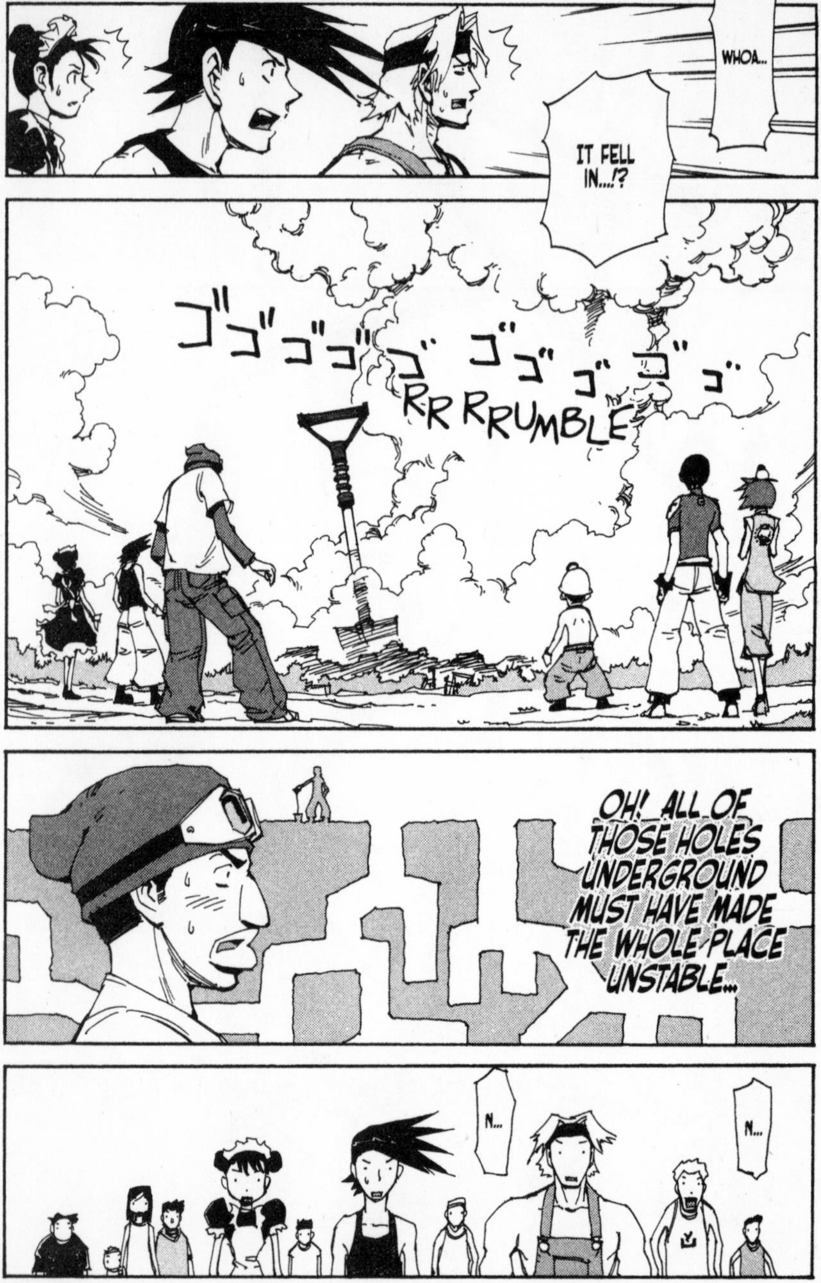
WHOA...
IT FELL IN...!?
ゴゴゴゴゴ ゴゴゴゴゴ
R-R RRRUMBLE
OH! ALL OF THOSE HOLES UNDERGROUND MUST HAVE MADE THE WHOLE PLACE UNSTABLE...
N...
N...

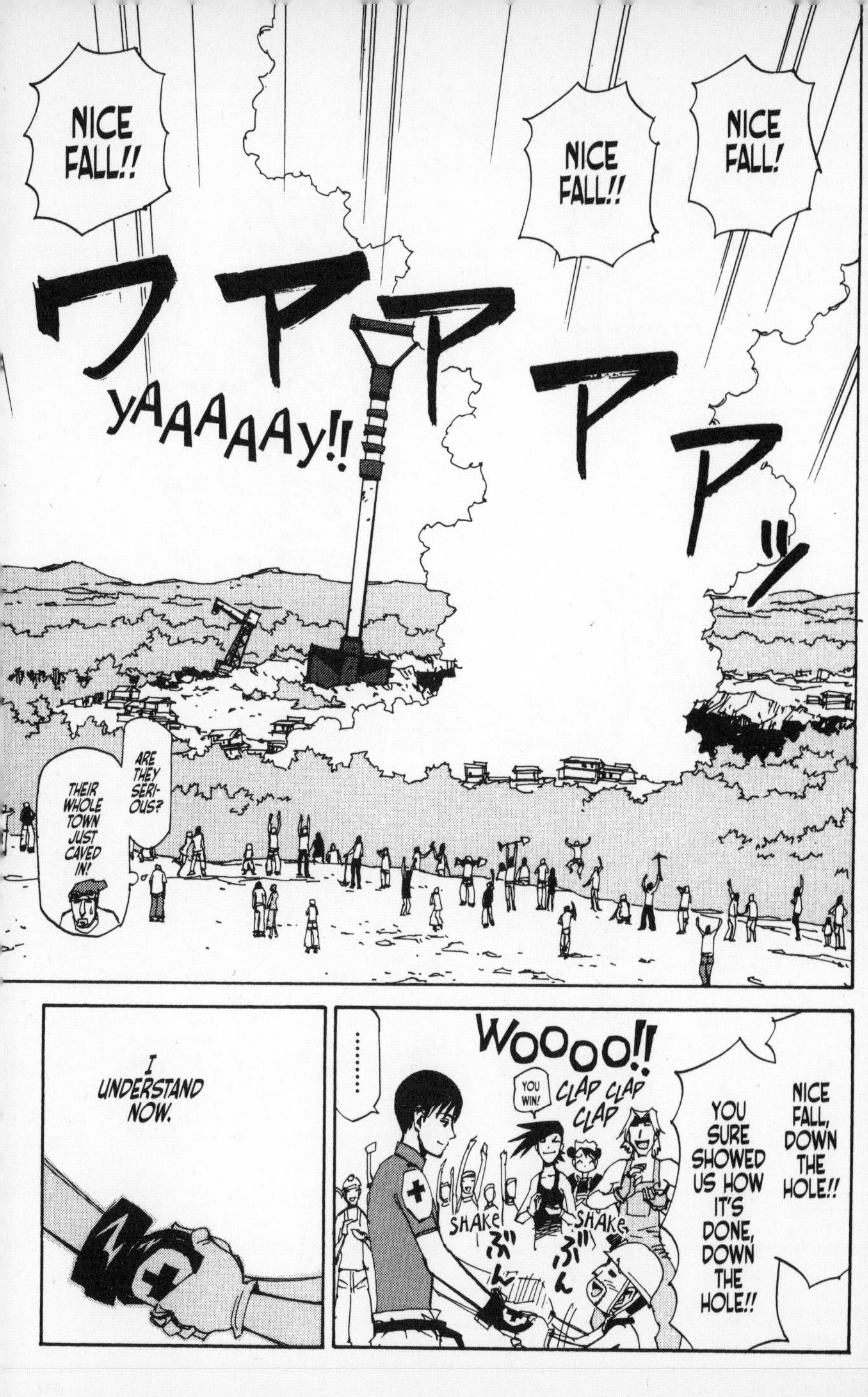
NICE FALL!
NICE FALL!!
NICE FALL!!
ワァァァァァッ
YAAAAAY!!
ARE THEY SERI-OUS?
THEIR WHOLE TOWN JUST CAVED IN!
NICE FALL, DOWN THE HOLE!!
YOU SURE SHOWED US HOW IT'S DONE, DOWN THE HOLE!!
WOOOO!!
CLAP CLAP CLAP
YOU WIN!
SHAKE ぶん
SHAKE ぶん
......
I UNDERSTAND NOW.

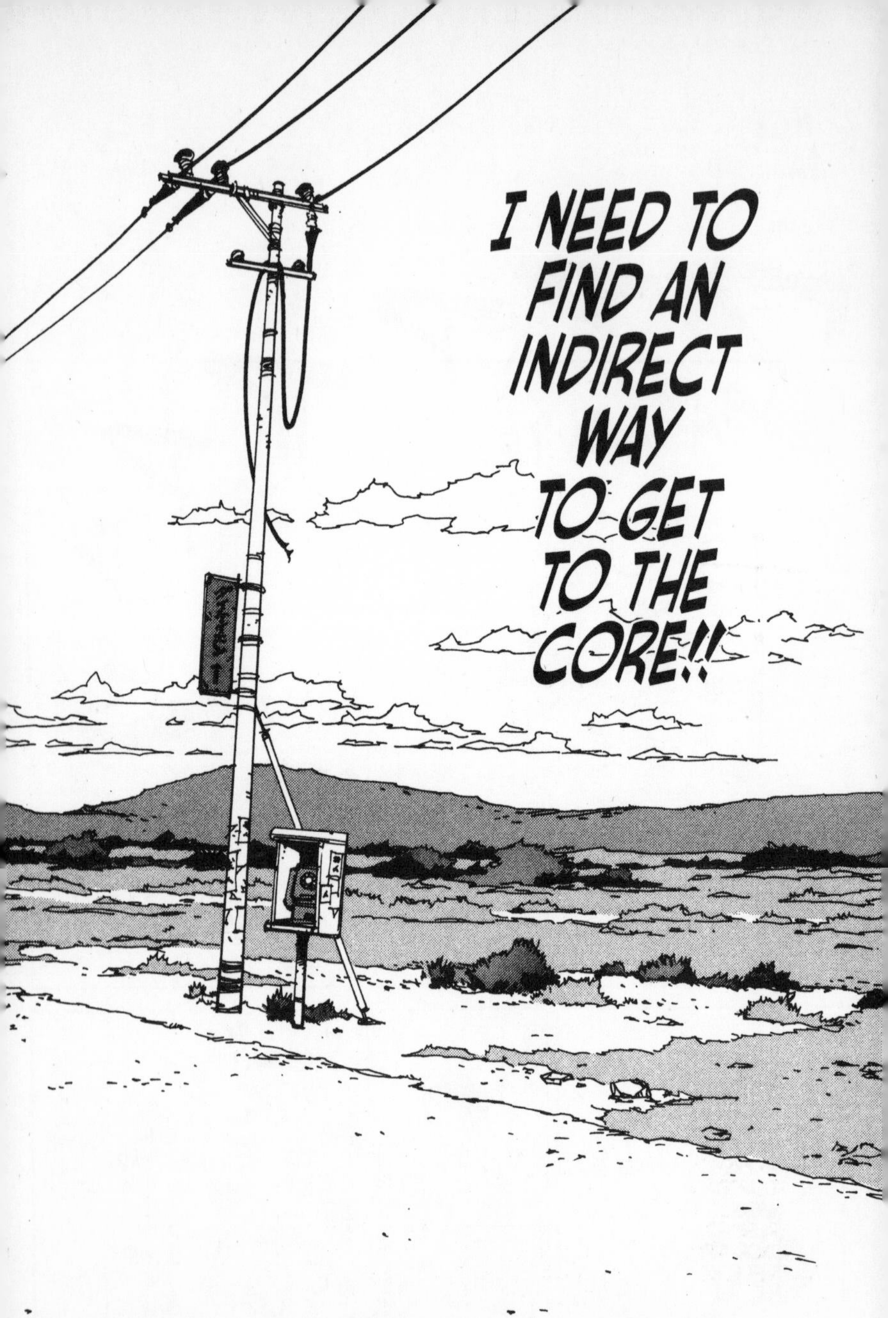
I NEED TO FIND AN INDIRECT WAY TO GET TO THE CORE!!

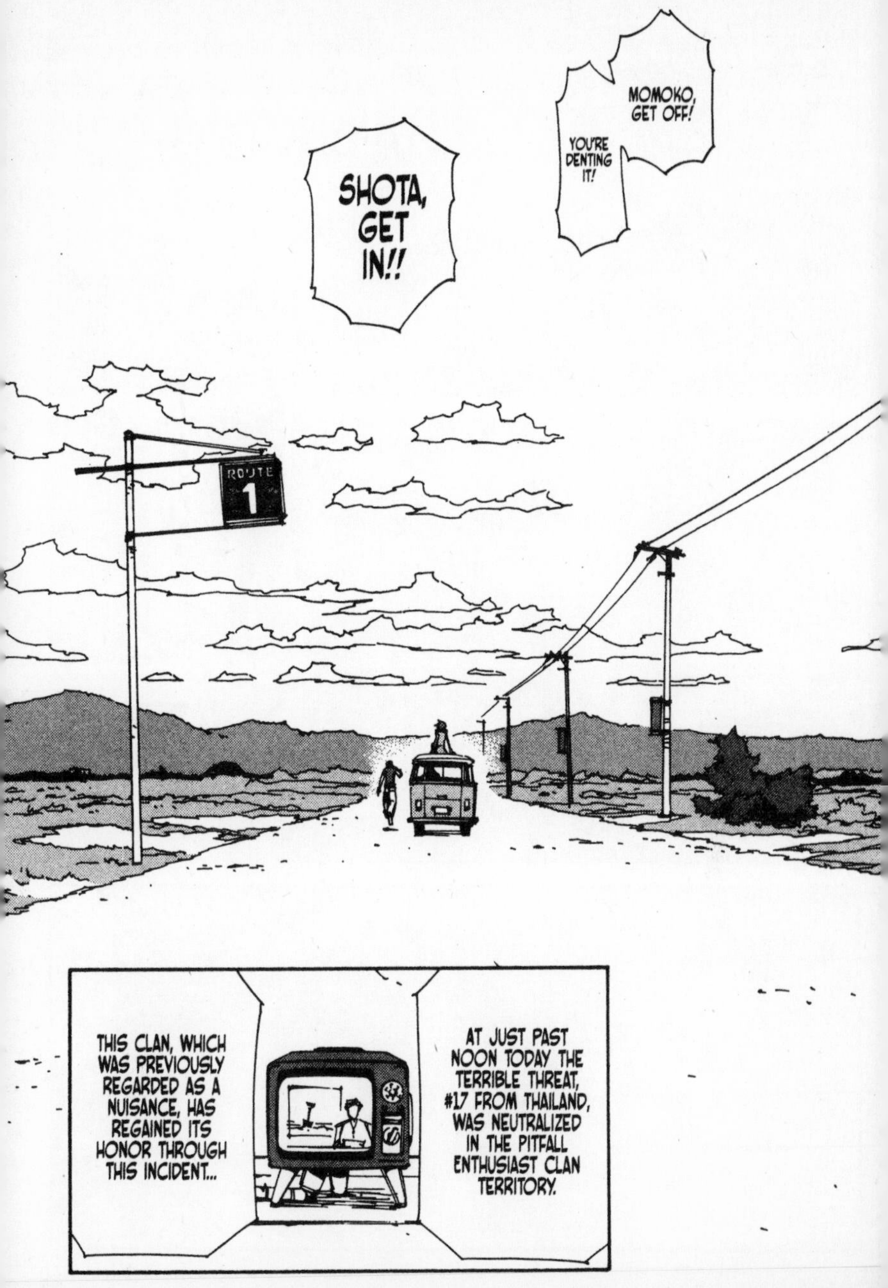
MOMOKO, GET OFF!
YOU'RE DENTING IT!
SHOTA, GET IN!!
ROUTE 1
AT JUST PAST NOON TODAY THE TERRIBLE THREAT, #17 FROM THAILAND, WAS NEUTRALIZED IN THE PITFALL ENTHUSIAST CLAN TERRITORY.
THIS CLAN, WHICH WAS PREVIOUSLY REGARDED AS A NUISANCE, HAS REGAINED ITS HONOR THROUGH THIS INCIDENT...

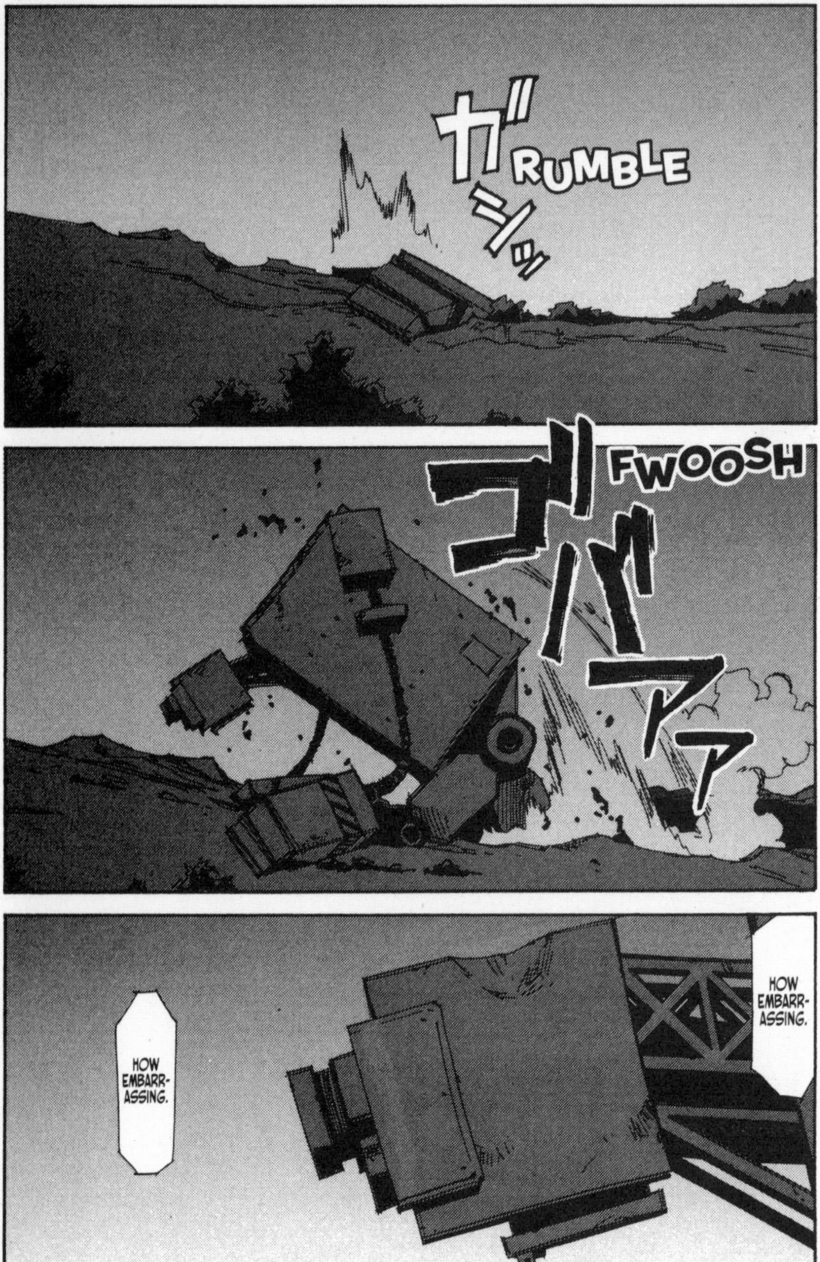
ガシッ
RUMBLE
ゴバァア
FWOOSH
HOW EMBARRASSING.
HOW EMBARRASSING.

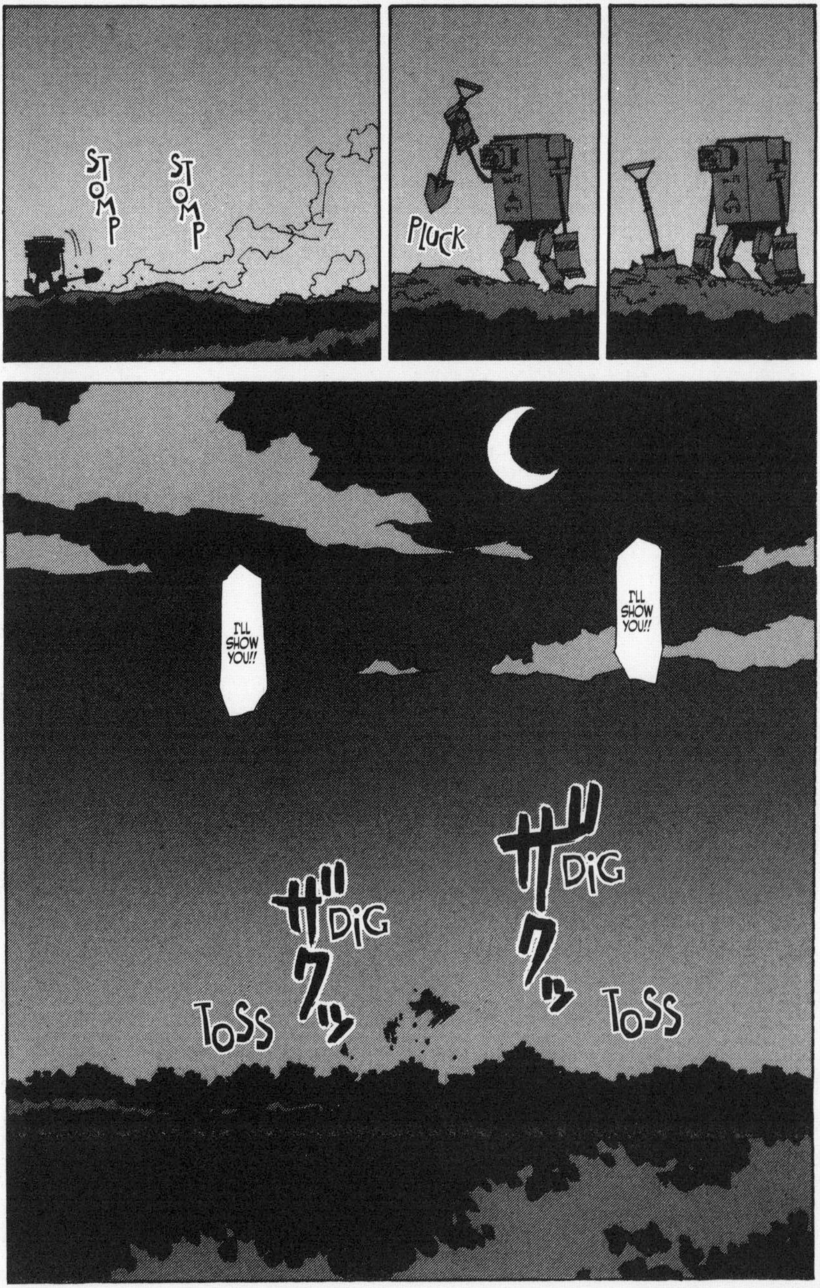
PLUCK
STOMP
STOMP
I'LL SHOW YOU!!
I'LL SHOW YOU!!
ザクッ
DIG
TOSS
ザクッ
DIG
TOSS

YAGAMI-SAN,
NICE FALL.

by Manager H

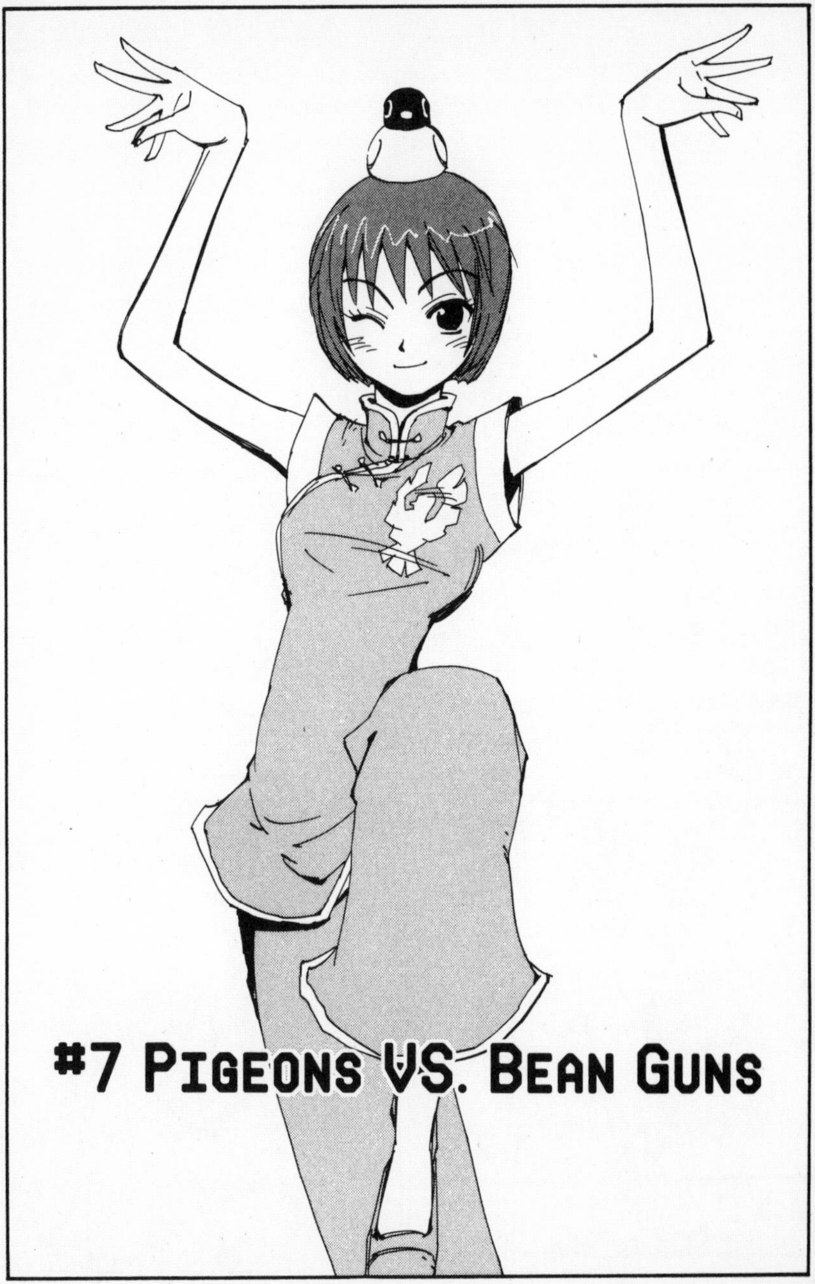
#7 Pigeons VS. Bean Guns

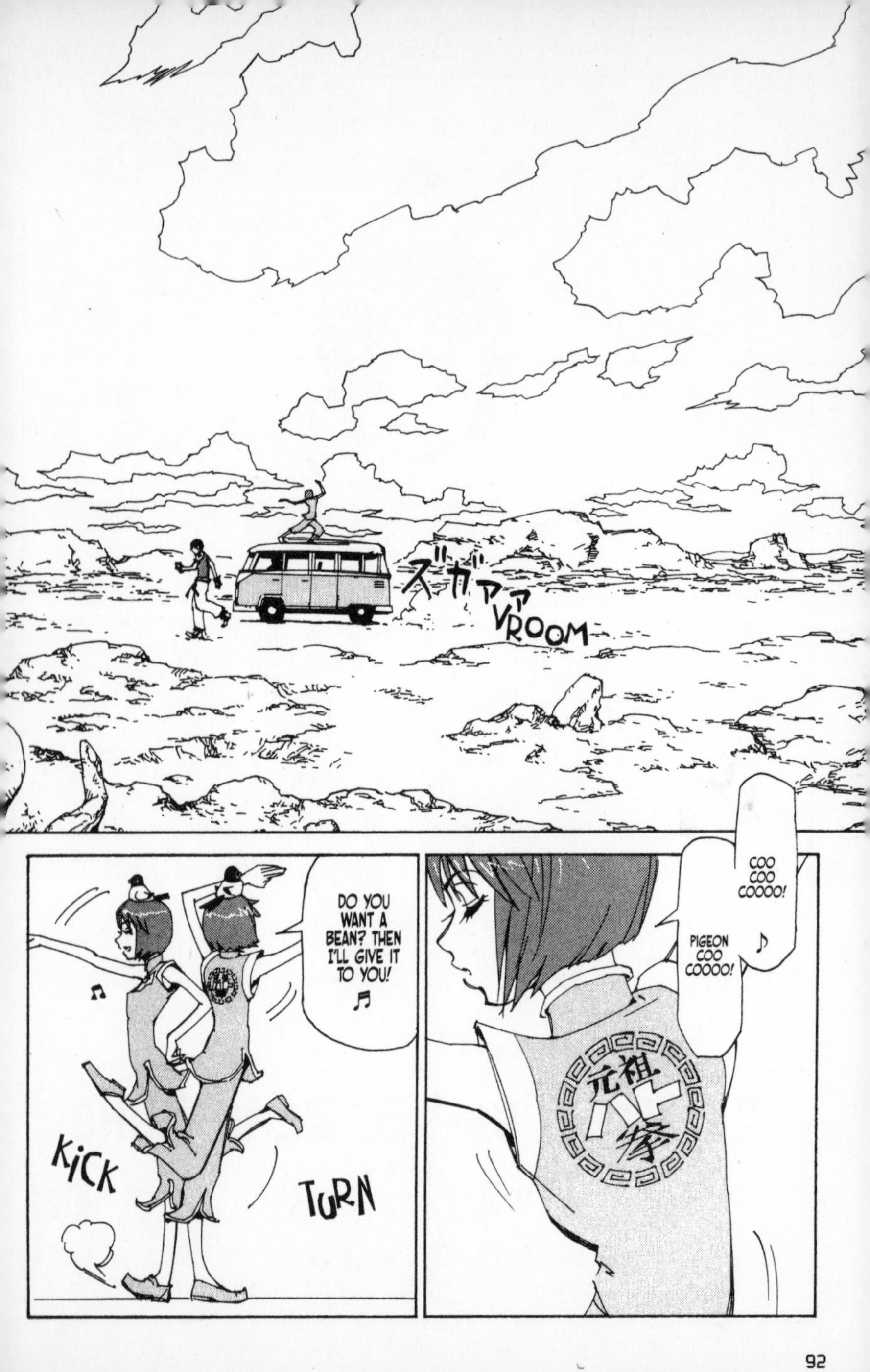
ズガァァ
VROOM
COO COO COOOO!
PIGEON COO COOOO!
♪
DO YOU WANT A BEAN? THEN I'LL GIVE IT TO YOU! ♫
KICK
TURN

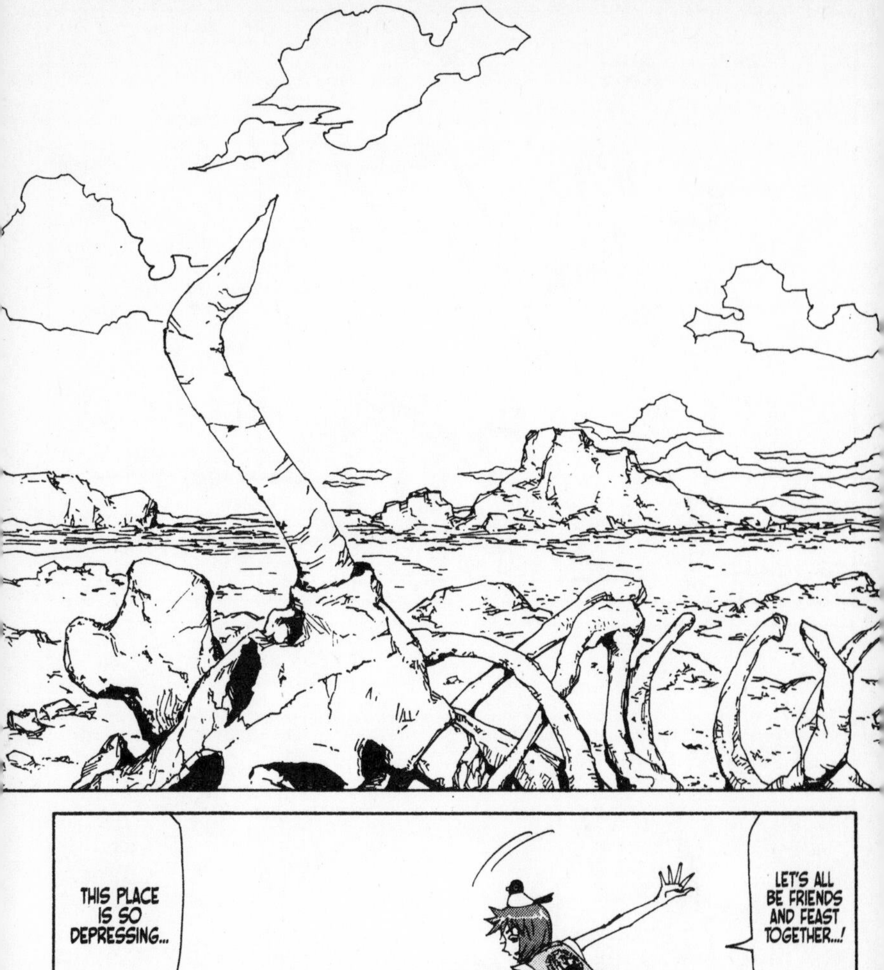
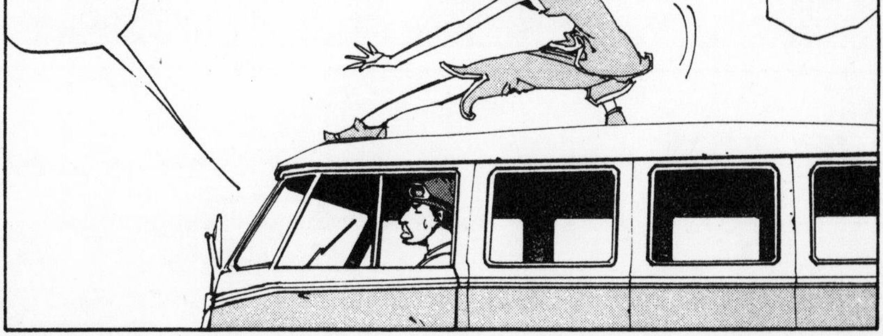
LET'S ALL BE FRIENDS AND FEAST TOGETHER...!
THIS PLACE IS SO DEPRESSING...

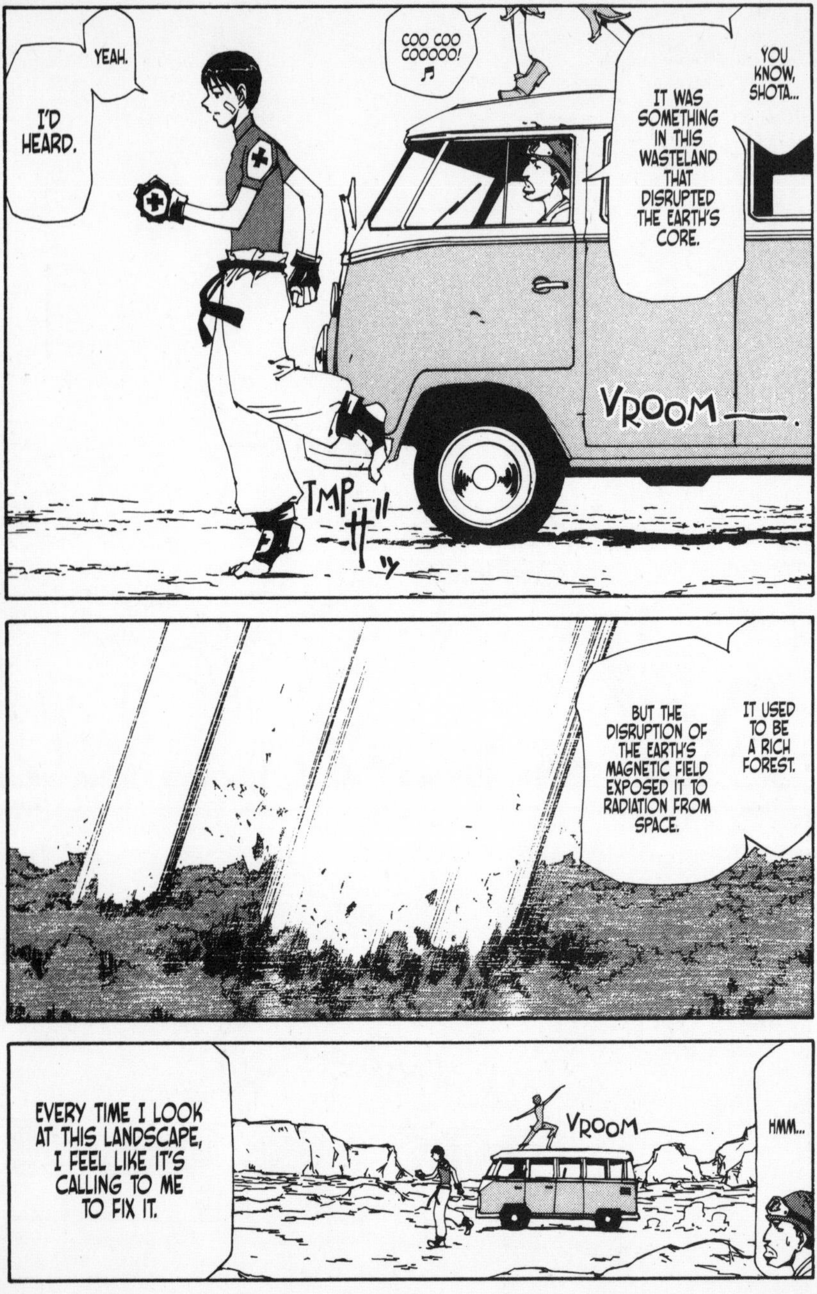
YOU KNOW, SHOTA...
IT WAS SOMETHING IN THIS WASTELAND THAT DISRUPTED THE EARTH'S CORE.
COO COO COOOOO! ♪
YEAH.
I'D HEARD.
VROOM___.
TMP
IT USED TO BE A RICH FOREST.
BUT THE DISRUPTION OF THE EARTH'S MAGNETIC FIELD EXPOSED IT TO RADIATION FROM SPACE.
HMM...
VROOM___
EVERY TIME I LOOK AT THIS LANDSCAPE, I FEEL LIKE IT'S CALLING TO ME TO FIX IT.

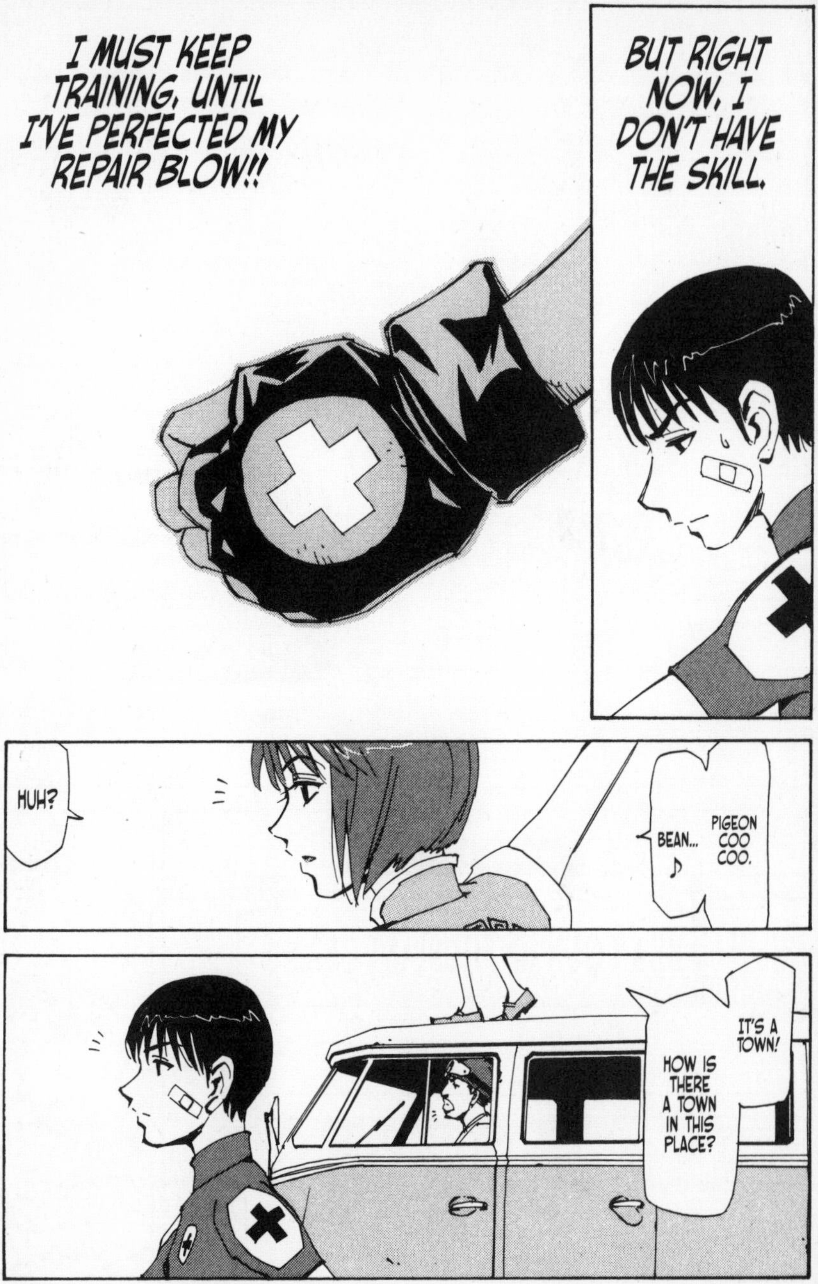
BUT RIGHT NOW, I DON'T HAVE THE SKILL.
I MUST KEEP TRAINING, UNTIL I'VE PERFECTED MY REPAIR BLOW!!
PIGEON COO COO.
BEAN... ♪
HUH?
IT'S A TOWN!
HOW IS THERE A TOWN IN THIS PLACE?

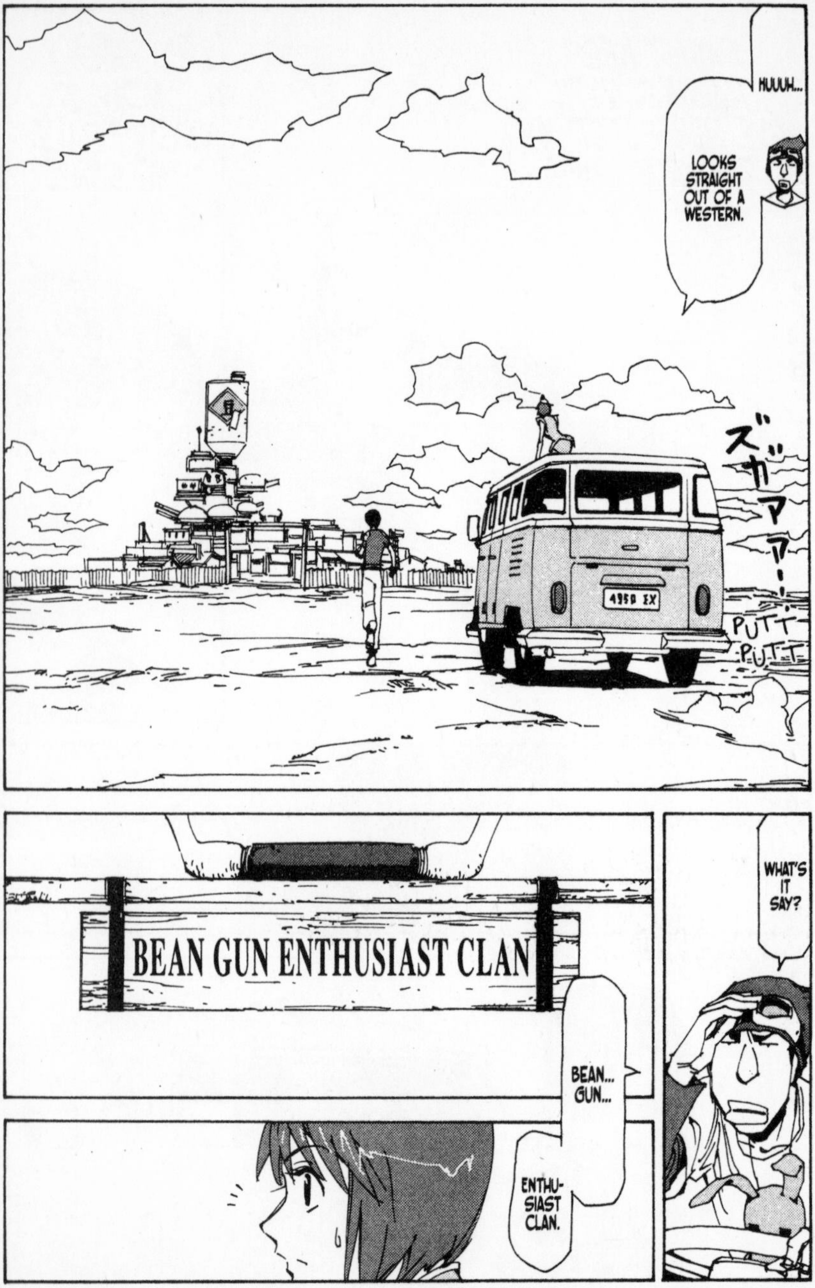
HUUUH...
LOOKS STRAIGHT OUT OF A WESTERN.
ズガァア…
PUTT PUTT
4350 EX
WHAT'S IT SAY?
BEAN GUN ENTHUSIAST CLAN
BEAN... GUN...
ENTHU-SIAST CLAN.

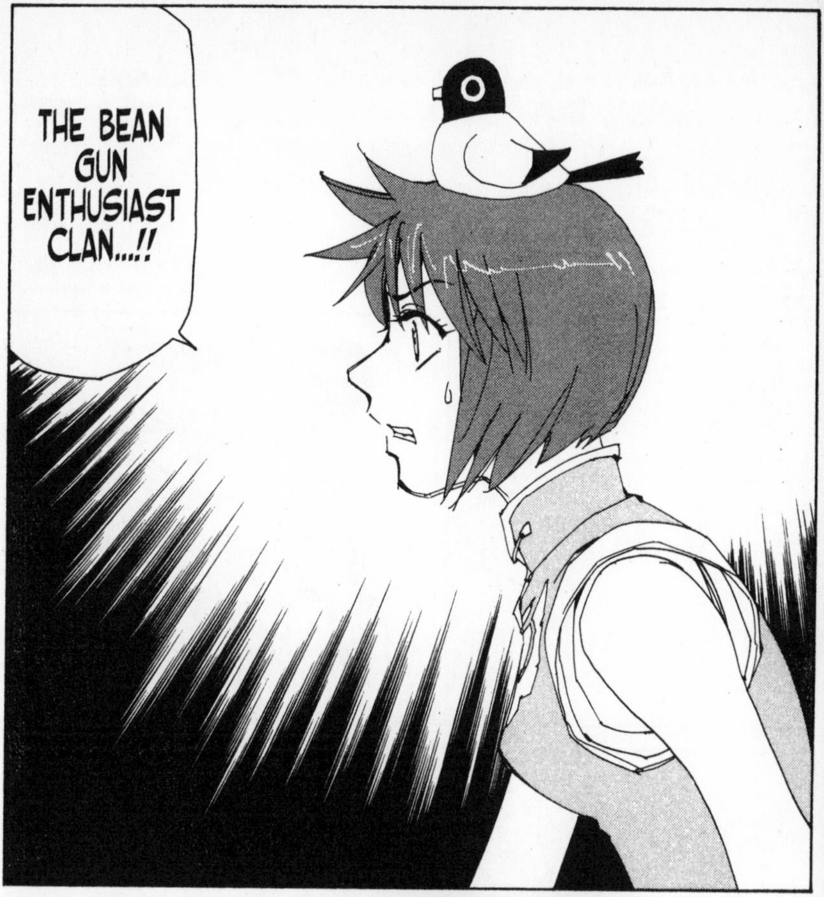
THE BEAN GUN ENTHUSIAST CLAN...!!
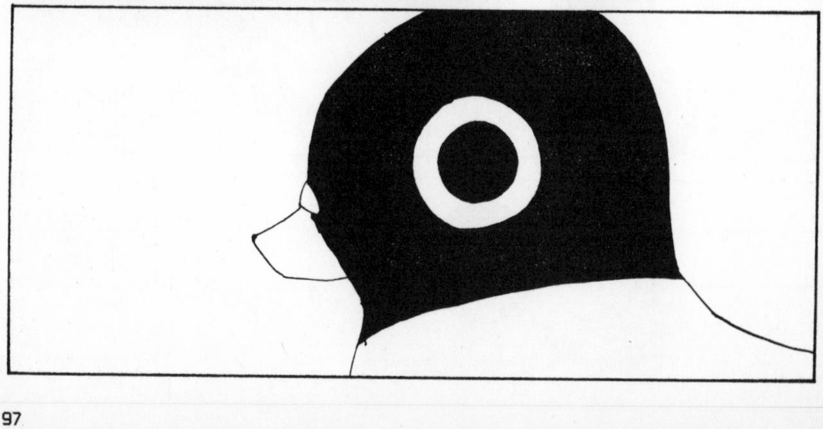

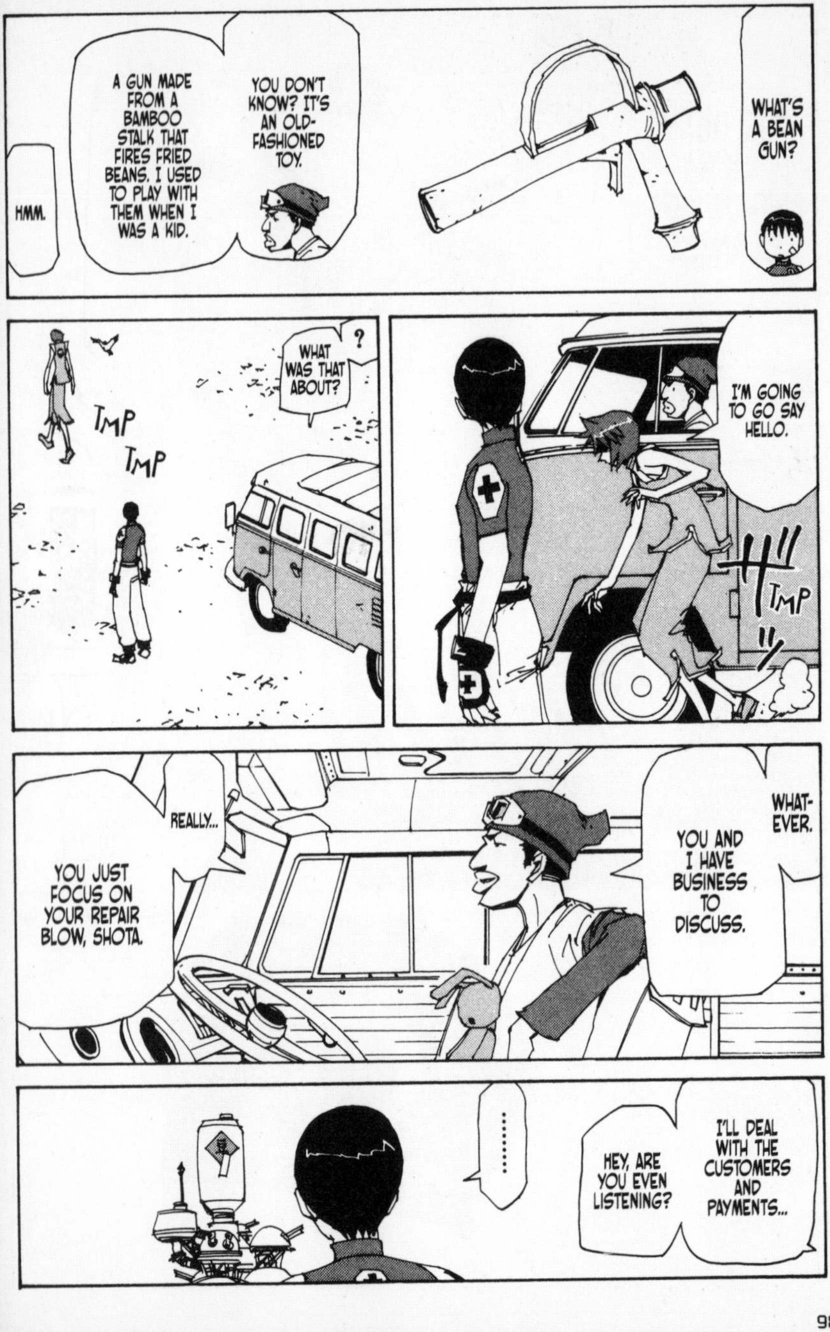
WHAT'S A BEAN GUN?
YOU DON'T KNOW? IT'S AN OLD-FASHIONED TOY.
A GUN MADE FROM A BAMBOO STALK THAT FIRES FRIED BEANS. I USED TO PLAY WITH THEM WHEN I WAS A KID.
HMM.
I'M GOING TO GO SAY HELLO.
TMP
?
WHAT WAS THAT ABOUT?
TMP
TMP
WHAT-EVER.
YOU AND I HAVE BUSINESS TO DISCUSS.
REALLY...
YOU JUST FOCUS ON YOUR REPAIR BLOW, SHOTA.
I'LL DEAL WITH THE CUSTOMERS AND PAYMENTS...
HEY, ARE YOU EVEN LISTENING?
....

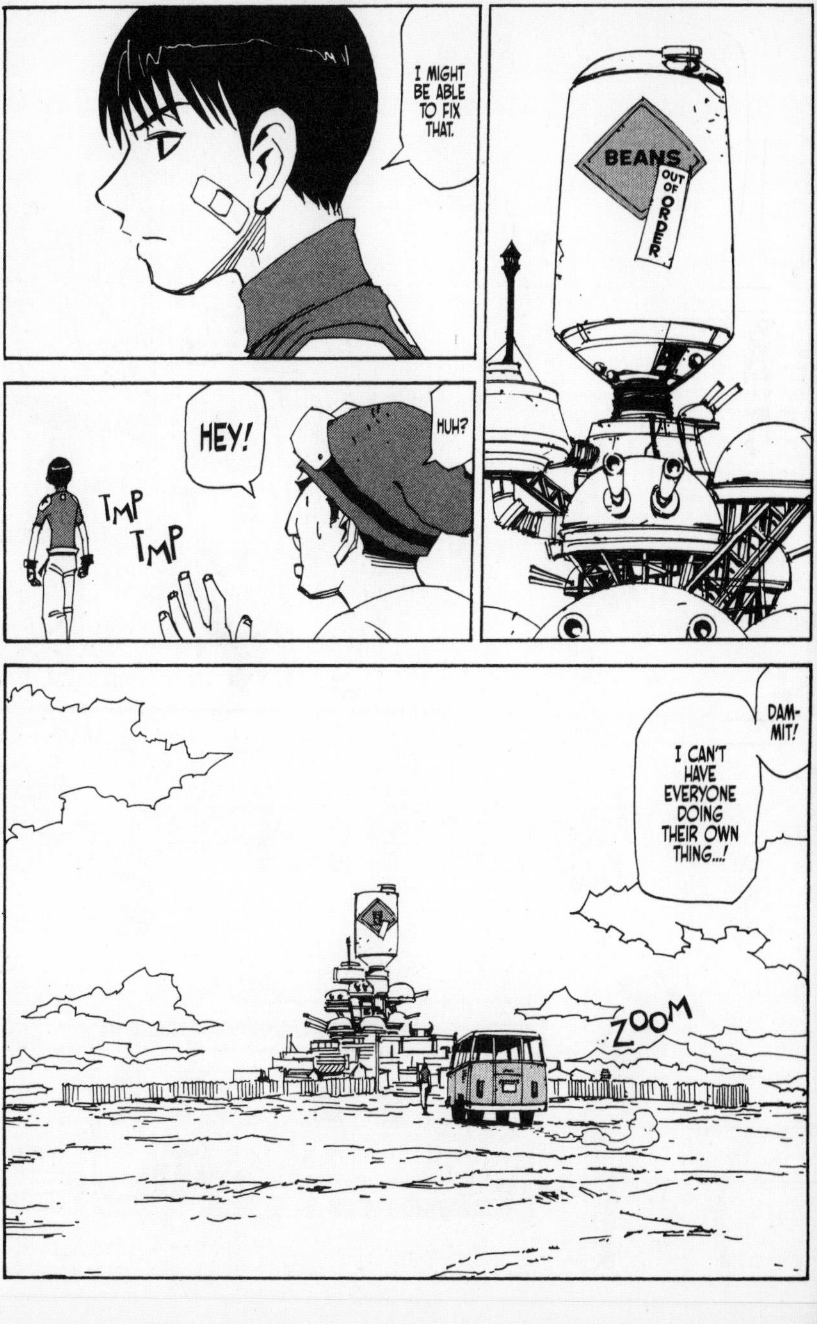
BEANS
OUT OF ORDER
I MIGHT BE ABLE TO FIX THAT.
HUH?
HEY!
TMP TMP
DAM-MIT!
I CAN'T HAVE EVERYONE DOING THEIR OWN THING...!
ZOOM

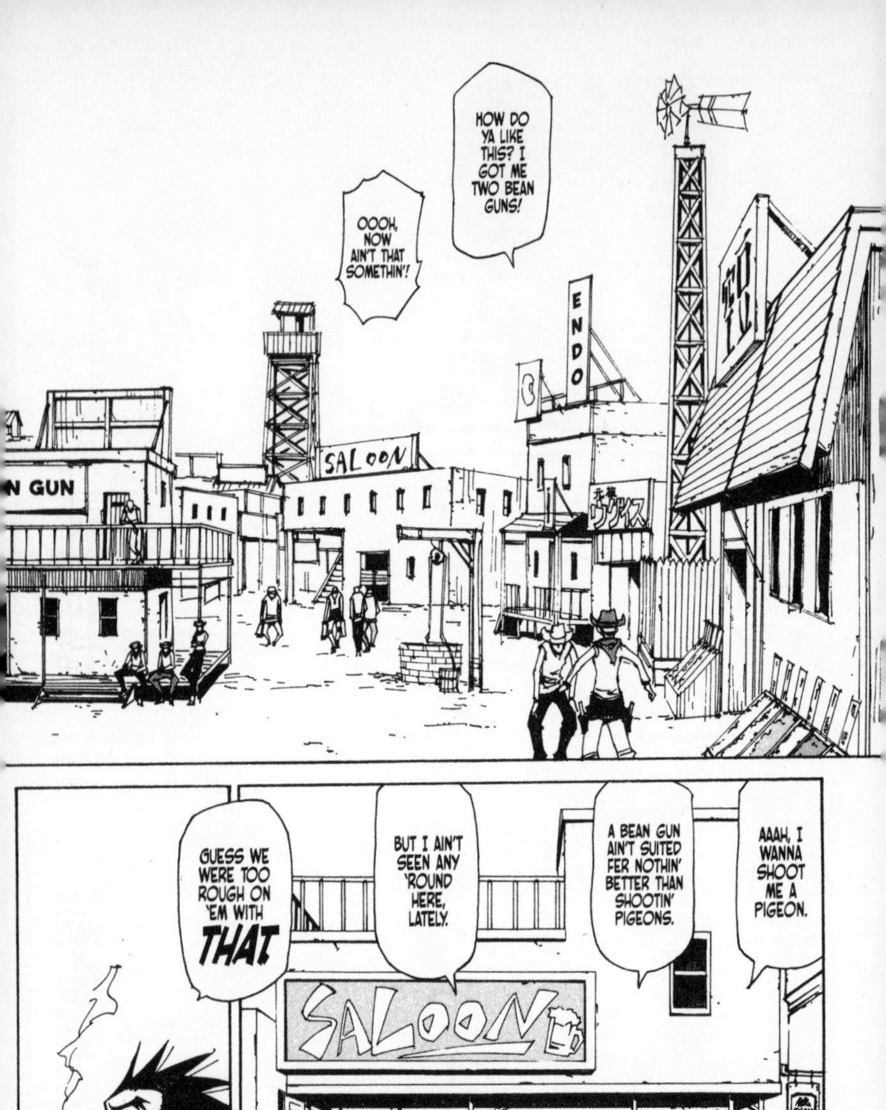
HOW DO YA LIKE THIS? I GOT ME TWO BEAN GUNS!
OOOH, NOW AIN'T THAT SOMETHIN'!
N GUN
SALOON
ENDO
AAAH, I WANNA SHOOT ME A PIGEON.
A BEAN GUN AIN'T SUITED FER NOTHIN' BETTER THAN SHOOTIN' PIGEONS.
BUT I AIN'T SEEN ANY 'ROUND HERE, LATELY.
GUESS WE WERE TOO ROUGH ON 'EM WITH THAT.
SALOON

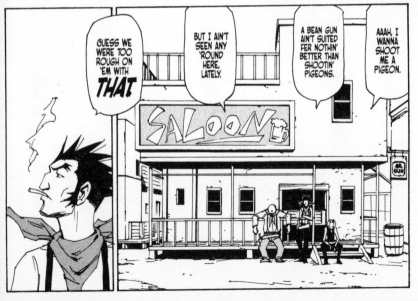

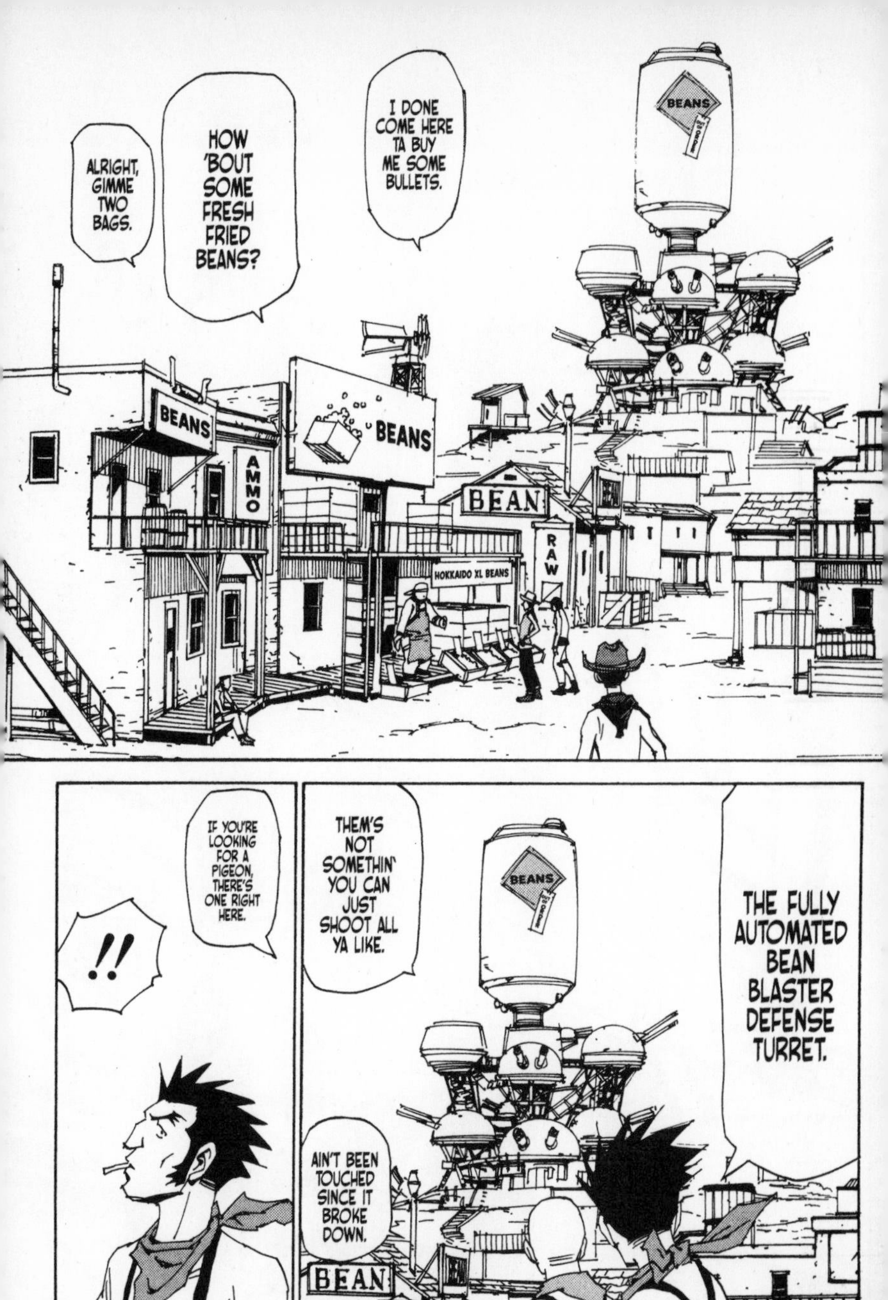
BEANS
I DONE COME HERE TA BUY ME SOME BULLETS.
HOW 'BOUT SOME FRESH FRIED BEANS?
ALRIGHT, GIMME TWO BAGS.
BEANS
BEANS
AMMO
BEAN
RAW
HOKKAIDO XL BEANS
THE FULLY AUTOMATED BEAN BLASTER DEFENSE TURRET.
THEM'S NOT SOMETHIN' YOU CAN JUST SHOOT ALL YA LIKE.
BEANS
AIN'T BEEN TOUCHED SINCE IT BROKE DOWN.
BEAN
RAW
IF YOU'RE LOOKING FOR A PIGEON, THERE'S ONE RIGHT HERE.
!!

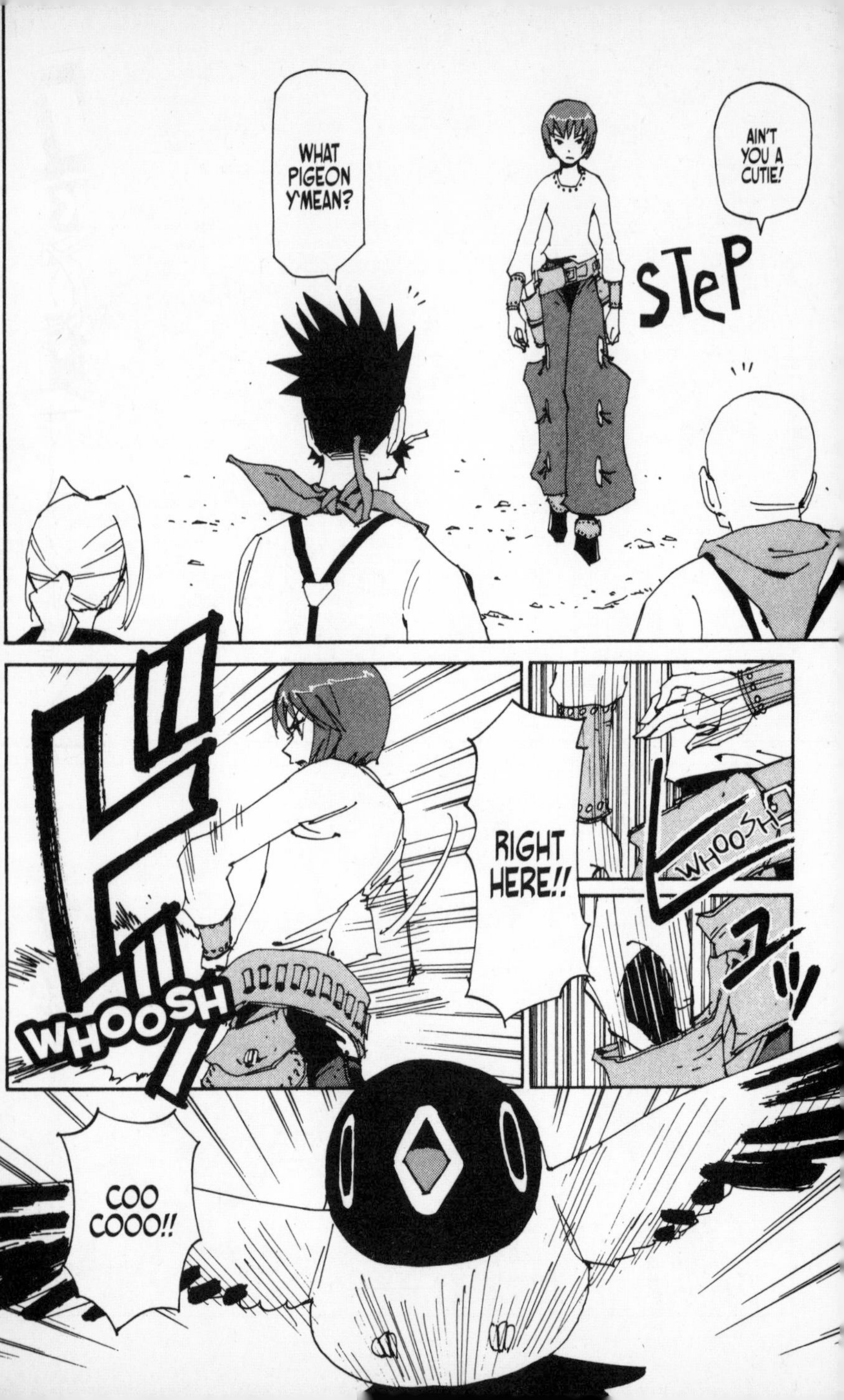
AIN'T YOU A CUTIE!
STEP
WHAT PIGEON Y'MEAN?
WHOOSH
RIGHT HERE!!
WHOOSH
COO COOO!!

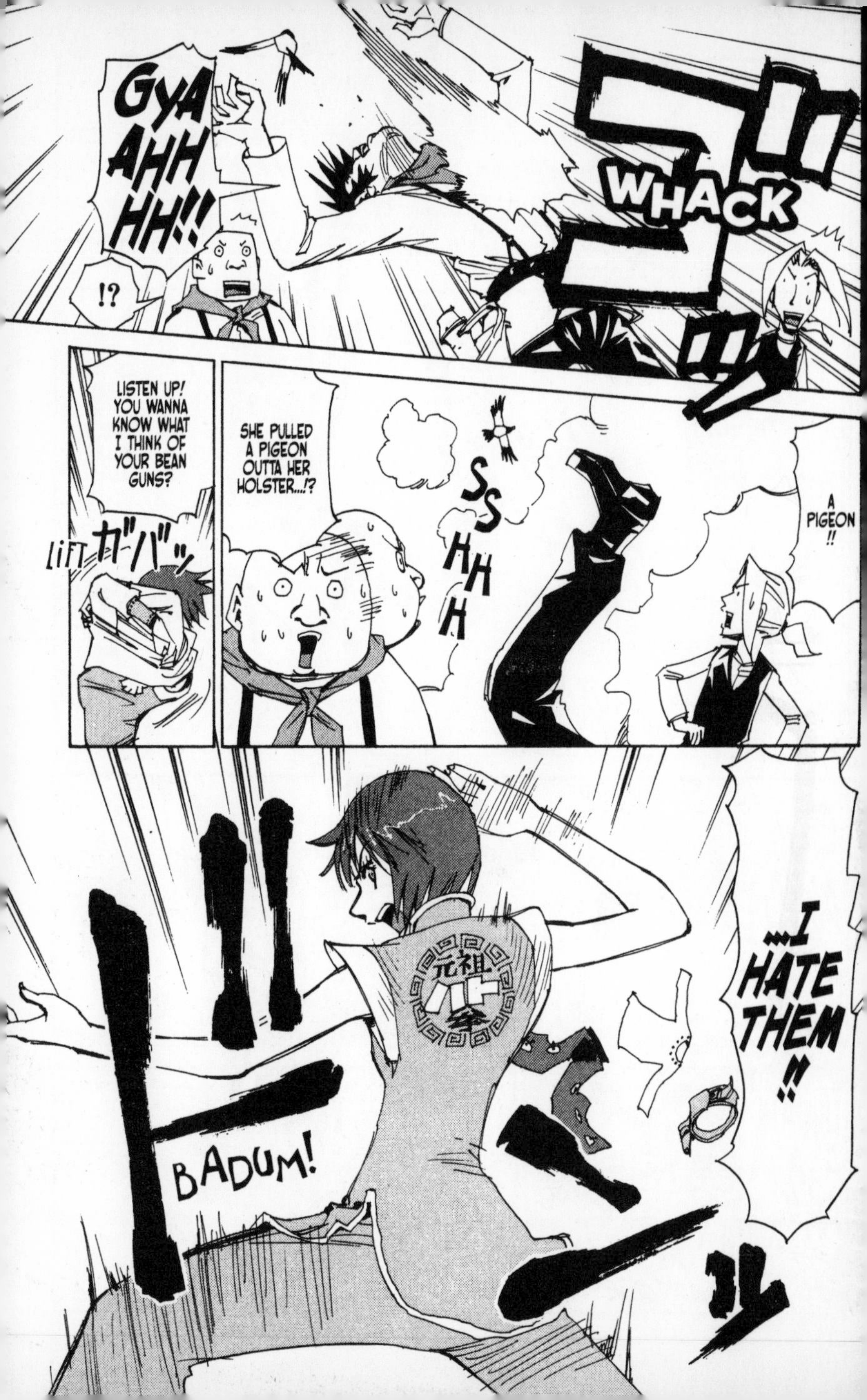
WHACK
GYAAHHHH!!
!?
A PIGEON!!
SSHHHH
SHE PULLED A PIGEON OUTTA HER HOLSTER...!?
LISTEN UP! YOU WANNA KNOW WHAT I THINK OF YOUR BEAN GUNS?
LIFT
...I HATE THEM!!
BADUM!

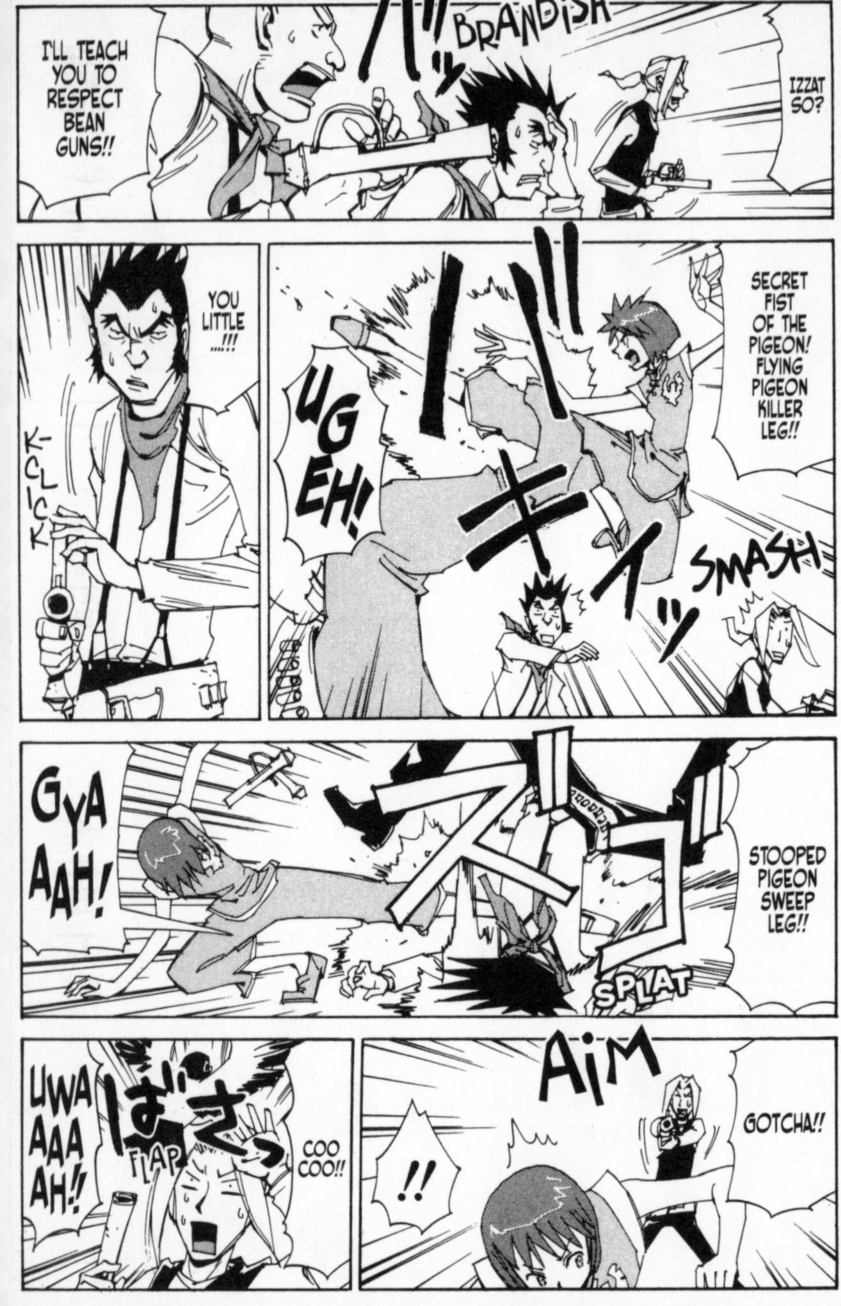

ハッ
BRANDISH
IZZAT SO?
I'LL TEACH YOU TO RESPECT BEAN GUNS!!
SECRET FIST OF THE PIGEON! FLYING PIGEON KILLER LEG!!
UGEH!
キィッ
SMASH
YOU LITTLE ...!!!
K-CLICK
STOOPED PIGEON SWEEP LEG!!
ズコッ
SPLAT
GYAAAH!
AIM
GOTCHA!!
!!
COO COO!!
ばさっ
FLAP
UWAAAAAH!!

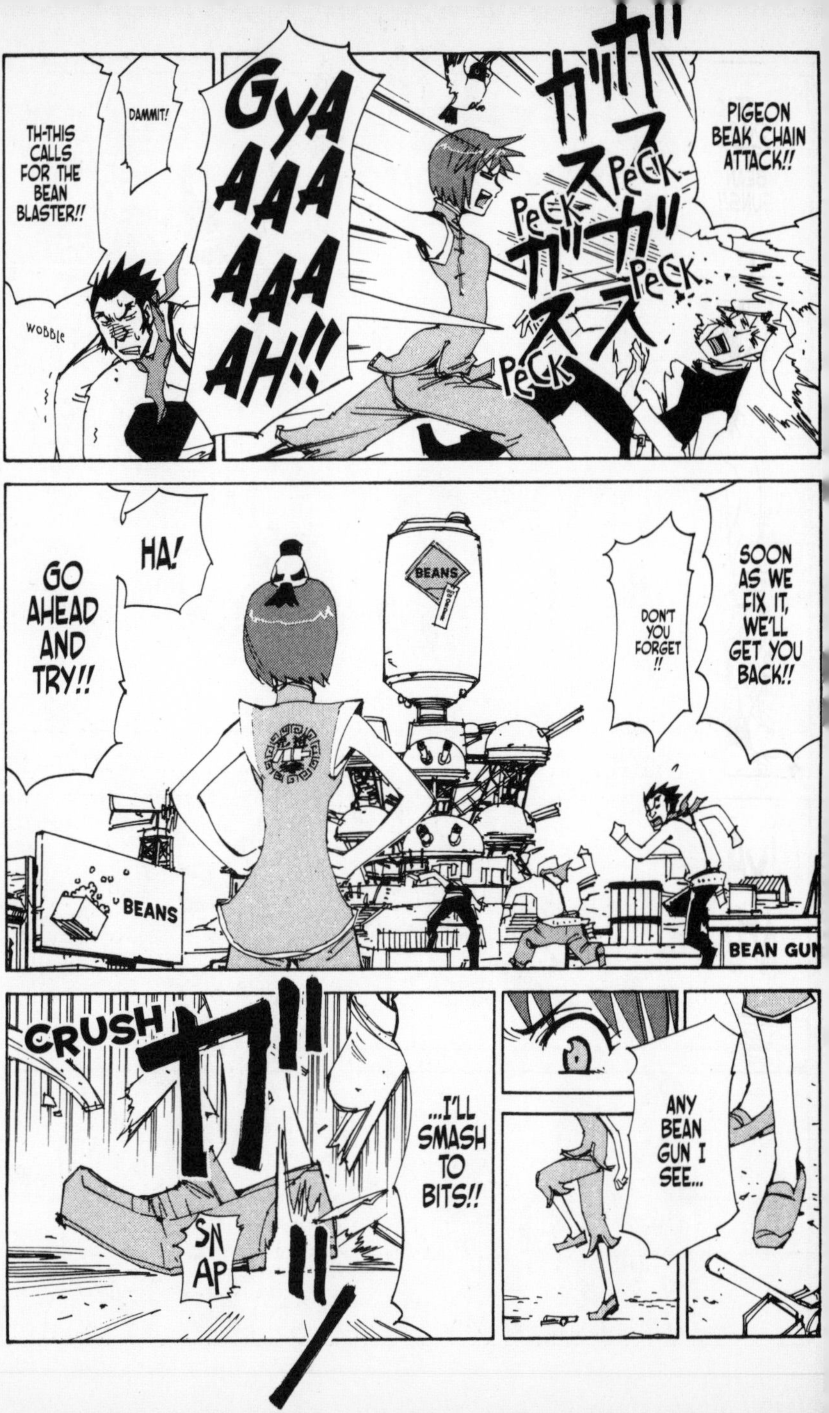
PIGEON BEAK CHAIN ATTACK!!
PECK
PECK
PECK
PECK
GYAAAAAAAAAH!!
DAMMIT!
TH-THIS CALLS FOR THE BEAN BLASTER!!
WOBBLE
SOON AS WE FIX IT, WE'LL GET YOU BACK!!
DON'T YOU FORGET!!
HA!
GO AHEAD AND TRY!!
BEANS
BEANS
BEAN GUN
ANY BEAN GUN I SEE...
...I'LL SMASH TO BITS!!
CRUSH
SNAP

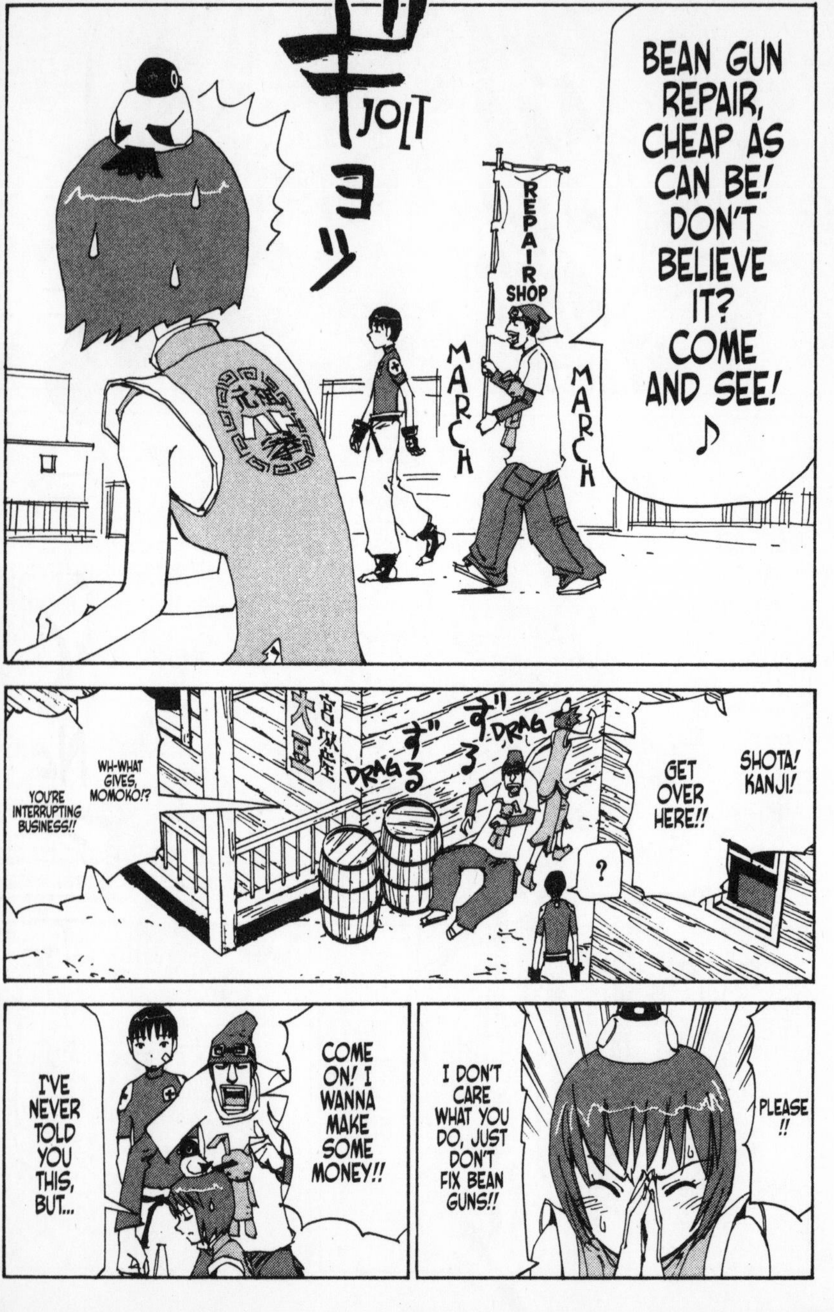
BEAN GUN REPAIR, CHEAP AS CAN BE! DON'T BELIEVE IT? COME AND SEE! ♪
MARCH
REPAIR SHOP
MARCH
ギョッ
JOLT
SHOTA! KANJI!
GET OVER HERE!!
ずる
DRAG
ずる
DRAG
?
宮城産 大豆
WH-WHAT GIVES, MOMOKO!?
YOU'RE INTERRUPTING BUSINESS!!
PLEASE!!
I DON'T CARE WHAT YOU DO, JUST DON'T FIX BEAN GUNS!!
COME ON! I WANNA MAKE SOME MONEY!!
I'VE NEVER TOLD YOU THIS, BUT...

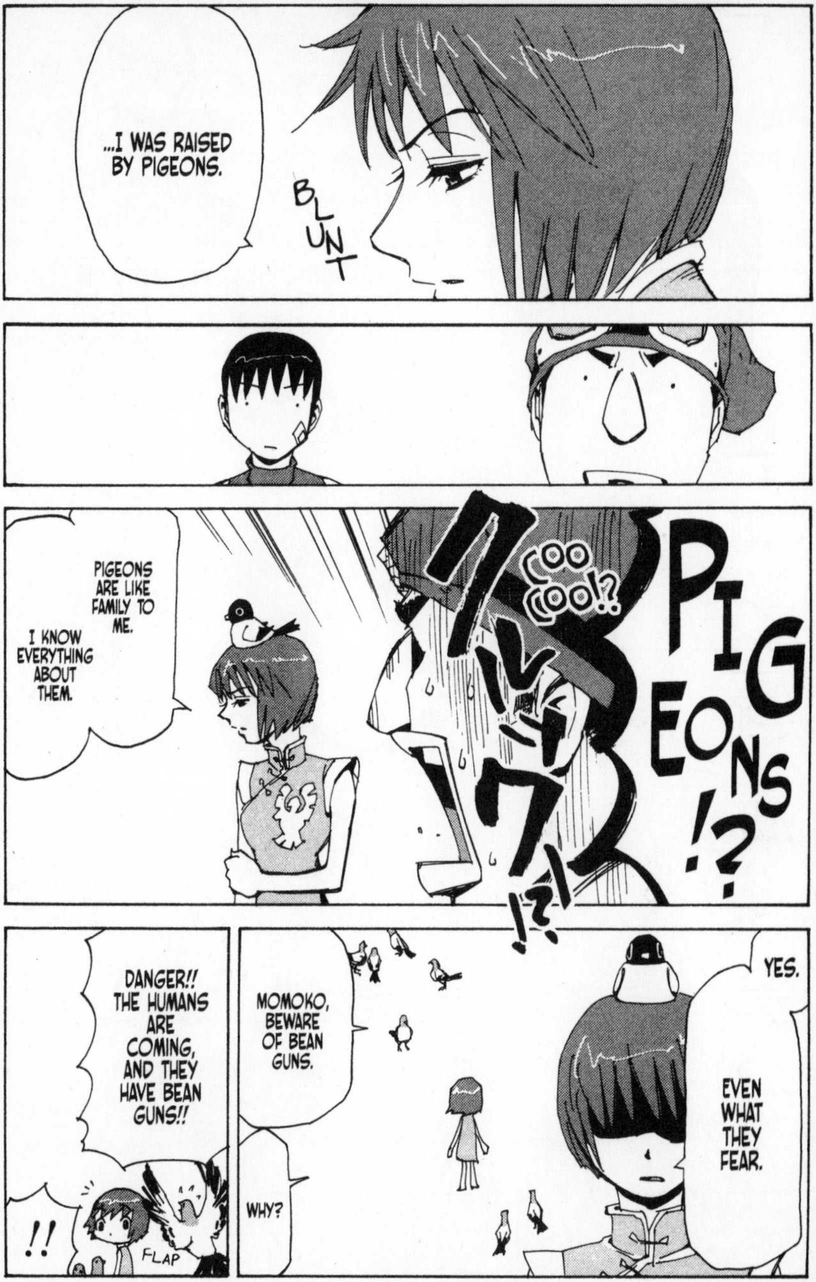

...I WAS RAISED BY PIGEONS.
BLUNT
PIGEONS!?
COO COO!?
PIGEONS ARE LIKE FAMILY TO ME.
I KNOW EVERYTHING ABOUT THEM.
YES.
EVEN WHAT THEY FEAR.
MOMOKO, BEWARE OF BEAN GUNS.
WHY?
DANGER!! THE HUMANS ARE COMING, AND THEY HAVE BEAN GUNS!!
!!
FLAP

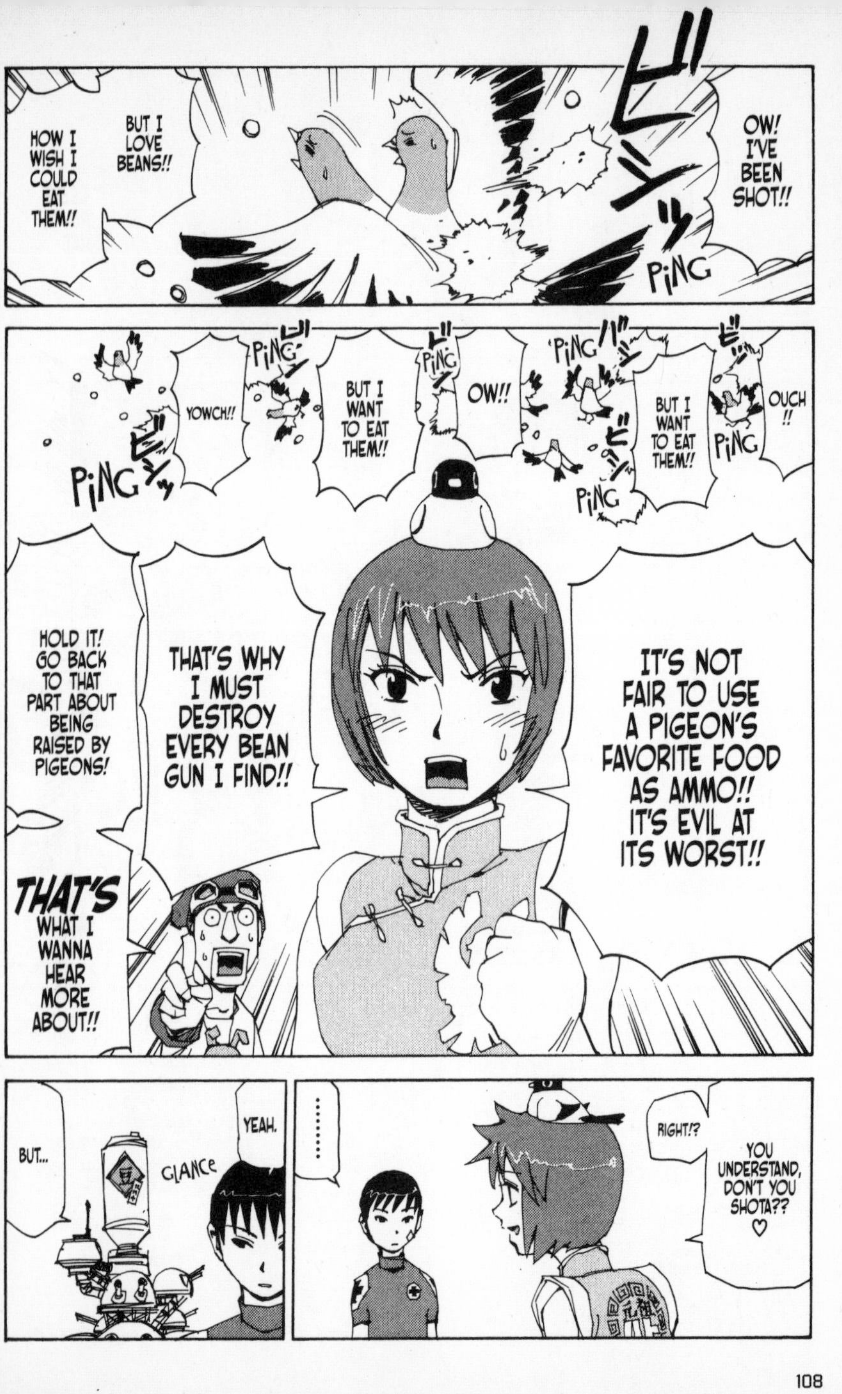
OW! I'VE BEEN SHOT!!
PING
BUT I LOVE BEANS!!
HOW I WISH I COULD EAT THEM!!
OUCH!!
PING
BUT I WANT TO EAT THEM!!
PING
'PING
OW!!
PING
BUT I WANT TO EAT THEM!!
PING
YOWCH!!
PING
IT'S NOT FAIR TO USE A PIGEON'S FAVORITE FOOD AS AMMO!! IT'S EVIL AT ITS WORST!!
THAT'S WHY I MUST DESTROY EVERY BEAN GUN I FIND!!
HOLD IT! GO BACK TO THAT PART ABOUT BEING RAISED BY PIGEONS!
THAT'S WHAT I WANNA HEAR MORE ABOUT!!
YOU UNDERSTAND, DON'T YOU SHOTA?? ♡
RIGHT!?
....
YEAH.
GLANCE
BUT...

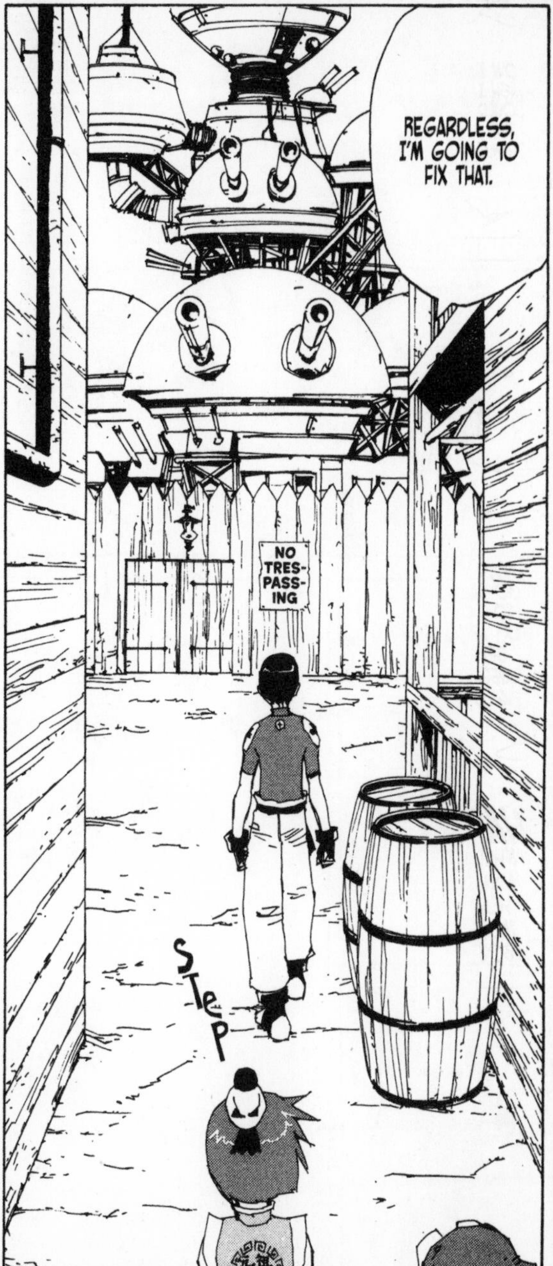
REGARDLESS, I'M GOING TO FIX THAT.
NO TRES-PASS-ING
STEP

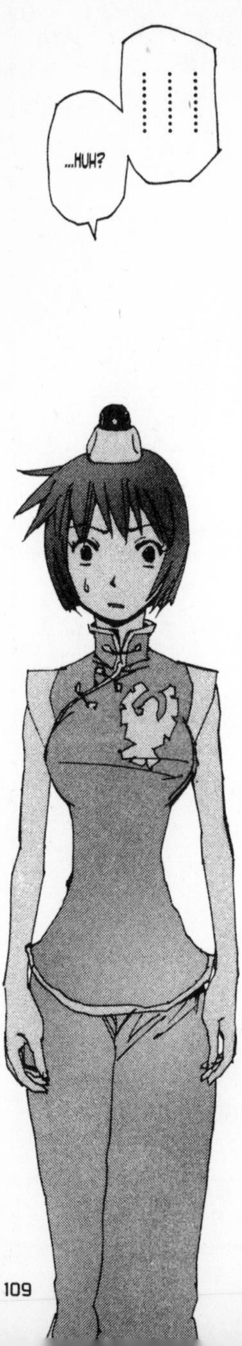
......
...HUH?

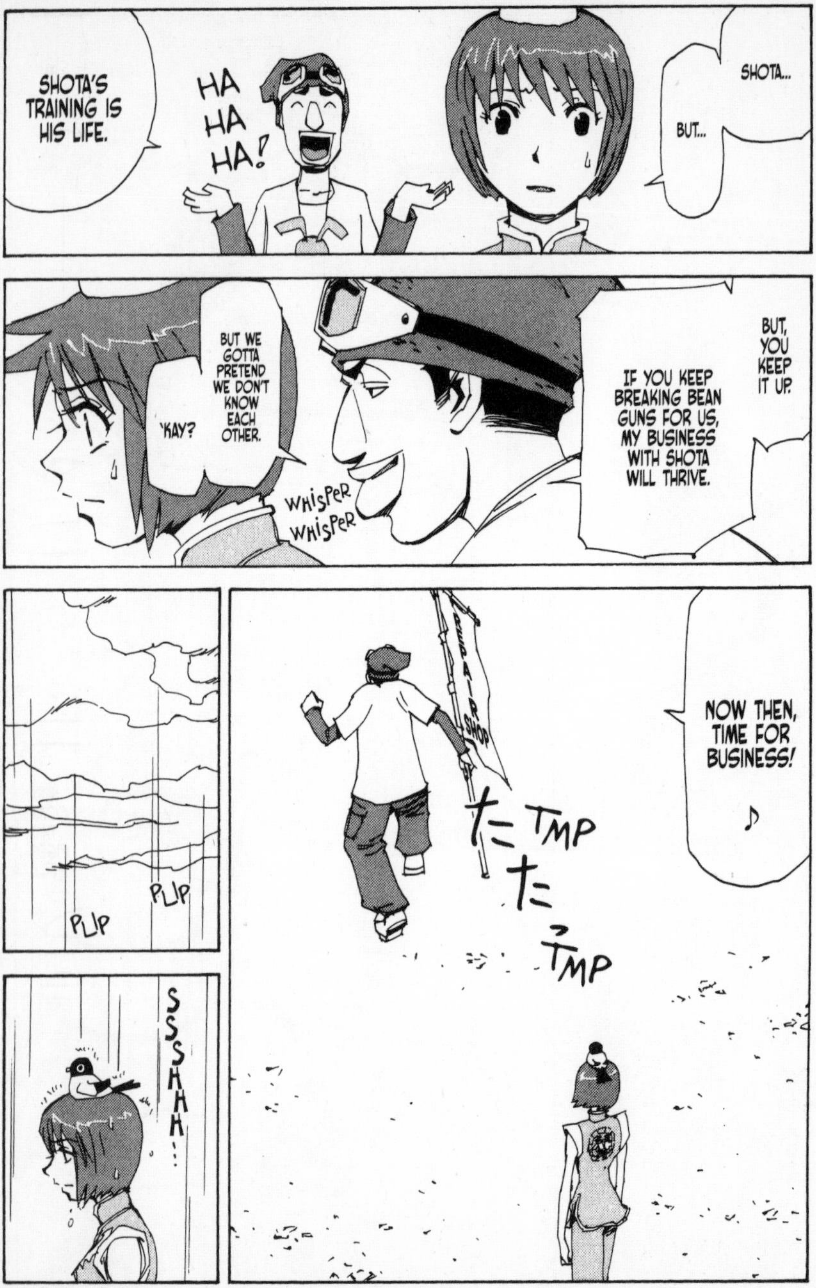
SHOTA... BUT...
HA HA HA!
SHOTA'S TRAINING IS HIS LIFE.
BUT, YOU KEEP IT UP.
IF YOU KEEP BREAKING BEAN GUNS FOR US, MY BUSINESS WITH SHOTA WILL THRIVE.
WHISPER WHISPER
BUT WE GOTTA PRETEND WE DON'T KNOW EACH OTHER.
'KAY?
NOW THEN, TIME FOR BUSINESS! ♪
REPAIR SHOP
た TMP
た TMP
PLIP
PLIP
SSSHHH...

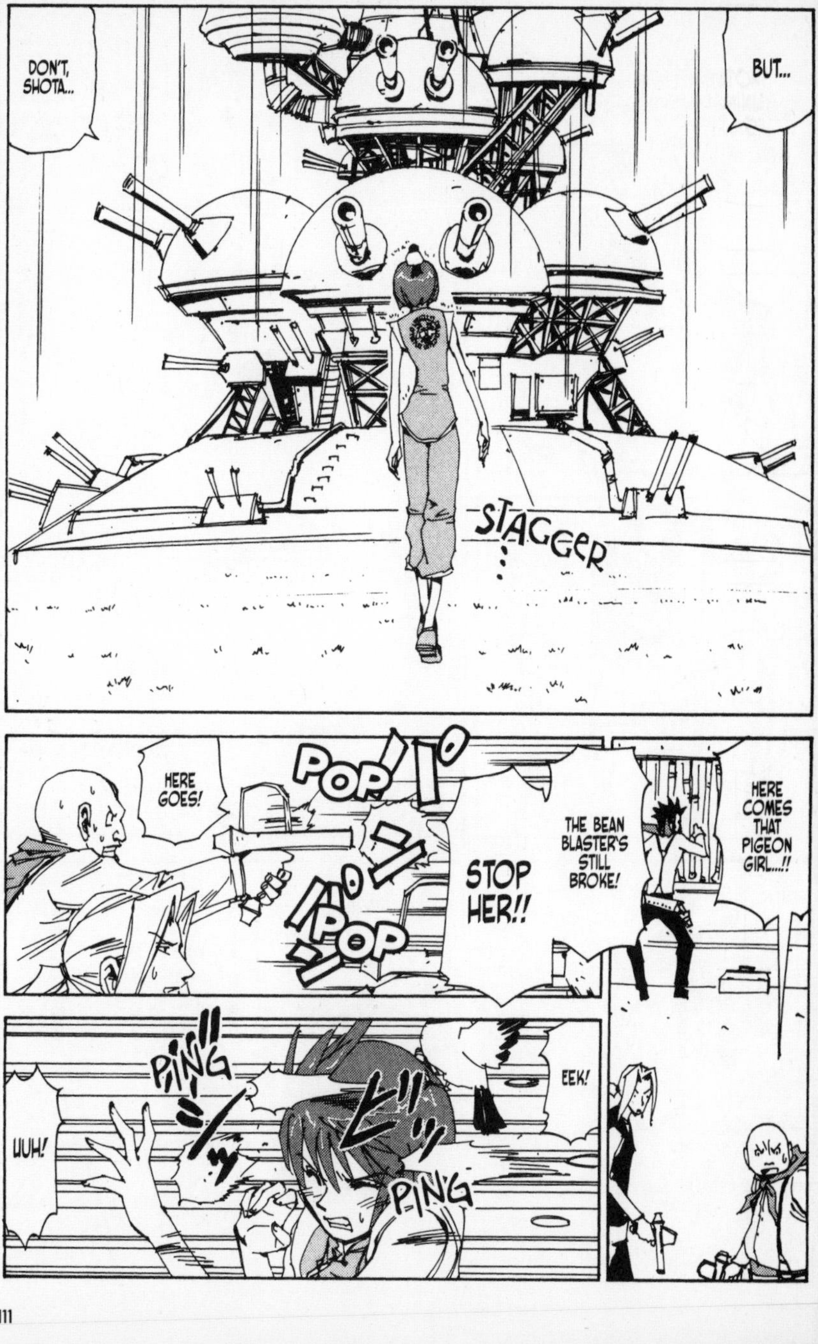
BUT...
DON'T, SHOTA...
STAGGER
HERE COMES THAT PIGEON GIRL...!!
THE BEAN BLASTER'S STILL BROKE!
STOP HER!!
HERE GOES!
POP!!
POP
PING!!
EEK!
PING
UUH!

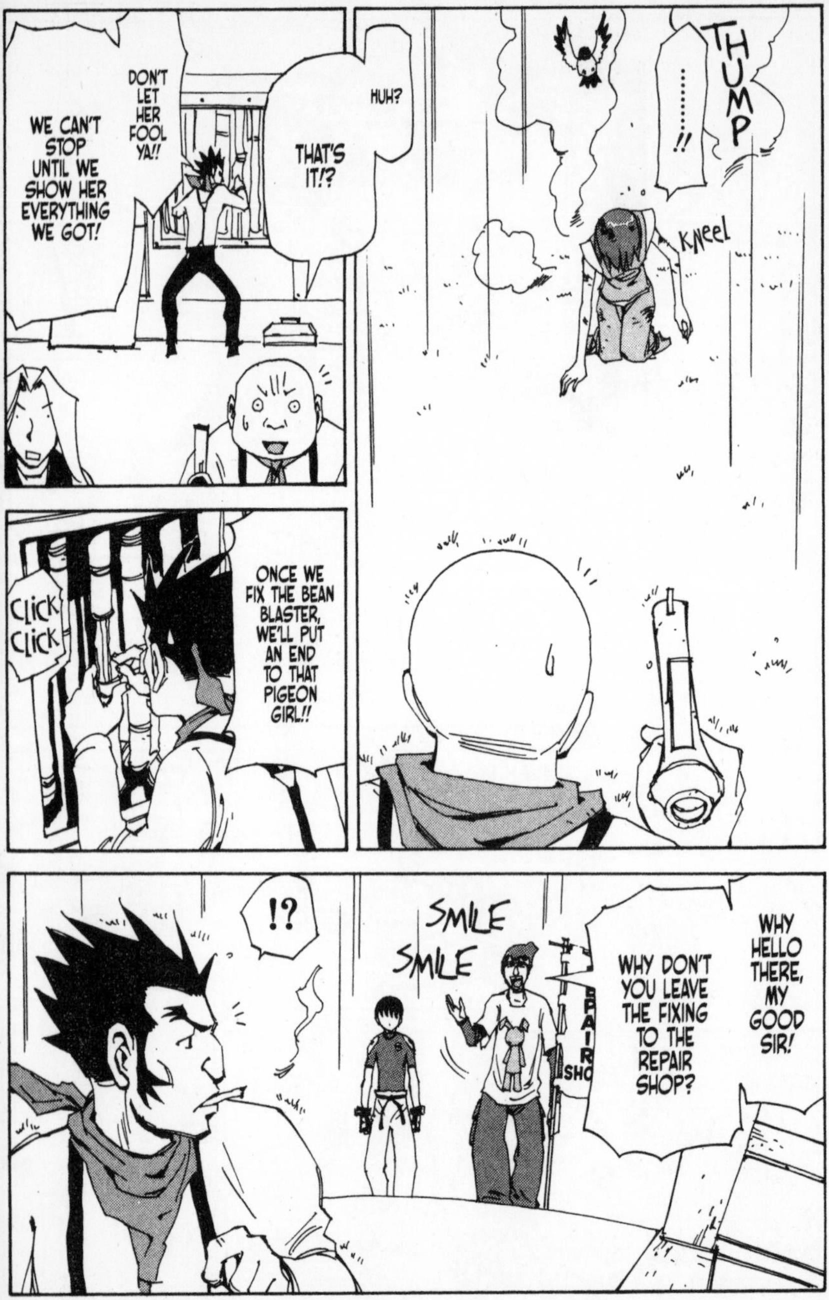
THUMP
......!!
Kneel
...
HUH?
THAT'S IT!?
DON'T LET HER FOOL YA!!
WE CAN'T STOP UNTIL WE SHOW HER EVERYTHING WE GOT!
ONCE WE FIX THE BEAN BLASTER, WE'LL PUT AN END TO THAT PIGEON GIRL!!
CLICK CLICK
WHY HELLO THERE, MY GOOD SIR!
WHY DON'T YOU LEAVE THE FIXING TO THE REPAIR SHOP?
SMILE
SMILE
!?

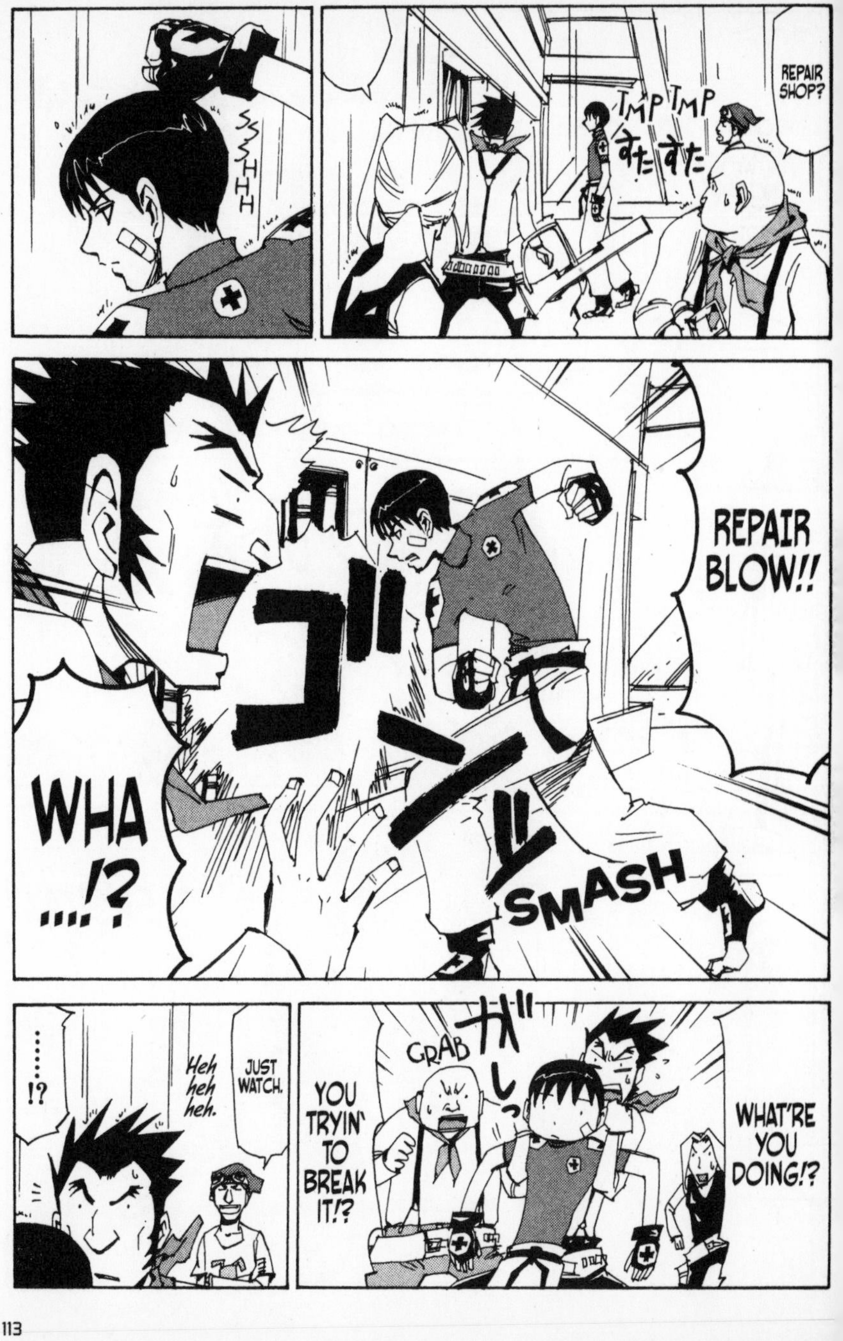
REPAIR SHOP?
TMP TMP
すたすた
SSSHHH
REPAIR BLOW!!
SMASH
WHA ....!?
WHAT'RE YOU DOING!?
GRAB
がしっ
YOU TRYIN' TO BREAK IT!?
JUST WATCH.
Heh heh heh.
......!?

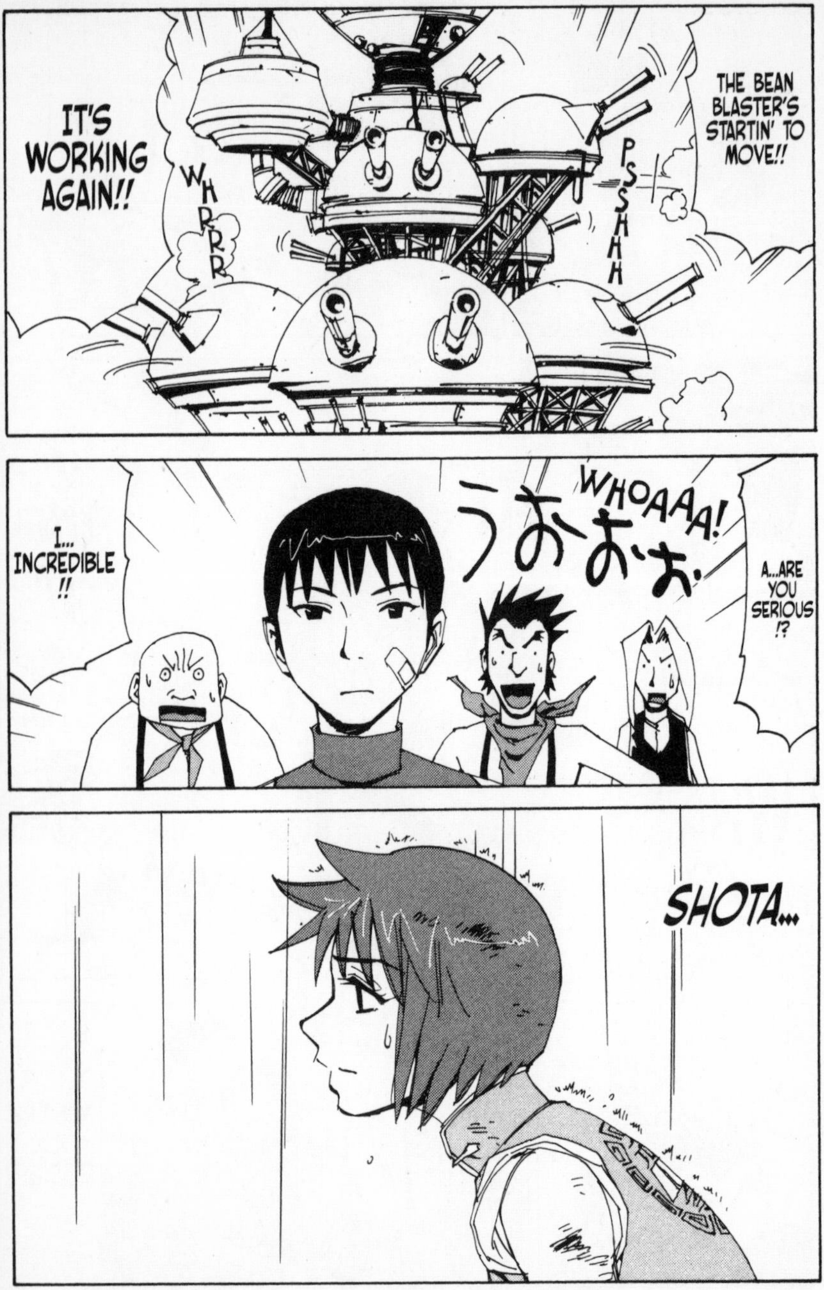
THE BEAN BLASTER'S STARTIN' TO MOVE!!
PSSHHH
WHRRRR
IT'S WORKING AGAIN!!
A...ARE YOU SERIOUS!?
WHOAAAA!
うおおぉ
I... INCREDIBLE!!
SHOTA...

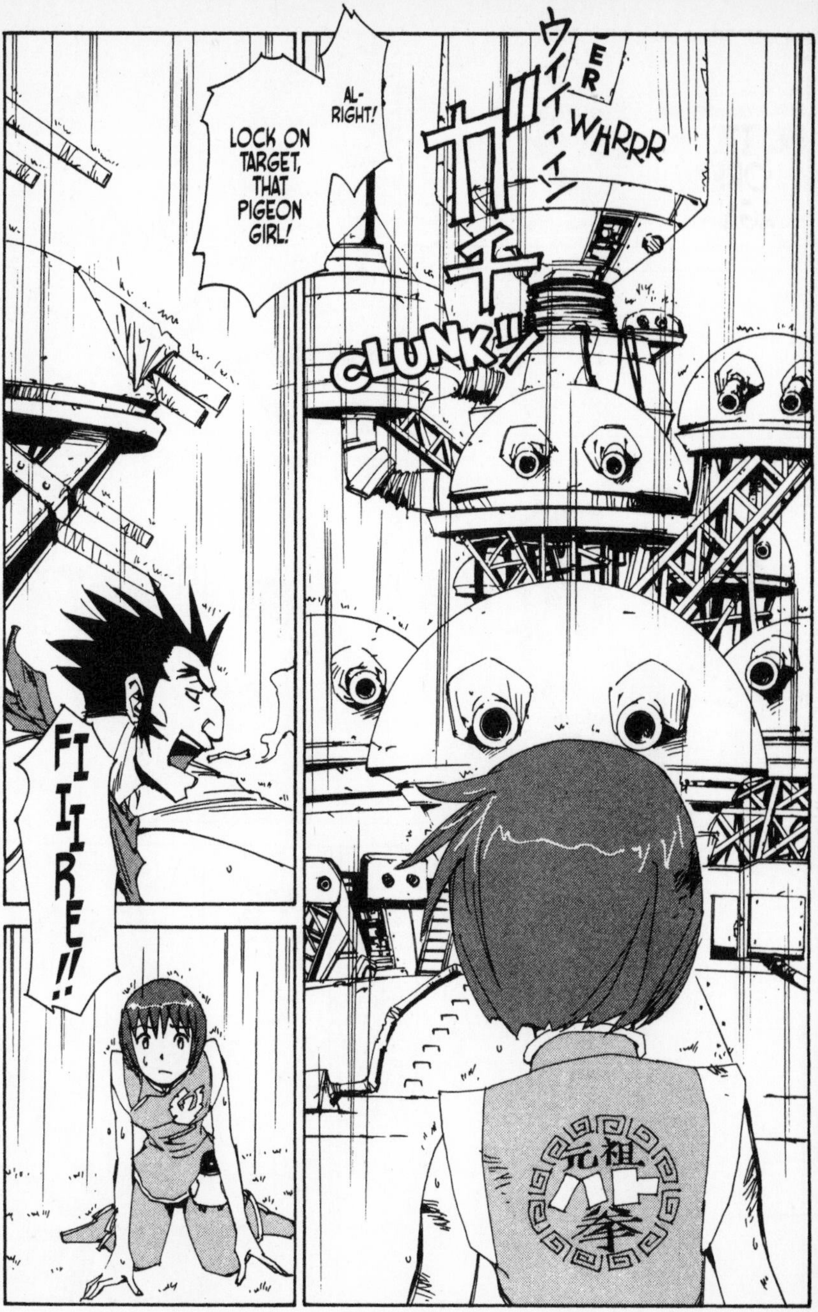
ウイイイイン
WHRRR
ガチ
CLUNK!!
元祖ハト拳
LOCK ON TARGET, THAT PIGEON GIRL!
AL-RIGHT!
FIIIRE!!

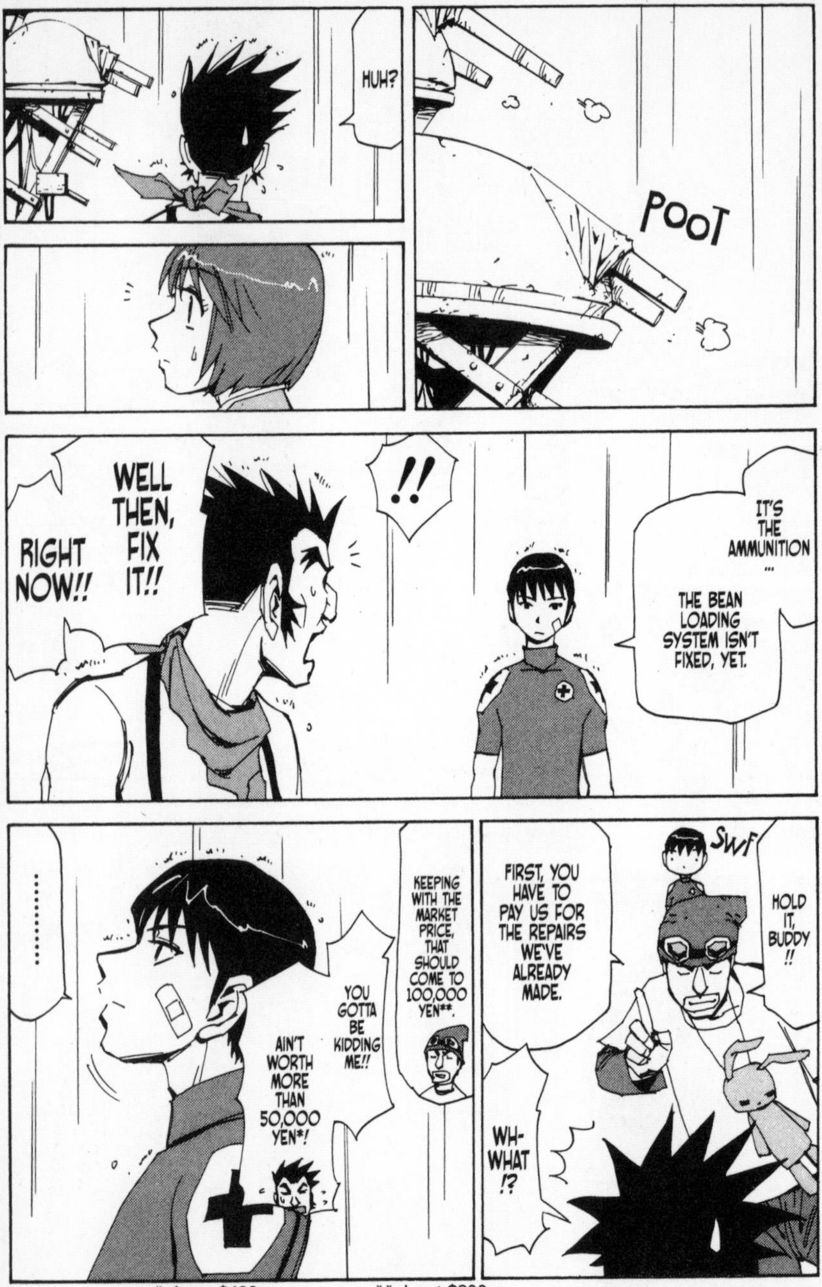
POOT
HUH?
IT'S THE AMMUNITION ...
THE BEAN LOADING SYSTEM ISN'T FIXED, YET.
!!
WELL THEN, FIX IT!!
RIGHT NOW!!
SWF
HOLD IT, BUDDY!!
FIRST, YOU HAVE TO PAY US FOR THE REPAIRS WE'VE ALREADY MADE.
WH-WHAT!?
KEEPING WITH THE MARKET PRICE, THAT SHOULD COME TO 100,000 YEN**.
YOU GOTTA BE KIDDING ME!!
AIN'T WORTH MORE THAN 50,000 YEN*!
....

*about $400

**about $800

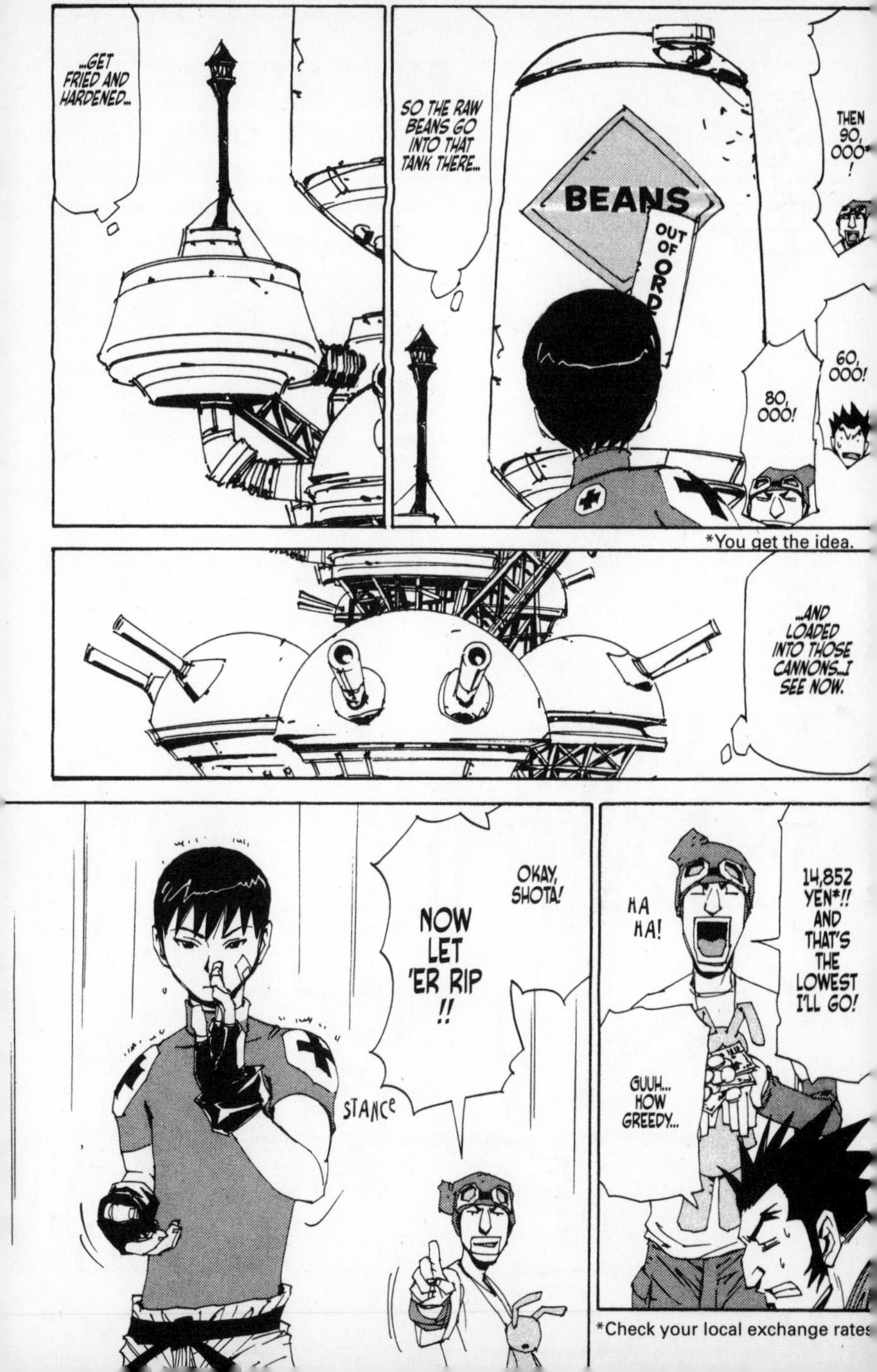
THEN 90, 000*!
SO THE RAW BEANS GO INTO THAT TANK THERE...
BEANS
OUT OF ORDE
60, 000!
80, 000!
...GET FRIED AND HARDENED...
...AND LOADED INTO THOSE CANNONS...I SEE NOW.
14,852 YEN*!! AND THAT'S THE LOWEST I'LL GO!
HA HA!
GUUH... HOW GREEDY...
OKAY, SHOTA!
NOW LET 'ER RIP!!
STANCE
*You get the idea.

*Check your local exchange rates

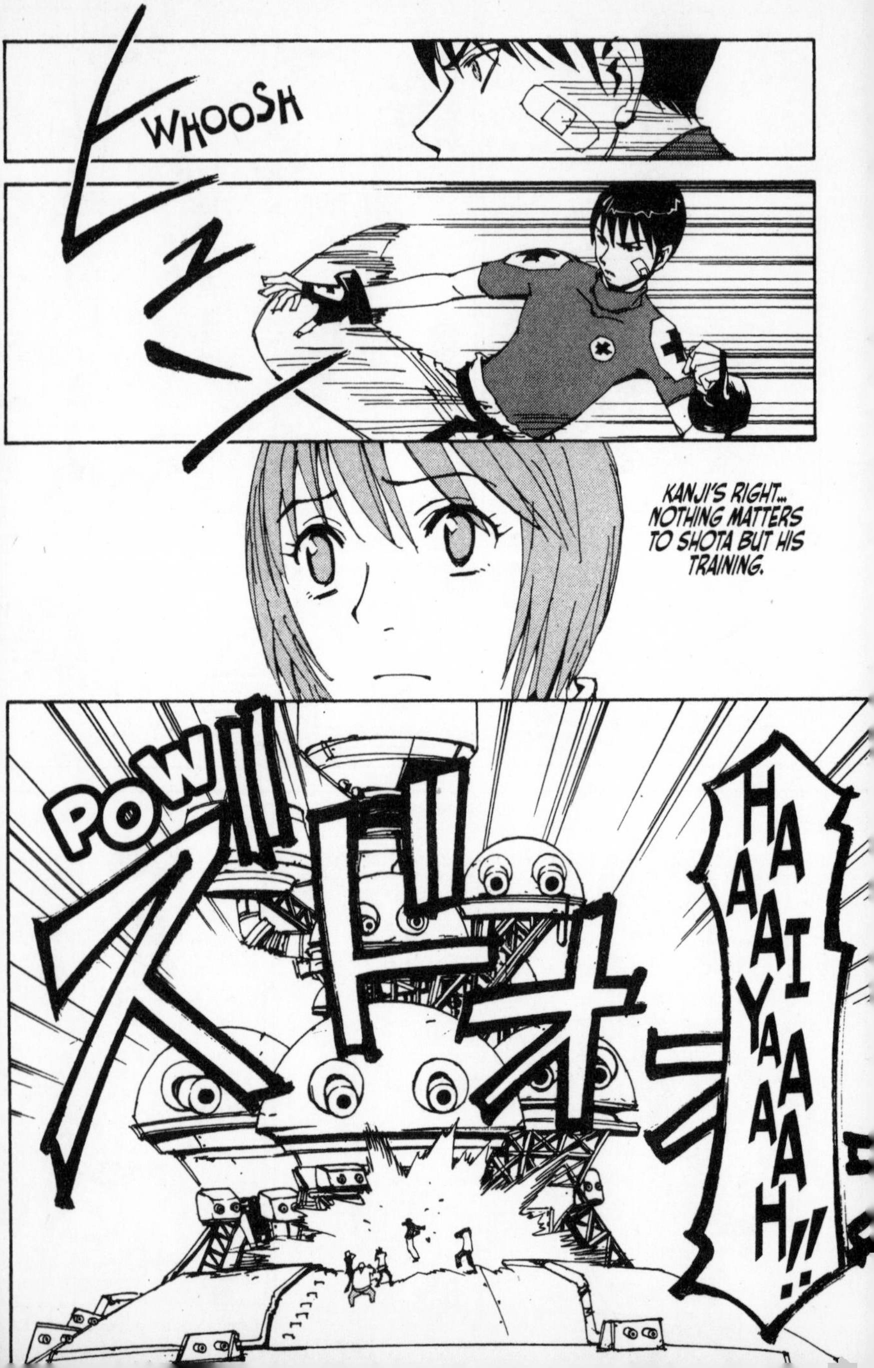
WHOOSH
KANJI'S RIGHT... NOTHING MATTERS TO SHOTA BUT HIS TRAINING.
HAAAIYAAAAAH!!
POW!!

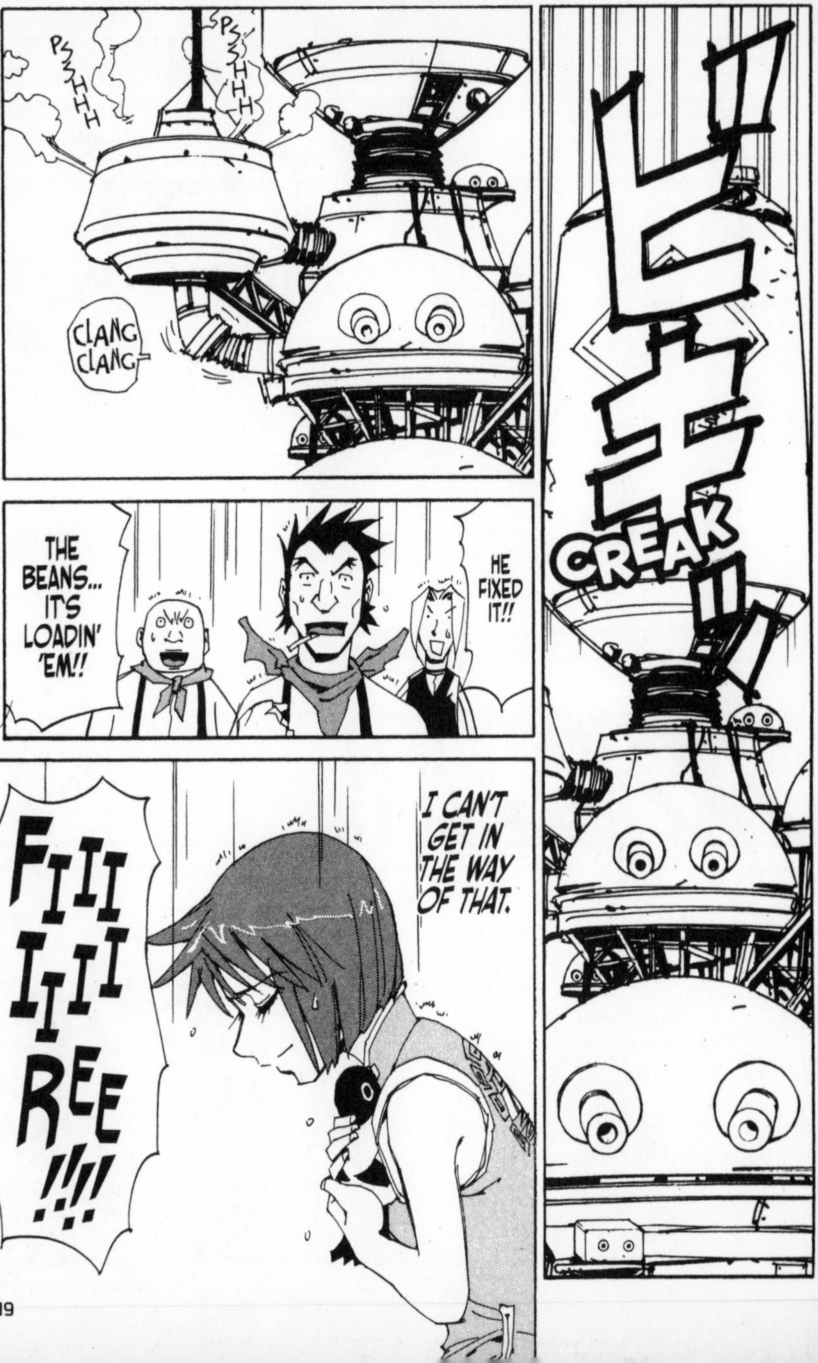
CREAK!!
PSSHHH
PSSHHH
CLANG CLANG
HE FIXED IT!!
THE BEANS... IT'S LOADIN' 'EM!!
I CAN'T GET IN THE WAY OF THAT.
FIIIIIIIREE!!!!

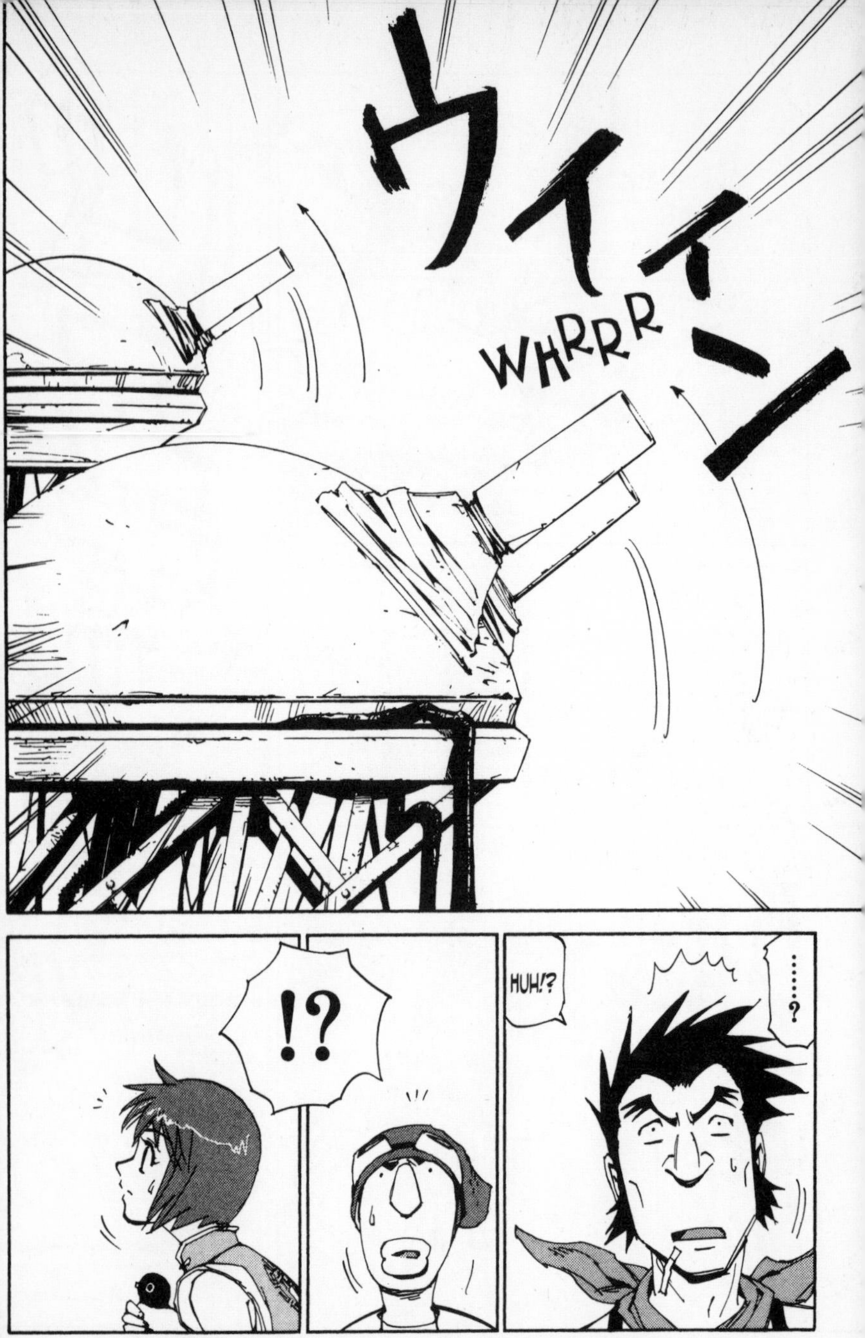
ウイイーン
WHRRR
......?
HUH!?
!?

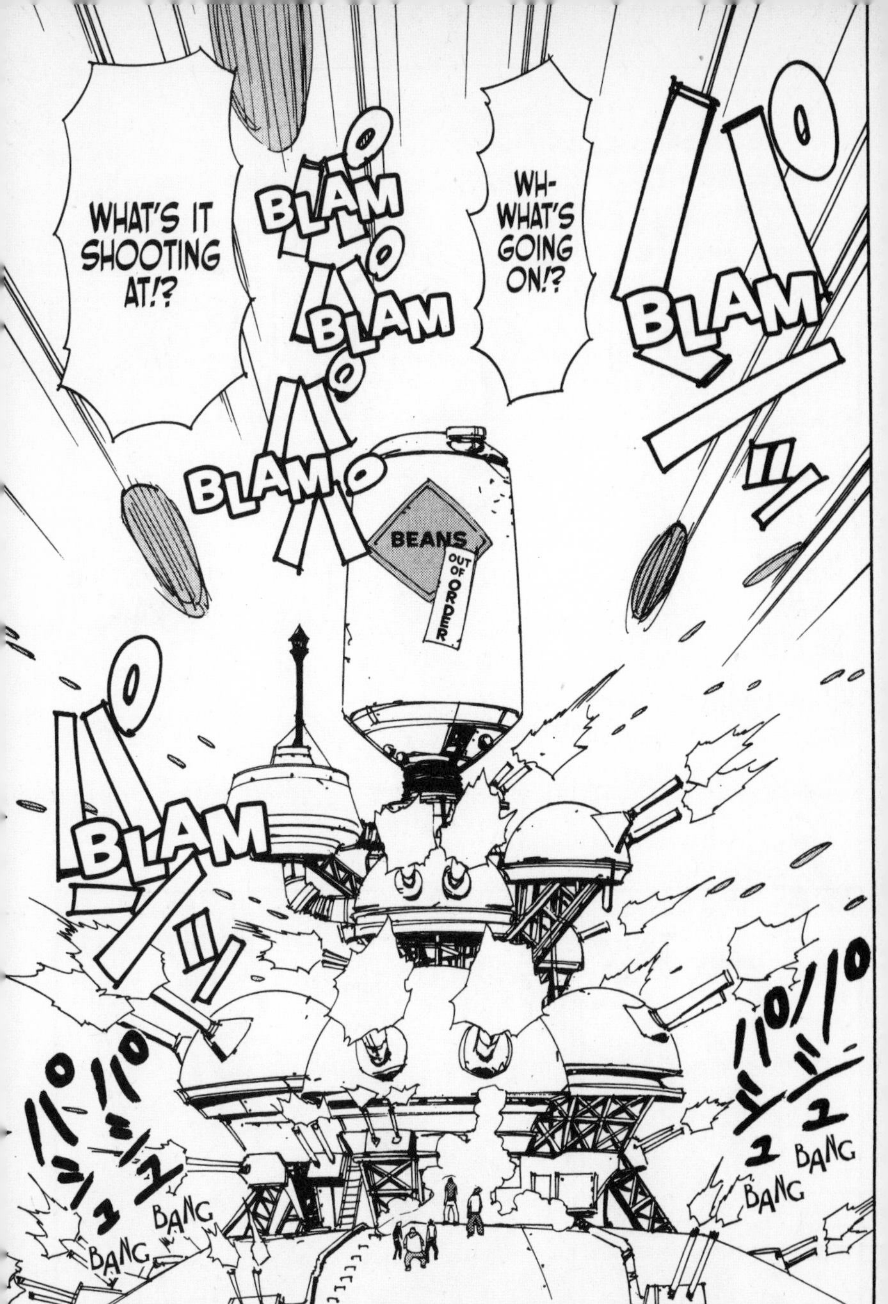
WH-WHAT'S GOING ON!?
BLAM
WHAT'S IT SHOOTING AT!?
BLAM
BLAM
BLAM
BEANS
OUT OF ORDER
BLAM
BANG
BANG
BANG
BANG

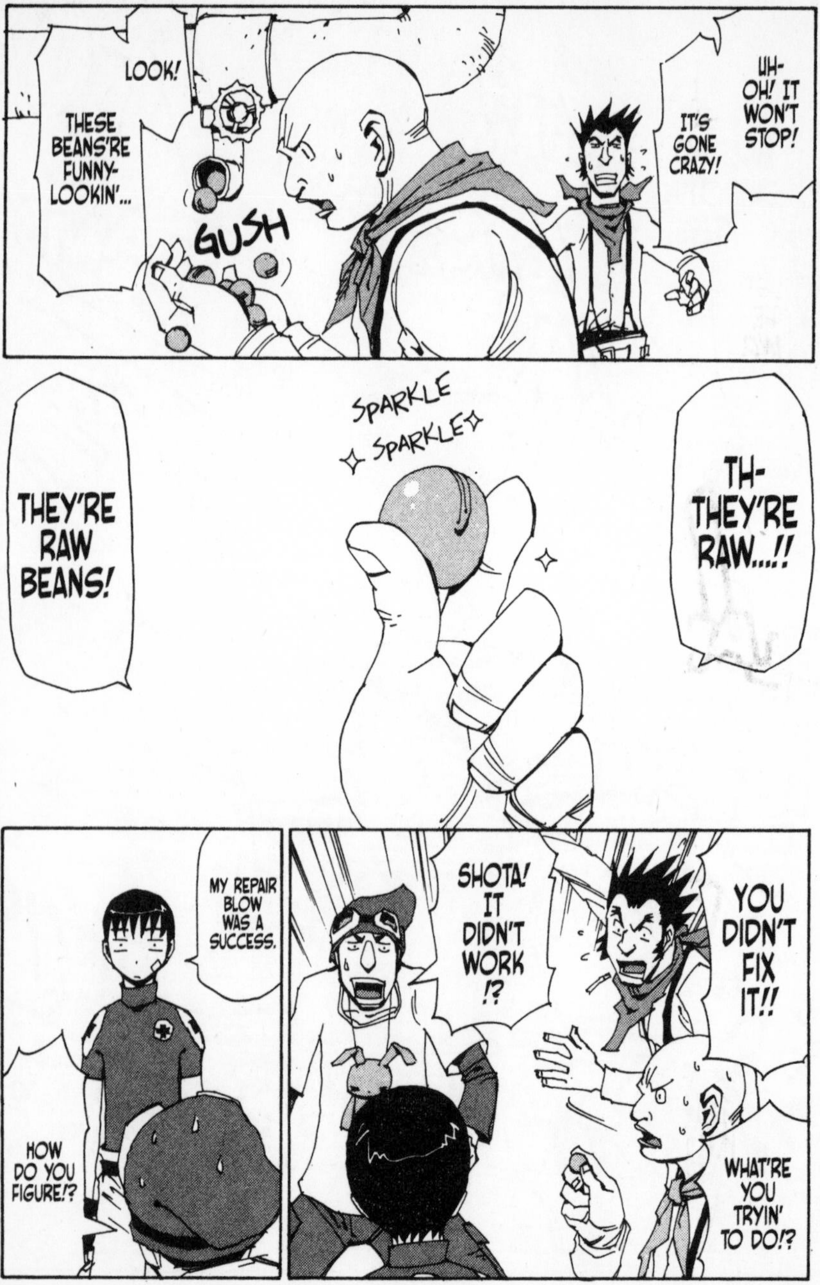
UH-OH! IT WON'T STOP!
IT'S GONE CRAZY!
LOOK!
THESE BEANS'RE FUNNY-LOOKIN'...
GUSH
TH-THEY'RE RAW...!!
SPARKLE
SPARKLE
THEY'RE RAW BEANS!
YOU DIDN'T FIX IT!!
SHOTA! IT DIDN'T WORK!?
WHAT'RE YOU TRYIN' TO DO!?
MY REPAIR BLOW WAS A SUCCESS.
HOW DO YOU FIGURE!?

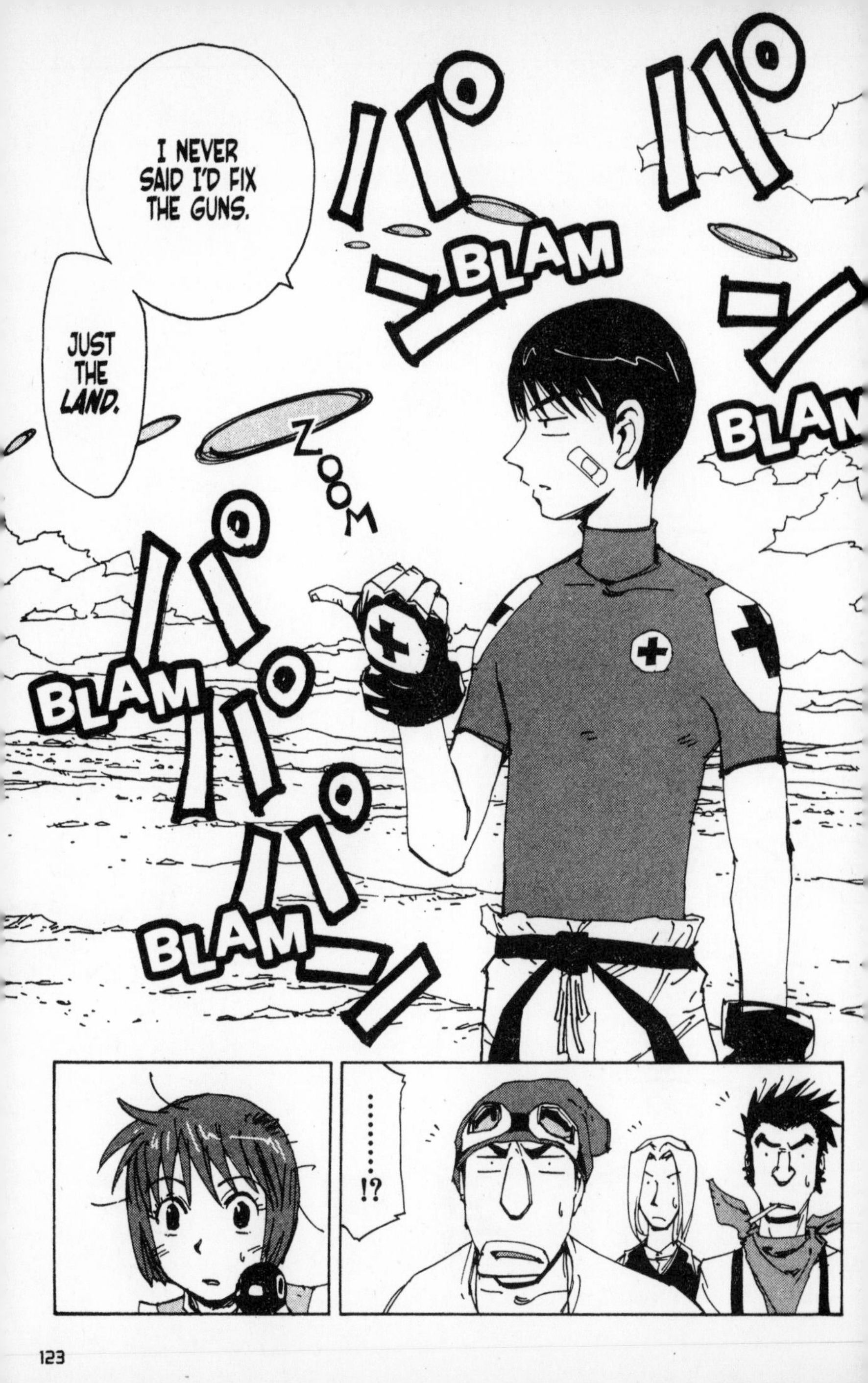
BLAM
BLAM
I NEVER SAID I'D FIX THE GUNS.
JUST THE *LAND.*
ZOOM
BLAM
BLAM
......!?

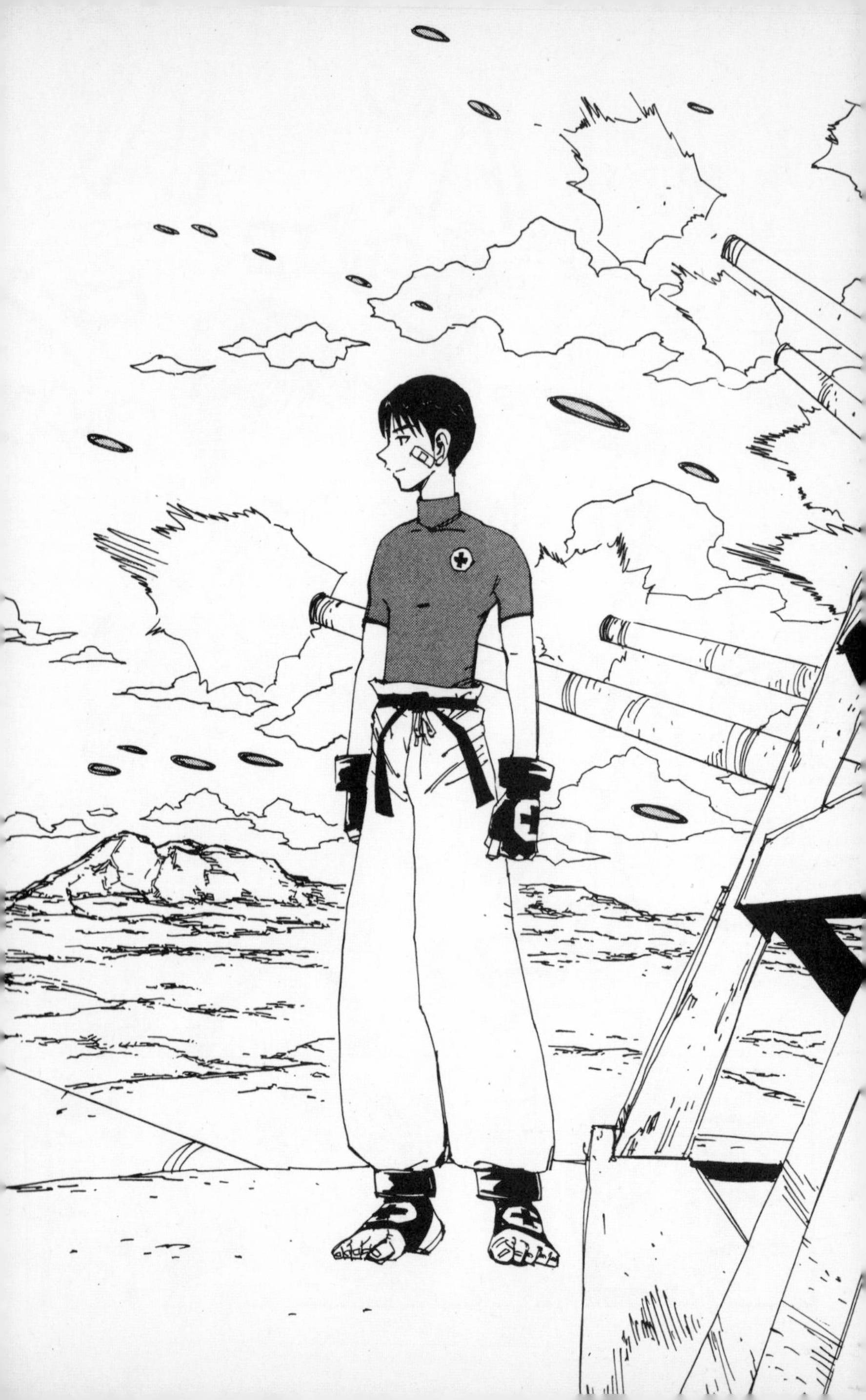

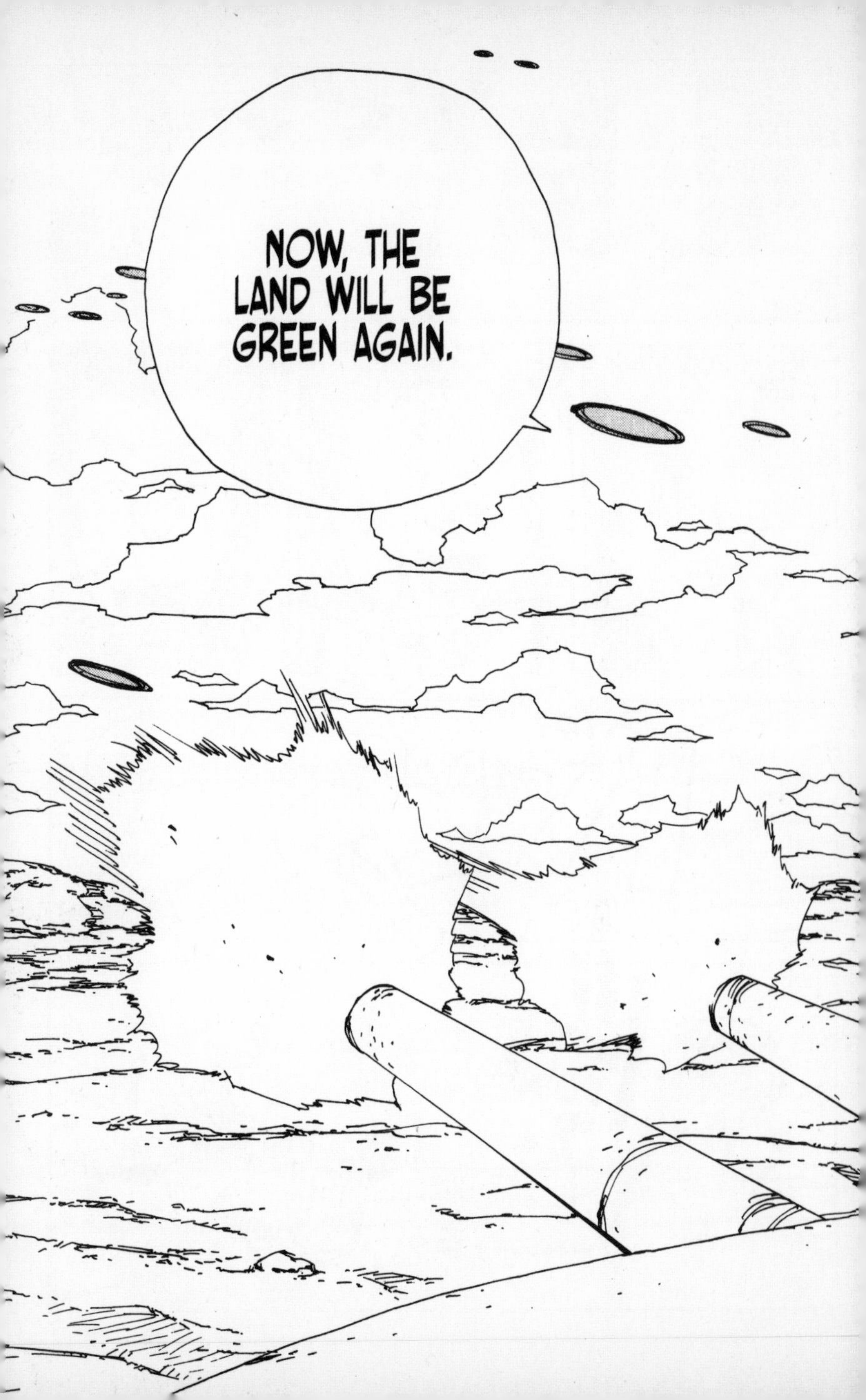
NOW, THE LAND WILL BE GREEN AGAIN.

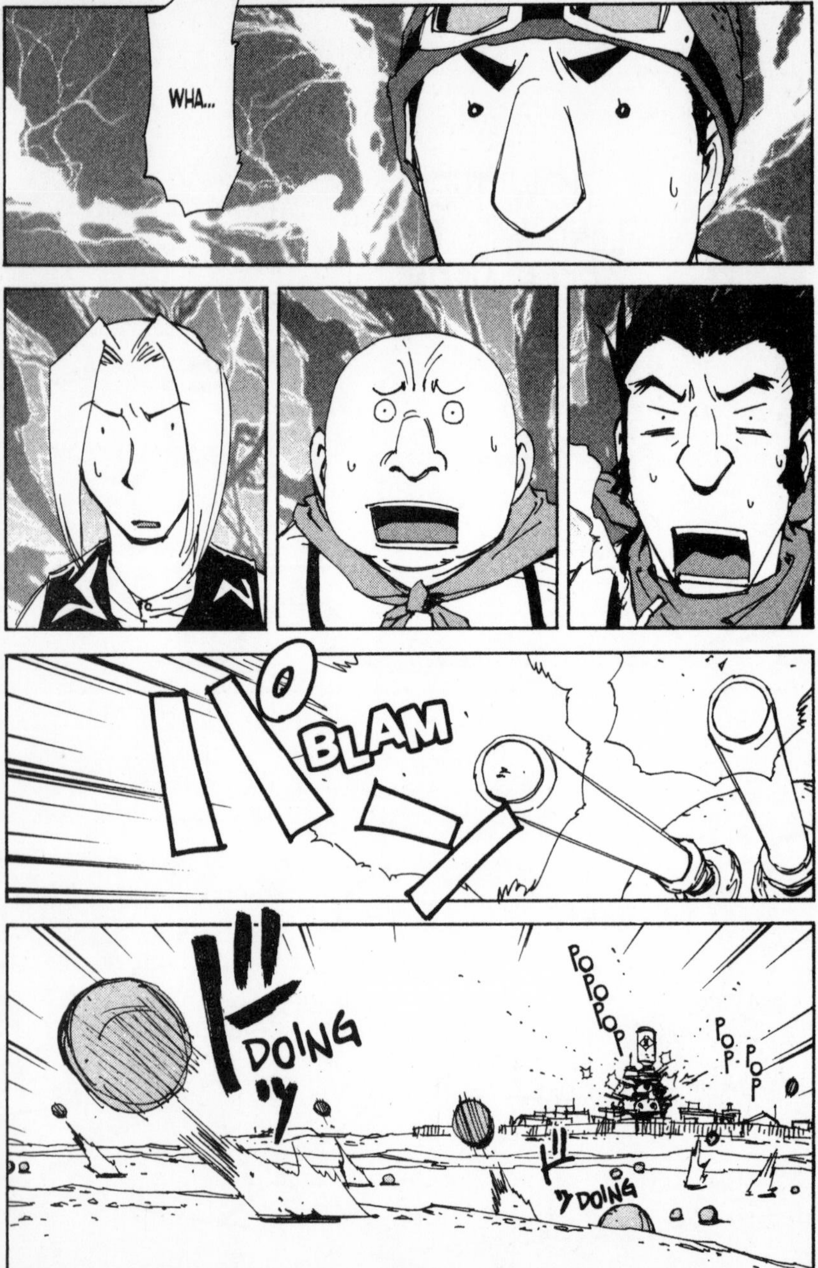
WHA...
BLAM
POPOPOP
POP POP
DOING
DOING

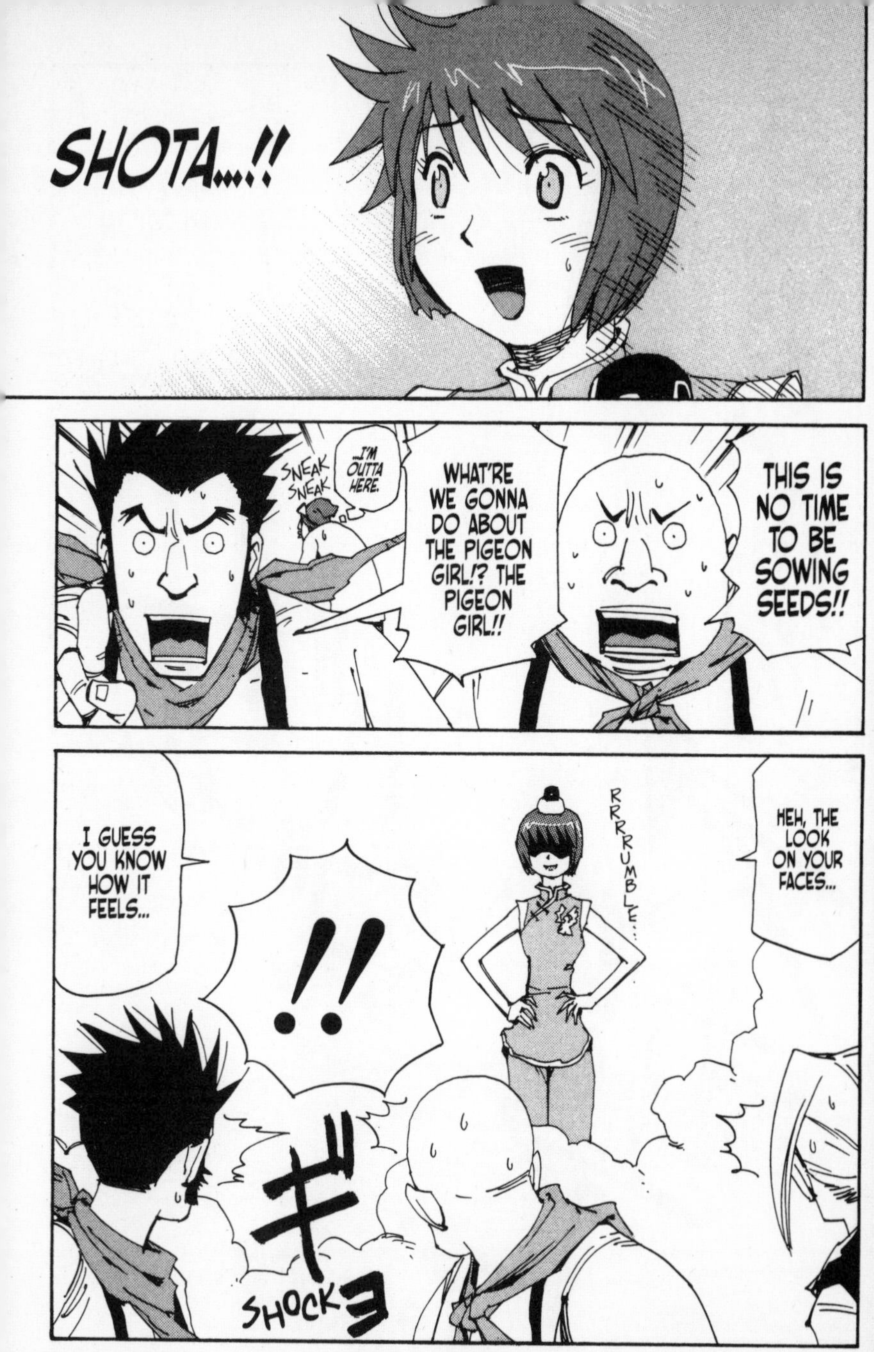
SHOTA...!!
THIS IS NO TIME TO BE SOWING SEEDS!!
WHAT'RE WE GONNA DO ABOUT THE PIGEON GIRL!? THE PIGEON GIRL!!
...I'M OUTTA HERE.
SNEAK SNEAK
HEH, THE LOOK ON YOUR FACES...
RRRRUMBLE...
I GUESS YOU KNOW HOW IT FEELS...
!!
SHOCK

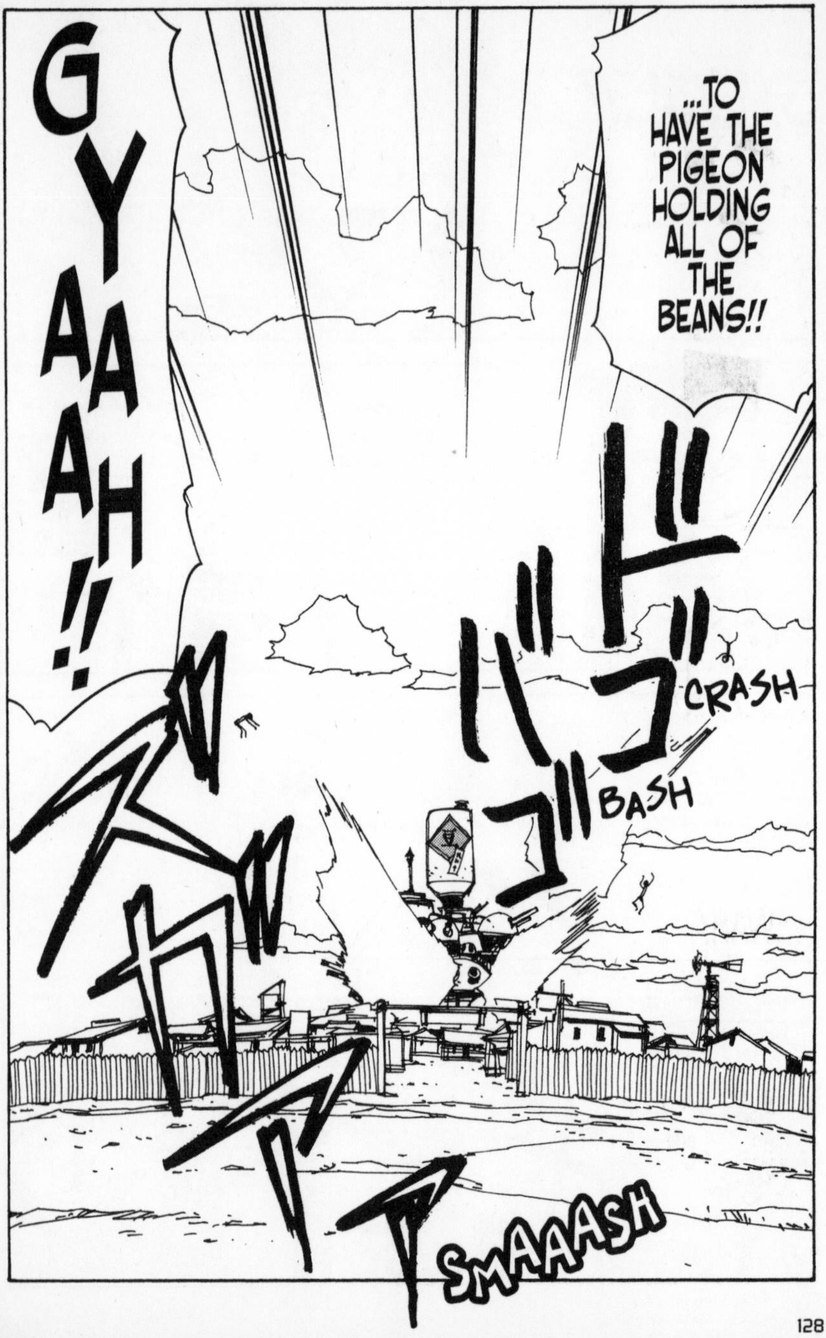
...TO HAVE THE PIGEON HOLDING ALL OF THE BEANS!!
GYAAAH!!
CRASH
BASH
SMAAASH

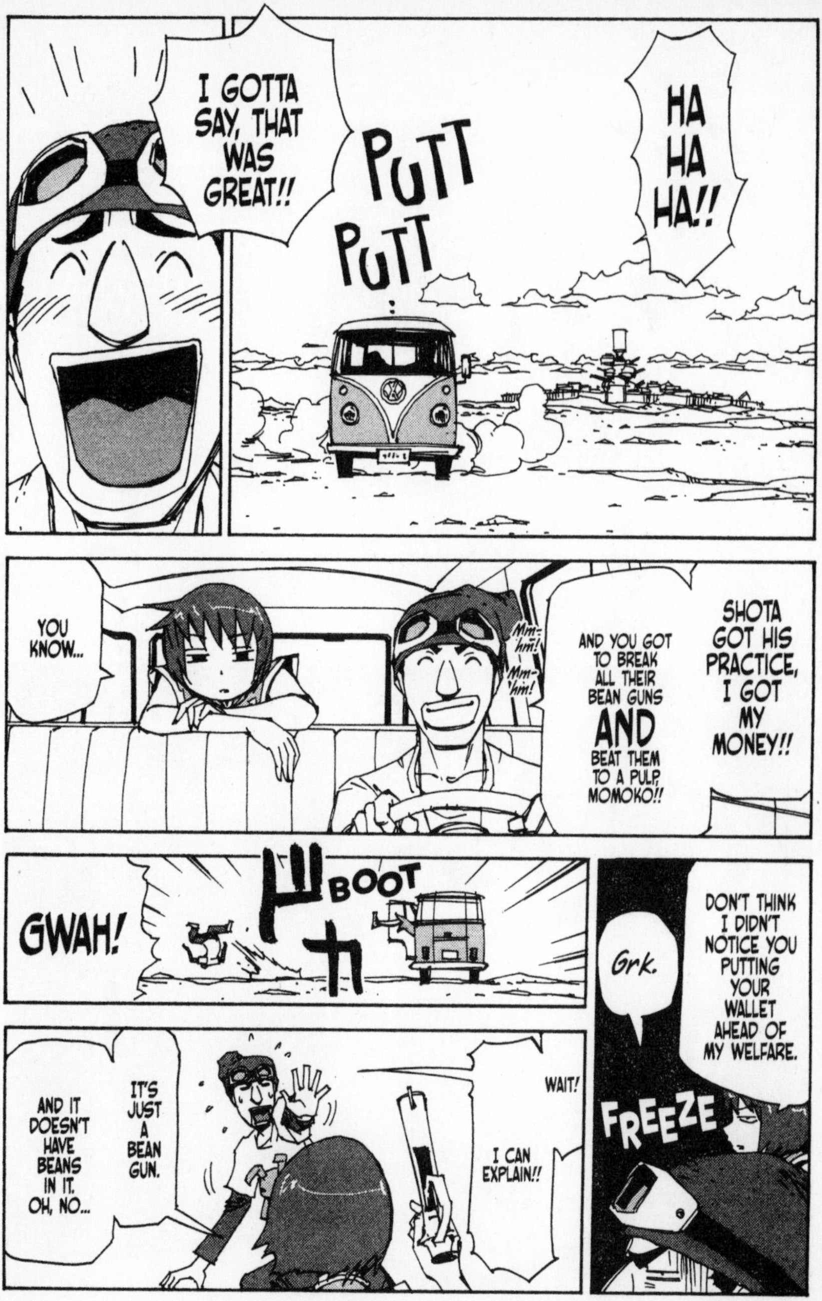

HA HA HA!!
PUTT PUTT
I GOTTA SAY, THAT WAS GREAT!!
SHOTA GOT HIS PRACTICE, I GOT MY MONEY!!
AND YOU GOT TO BREAK ALL THEIR BEAN GUNS AND BEAT THEM TO A PULP, MOMOKO!!
Mm-hm! Mm-hm!
YOU KNOW...
DON'T THINK I DIDN'T NOTICE YOU PUTTING YOUR WALLET AHEAD OF MY WELFARE.
Grk.
FREEZE
BOOT
GWAH!
WAIT!
I CAN EXPLAIN!!
IT'S JUST A BEAN GUN.
AND IT DOESN'T HAVE BEANS IN IT. OH, NO...

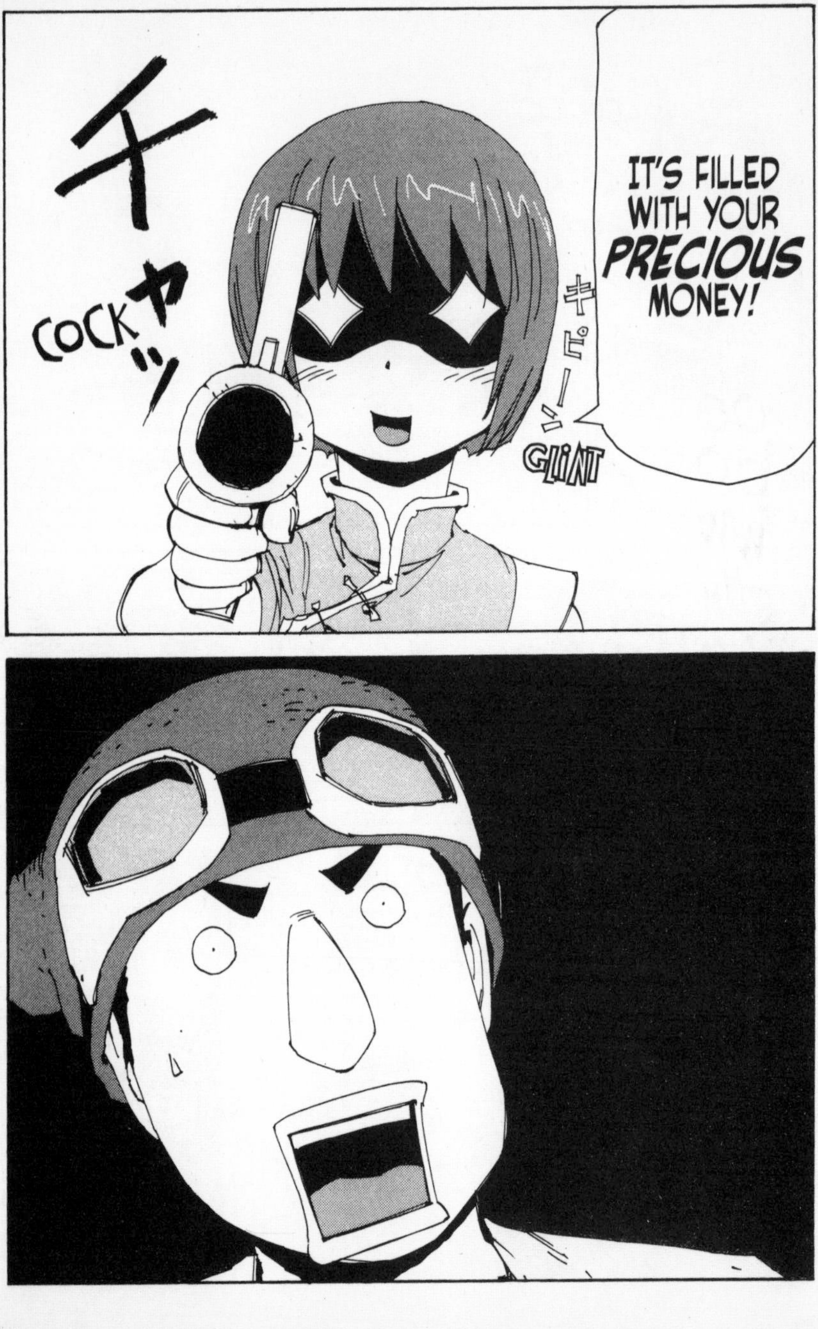
IT'S FILLED WITH YOUR PRECIOUS MONEY!
キピーン
GLINT
チャッ
COCK

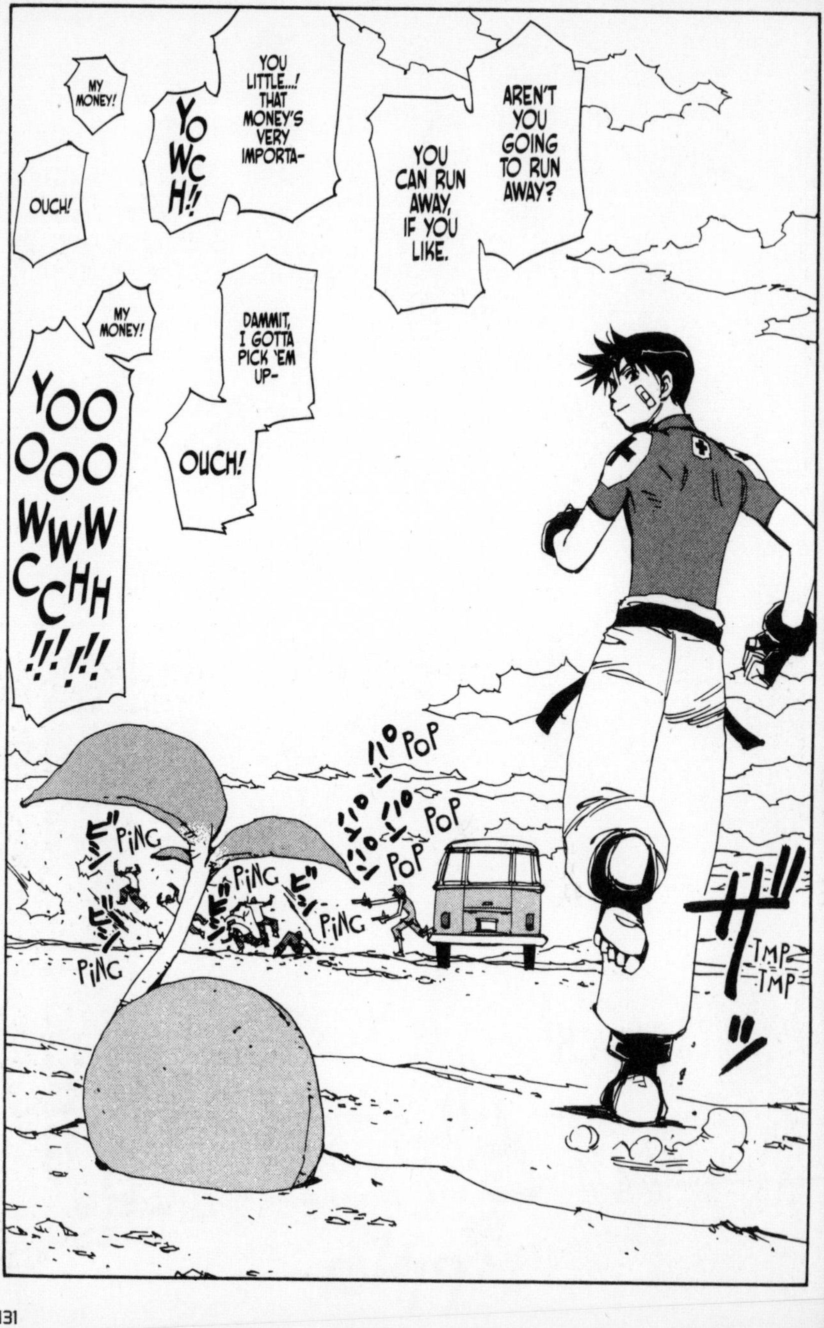
AREN'T YOU GOING TO RUN AWAY?
YOU CAN RUN AWAY, IF YOU LIKE.
YOU LITTLE...! THAT MONEY'S VERY IMPORTA-
YOWCH!!
MY MONEY!
OUCH!
DAMMIT, I GOTTA PICK 'EM UP-
MY MONEY!
OUCH!
YOOOOOWWWCCHH!!!!!!
TMP TMP
POP
POP
POP
PING
PING
PING
PING

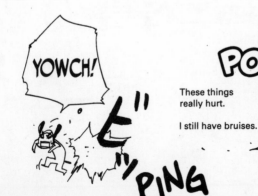

Reference materials
This is the bean gun I bought at Asakusa.
POP
These things really hurt.
I still have bruises.
YOWCH!
PING

#8 A Match of Insides!

王

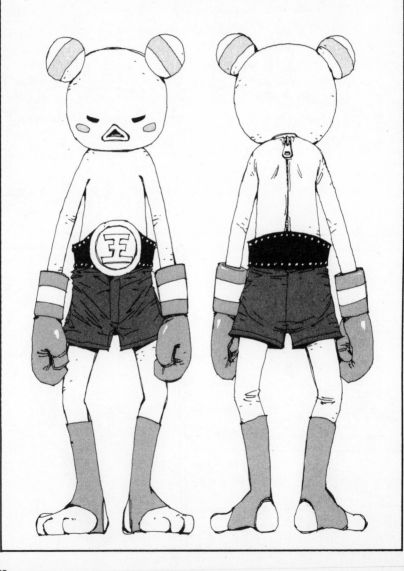

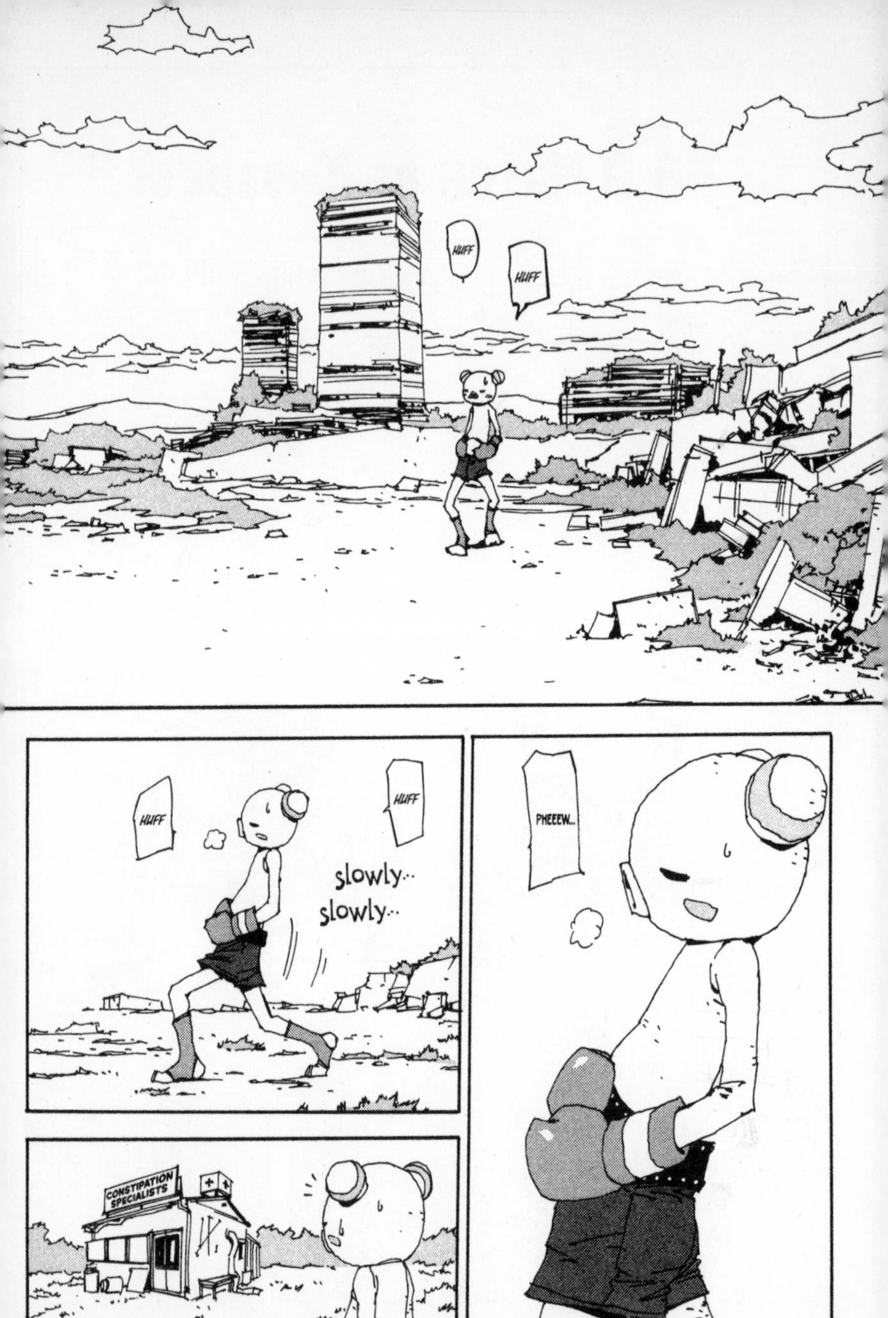
HUFF
HUFF
PHEEEW...
HUFF
HUFF
slowly...
slowly...
CONSTIPATION SPECIALISTS

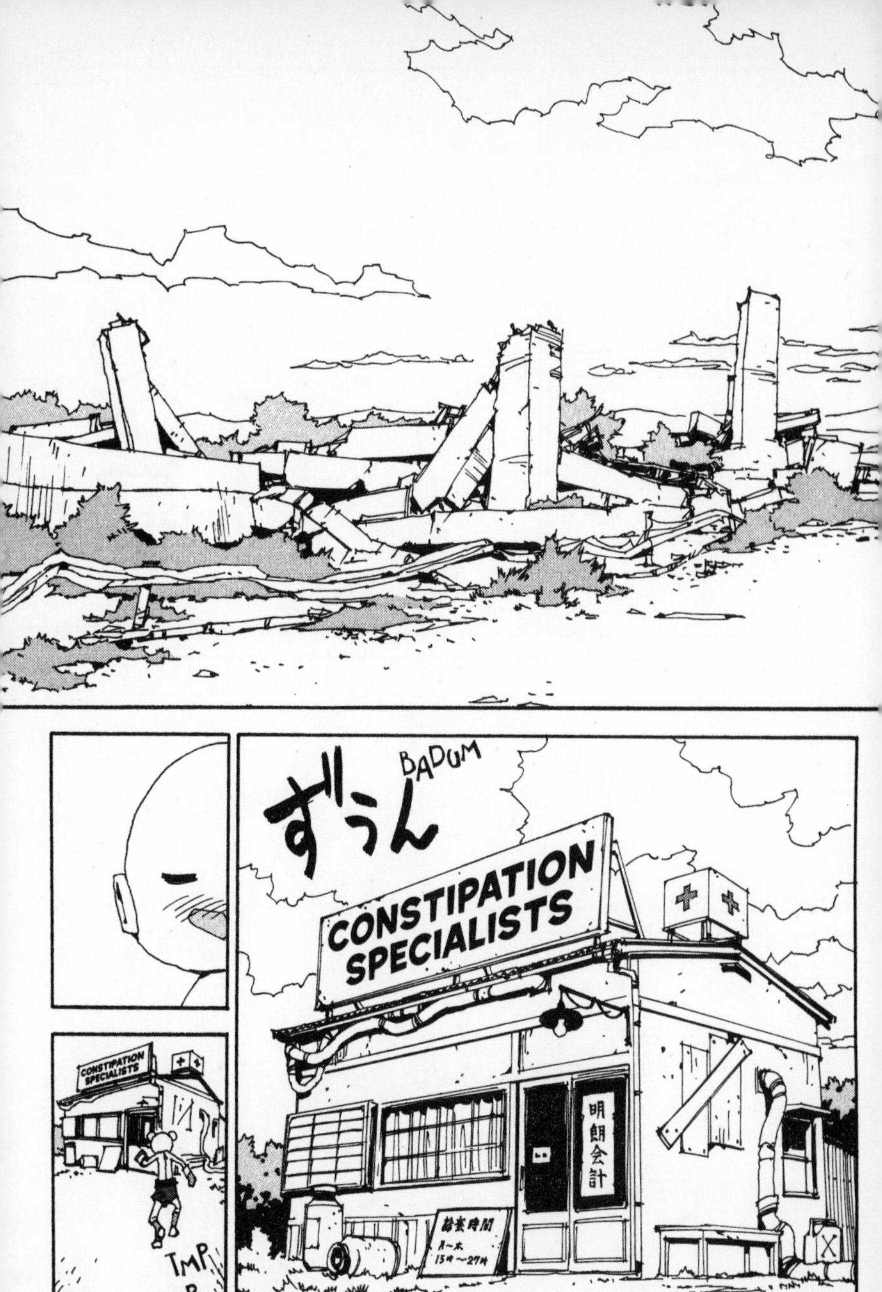

ずぅん
BADUM
CONSTIPATION SPECIALISTS
明朗会計
CONSTIPATION SPECIALISTS
TMP
TMP

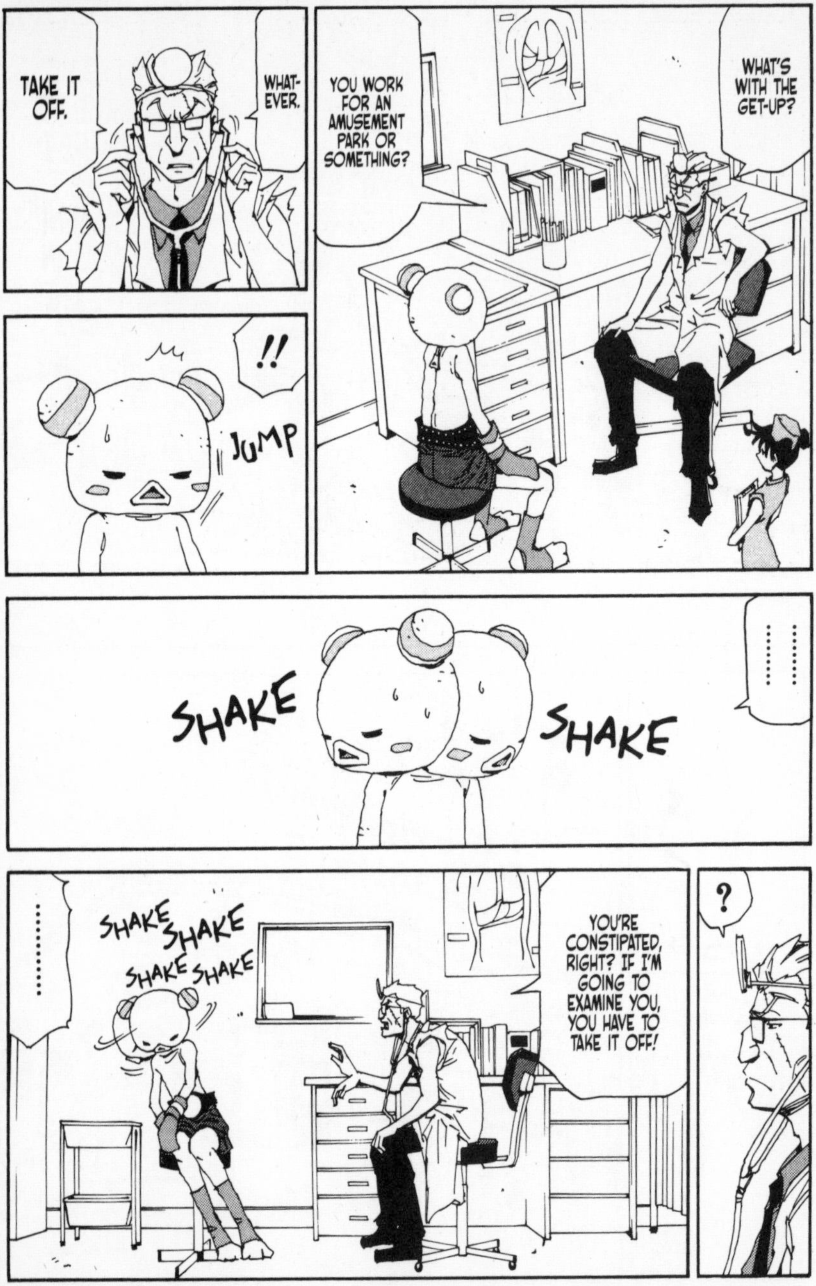
WHAT'S WITH THE GET-UP?
YOU WORK FOR AN AMUSEMENT PARK OR SOMETHING?
WHAT-EVER.
TAKE IT OFF.
!!
JUMP
......
SHAKE
SHAKE
?
YOU'RE CONSTIPATED, RIGHT? IF I'M GOING TO EXAMINE YOU, YOU HAVE TO TAKE IT OFF!
SHAKE SHAKE SHAKE SHAKE
....

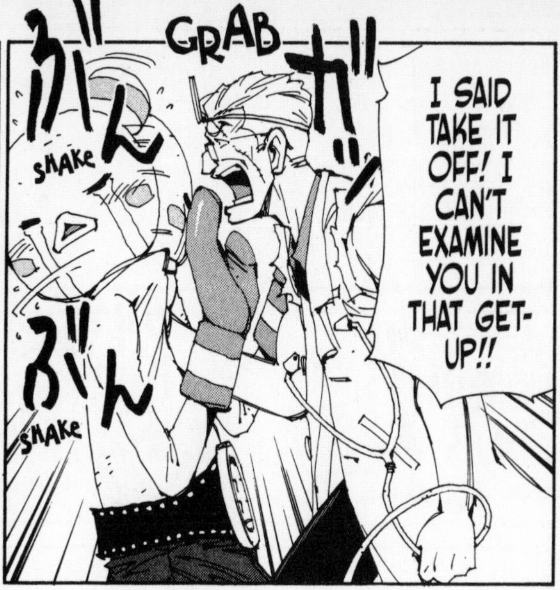
GRAB
I SAID TAKE IT OFF! I CAN'T EXAMINE YOU IN THAT GET-UP!!
SHAKE
SHAKE

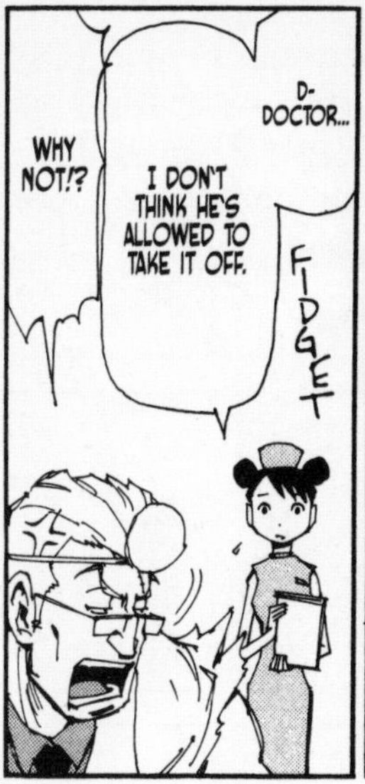
D-DOCTOR...
I DON'T THINK HE'S ALLOWED TO TAKE IT OFF.
WHY NOT!?
FIDGET

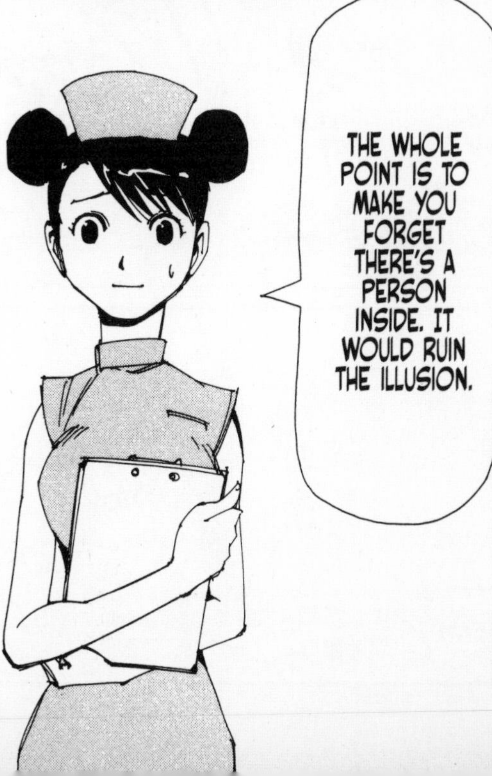
THE WHOLE POINT IS TO MAKE YOU FORGET THERE'S A PERSON INSIDE. IT WOULD RUIN THE ILLUSION.

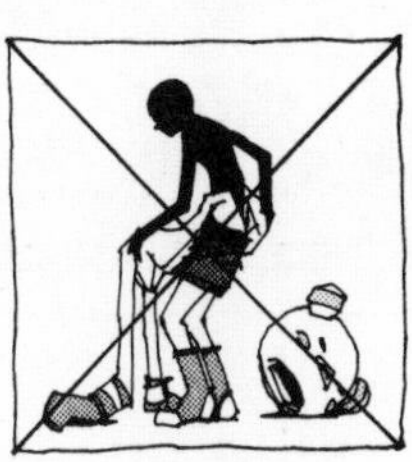

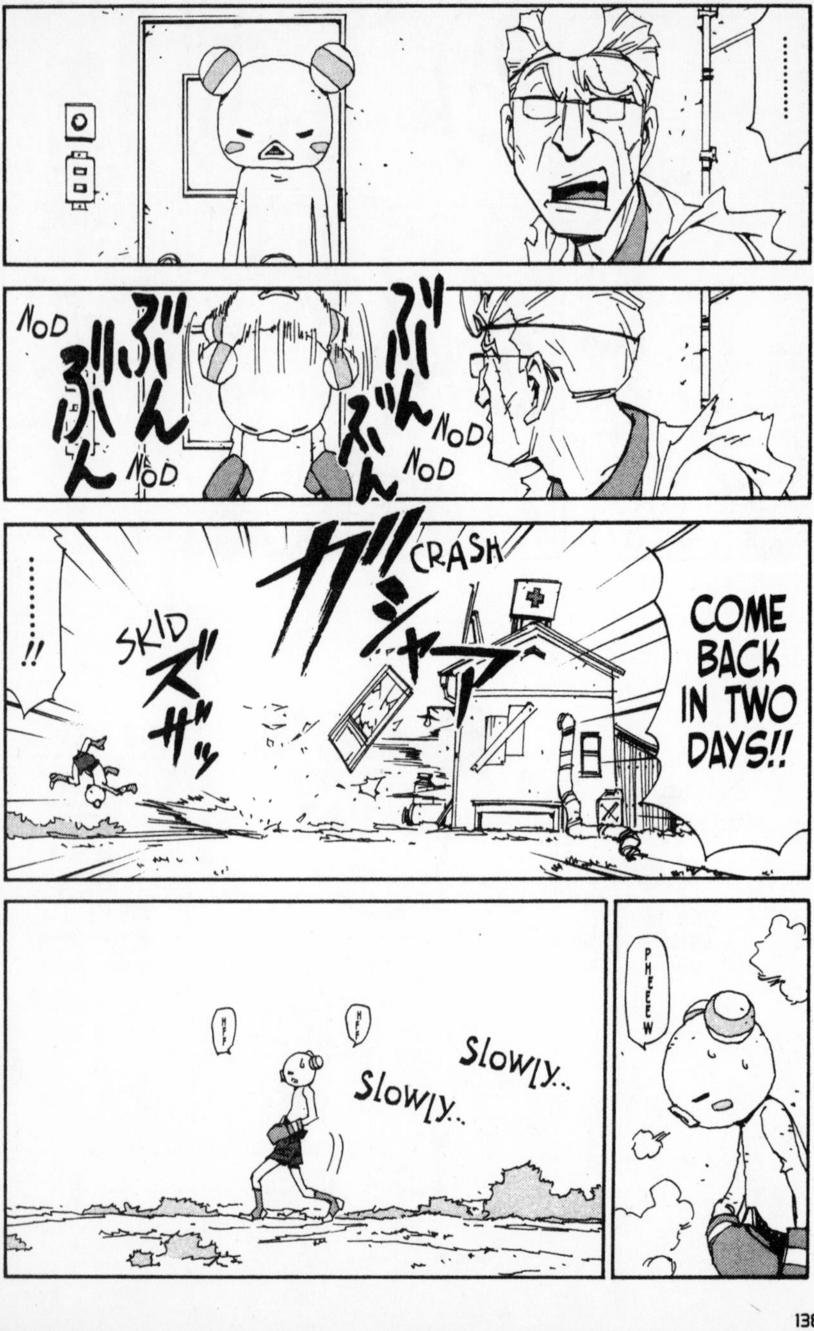
......
ぶんぶん
NOD
NOD
ぶんぶん
NOD
NOD
COME BACK IN TWO DAYS!!
ガシャア
CRASH
ズザッ
SKID
......!!
PHEEEW
MFF
MFF
SLOWLY...
SLOWLY...

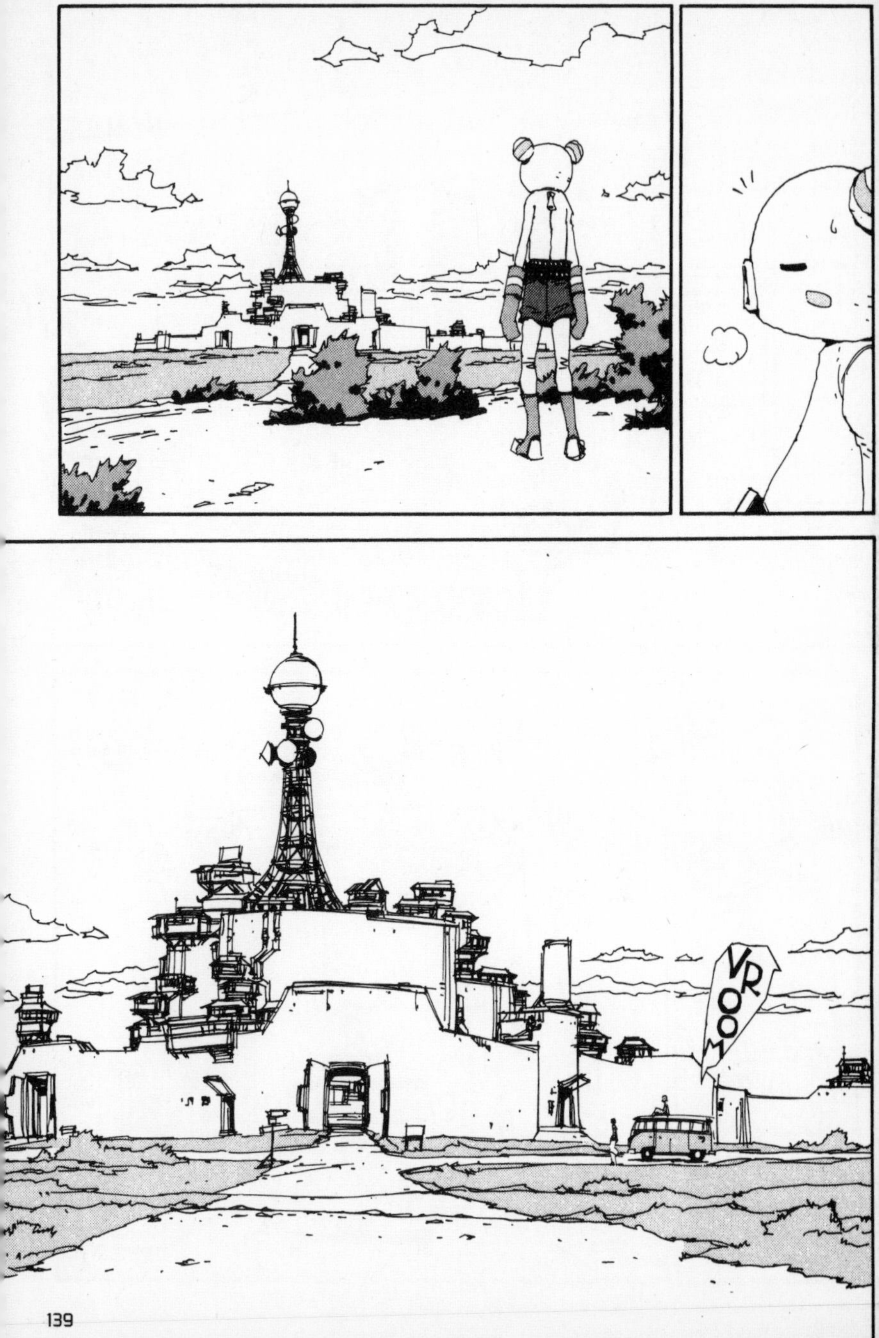
VROOOM

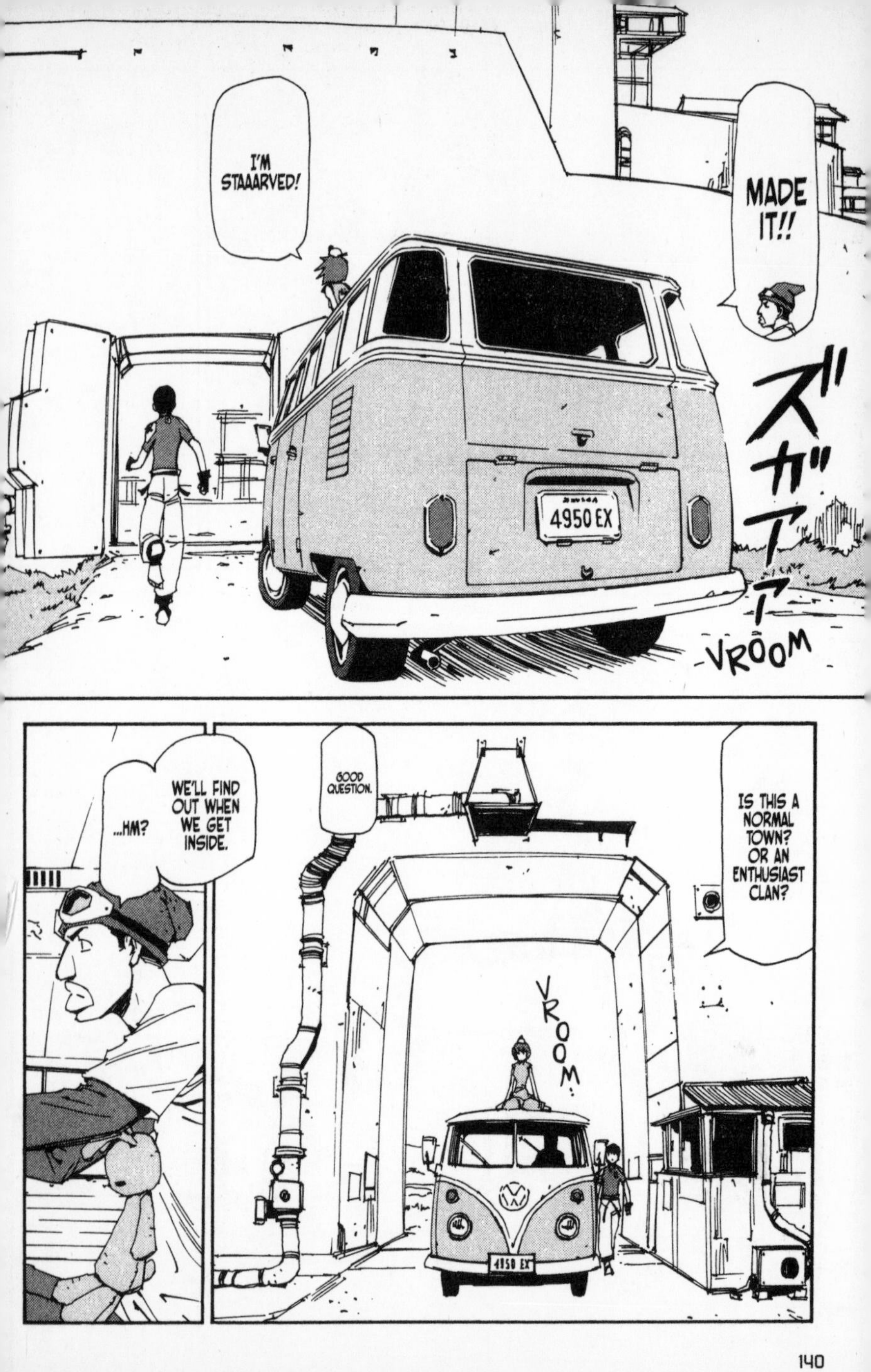
MADE IT!!
I'M STAAARVED!
ズガァァァ
VROOM
IS THIS A NORMAL TOWN? OR AN ENTHUSIAST CLAN?
GOOD QUESTION.
VROOM.
WE'LL FIND OUT WHEN WE GET INSIDE.
...HM?

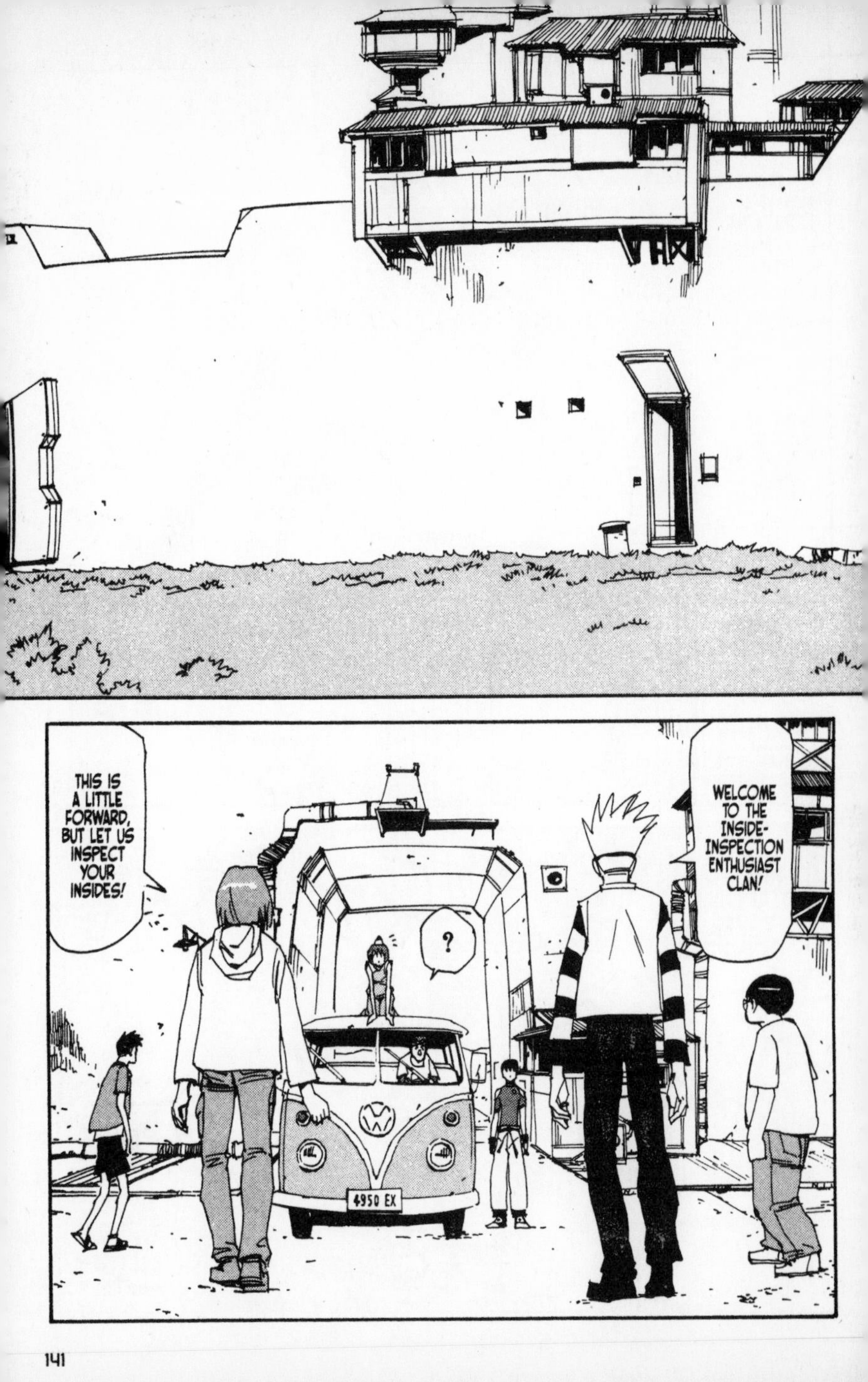
WELCOME TO THE INSIDE-INSPECTION ENTHUSIAST CLAN!
?
THIS IS A LITTLE FORWARD, BUT LET US INSPECT YOUR INSIDES!
4950 EX

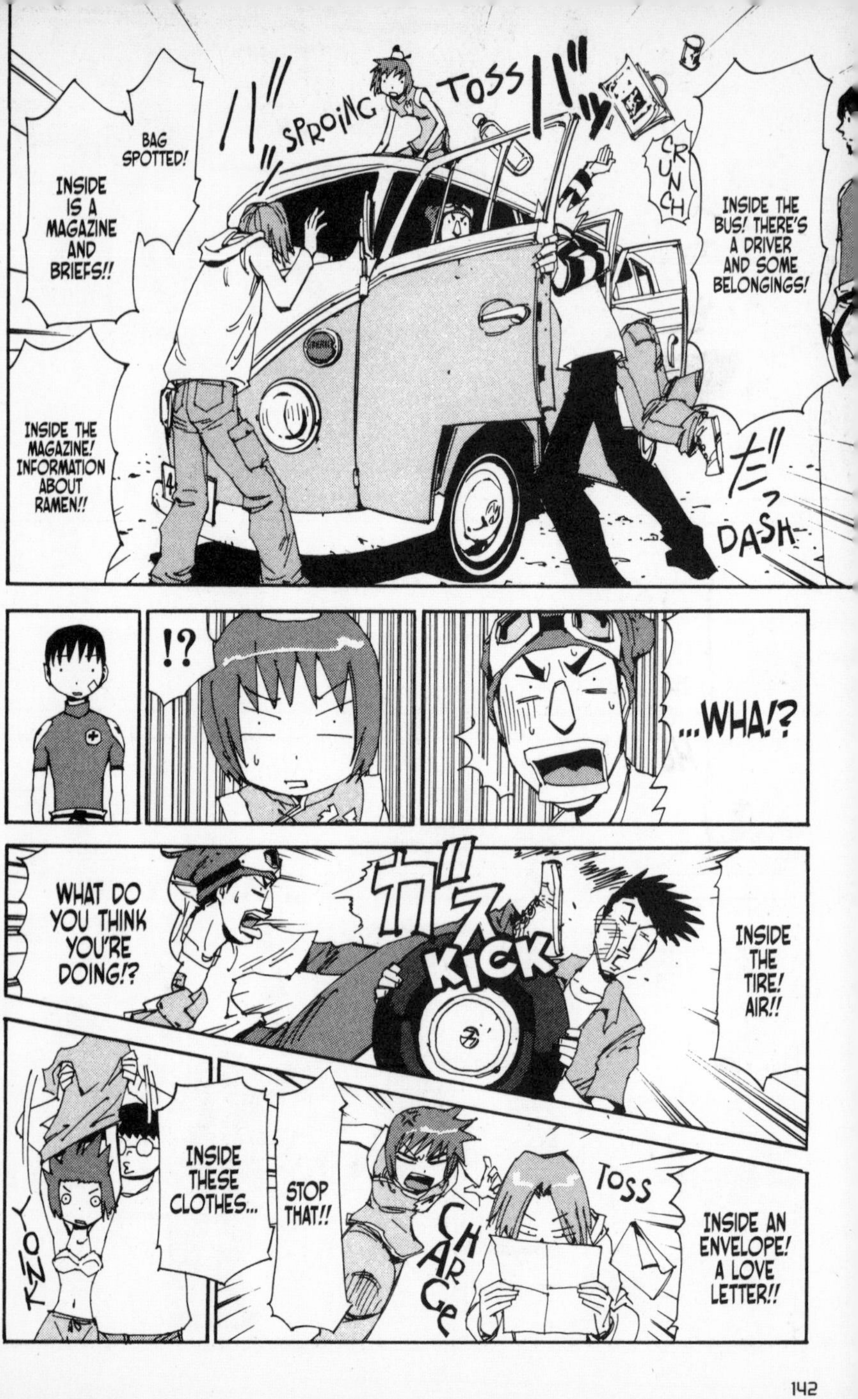
INSIDE THE BUS! THERE'S A DRIVER AND SOME BELONGINGS!
CRUNCH
TOSS
SPROING
BAG SPOTTED!
INSIDE IS A MAGAZINE AND BRIEFS!!
DASH
INSIDE THE MAGAZINE! INFORMATION ABOUT RAMEN!!
...WHA!?
!?
INSIDE THE TIRE! AIR!!
KICK
WHAT DO YOU THINK YOU'RE DOING!?
INSIDE AN ENVELOPE! A LOVE LETTER!!
TOSS
CHARGE
STOP THAT!!
INSIDE THESE CLOTHES...
YOINK

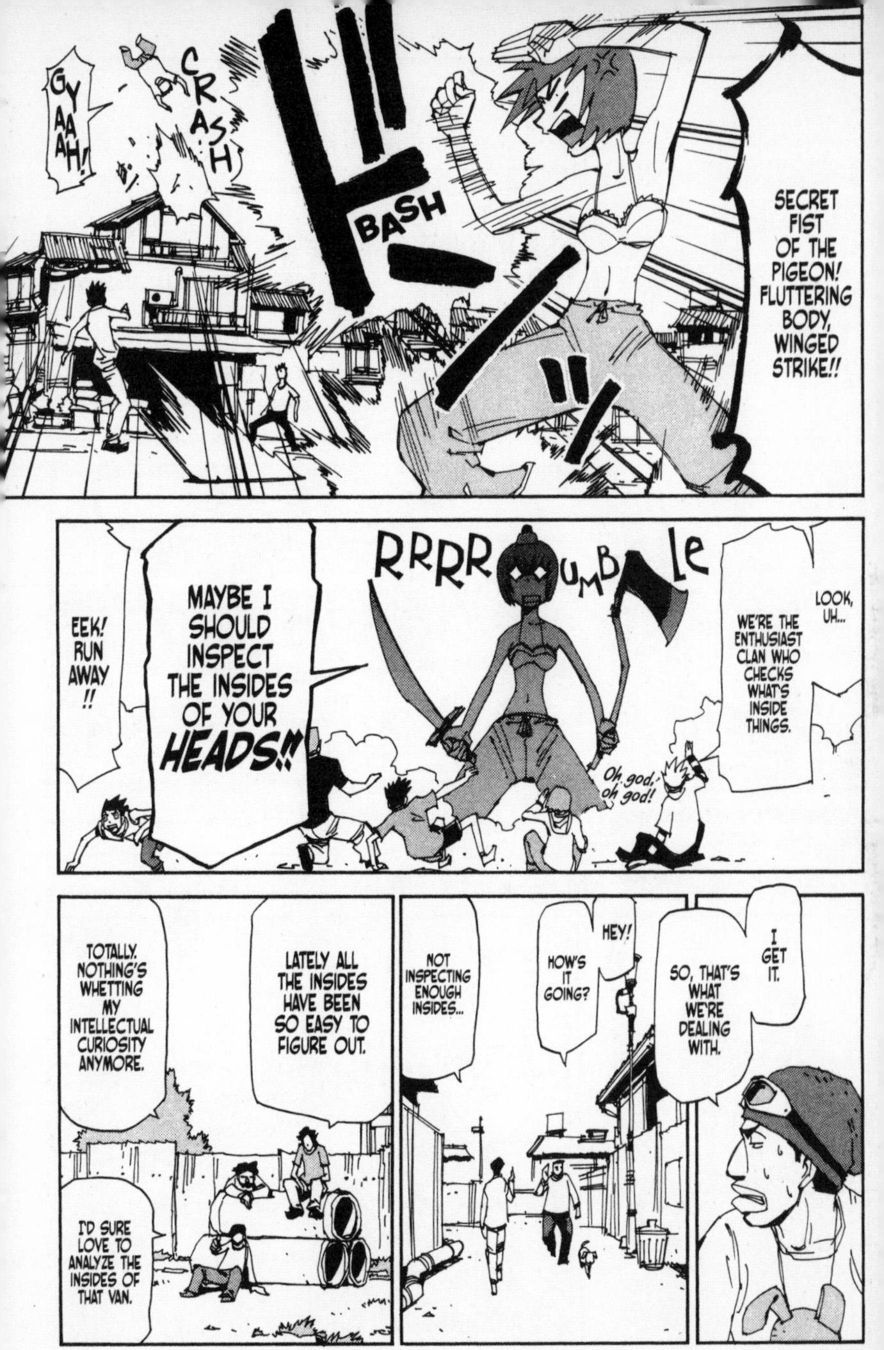
SECRET FIST OF THE PIGEON! FLUTTERING BODY, WINGED STRIKE!!
BASH
CRASH
GYAAAH!
LOOK, UH...
WE'RE THE ENTHUSIAST CLAN WHO CHECKS WHAT'S INSIDE THINGS.
RRRRUMBLE
Oh god, oh god!
MAYBE I SHOULD INSPECT THE INSIDES OF YOUR HEADS!!
EEK! RUN AWAY!!
I GET IT.
SO, THAT'S WHAT WE'RE DEALING WITH.
HEY!
HOW'S IT GOING?
NOT INSPECTING ENOUGH INSIDES...
LATELY ALL THE INSIDES HAVE BEEN SO EASY TO FIGURE OUT.
TOTALLY. NOTHING'S WHETTING MY INTELLECTUAL CURIOSITY ANYMORE.
I'D SURE LOVE TO ANALYZE THE INSIDES OF THAT VAN.

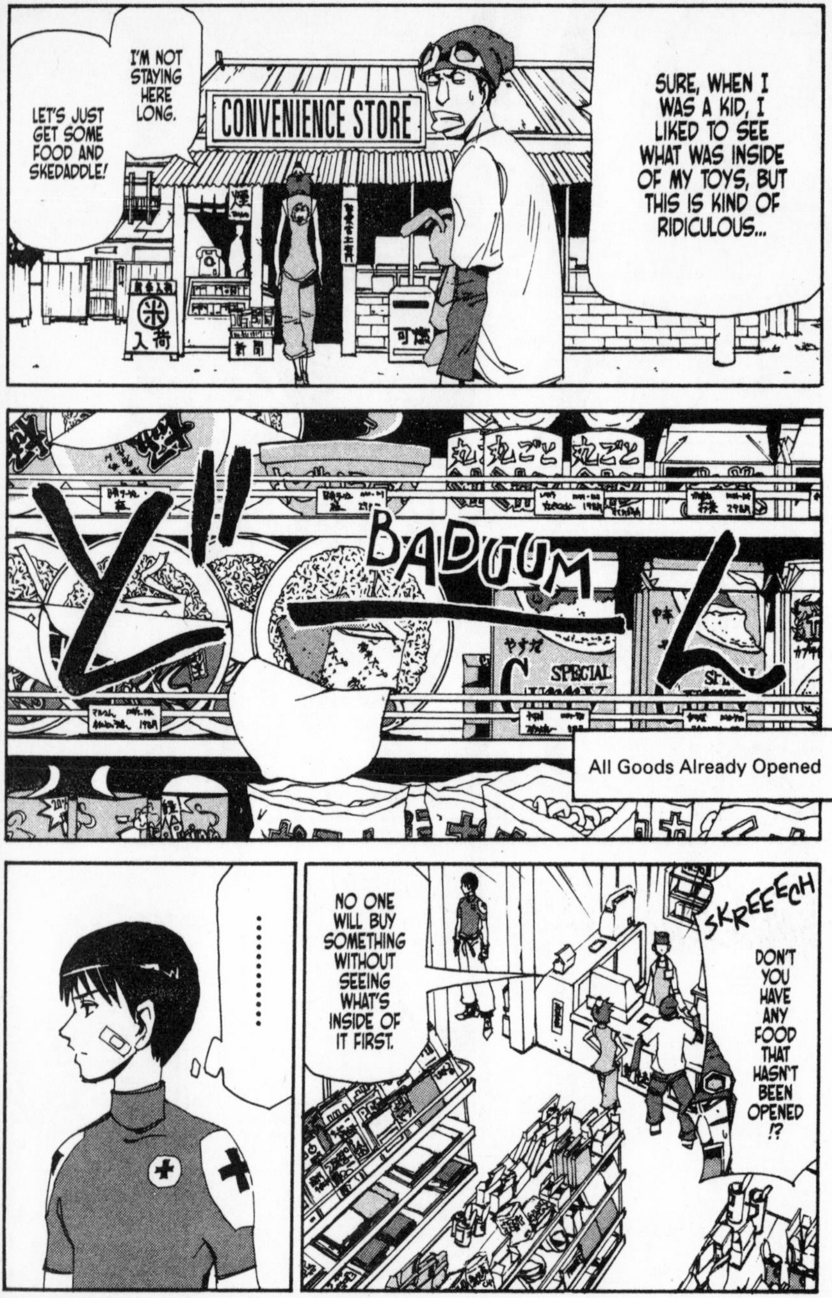
SURE, WHEN I WAS A KID, I LIKED TO SEE WHAT WAS INSIDE OF MY TOYS, BUT THIS IS KIND OF RIDICULOUS...
CONVENIENCE STORE
I'M NOT STAYING HERE LONG.
LET'S JUST GET SOME FOOD AND SKEDADDLE!
BADUUM
All Goods Already Opened
SKREEECH
DON'T YOU HAVE ANY FOOD THAT HASN'T BEEN OPENED!?
NO ONE WILL BUY SOMETHING WITHOUT SEEING WHAT'S INSIDE OF IT FIRST.
......

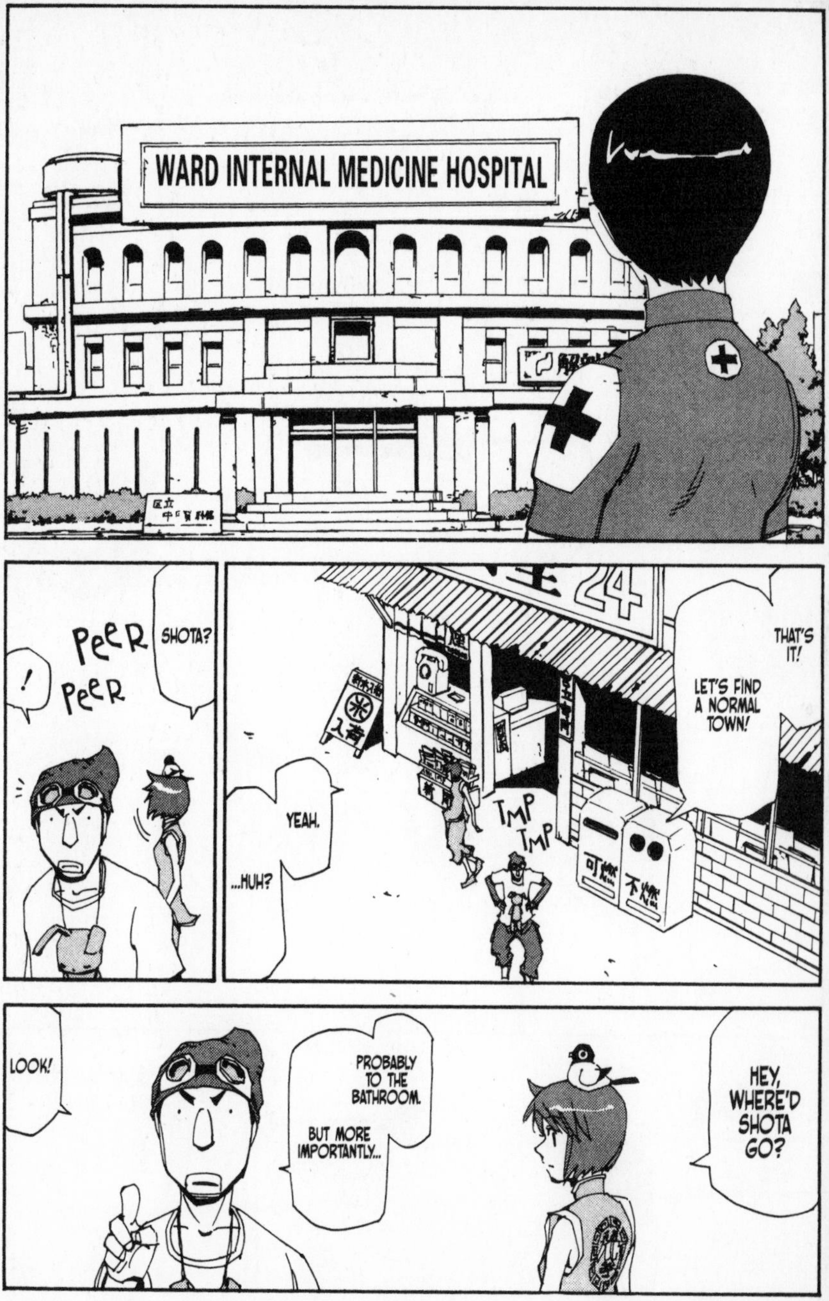
WARD INTERNAL MEDICINE HOSPITAL
THAT'S IT!
LET'S FIND A NORMAL TOWN!
TMP TMP
可燃
不燃
YEAH.
...HUH?
SHOTA?
PeeR PeeR
!
HEY, WHERE'D SHOTA GO?
PROBABLY TO THE BATHROOM.
BUT MORE IMPORTANTLY...
LOOK!

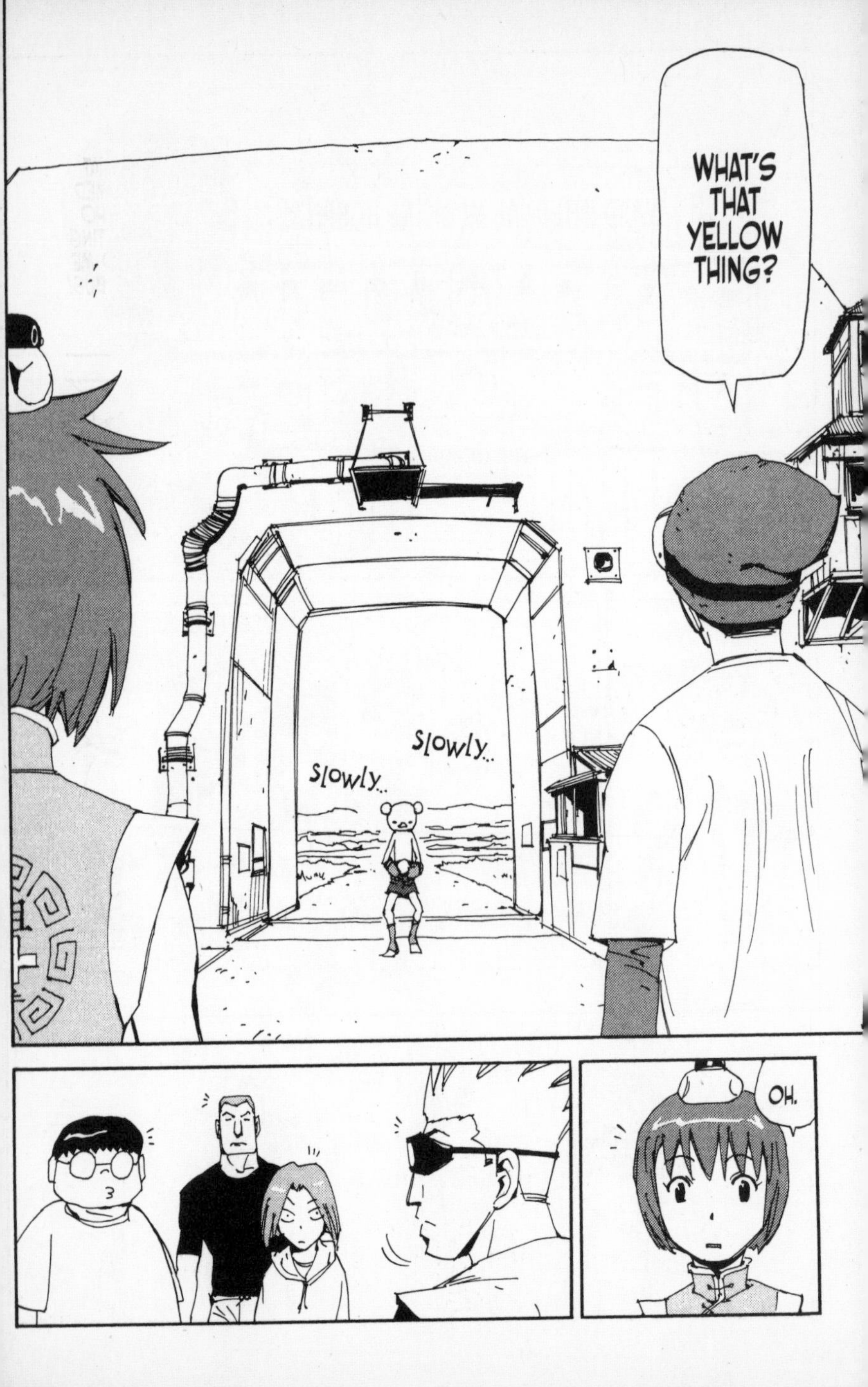
WHAT'S THAT YELLOW THING?
SLOWLY...
SLOWLY...
OH.

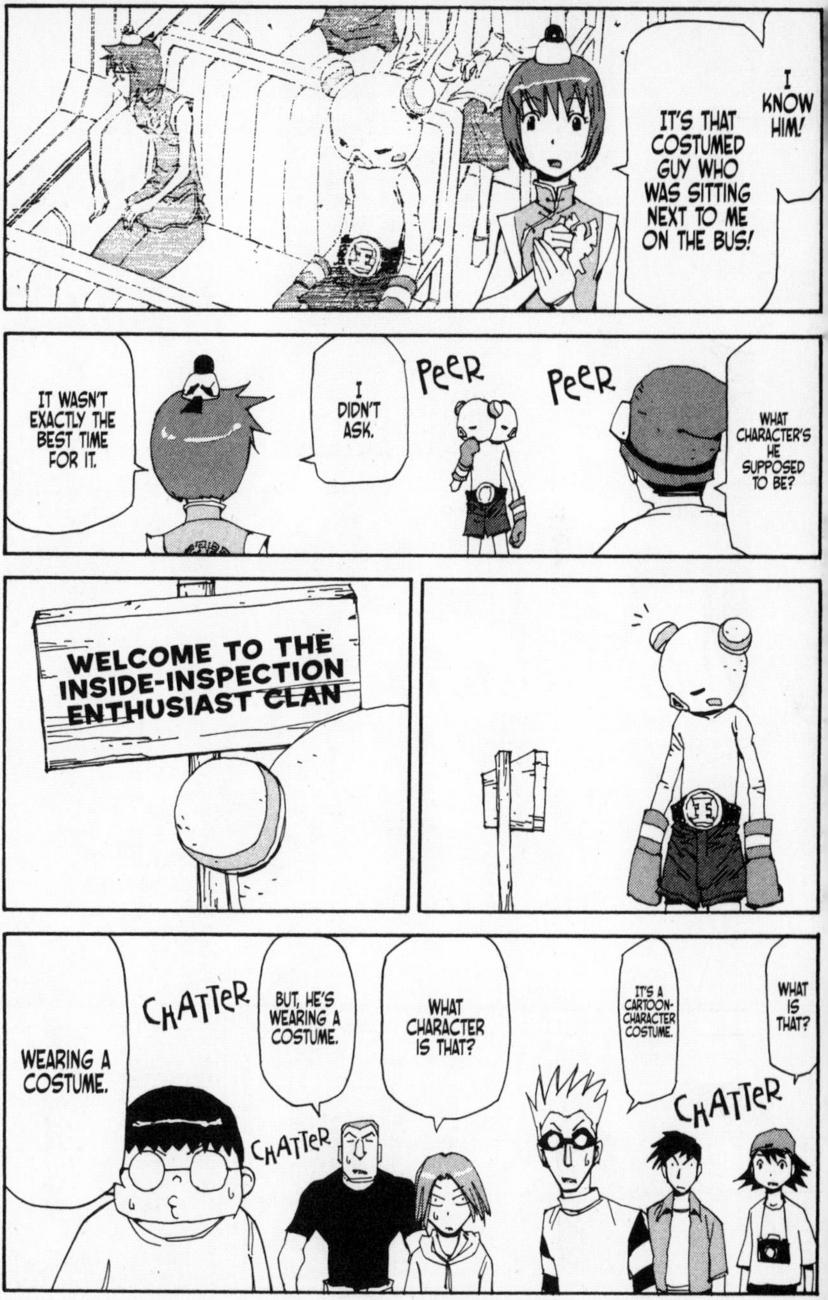
I KNOW HIM!
IT'S THAT COSTUMED GUY WHO WAS SITTING NEXT TO ME ON THE BUS!
WHAT CHARACTER'S HE SUPPOSED TO BE?
PEER
PEER
I DIDN'T ASK.
IT WASN'T EXACTLY THE BEST TIME FOR IT.
WELCOME TO THE INSIDE-INSPECTION ENTHUSIAST CLAN
WHAT IS THAT?
IT'S A CARTOON-CHARACTER COSTUME.
CHATTER
WHAT CHARACTER IS THAT?
BUT, HE'S WEARING A COSTUME.
CHATTER
CHATTER
WEARING A COSTUME.

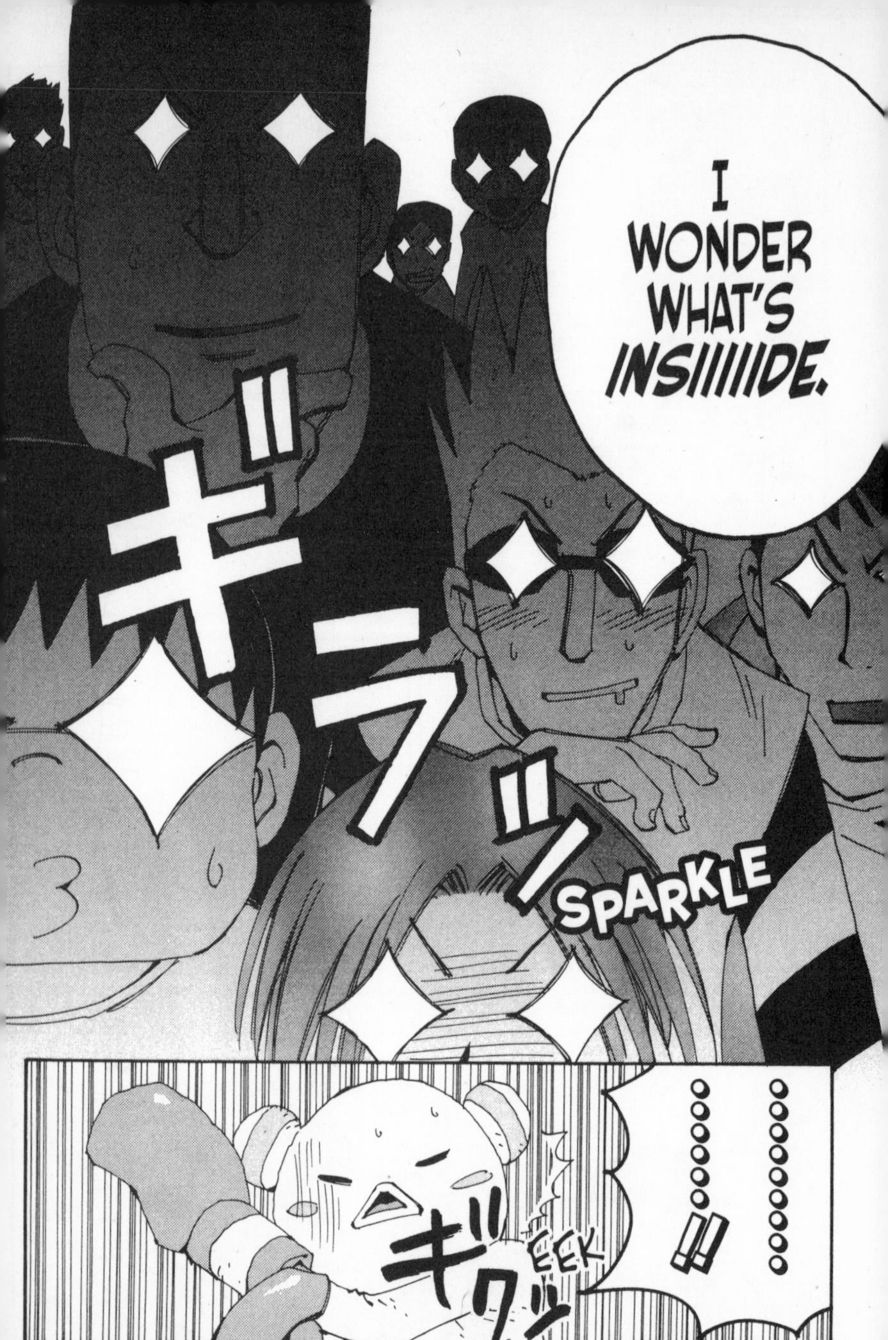
I WONDER WHAT'S INSIIIIIDE.
SPARKLE
OOOOOOOOOO
OOOOOOOO!!
EEK

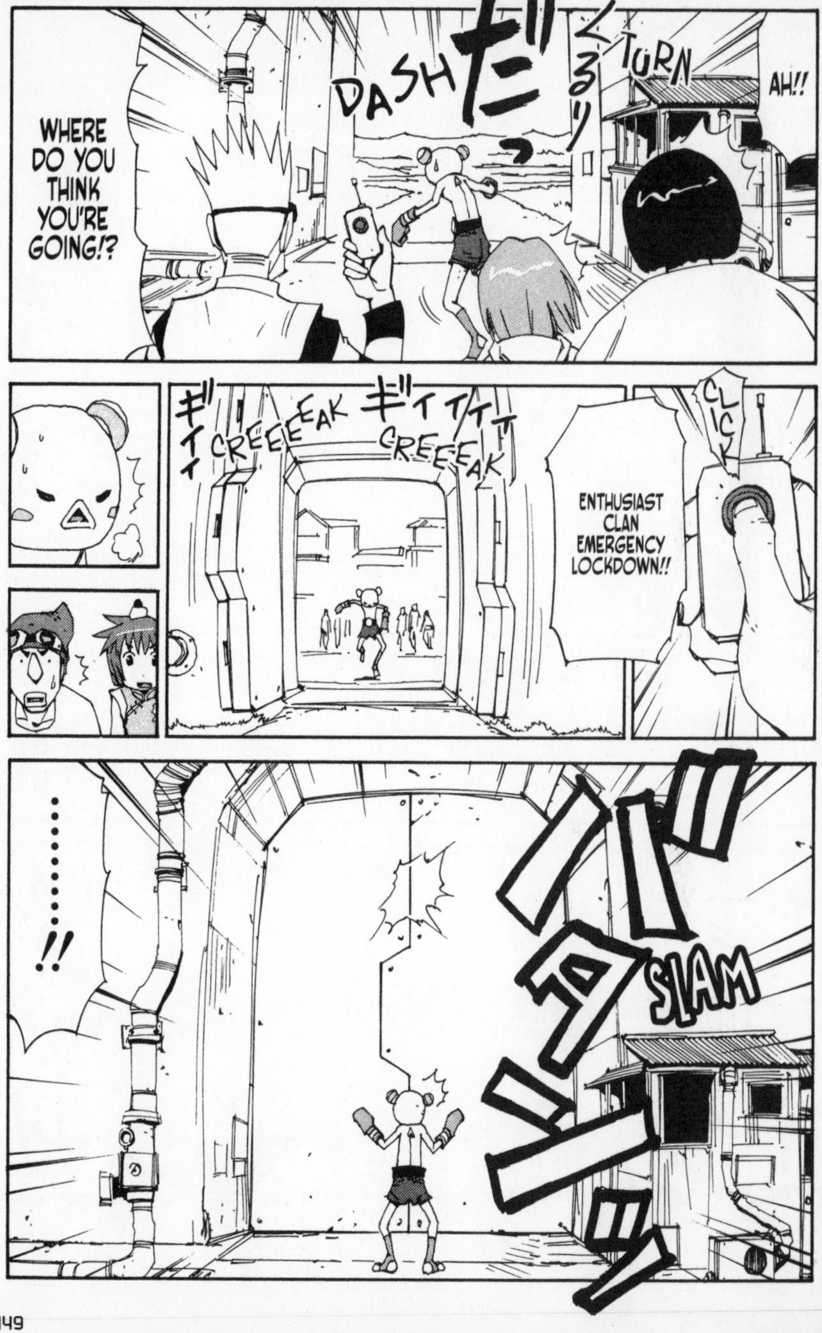

AH!!
くるり
TURN
だっ
DASH
WHERE DO YOU THINK YOU'RE GOING!?
CLICK
ENTHUSIAST CLAN EMERGENCY LOCKDOWN!!
ギィィ
CREEEEAK
ギィィィィ
CREEEEAK
バタンッ
SLAM
......!!

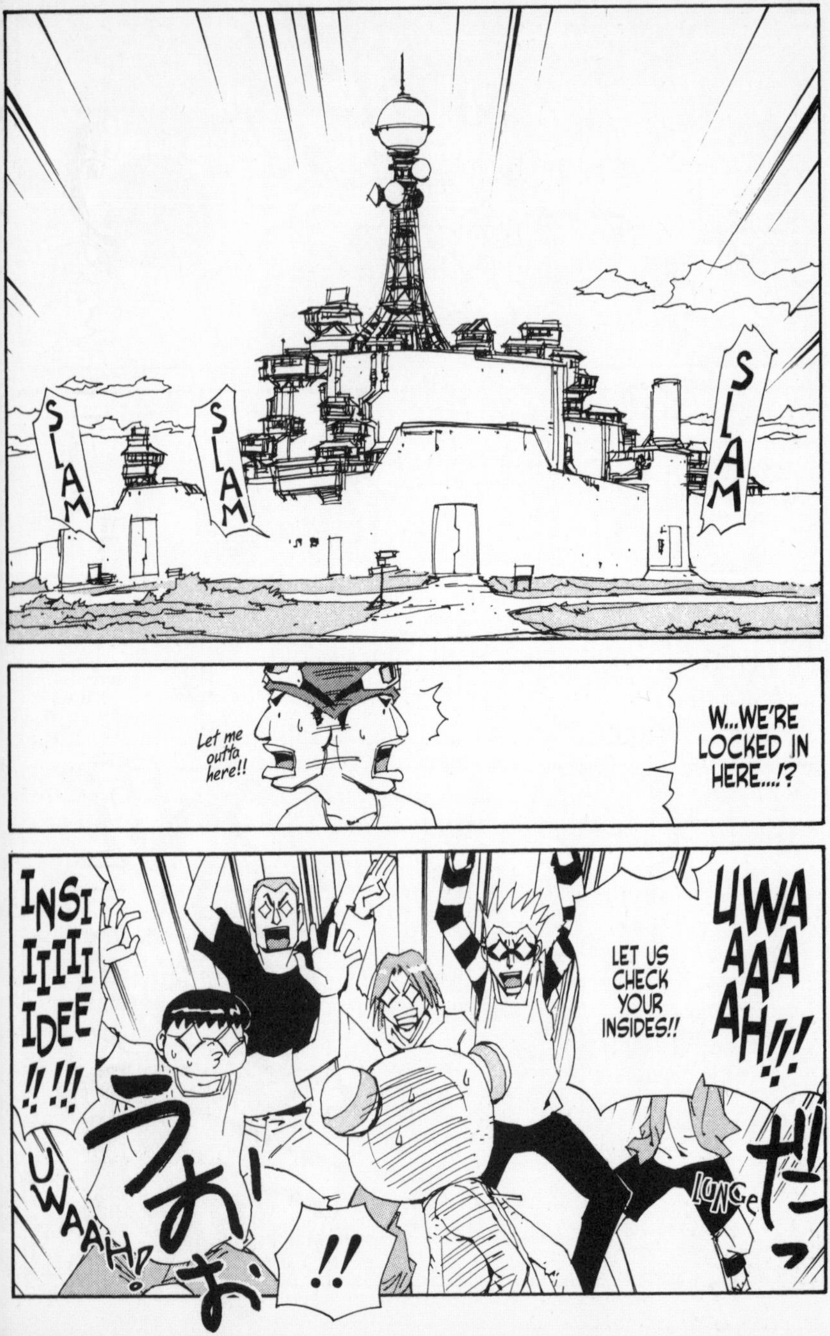
SLAM
SLAM
SLAM
W...WE'RE LOCKED IN HERE...!?
Let me outta here!!
UWAAAAAH!!!!
LET US CHECK YOUR INSIDES!!
だっ
LUNGE
INSIIIIIIDEE!!!!!
!!
うおお
UWAAAH!!

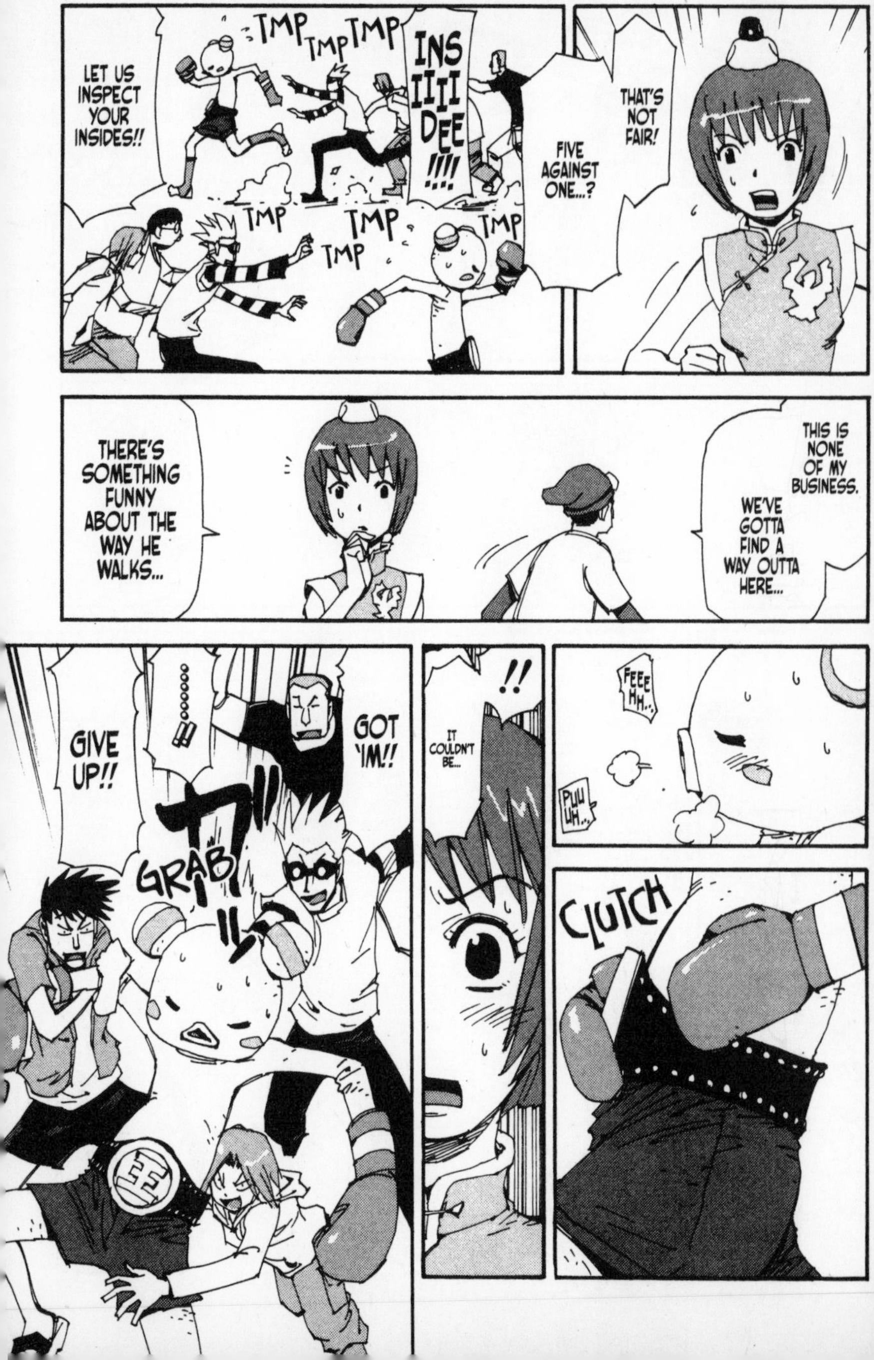
THAT'S NOT FAIR!
FIVE AGAINST ONE...?
INSIIIIDEE!!!!
TMP TMP TMP
LET US INSPECT YOUR INSIDES!!
TMP
TMP
TMP
TMP
THIS IS NONE OF MY BUSINESS.
WE'VE GOTTA FIND A WAY OUTTA HERE...
THERE'S SOMETHING FUNNY ABOUT THE WAY HE WALKS...
FEEEHH...
PUUUH...
CLUTCH
!!
IT COULDN'T BE...
GOT 'IM!!
.......!!
GIVE UP!!
GRAB

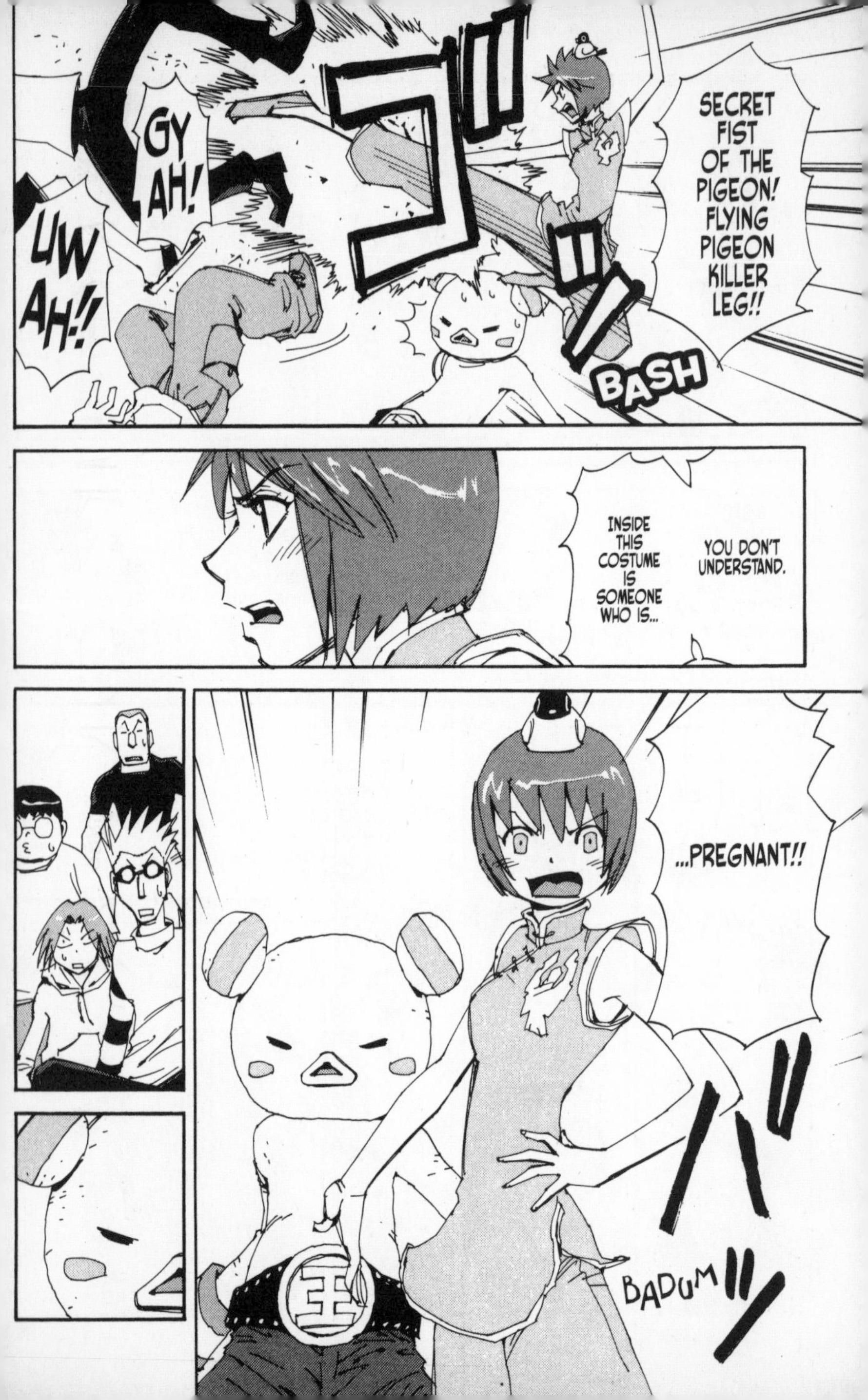
SECRET FIST OF THE PIGEON! FLYING PIGEON KILLER LEG!!
GYAH!
UWAH!!
BASH
YOU DON'T UNDERSTAND.
INSIDE THIS COSTUME IS SOMEONE WHO IS...
...PREGNANT!!
BADUM

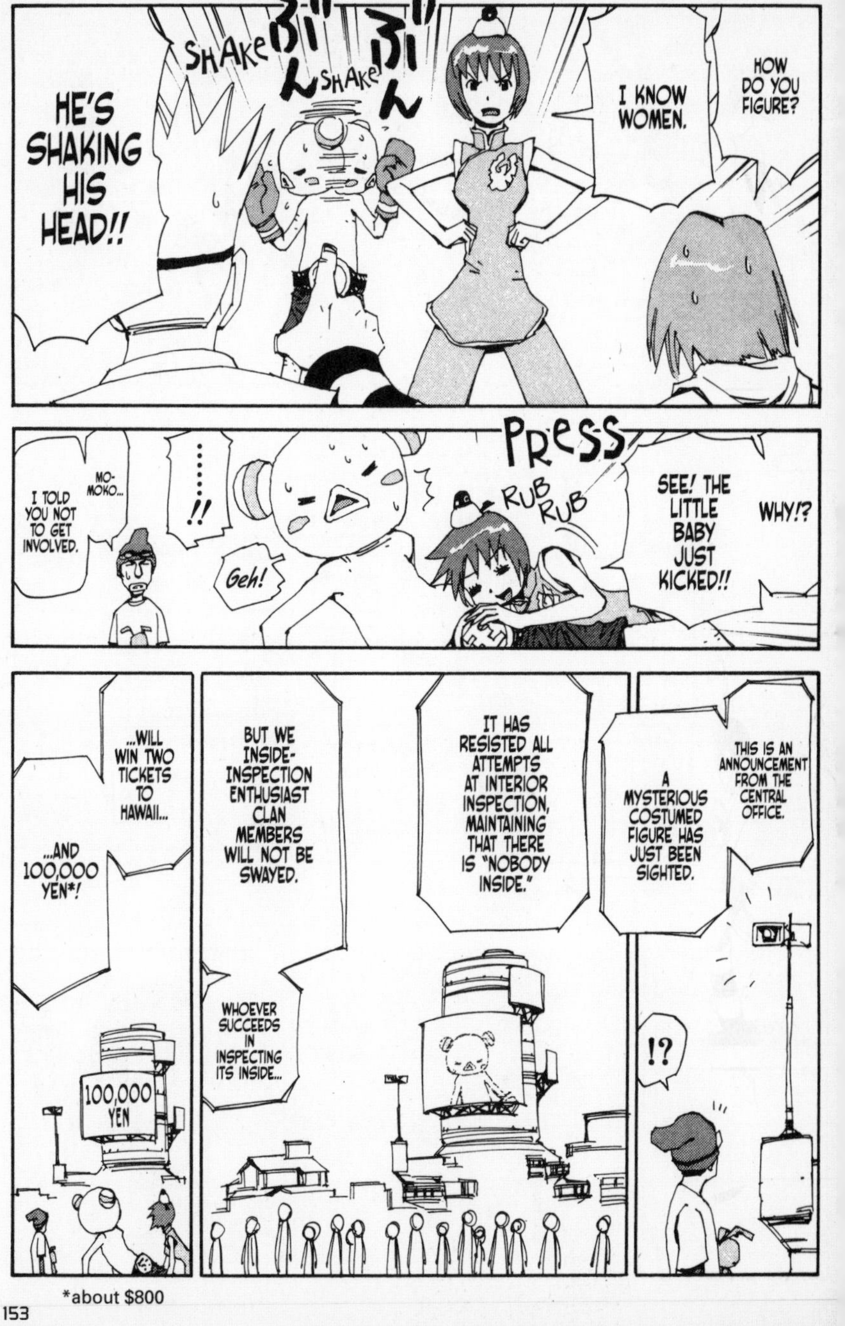
HOW DO YOU FIGURE?
I KNOW WOMEN.
SHAKE ぶん SHAKE ぶん
HE'S SHAKING HIS HEAD!!
WHY!?
SEE! THE LITTLE BABY JUST KICKED!!
PRESS
RUB RUB
Geh!
......!!
MO-MOKO...
I TOLD YOU NOT TO GET INVOLVED.
THIS IS AN ANNOUNCEMENT FROM THE CENTRAL OFFICE.
A MYSTERIOUS COSTUMED FIGURE HAS JUST BEEN SIGHTED.
!?
IT HAS RESISTED ALL ATTEMPTS AT INTERIOR INSPECTION, MAINTAINING THAT THERE IS "NOBODY INSIDE."
BUT WE INSIDE-INSPECTION ENTHUSIAST CLAN MEMBERS WILL NOT BE SWAYED.
WHOEVER SUCCEEDS IN INSPECTING ITS INSIDE...
...WILL WIN TWO TICKETS TO HAWAII...
...AND 100,000 YEN*!
100,000 YEN

*about $800

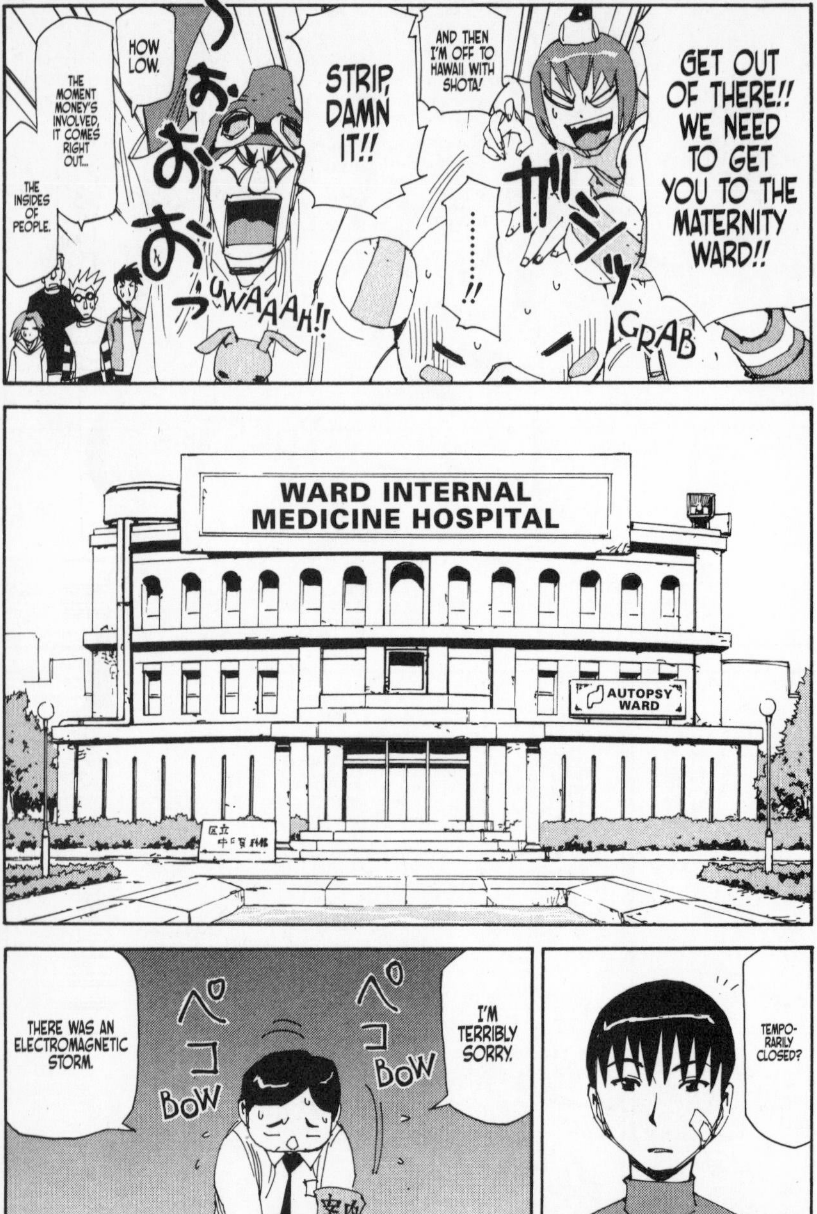
GET OUT OF THERE!! WE NEED TO GET YOU TO THE MATERNITY WARD!!
ガシッ
GRAB
AND THEN I'M OFF TO HAWAII WITH SHOTA!
......!!
STRIP, DAMN IT!!
うぉぉぉっ
UWAAAAH!!
HOW LOW.
THE MOMENT MONEY'S INVOLVED, IT COMES RIGHT OUT...
THE INSIDES OF PEOPLE.
WARD INTERNAL MEDICINE HOSPITAL
AUTOPSY WARD
TEMPO-RARILY CLOSED?
I'M TERRIBLY SORRY.
ペコ
BOW
ペコ
BOW
案内
THERE WAS AN ELECTROMAGNETIC STORM.

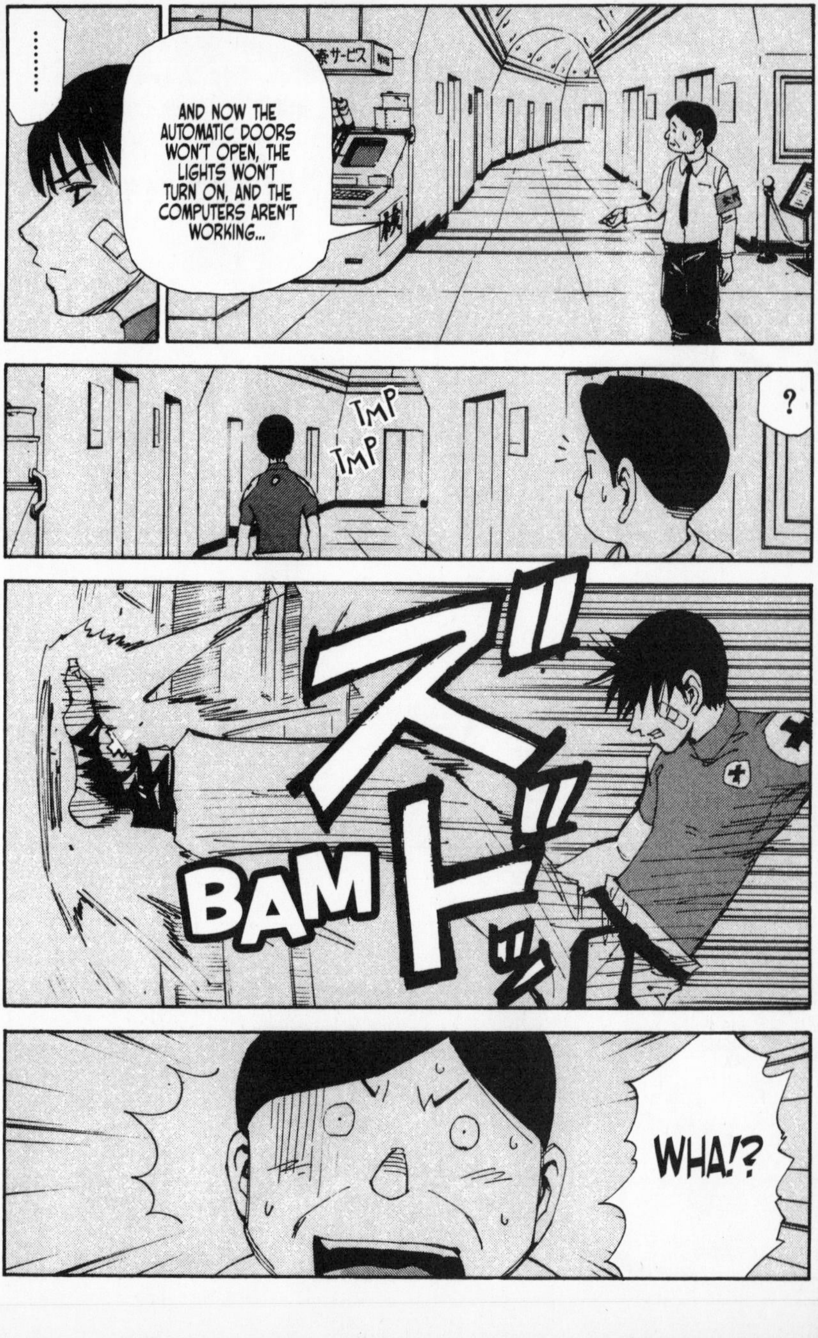
AND NOW THE AUTOMATIC DOORS WON'T OPEN, THE LIGHTS WON'T TURN ON, AND THE COMPUTERS AREN'T WORKING...
......
?
TMP
TMP
ズ
ドッ
BAM
WHA!?

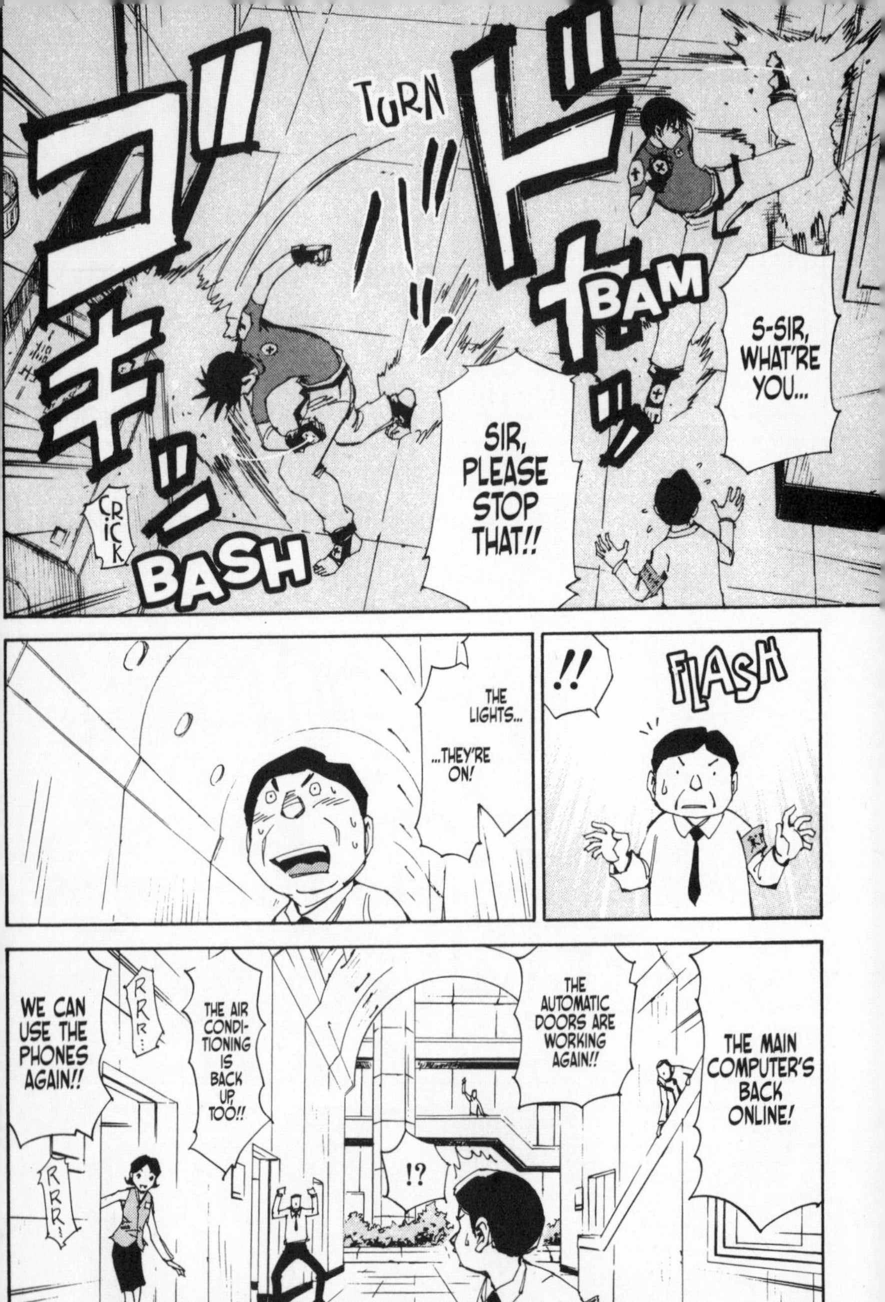
S-SIR, WHAT'RE YOU...
BAM
TURN
SIR, PLEASE STOP THAT!!
BASH
CRICK
FLASH
!!
THE LIGHTS...
...THEY'RE ON!
THE MAIN COMPUTER'S BACK ONLINE!
THE AUTOMATIC DOORS ARE WORKING AGAIN!!
!?
THE AIR CONDI-TIONING IS BACK UP, TOO!!
RRR...
WE CAN USE THE PHONES AGAIN!!
RRR...

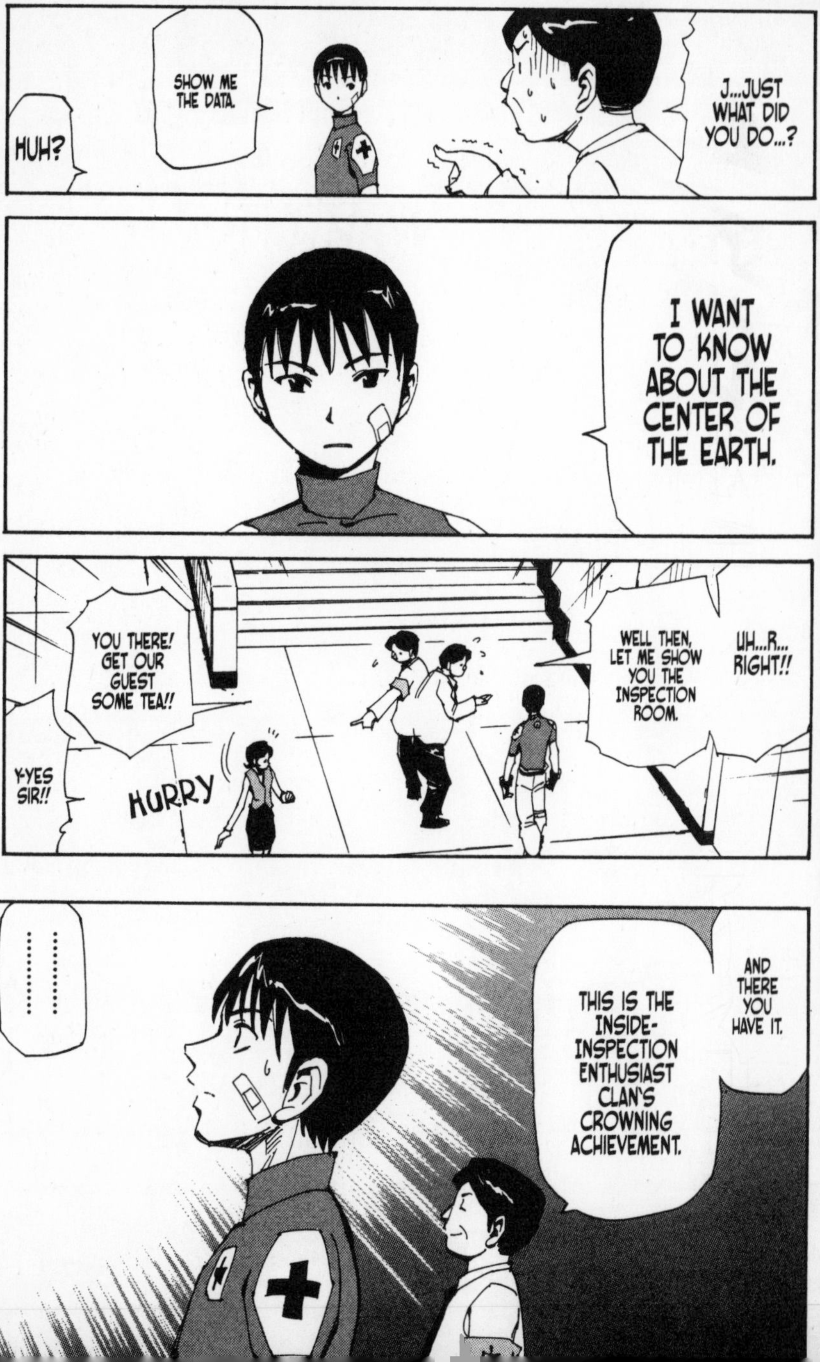
J...JUST WHAT DID YOU DO...?
SHOW ME THE DATA.
HUH?
I WANT TO KNOW ABOUT THE CENTER OF THE EARTH.
UH...R... RIGHT!!
WELL THEN, LET ME SHOW YOU THE INSPECTION ROOM.
YOU THERE! GET OUR GUEST SOME TEA!!
HURRY
Y-YES SIR!!
AND THERE YOU HAVE IT.
THIS IS THE INSIDE-INSPECTION ENTHUSIAST CLAN'S CROWNING ACHIEVEMENT.
....
....

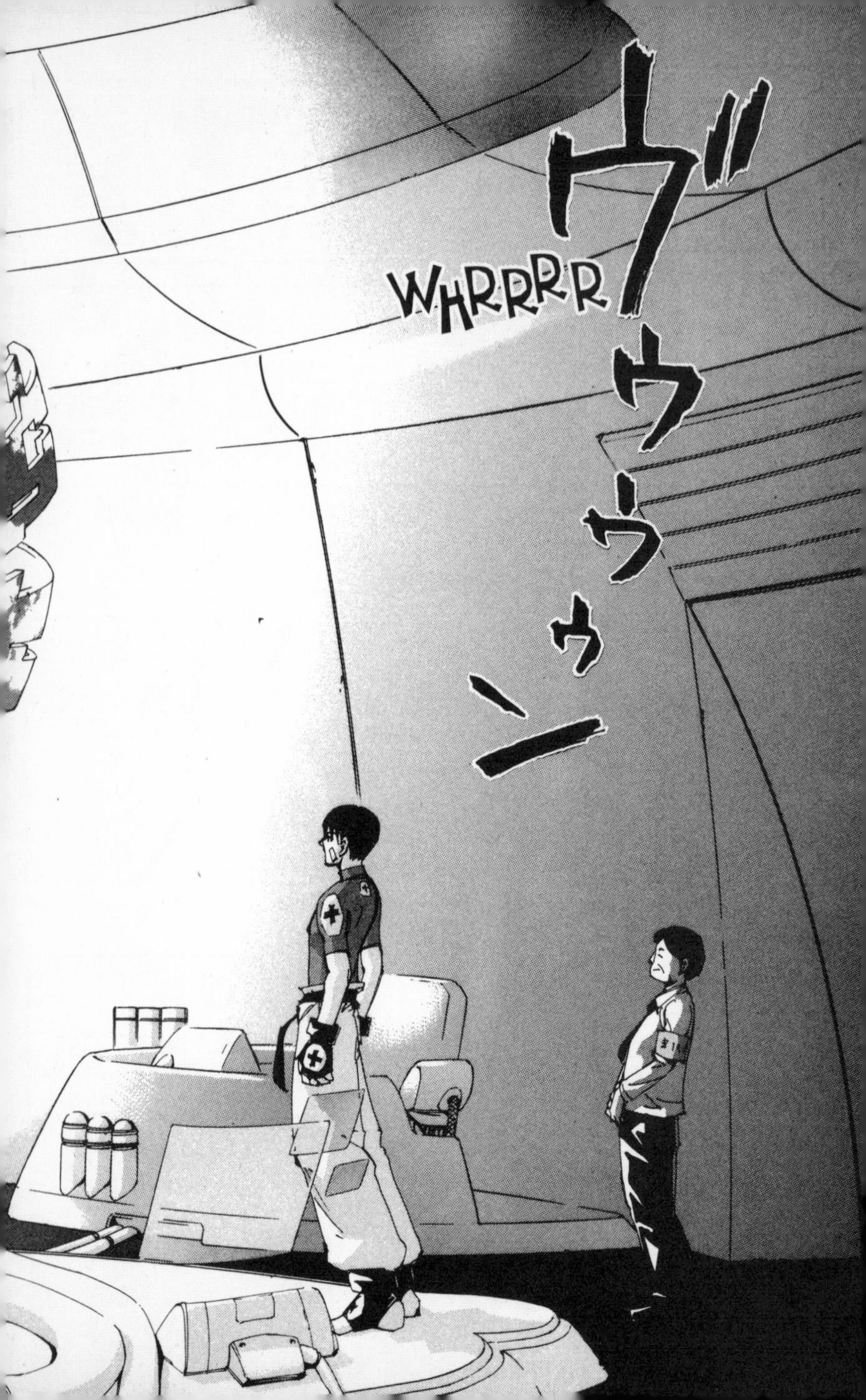

ヴヴゥゥゥーン
WHRRRR

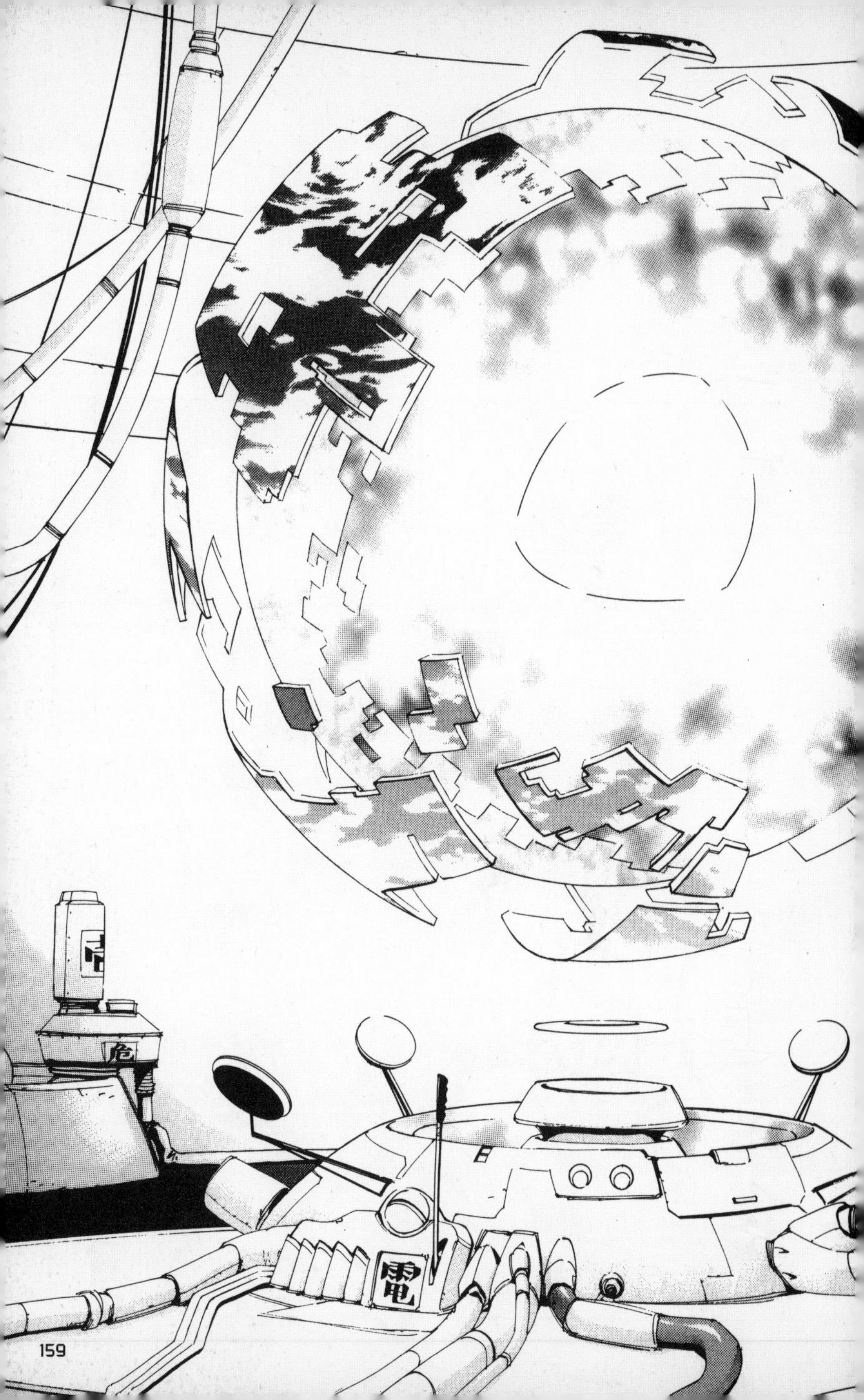
危
電

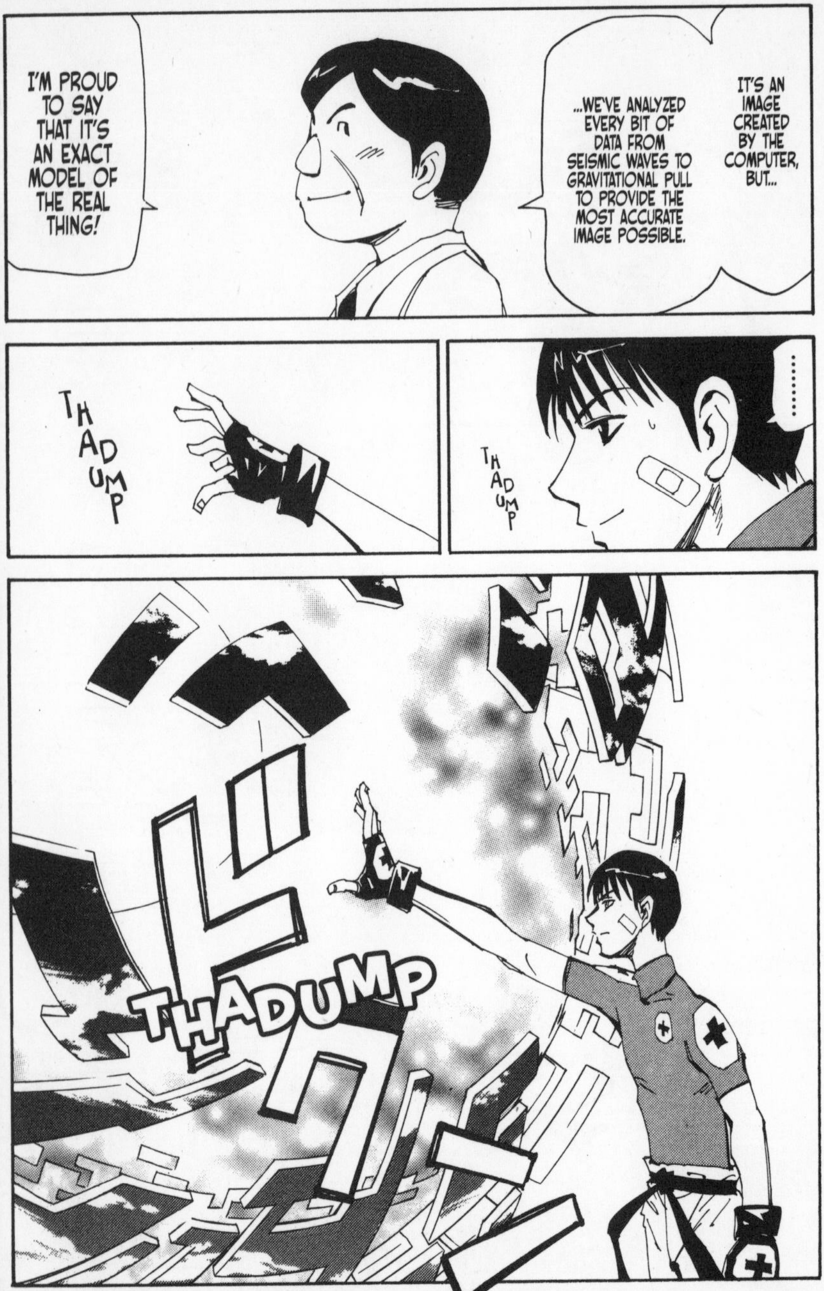
IT'S AN IMAGE CREATED BY THE COMPUTER, BUT...
...WE'VE ANALYZED EVERY BIT OF DATA FROM SEISMIC WAVES TO GRAVITATIONAL PULL TO PROVIDE THE MOST ACCURATE IMAGE POSSIBLE.
I'M PROUD TO SAY THAT IT'S AN EXACT MODEL OF THE REAL THING!
......
THADUMP
THADUMP
THADUMP

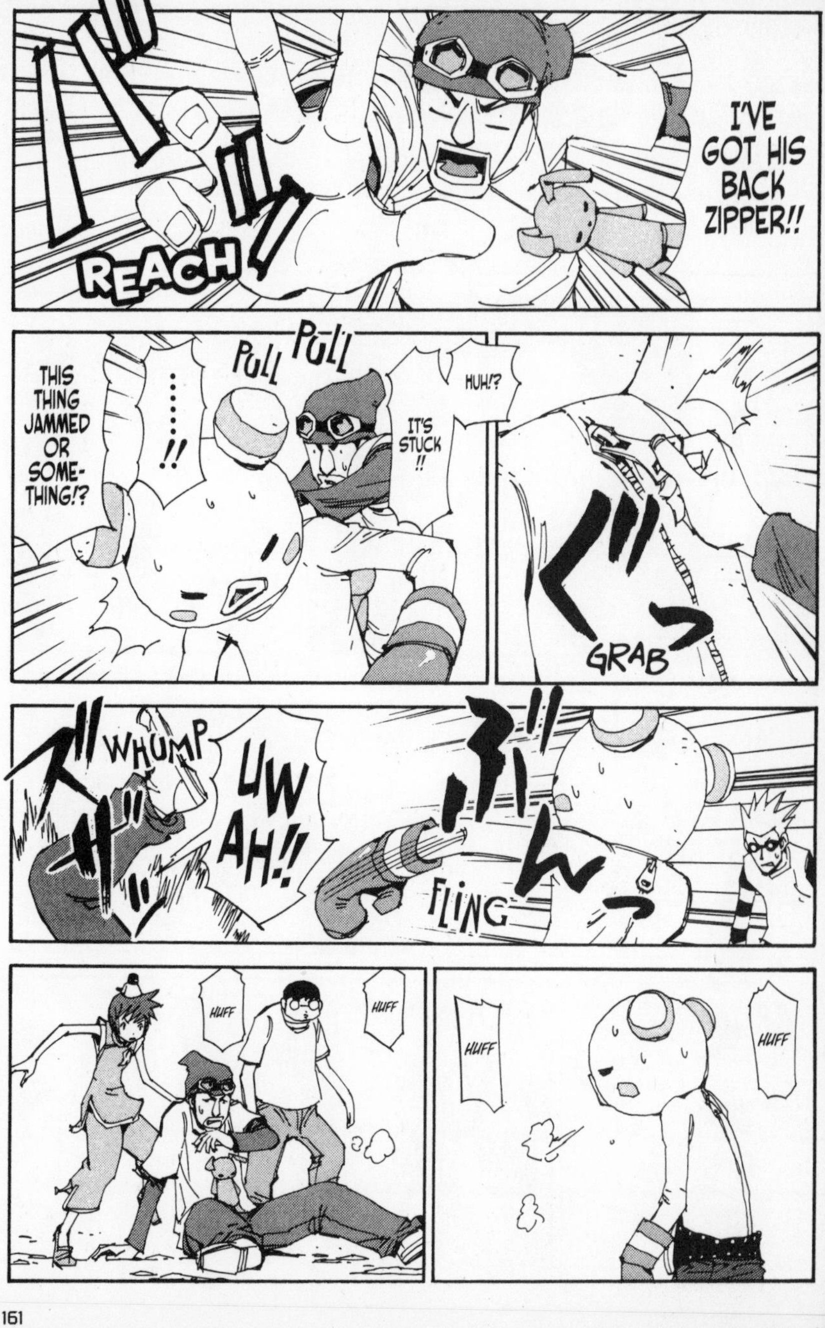
I'VE GOT HIS BACK ZIPPER!!
REACH
GRAB
HUH!?
IT'S STUCK!!
PULL PULL
......!!
THIS THING JAMMED OR SOME-THING!?
FLING
UWAH!!
WHUMP
HUFF
HUFF
HUFF
HUFF

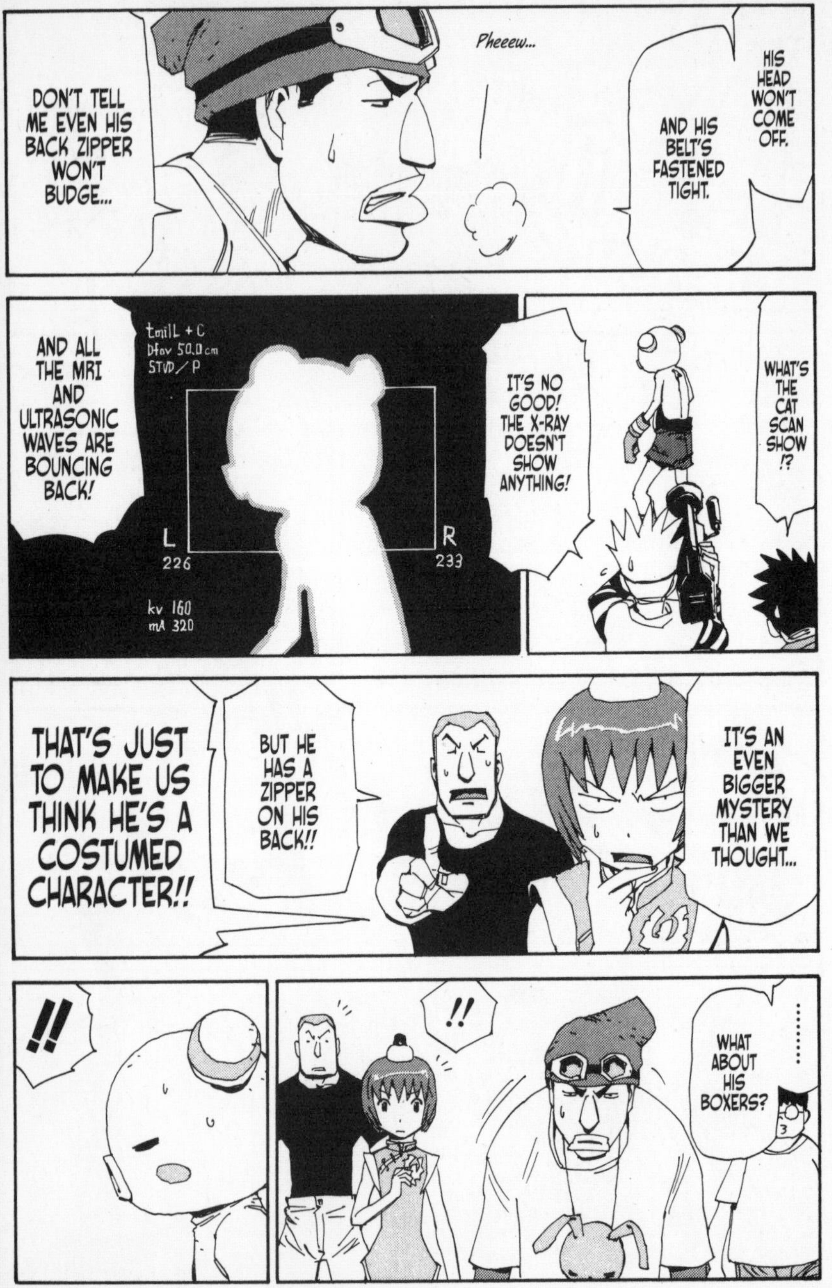
HIS HEAD WON'T COME OFF.
AND HIS BELT'S FASTENED TIGHT.
Pheeew...
DON'T TELL ME EVEN HIS BACK ZIPPER WON'T BUDGE...
WHAT'S THE CAT SCAN SHOW!?
IT'S NO GOOD! THE X-RAY DOESN'T SHOW ANYTHING!
tmilL + C
Dfov 50.0cm
STVD / P
L
226
R
233
kv 160
mA 320
AND ALL THE MRI AND ULTRASONIC WAVES ARE BOUNCING BACK!
IT'S AN EVEN BIGGER MYSTERY THAN WE THOUGHT...
BUT HE HAS A ZIPPER ON HIS BACK!!
THAT'S JUST TO MAKE US THINK HE'S A COSTUMED CHARACTER!!
......
WHAT ABOUT HIS BOXERS?
!!
!!

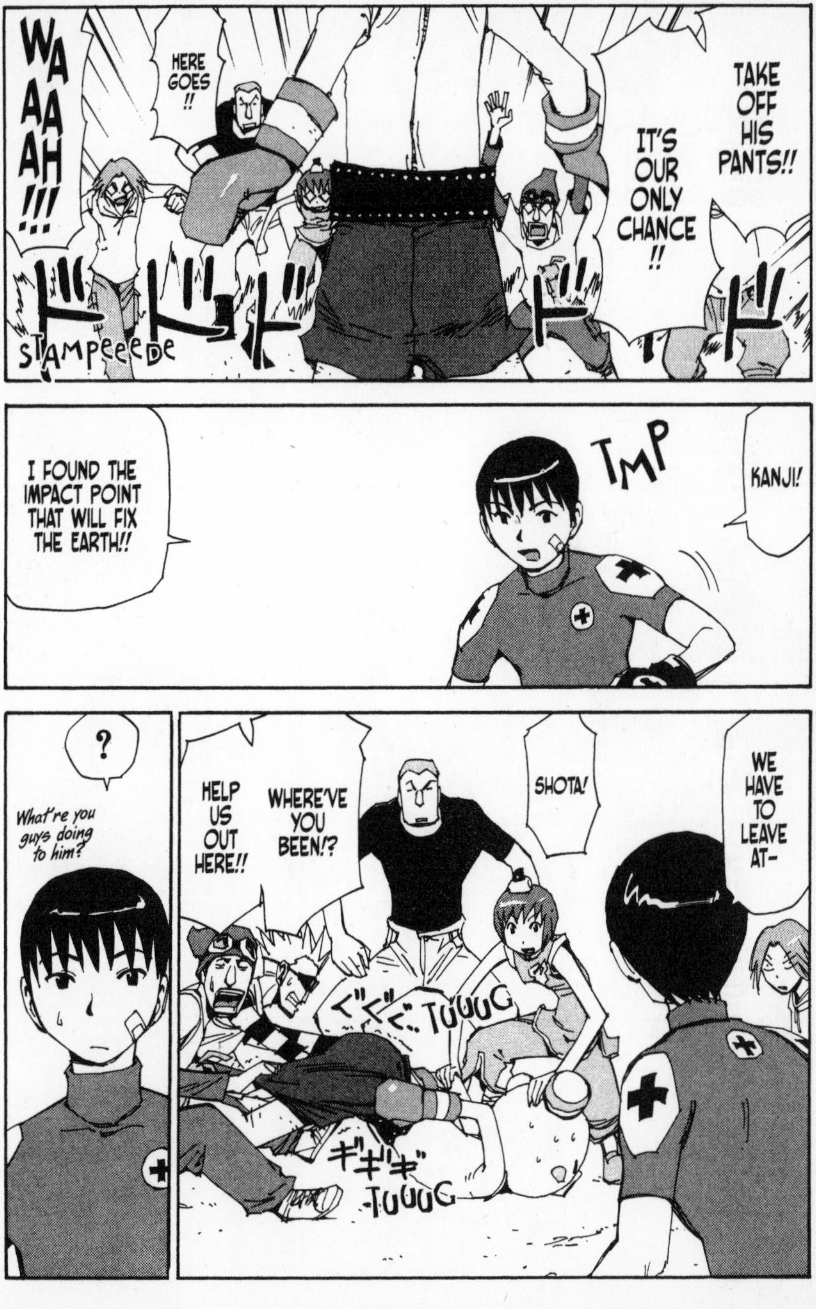
TAKE OFF HIS PANTS!!
IT'S OUR ONLY CHANCE!!
HERE GOES!!
WAAAAH!!!
ドドドド
STAMPEEEDE
KANJI!
TMP
I FOUND THE IMPACT POINT THAT WILL FIX THE EARTH!!
WE HAVE TO LEAVE AT-
SHOTA!
WHERE'VE YOU BEEN!?
HELP US OUT HERE!!
ぐぐぐ.. TUUUG
ギギギ TUUUG
?
What're you guys doing to him?

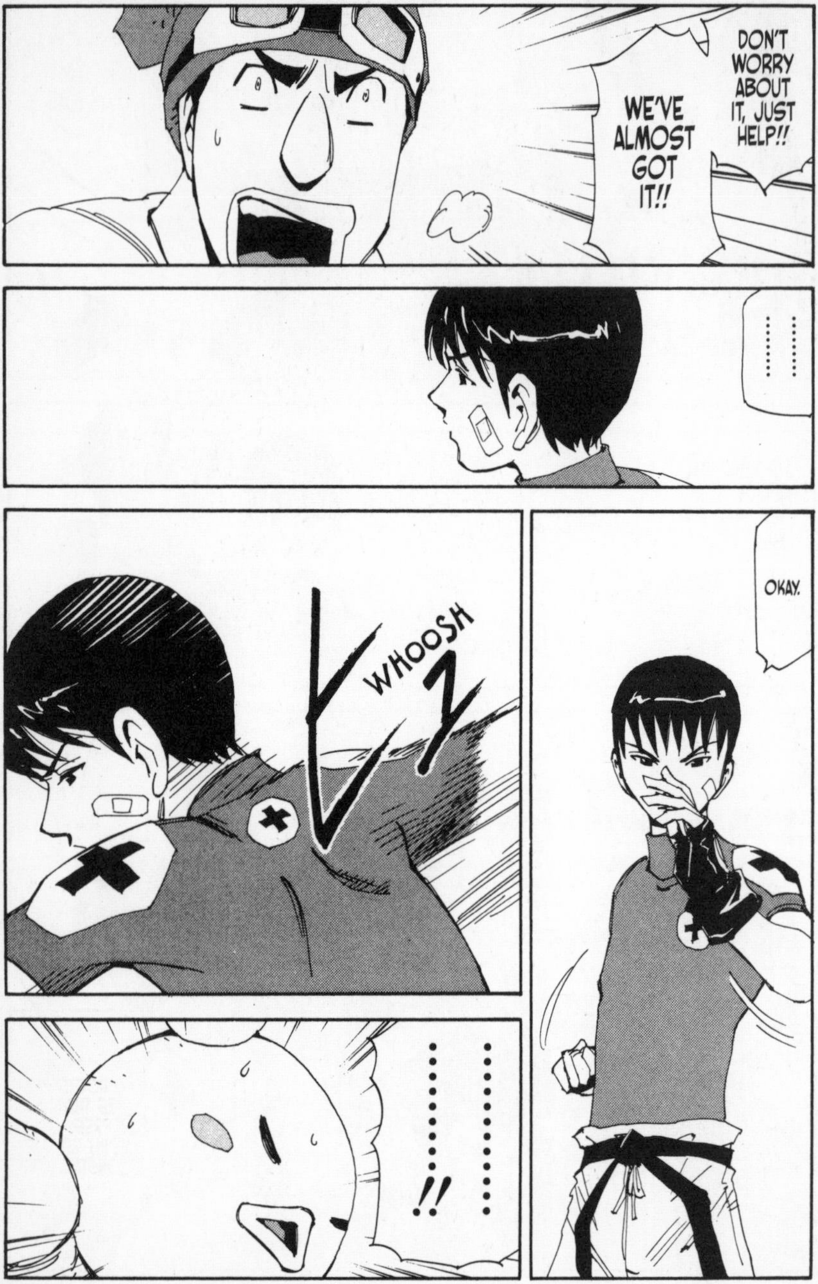
DON'T WORRY ABOUT IT, JUST HELP!!
WE'VE ALMOST GOT IT!!
......
OKAY.
WHOOSH
......
......!!

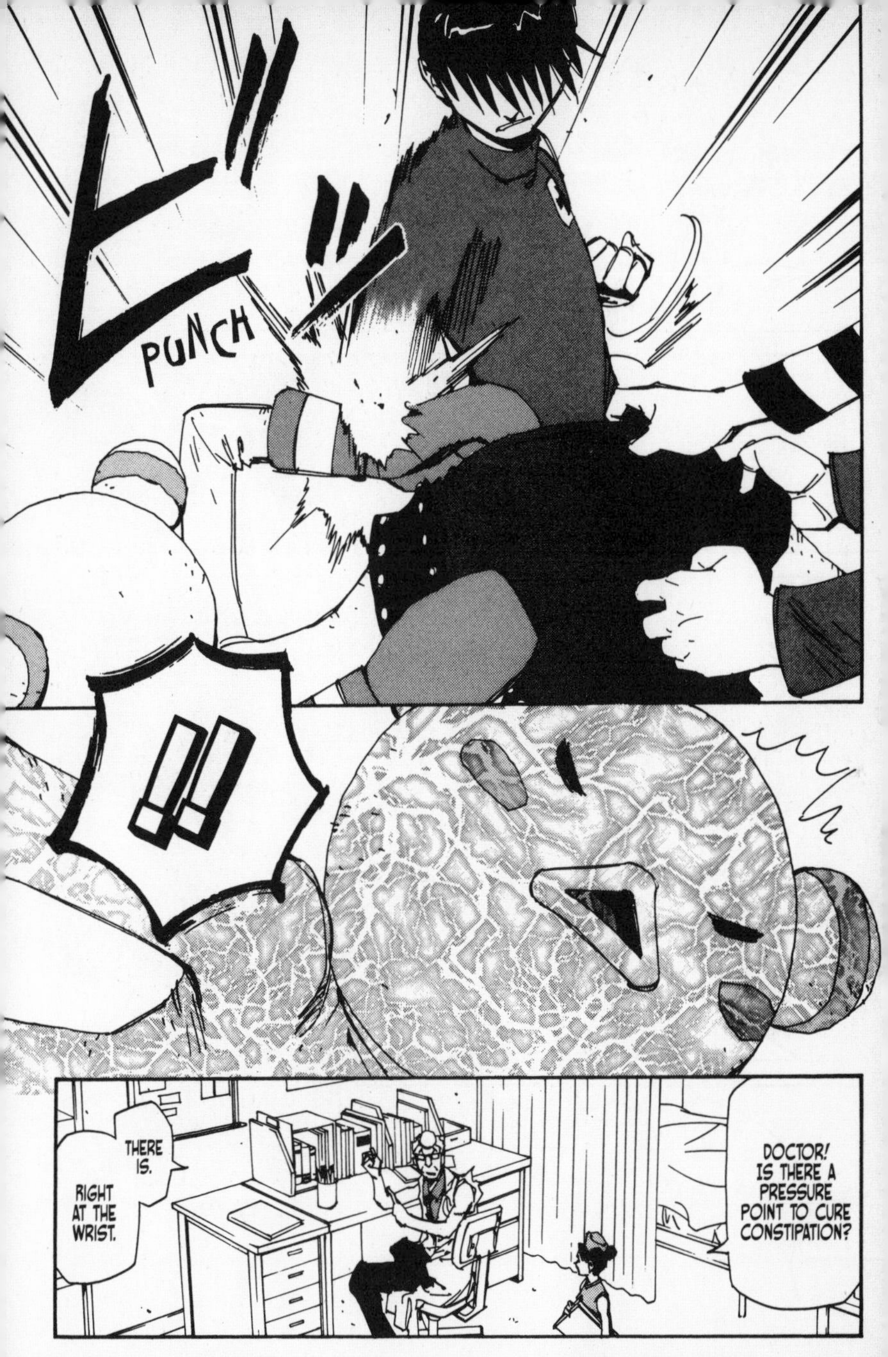
ド
PUNCH
!!
DOCTOR! IS THERE A PRESSURE POINT TO CURE CONSTIPATION?
THERE IS.
RIGHT AT THE WRIST.

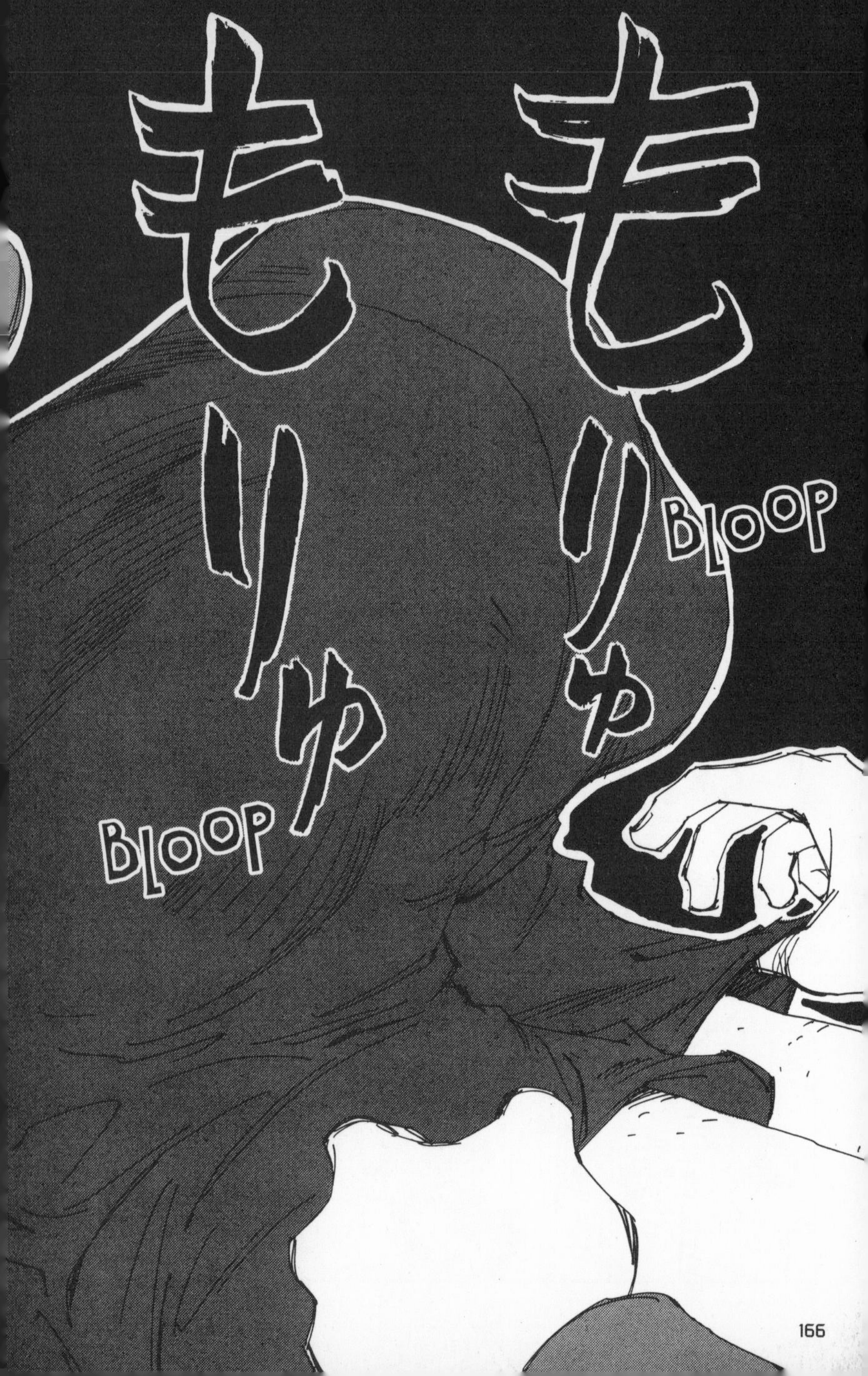
もりゅ
BLOOP
もりゅ
BLOOP

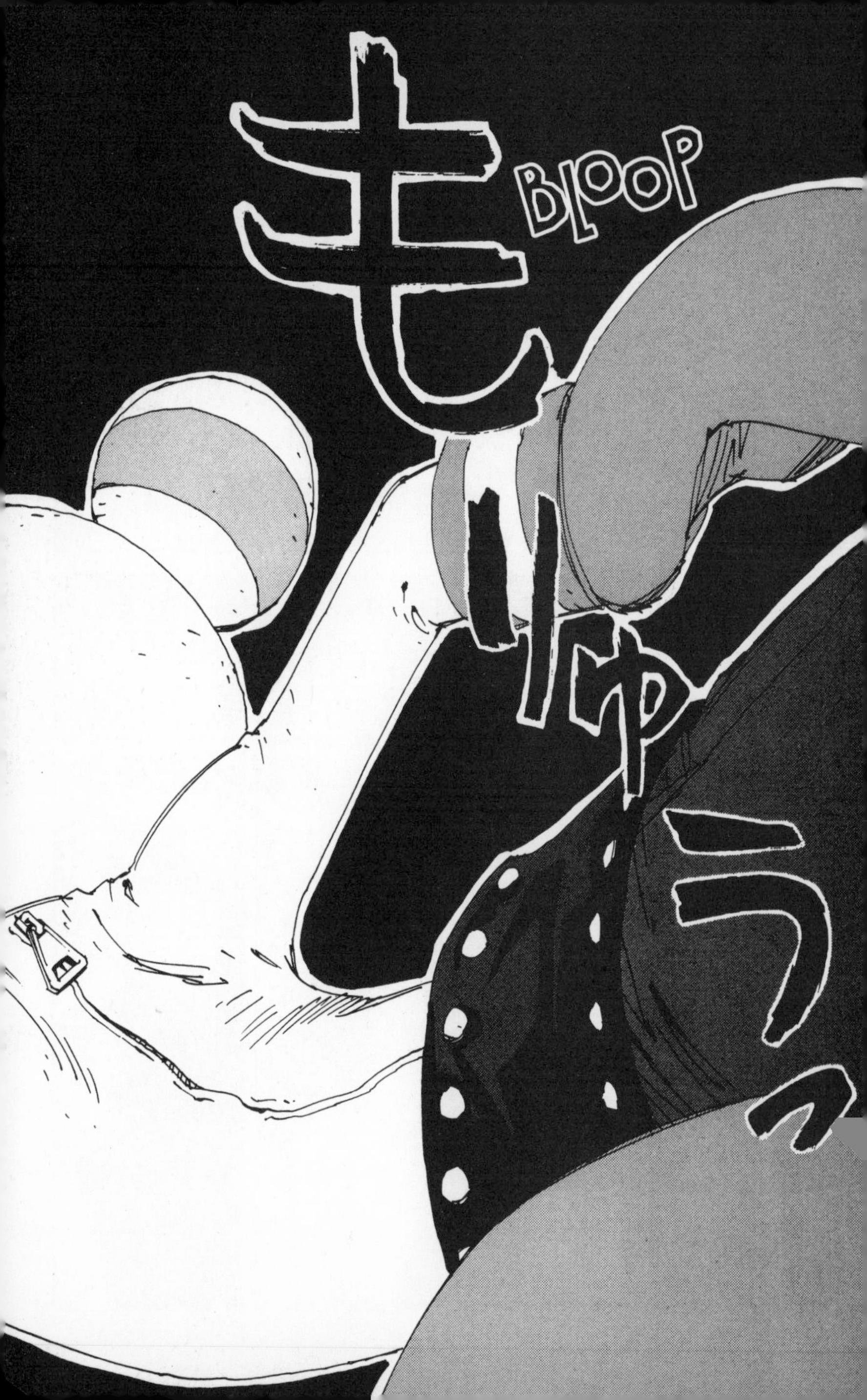
もにゅううん
BLOOP

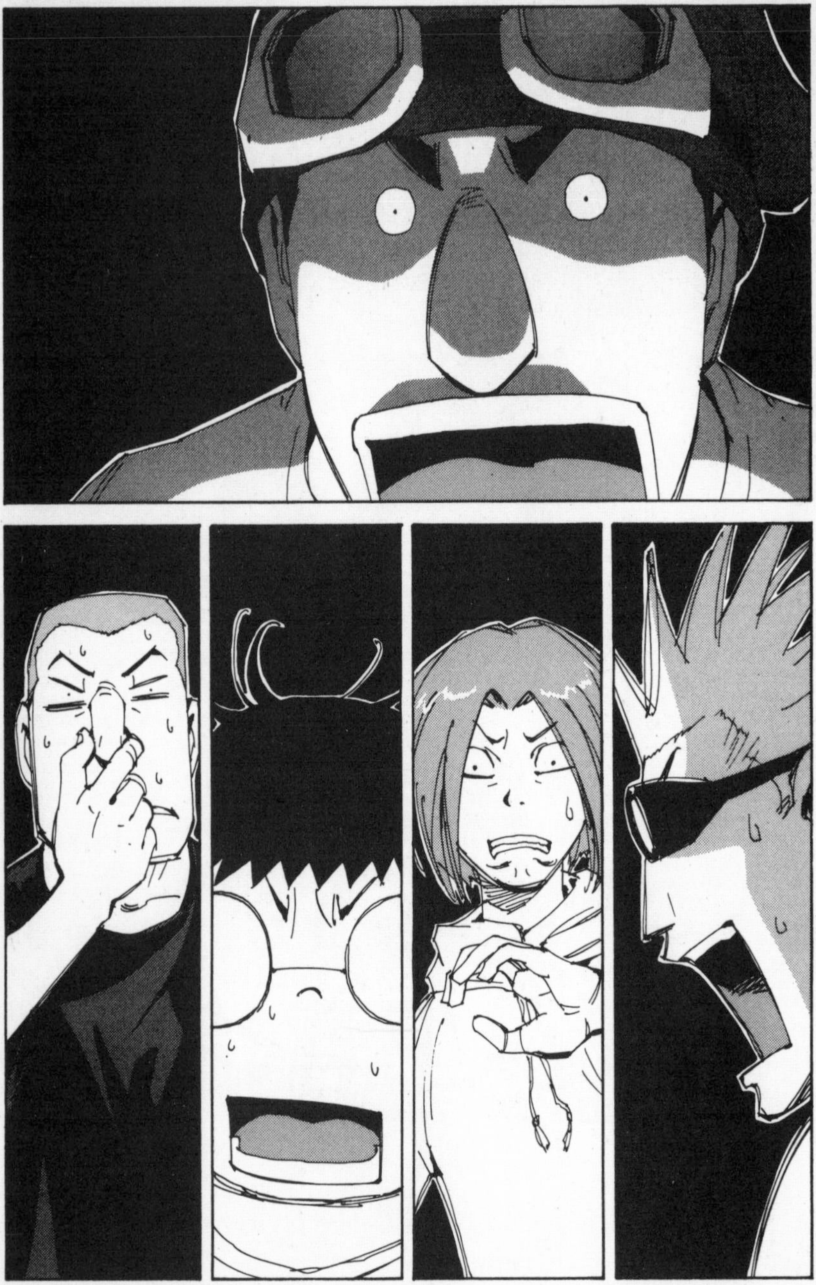

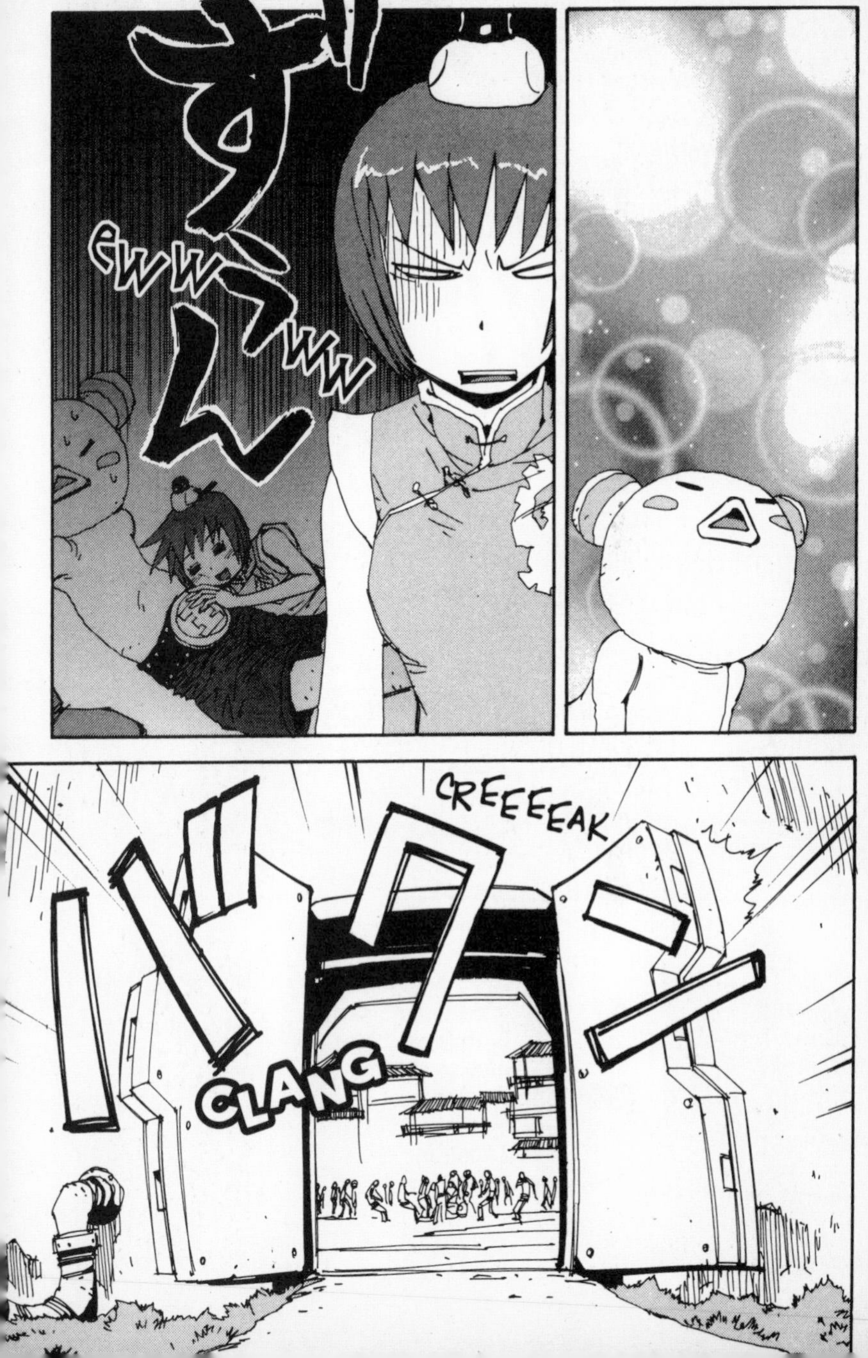
EWWWWW
CREEEEEAK
CLANG

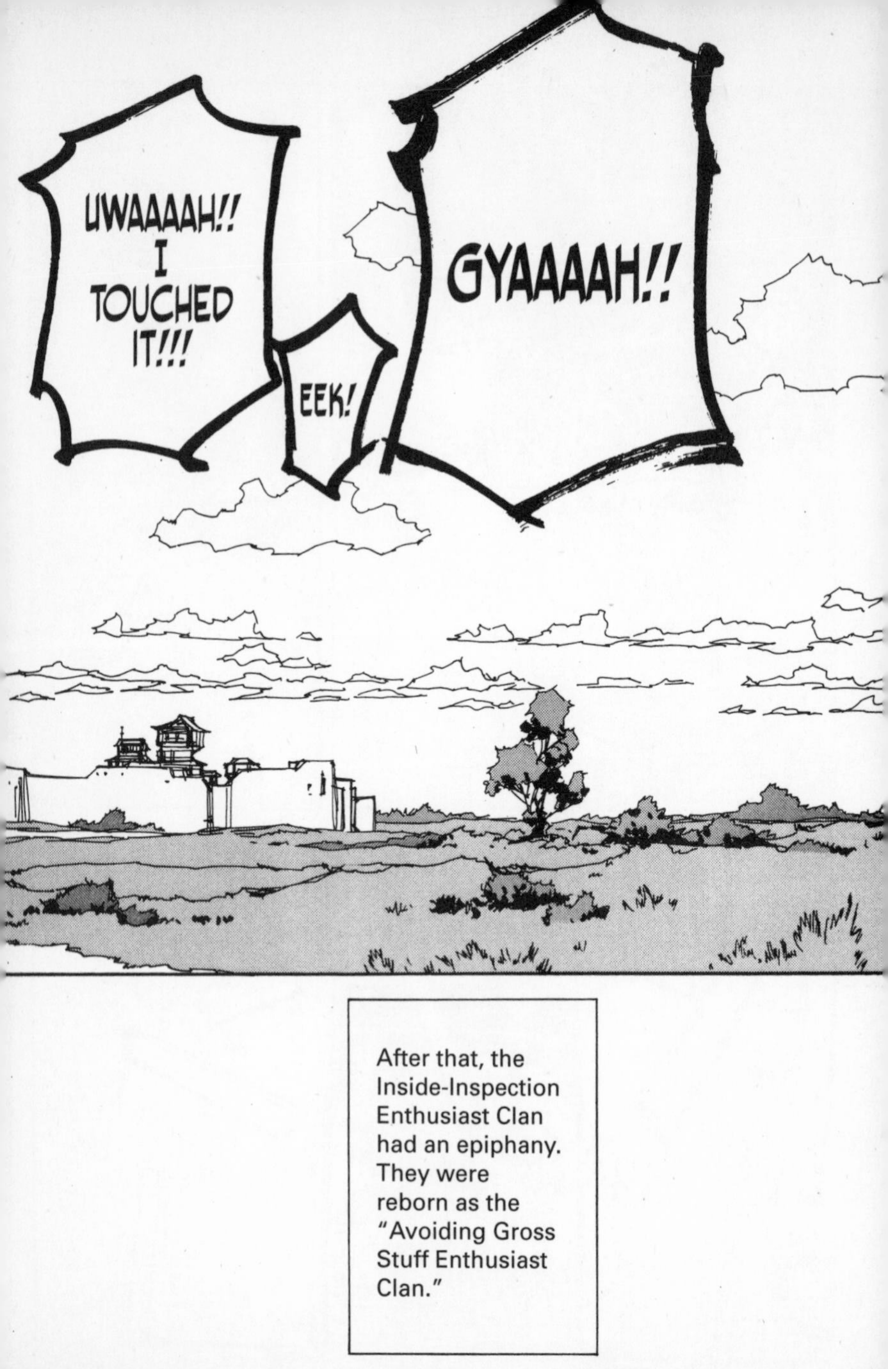
GYAAAAH!!
EEK!
UWAAAAH!! I TOUCHED IT!!!
After that, the Inside-Inspection Enthusiast Clan had an epiphany. They were reborn as the "Avoiding Gross Stuff Enthusiast Clan."

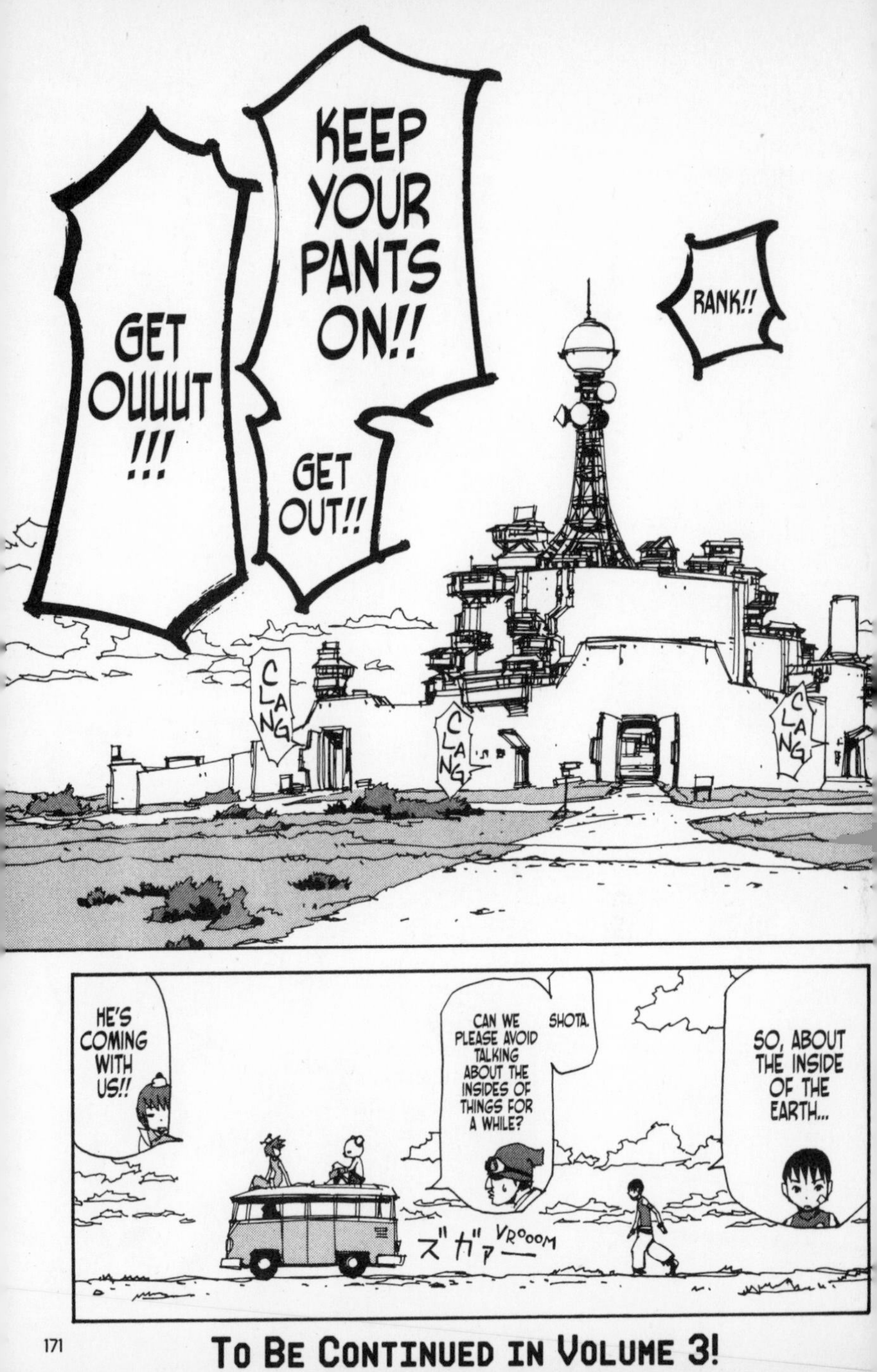
RANK!!
KEEP YOUR PANTS ON!!
GET OUT!!
GET OUUUT!!!
CLANG
CLANG
CLANG
SO, ABOUT THE INSIDE OF THE EARTH...
SHOTA.
CAN WE PLEASE AVOID TALKING ABOUT THE INSIDES OF THINGS FOR A WHILE?
ズガァー
VROOOM
HE'S COMING WITH US!!

To Be Continued in Volume 3!

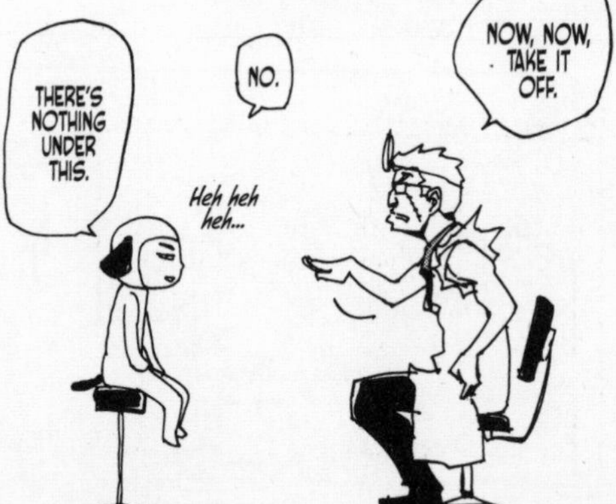
NOW, NOW, TAKE IT OFF.
NO.
THERE'S NOTHING UNDER THIS.
Heh heh heh...

End of Book Bonus Four-Panel Funnies

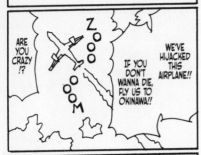

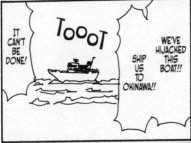

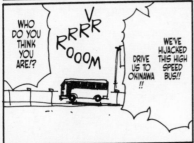

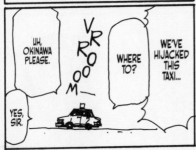

SYNTHESIZED PERFUME

What is Synthesized Perfume?

Four-Panel Funnies that I make for fun when I have free time.

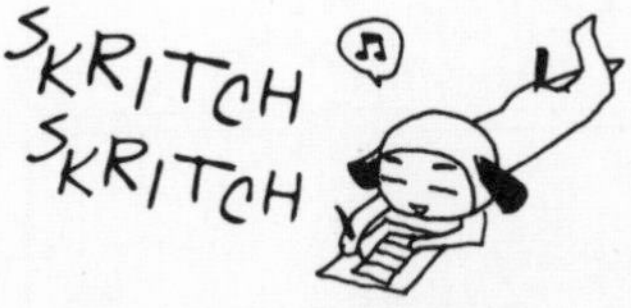

SKRITCH
SKRITCH

BY YU YAGAMI

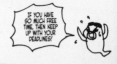

IF YOU HAVE SO MUCH FREE TIME, THEN KEEP UP WITH YOUR DEADLINES!

HIJACKING IS HARD
WE'VE HIJACKED THIS AIRPLANE!!
IF YOU DON'T WANNA DIE, FLY US TO OKINAWA!!
ZOOOOOOM
ARE YOU CRAZY!?
WE'VE HIJACKED THIS BOAT!!
SHIP US TO OKINAWA!!
TOOOT
IT CAN'T BE DONE!
WE'VE HIJACKED THIS HIGH SPEED BUS!!
DRIVE US TO OKINAWA!!
VRRRR ROOOM
WHO DO YOU THINK YOU ARE!?
WE'VE HIJACKED THIS TAXI...
WHERE TO?
VROOOM—
UH, OKINAWA PLEASE.
YES, SIR.

HOW TO BECOME A COW

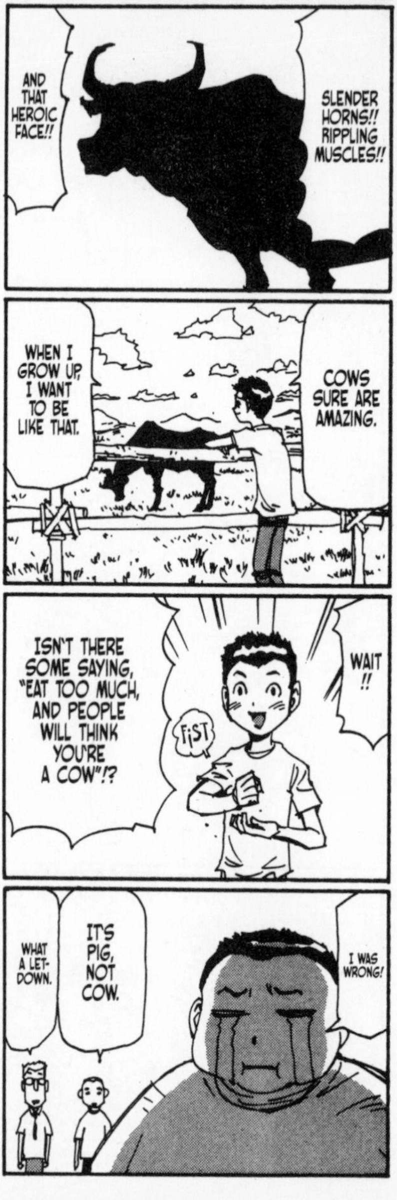
SLENDER HORNS!! RIPPLING MUSCLES!!
AND THAT HEROIC FACE!!
COWS SURE ARE AMAZING.
WHEN I GROW UP, I WANT TO BE LIKE THAT.
WAIT !!
FiST
ISN'T THERE SOME SAYING, "EAT TOO MUCH, AND PEOPLE WILL THINK YOU'RE A COW"!?
I WAS WRONG!
IT'S PIG, NOT COW.
WHAT A LET-DOWN.

WISH ON A STAR

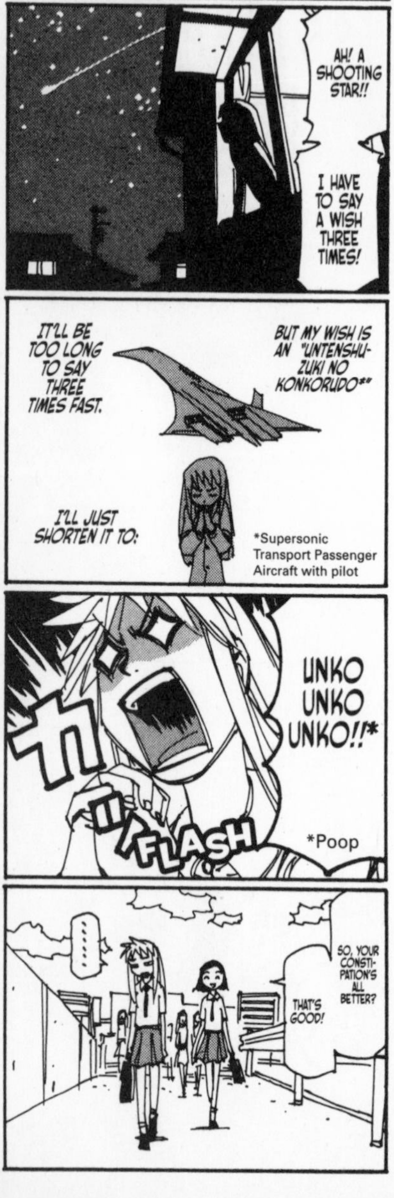
AH! A SHOOTING STAR!!
I HAVE TO SAY A WISH THREE TIMES!
BUT MY WISH IS AN "UNTENSHU-ZUKI NO KONKORUDO*"
IT'LL BE TOO LONG TO SAY THREE TIMES FAST.
I'LL JUST SHORTEN IT TO:
*Supersonic Transport Passenger Aircraft with pilot
UNKO UNKO UNKO!!*
FLASH
*Poop
SO, YOUR CONSTI-PATION'S ALL BETTER?
THAT'S GOOD!
......

SOCCER TERM

HAT TRICK → WHEN A PLAYER SCORES THREE POINTS IN A SINGLE GAME

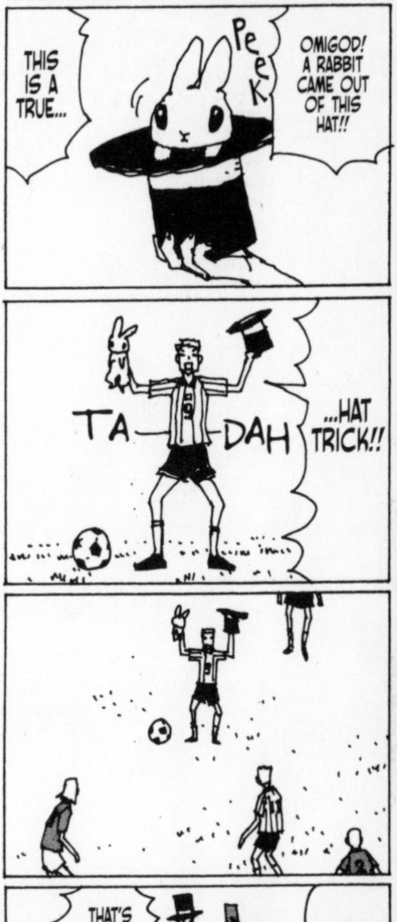
OMIGOD! A RABBIT CAME OUT OF THIS HAT!!
PEEK
THIS IS A TRUE...
...HAT TRICK!!
TA—DAH
AND A RED CARD FROM THIS POCKET.
THAT'S NOT A MAGIC TRI-
SHUT UP!

TWO OPTIONS

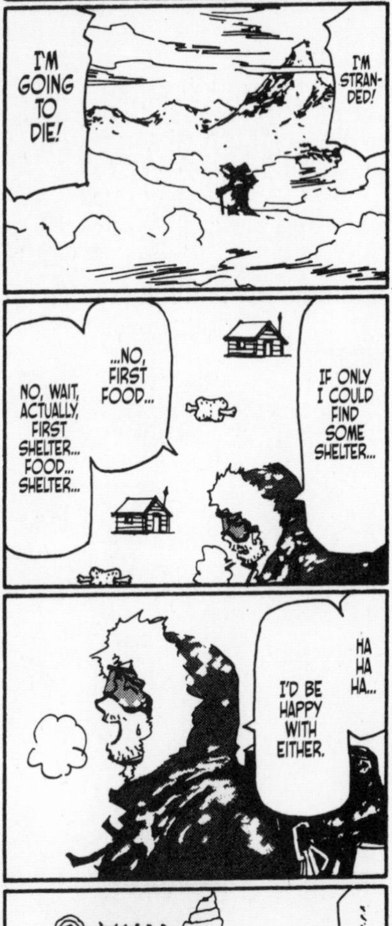
I'M STRANDED!
I'M GOING TO DIE!
IF ONLY I COULD FIND SOME SHELTER...
...NO, FIRST FOOD...
NO, WAIT, ACTUALLY, FIRST SHELTER... FOOD... SHELTER...
HA HA HA...
I'D BE HAPPY WITH EITHER.
House made of candy
WOOOO

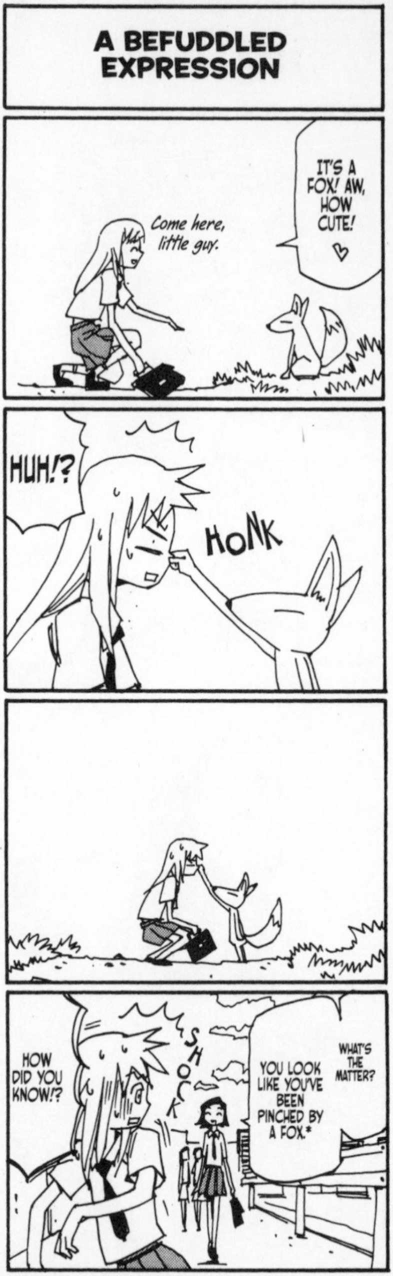
A BEFUDDLED EXPRESSION
IT'S A FOX! AW, HOW CUTE!
Come here, little guy.
HUH!?
HONK
WHAT'S THE MATTER?
YOU LOOK LIKE YOU'VE BEEN PINCHED BY A FOX.*
SHOCK
HOW DID YOU KNOW!?

*See translator's notes

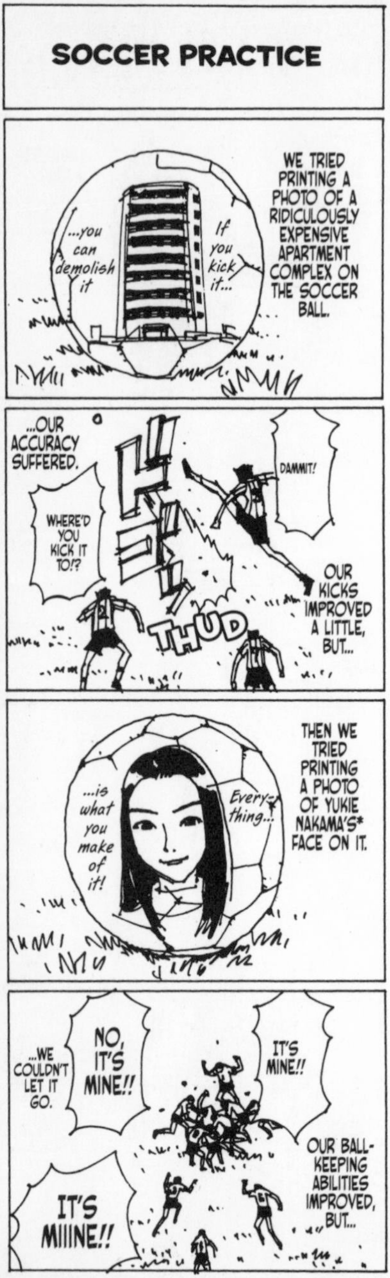
SOCCER PRACTICE
WE TRIED PRINTING A PHOTO OF A RIDICULOUSLY EXPENSIVE APARTMENT COMPLEX ON THE SOCCER BALL.
If you kick it...
...you can demolish it
DAMMIT!
OUR KICKS IMPROVED A LITTLE, BUT...
...OUR ACCURACY SUFFERED.
WHERE'D YOU KICK IT TO!?
THUD
THEN WE TRIED PRINTING A PHOTO OF YUKIE NAKAMA'S* FACE ON IT.
Every-thing...
...is what you make of it!
IT'S MINE!!
OUR BALL-KEEPING ABILITIES IMPROVED, BUT...
NO, IT'S MINE!!
...WE COULDN'T LET IT GO.
IT'S MIIINE!!

*See translator's notes

TRANSLATOR'S NOTES

Pg. 57 – "down the hole!!"
A meaningless catchphrase of the Pitfall Enthusiast
Clan, used to end sentences rather like the Canadian use
of "eh?", or Monty Python's "Y'know what I mean?"

Pg. 58 – "My name's Orinosuke."
His name is derived from the word "*oriru*" which
means "to go down" or "descend" and "*suke*" is a
common ending for a guy's name.

Pg. 176 – "pinched by a fox"
A Japanese colloquialism meaning to be befuddled,
confused or at a loss about what to do.

Pg. 176 – Yukie Nakama
A beautiful Japanese actress and model.

Pg. 177 – Yasutaka Tsutsui
A Japanese novelist famed for his dark humor.

Pg. 177 – "Moe-tan!"
The suffix "-tan" is a cute version of "-chan", and Moe
is a cute little girl.

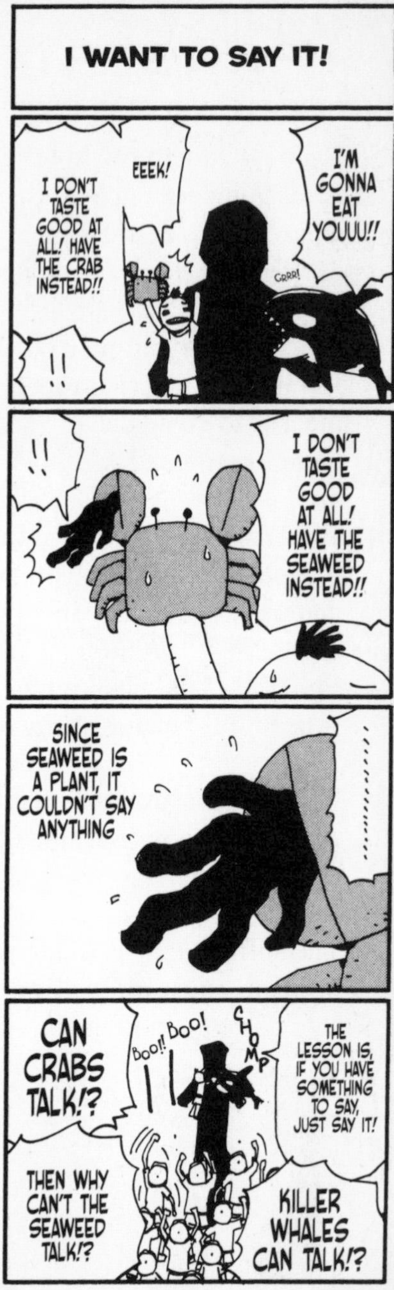
I WANT TO SAY IT!
I'M GONNA EAT YOUUU!!
GRRR!
EEEK!
I DON'T TASTE GOOD AT ALL! HAVE THE CRAB INSTEAD!!
!!
I DON'T TASTE GOOD AT ALL! HAVE THE SEAWEED INSTEAD!!
!!
......
SINCE SEAWEED IS A PLANT, IT COULDN'T SAY ANYTHING
THE LESSON IS, IF YOU HAVE SOMETHING TO SAY, JUST SAY IT!
CHOMP
BOO! BOO!!
CAN CRABS TALK!?
KILLER WHALES CAN TALK!?
THEN WHY CAN'T THE SEAWEED TALK!?

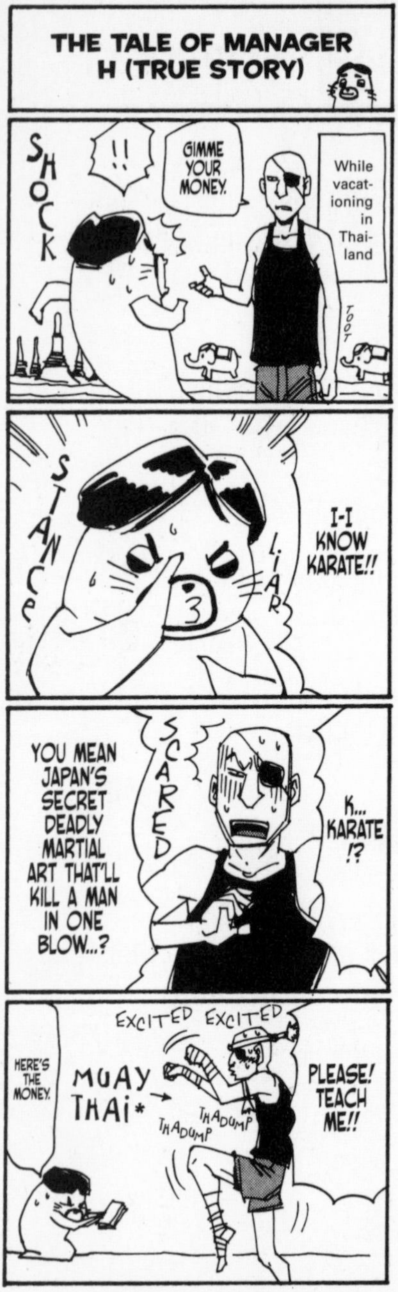
THE TALE OF MANAGER H (TRUE STORY)
While vacationing in Thailand
GIMME YOUR MONEY.
!!
SHOCK
TOOT
I-I KNOW KARATE!!
LIAR
STANCE
K... KARATE!?
SCARED
YOU MEAN JAPAN'S SECRET DEADLY MARTIAL ART THAT'LL KILL A MAN IN ONE BLOW...?
PLEASE! TEACH ME!!
EXCITED EXCITED
THADUMP THADUMP
MUAY THAI*
HERE'S THE MONEY.

*Thailand's deadly kickboxing martial arts style

HIJACK?

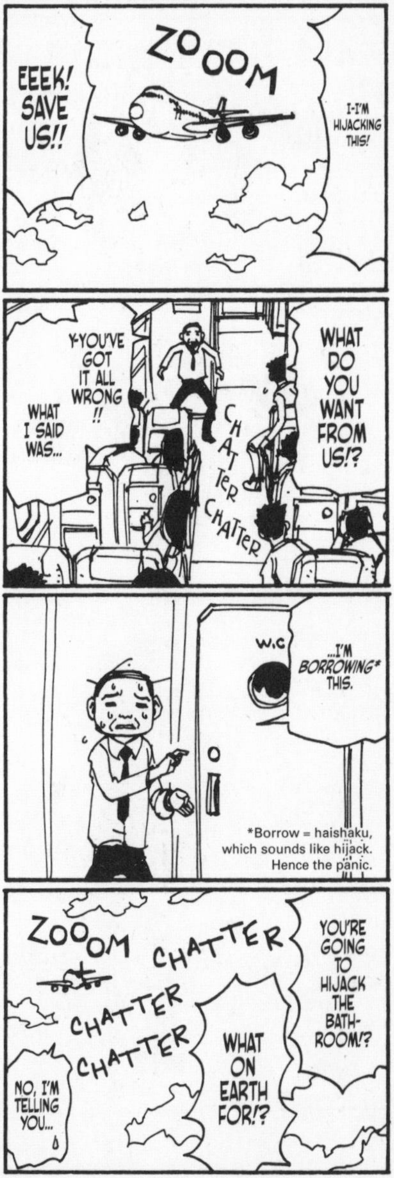
ZOOOM
I-I'M HIJACKING THIS!
EEEK! SAVE US!!
WHAT DO YOU WANT FROM US!?
Y-YOU'VE GOT IT ALL WRONG!!
CHATTER CHATTER
WHAT I SAID WAS...
...I'M BORROWING* THIS.
W.C
*Borrow = haishaku, which sounds like hijack. Hence the panic.
YOU'RE GOING TO HIJACK THE BATHROOM!?
ZOOOM
CHATTER
WHAT ON EARTH FOR!?
CHATTER CHATTER
NO, I'M TELLING YOU...

ROLLERCOASTER

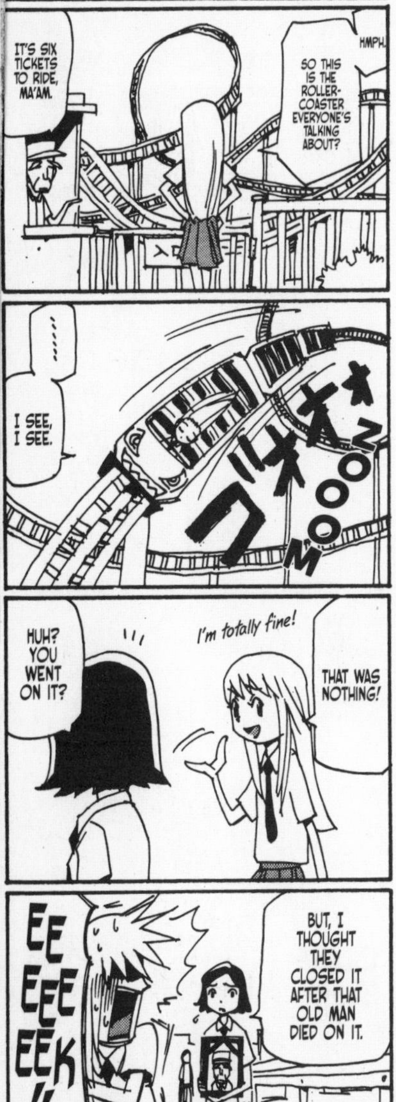
HMPH.
SO THIS IS THE ROLLERCOASTER EVERYONE'S TALKING ABOUT?
IT'S SIX TICKETS TO RIDE, MA'AM.
......
I SEE, I SEE.
ZOOOOOM
THAT WAS NOTHING!
I'm totally fine!
HUH? YOU WENT ON IT?
BUT, I THOUGHT THEY CLOSED IT AFTER THAT OLD MAN DIED ON IT.
EEEEEEEEEK!!

NATURAL PROVIDENCE

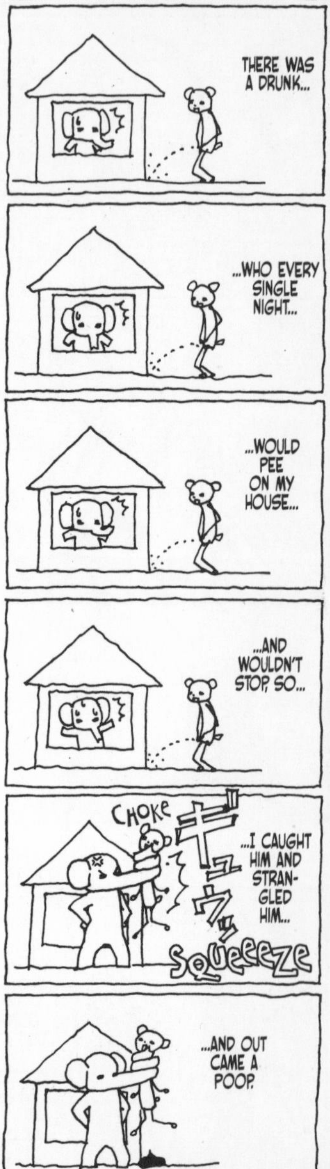
THERE WAS A DRUNK...
...WHO EVERY SINGLE NIGHT...
...WOULD PEE ON MY HOUSE...
...AND WOULDN'T STOP, SO...
CHOKE
...I CAUGHT HIM AND STRAN-GLED HIM...
SQUEEEZE
...AND OUT CAME A POOP.

© 筒井康隆 © Yasutaka Tsutsui*

*See translator's notes

PLAYOFF FOR THE TOURNAMENT WIN

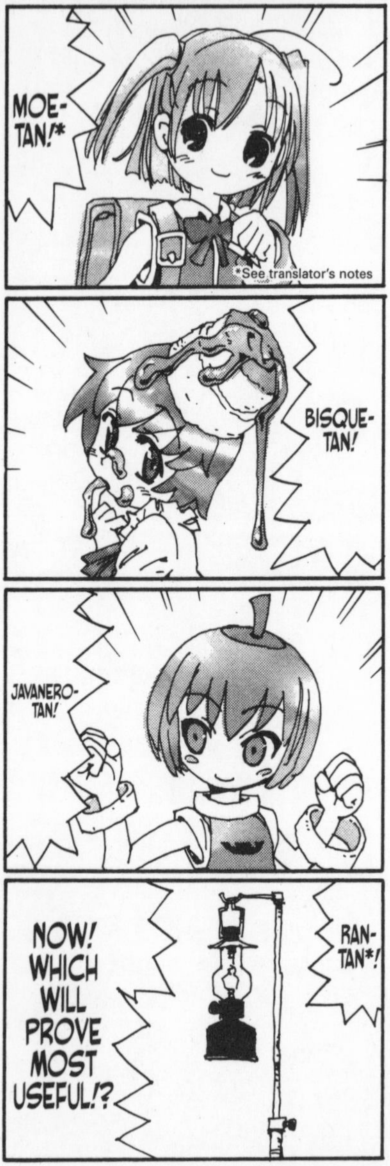
MOE-TAN!*
*See translator's notes
BISQUE-TAN!
JAVANERO-TAN!
RAN-TAN*!
NOW! WHICH WILL PROVE MOST USEFUL!?

*Japanese pronunciation of "lantern."

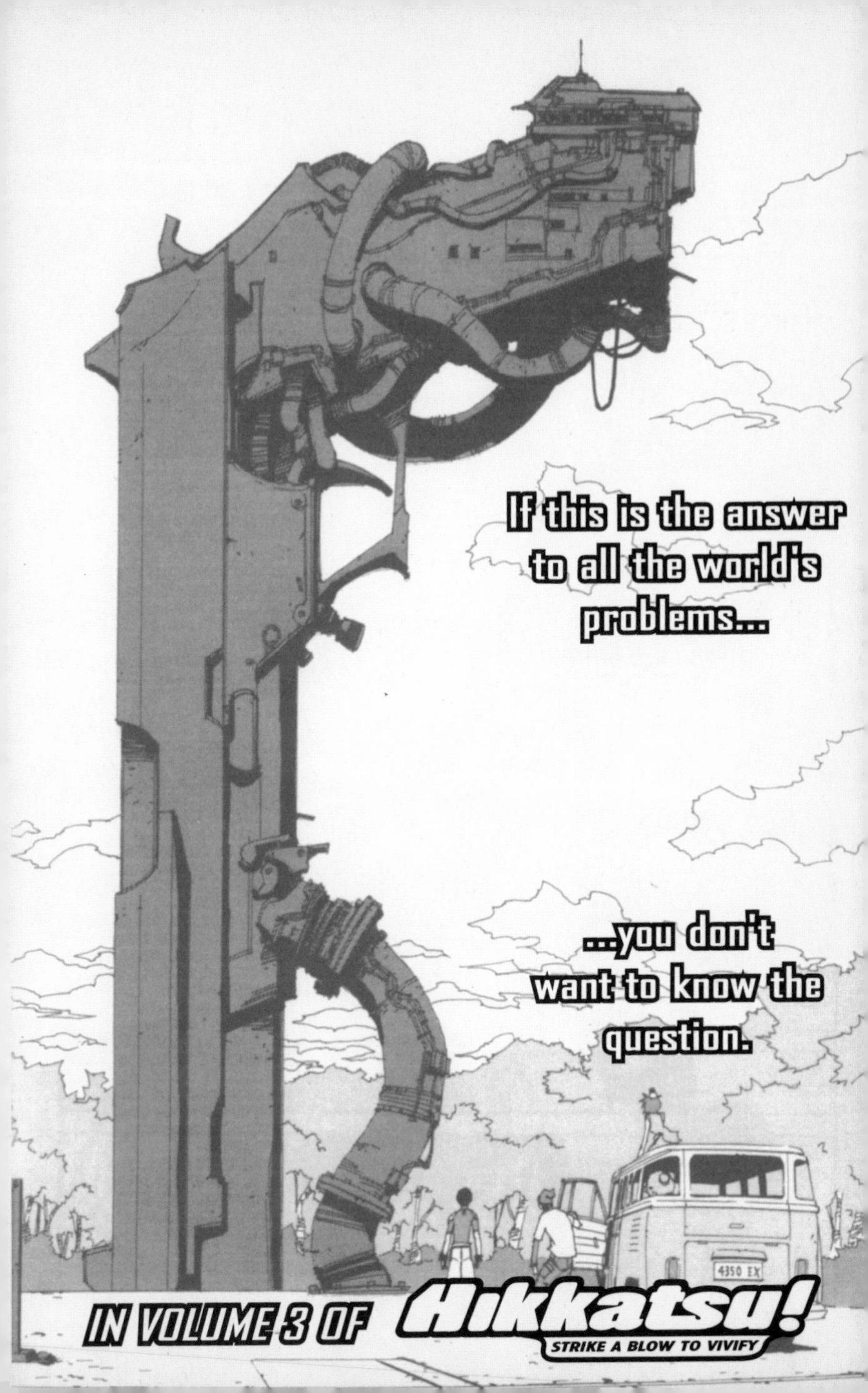
If this is the answer to all the world's problems...
...you don't want to know the question.
4350 EX
IN VOLUME 3 OF
Hikkatsu!
STRIKE A BLOW TO VIVIFY

from the creator of
HER MAJESTY'S DOG
Sometimes a diamond in the rough is PURE GOLD!
A Wise Man Sleeps
go!comi
THE SOUL OF MANGA
www.gocomi.com
© Mick Takeuchi/ AKITASHOTEN

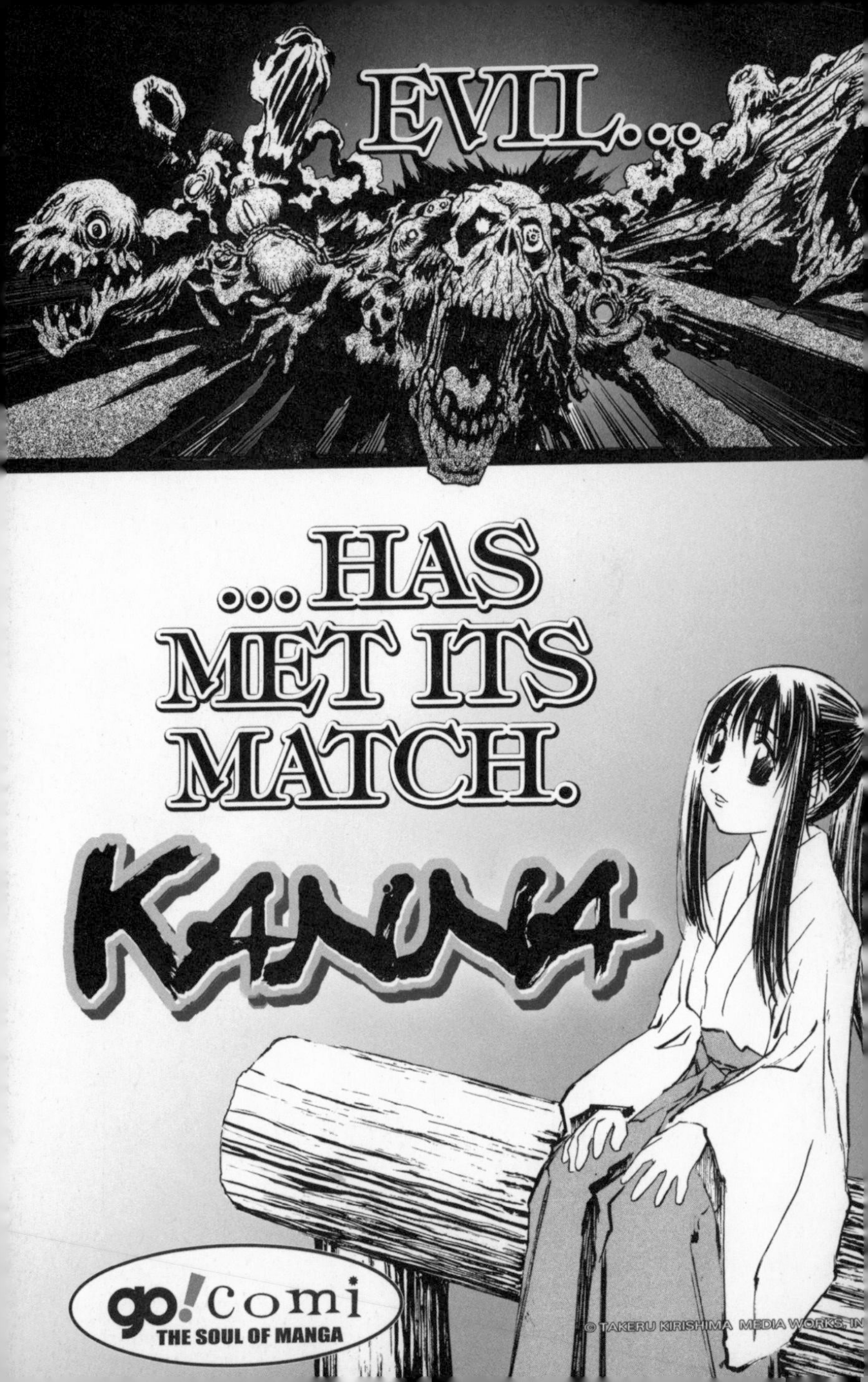
EVIL...
...HAS MET ITS MATCH.
KANNA
go!comi
THE SOUL OF MANGA
© TAKERU KIRISHIMA MEDIA WORKS, IN

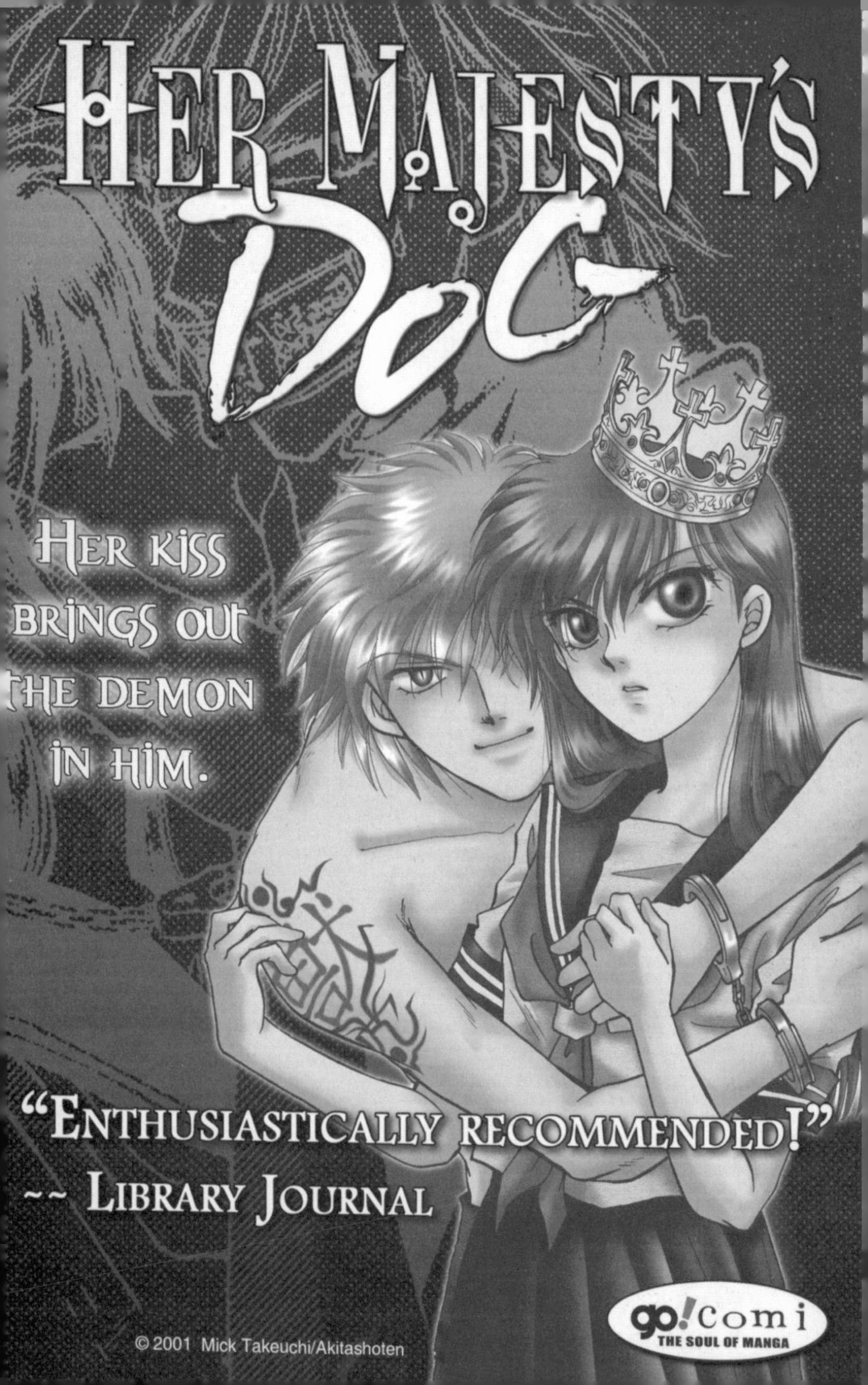

HER MAJESTY'S DOG
HER KISS BRINGS OUT THE DEMON IN HIM.
"ENTHUSIASTICALLY RECOMMENDED!"
~~ LIBRARY JOURNAL
go!comi THE SOUL OF MANGA
© 2001 Mick Takeuchi/Akitashoten

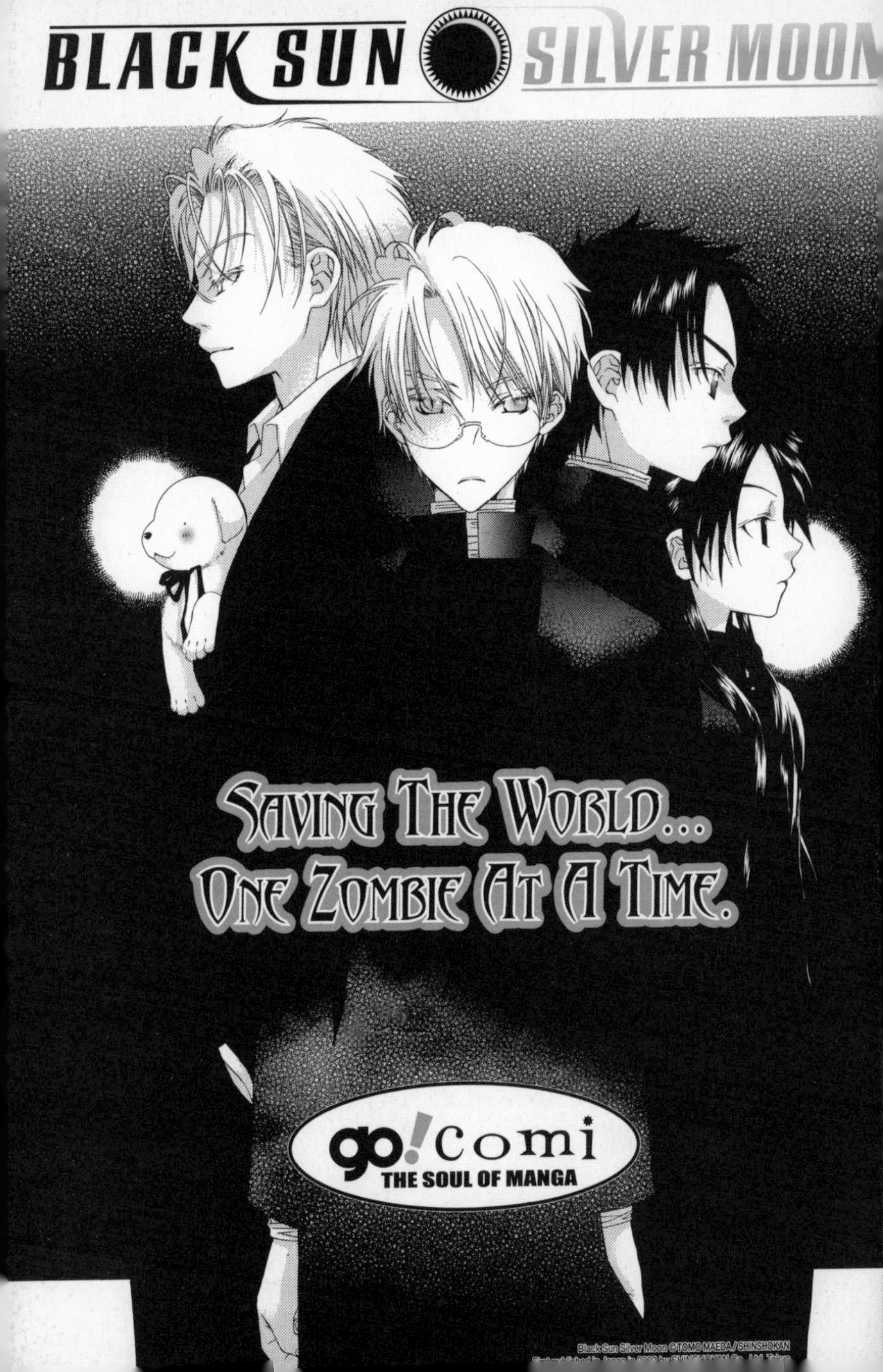
BLACK SUN SILVER MOON
SAVING THE WORLD...
ONE ZOMBIE AT A TIME.
go! comi
THE SOUL OF MANGA
Black Sun Silver Moon ©TOMO MAEDA / SHINSHOKAN

Ctrl+Alt+Deleting
All the Rules!
ER
CY-BELIEVERS
From the creator of
crossroad
go!comi
THE SOUL OF MANGA
© Shioko Mizuki / AKITASHOTEN
www.gocomi.com

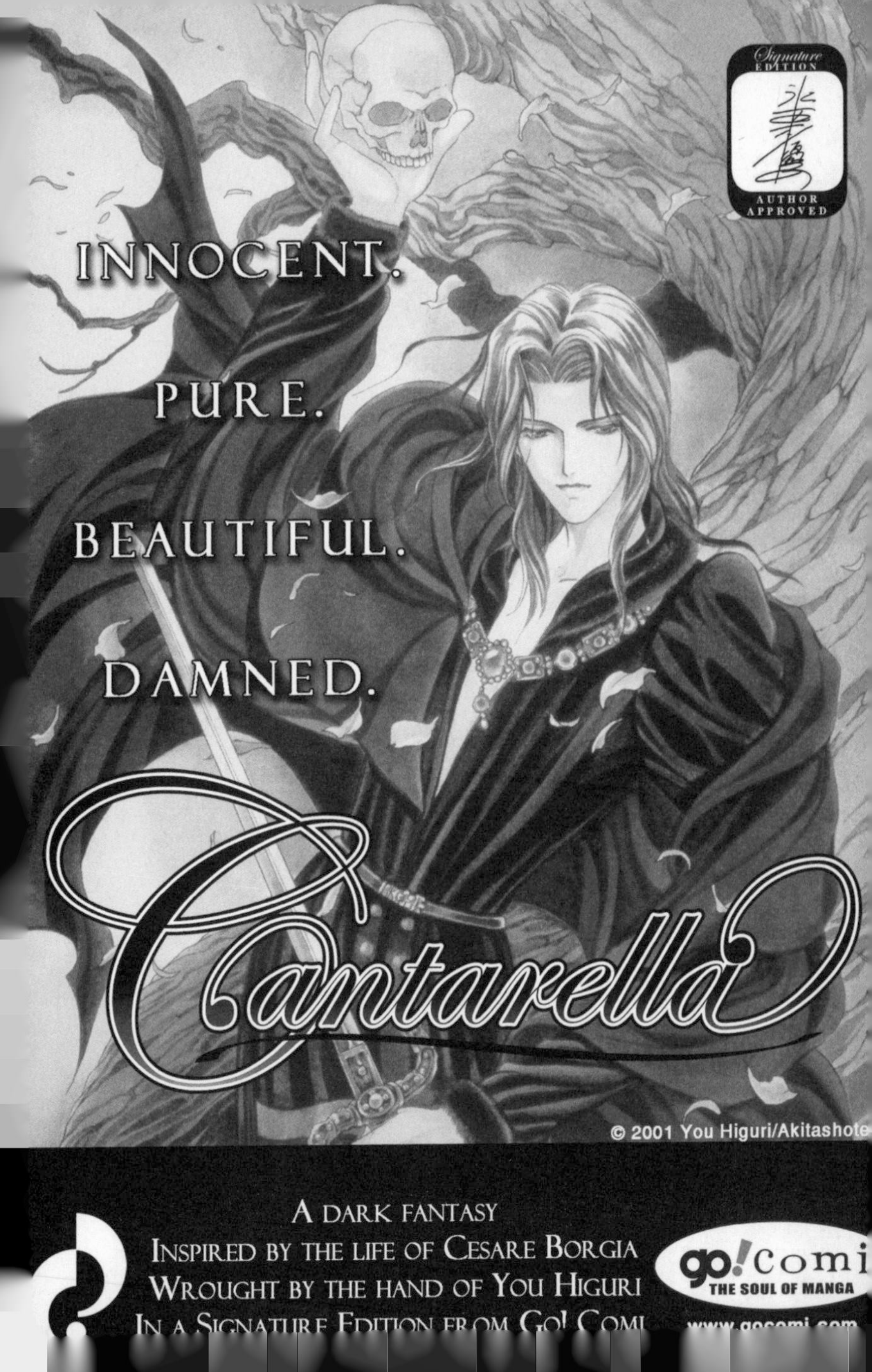
INNOCENT.
PURE.
BEAUTIFUL.
DAMNED.
Signature EDITION
AUTHOR APPROVED
Cantarella
© 2001 You Higuri/Akitashoten
A DARK FANTASY
INSPIRED BY THE LIFE OF CESARE BORGIA
WROUGHT BY THE HAND OF YOU HIGURI
IN A SIGNATURE EDITION FROM GO! COMI
go!comi
THE SOUL OF MANGA
www.gocomi.com

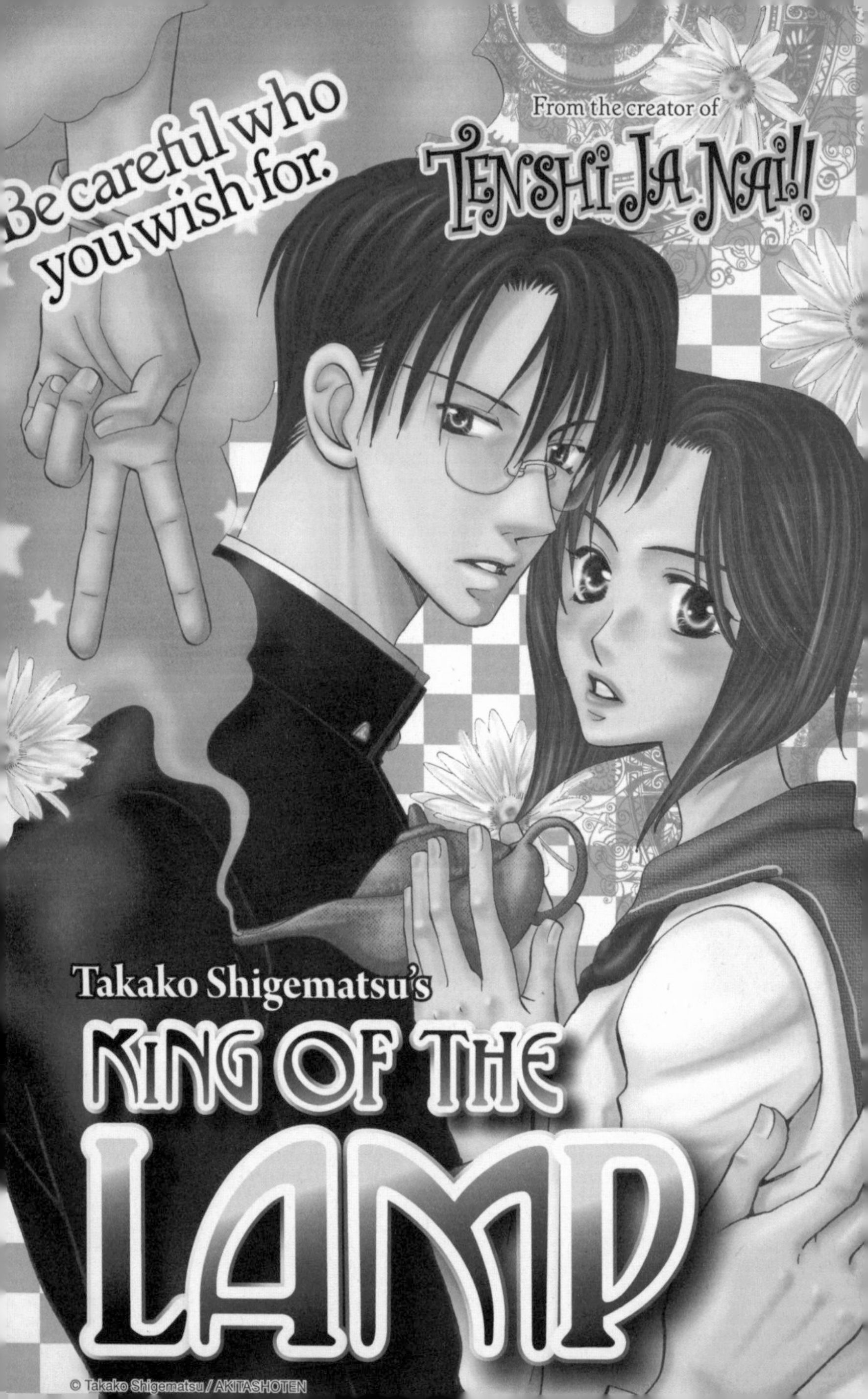
Be careful who you wish for.
From the creator of
TENSHI JA NAI!!
Takako Shigematsu's
KING OF THE LAMP
© Takako Shigematsu / AKITASHOTEN

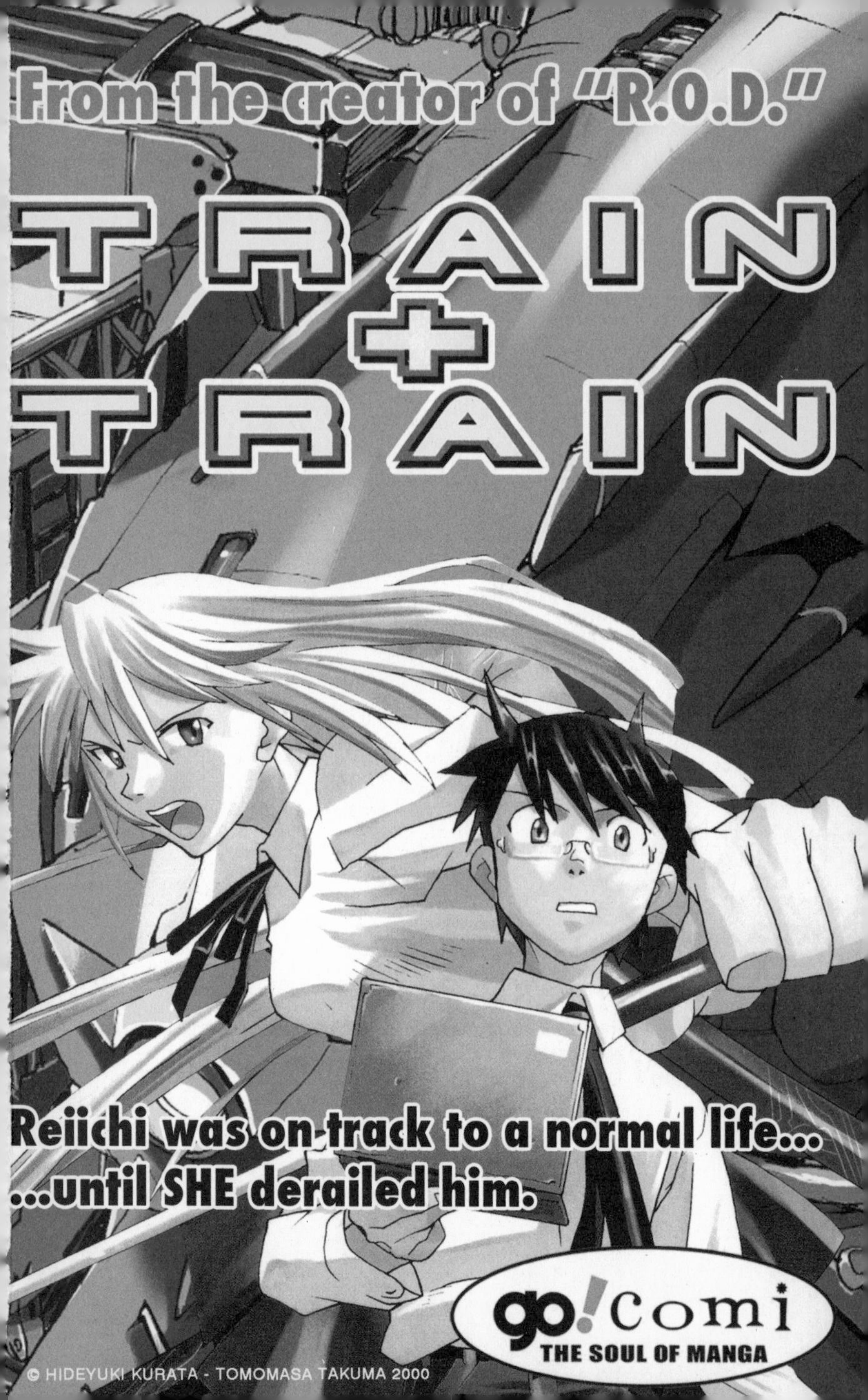